D0521885

Praise for Speaking in Thumbs

'Expertly cuts right through the confusion of modern dating. A fantastic guide for anyone looking for real connection, but struggling to understand what messages really mean.'

Thomas Erikson, multi-million-copy bestselling
author of *Surrounded by Idiots*

'Mimi Winsberg's *Speaking in Thumbs* is an entertaining, essential, and ultimately practical guide for anyone navigating the most vexing feature of modern romance: text messages. Winsberg has compiled research and real-life examples, including texts from her own life, to help readers spot red flags, discern compatibility, and recognize where they are pushing potential partners away. By analyzing texts from the entire life cycle of a romance – from initial exchanges to the gut-wrenching end-of-relationship goodbyes – Winsberg empowers readers to understand both themselves and the people on the other end of their text messages. Winsberg's book entertains as it enlightens, and empowers as it analyzes. Don't even think of swiping right again until you read this book.'

Christie Tate, *New York Times* bestselling author of *Group: How One Therapist and a Circle of Strangers Saved My Life*

'Mimi Winsberg uses her incredible knowledge and research to help us understand that communication is a practice and vital to setting a relationship up for success.'

Eve Rodsky, *New York Times* bestselling author of *Fair Play: A Game-Changing Solution for When You Have Too Much to Do (and More Life to Live)*

'For riveting insights into what your prospective suitor's texts really mean, look no further than this irresistibly titled guide . . . unputdownable.'

Caroline Sanderson, Editor's Choice, *The Bookseller*

Speaking
in Thumbs

A Psychiatrist Decodes

Your Relationship Texts

So You Don't Have To

DR MIMI WINSBERG

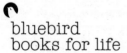

bluebird
books for life

First published 2021 by Doubleday
an imprint of Penguin Random House LLC New York.

First published in the UK 2022 by Bluebird
an imprint of Pan Macmillan
The Smithson, 6 Briset Street, London EC1M 5NR
EU representative: Macmillan Publishers Ireland Ltd, 1st Floor,
The Liffey Trust Centre, 117–126 Sheriff Street Upper,
Dublin 1, D01 YC43
Associated companies throughout the world
www.panmacmillan.com

TPB ISBN 978-1-5290-5969-4
HB ISBN 978-1-5290-9460-2

Contents

Introduction

If a pair of Bottega Veneta ballet flats could stomp, then I would say Agnes stomped down the long hallway and into the cavernous room that is my office. Instead of flinging herself onto the gray sectional, she leaned stiffly against a drafting chair, clutching her phone like a sacred tablet. Her nails were the color of the accent wall, the carpet, and the cigarette pack peeking out of the purse slung low against the thigh of her white capri pants: celadon.

I had acknowledged her arrival and was waiting for a response. At thirty-two, Agnes was used to being the smartest person in the room, and it showed in the way she carried herself. She was an MIT graduate and a level-six engineer at Facebook, making more money than a surgeon or a top corporate lawyer. Now she was wearing a mixture of scowl and pout.

"I don't get it," she said, thrusting the ridiculously dim screen of her phone at me. I put on my glasses, which I seldom do around my patients. A text message from a man named Jason read, "Let's talk when you are back from your trip."

"What's the matter?" I ventured.

They had met online recently and had just spent a lovely weekend together, talking, hiking, cooking, *feeling*. She was hurt and annoyed by his text and wasn't sure why. "What does this mean, how should I respond?" she asked. I could read the subtext: Why isn't the relationship developing the way I think it should?

"You know about sharks, how they have to stay in motion?" I said.

"Otherwise they die," she replied.

"Exactly. People assume relationships are like sharks—that they need to move forward to survive. Well, they're not; they move in mysterious ways, or sometimes not at all."

Agnes slumped into the drafting chair, rolled it beside me, and handed me her phone. We began to dissect her online chats with Jason to see if we were dealing with a shark, or perhaps an animal with a better chance of survival.

I've got a story for you.

It's my own story, but I've been a psychiatrist long enough to know that it's a common one. Over twenty-five years of practice, my couch has provided me with a window into people's intimate lives—their hopes, their dreams, and their worries. It has shown that we are all creatures of romantic attachment, not to mention the victims of epic dating fails. I have listened to countless colorful accounts of my patients' online dating—just like Agnes's— their heartening successes and their heart-stopping failures. The thrill of connection, and the agony of rejection.

So if I've got a story, it's only because you've had so many stories for me.

Those narratives themselves have always been psychiatry's bread and butter. While medicine continues to grasp for the biological and genetic underpinnings of mental illness—which neurochemicals cause us to be depressed, anxious, compulsive— our stories remain a quick and reliable tool for understanding ourselves, available to one and all.

In psychiatry we call it the heuristic approach. A heuristic is a problem-solving method that uses shortcuts to come to quick conclusions. We can't analyze every synapse, download every experience, and sum up a person. We likely never will. But the heuristic approach offers us something else. Through stories and the way we make them meaningful, we can engage in a fruitful process of learning and discovery.

Scientifically speaking, stories have a bad rap. Anecdotal evidence is considered by science a lesser form of knowledge when compared with cold, hard data. Feelings, impressions, unsupported theories—they abound in the writings of psychiatry's forefathers, largely dismissed today. Freud himself acknowledged that his case histories should read like short stories; they lack the emphasis on data that we've come to expect, the serious stamp of science. He focused instead on the connection between our narratives and our symptoms—the idea that our psychiatric conditions could be understood by analyzing the stories we tell ourselves about life events.

I witnessed firsthand the role that stories can play in understanding symptoms when I was in medical school. I had elected to do some work in refugee camps in Asia, as well as a rotation at a local clinic that served Southeast Asian refugees. Many of the patients had not only been displaced but suffered significant trauma. Their stories, relayed through an interpreter, were both tragic and compelling. One Cambodian woman described a psychosomatic blindness—losing her sight after watching her husband being stabbed to death with sharp sticks. As Freud suggested, her symptoms could only be understood through her recollections; no eye exam or CT scan could do them justice. This experience brought my interest in mental health into sharp focus. Even when I was a young medical student, my willingness to listen to people's stories could be powerful and life changing, for them and for me.

It is what we do as humans, after all. We tell stories about ourselves and the people in our lives. Some of the stories are true, some distorted, some frankly false. As a psychiatrist, I am trained to listen to patients' stories in a specific way: to draw out their histories, their family backgrounds, their symptoms and struggles. Some of what I do is to help patients tell a new story about themselves.

And of course many of the stories I have heard in my practice have been about love—love being one of the greatest stories, one that gives our lives meaning. Love is always a story we tell first to ourselves and then to each other.

For three years, I did my listening at the very place that is credited (or blamed) for inventing the predominant means of online human communication today. At Facebook, I listened to Silicon Valley's alpha and beta testers, its disrupters and innovators. The inventors and shepherds of *the algorithm*—that impenetrable sequence of code that promises deeper and more profound connection with our fellow humans—they were and still are my patients. Those geniuses who know how you tick? I know how they tick.

Now, I should admit that for all this talk of stories and their primacy, I'm not immune to the lure of technology. At Facebook and beyond, I've seen the power of data firsthand. In the age of Big Data and measurable outcomes, now even psychiatry—founded on the intangibles of emotion—has felt the pull. The field has gone digital. I've been fortunate enough to be at the center of it, helping to lead the charge as digital health companies attempt to apply data science, measurement-based care, and even artificial intelligence to the study of human behavior and its associated illnesses. I co-founded Brightside Health, a digital behavioral health company at the convergence of technology and mental health. At Brightside we treat depression and anxiety over telemedicine, using state-of-the-art technology to help patients and providers select treatment plans and manage care. While patients have long relied on trained clinicians for diagnostic impressions and treatment selections, we are now more and more turning to machines, which can help us recognize patterns that humans routinely miss.

The past five years of my work in digital health have centered on training machines to recognize symptom clusters in text messages—in other words, using technology to pore over our digital communication and reveal crucial facts about behavioral health. As a leader in mental health, Brightside has pioneered advances in both diagnosis (recognizing the telltale signs of mental illness) and triage (judging how urgent a patient's illness is), as well as the selection of appropriate psychiatric treatments. Effectively, we're wrangling data to understand both internal psychology and external behavior, training machines not only how to think but how to "shrink."

Alongside all this Big Data, I've seen the rise of Big Dating. Any technology of real value has always been quickly adapted to suit our most primal desires. So with the advent of personal and mobile computing, it's perhaps inevitable that online dating has, in a matter of a decade or two, gone from the fringes to the norm. More than fifty million American adults say they either have used or continue to use a dating app in the pursuit of romance. Tinder alone processes 1.6 billion swipes per day. In less than a single generation, Big Data has upended the courtship process.

I've felt its effects firsthand. Shortly before I began my tenure as Facebook's resident psychiatrist, my marriage of sixteen years ended. Our partnership had become all about the business of running a family, and while we could still connect intellectually, we had drifted apart romantically. And so we amicably parted ways.

I knew what was in store for me—dating apps—and I was fine with it. In no time I was swiping daily, looking to find that special someone . . . or just looking. What I discovered was something I hadn't expected: that all my training had prepared me extraordinarily well for this. My clinical practice informed the way I approached dating, and vice versa. My familiarity with data analysis seeped through too. Soon I was sifting through bursts of text messaging to find the golden nuggets of information hidden within. I found myself with an uncanny ability to see through (even sometimes, if I'm being honest, to provisionally *diagnose*) those I engaged with on these dating apps, often after exchanging just a few messages.

It was here at the intersection of psychology, tech, and romance that I began to see the human condition up close, in high resolution. It is where I truly, and literally, had skin in the game. I started developing my own heuristic approach, translating intimate exchanges like a text whisperer.

"U still up?" an incoming message reads.

Up for what? What do they really mean?

We've all done it: obsessively parsing the words from a prospective partner. Looking for clues in their response times, whether too fast or too slow. Wondering why that three-dot ellipsis came . . . and went. To inject meaning into these fleeting moments is a romantic comedy cliché.

Well, it turns out that this cliché, like so many others, is grounded in reality. The changes in the way we communicate accompany a broader fact: romantic relationships have become more complicated. Now it's not just "Whom should I be dating?" but "How many people should I be dating at once?" "How do I define myself along lines of gender and orientation?" We wonder who is going to initiate the conversation and who will be the one to deepen it. We wrestle with the nuances of the past, overlaid with shifting gender norms and our complex, evolving identities. We seek contact. We crave connection. We are talking about stuff that we have never talked about before.

And we are doing it over text. Texting is now the dominant mode of communication. It forces us to rely exclusively on our written language (and of course our emojis). Word choice, semantics, and grammar have to communicate ever more meaning in the absence of the cues we derive from body language, eye contact, and stance, to say nothing of vocal cues like tone, cadence, and volume. Now our words alone do the heavy lifting. The act of writing—with just our thumbs, no less—forces the compression of these emotional cues into tiny chat bubbles, which then require a new skill set to unpack and understand.

The word "data" derives from the Latin verb *dare,* "to give." The French word for data is *les données,* "the givens." Let's not forget, in our technology-ridden lives, that with every thumb tap and keystroke we are giving away little pieces of ourselves. We leave behind contrails of digital exhaust, signatures of ourselves, our desires, our states of mind, even our character.

Does online *dating* translate into online *data?* Can the thumbprints encoded in individual text messages help us make sense of our online conversations as a whole and shed light on our subsequent courtships, on-screen and in person?

Sometimes our clearest, most unbiased view of a person is in our first meeting with them. It's before the storytelling aspects of our brains have begun to spin a narrative about them, before we've become attached, our noses pressed up against the glass of our budding relationship, without our objectivity or perspective. What better first glimpse of a person than their initial text messages? Armed with the right tools, these chat bubbles offer peepholes into the psyche.

Our text messages also reflect key factors in the creation of healthy communication patterns throughout the courtship process. The unique features of an individual, and even a couple, are sitting there on our phones, visible to the trained naked eye. The narcissism of the guy who broke your heart was evident in his use of possessive pronouns. The guy who had the attention span of a puppy cursed too much from the start. When the man who eventually shows up for dinner looks nothing like his profile picture, or when a delightful connection disappears like a ghost, traces of those fatal flaws might have been hiding in plain text.

This book is a guide to analyzing dating and relationship text threads. It will provide tools to help you avoid the bad experiences that pollute our dating world and the clarity to better understand and identify key elements of personality, attachment style, and even psychopathology.

I'll be honest, transparent, revealing. We'll look over my shoulder at text exchanges, and I'll show you how to read between the lines. We'll examine the chats that you've probably had, the ones you will have, and the ones you will want to have. These are private conversations, but they are part of our collective yearning to communicate, to comprehend the frustrations, pains, and joys that we endure in finding romantic connection.

Based on my real-life experience and professional expertise, we'll gather insights on finding the person with the right psychological profile for you, one chat bubble at a time. The first section of the book examines what text can reveal about the traits of the individual; the second section is focused on uncovering traits of the pair-bond; and in the third section we'll use text exchanges as the written medical record of the arc of the relationship so that we can recognize important inflection points—as well as breaking points. We'll decipher the real meaning of our romantic text messages.

Together, we'll go from speaking in tongues to *speaking in thumbs.*

PART 1

Swiping

CHAPTER 1

Mixed Emojis

OUR LOVE/HATE RELATIONSHIP WITH ONLINE DATING

Sinead: My app says we are a 94% match!

Rosalyn: Mine too. Maybe our profiles should go out on a date while we just keep texting here 😜

The pictures are cute. The bio clever. The face that beams up at you from the open app on your phone seems to want all the same things you do. Someone somewhere, or maybe it was an algorithm, determined that you're 94 percent compatible—whatever that means. Your finger is poised to swipe right, with all the anticipation that they'll swipe right as well; I mean, 94 percent compatible, surely they noticed that too. You'll match, meet, and the rest will be history.

If only it were so easy.

Endless strings of texts, fleeting trysts, an online crush on the person you imagine will be the future love of your life—they all form the mainstays of the online dating experience. There is excitement, anticipation, and enthusiasm. There is also ennui, alienation, and just plain exhaustion. If there is one thing that can be said about online dating, it's that it's rife with contradictions.

Even though it's my job to understand human behavior, I too have felt buffeted by the ups and downs of online dating. We can't help but embark on the journey with inflated expectations.

We're promised a whirlwind of choices, a crowd of suitors, a wondrous wizard of technology pulling the strings behind the curtain. But knowing that the process can be a drag, we simultaneously brace ourselves for disappointment. It's a story of mismatched expectations, a journey rife with paradoxes.

I once had a text exchange start like this:

Me: Hi Mark

Mark: Hello Mimi. Nice to connect with you

Me: Likewise. Always fun to meet interesting people.

Mark: I'll certainly try not to disappoint you.

I led with "fun" and "interesting"; Mark countered with "disappoint." Right out of the gate, he called out this tendency that many of us share, to brace for disappointment in the face of hope. He did so in a facetious way, flirtatiously acknowledging that the hand was his to lose—explicitly calling a low-stakes game as he diminished my expectations. Still, Mark was pointing to a truth about romance: the most perilous aspect is certainly its uncertainty. We say that we "fall" in love because the process feels inherently out of control.

One patient, after a nasty breakup, described to me her secret desire to "win at dating apps." While this is a nice fantasy, the reality is more akin to walking into a casino, where we might entertain ideas of life-changing jackpots, but it's the house that always wins. Online dating involves chance; players face unavoidable risk when they follow the usual advice to "put yourself out there." Bracing for disappointment may just be the price of admission for using the app.

Because online dating involves technology, and technology has reduced friction in so much of our lives, from ordering a pizza to calling a cab, we expect, consciously or not, that dating apps should somehow spare us all this uncertainty. Once our expectations are permitted to soar, no outcome is likely to please.

When I listen to people talk about their experiences with dating apps, I hear a litany of complaints: about conversations going nowhere, not getting second dates, ghosting, the notorious "bad algorithm." I also find a relentless pursuit of perfection, coupled with a lot of churn. "Men are like buses," said one of my patients. "There's another one every few minutes." Matches sound oddly disposable, rather than representations of actual human beings; chats are treated as transactional and fungible. People form an index of false assumptions, cognitive distortions, and puzzling conclusions. We are prisoners of the paradox.

In this chapter, we'll dig into the contradictions that surround online dating, how they affect us, and the neuroscience behind them. We'll also discover how the app that sits in the palm of our hand can be used as our tool, and not the reverse. Along the way we'll look at real-life examples, showing how we can put our words to work for us. It is only once we've grappled with our mixed feelings about the *medium* that we can get to the *messages*.

The Paradox of Familiarity

What are we most attracted to, the familiar or the novel?

> **Duncan:** Hi there—loved your profile. It was very authentic!

> **Duncan:** Has London always been your home?

> **Duncan:** I really want to hear back from you!

Sarah: Hey . . .

Sarah: No, London has not always been my home, I'm originally from California

Duncan: Ah, I lived in California for ten years. Loved it.

Duncan: What are you up to tonight?

Sarah: I'm going out. Having a few drinks with friends

Duncan: well, I'd love to buy you a cocktail . . .

Duncan: is it a girls night?

Sarah: it is a girls night . . .

Duncan: I'll be grabbing a lovely dinner at the Hawksmoor

Sarah: Oh no, not a lovely dinner at Hawksmoor. At least the steak is good company 😣

Duncan: I'll be in Soho in the AM, if you are close we could grab a coffee

Sarah: Ah, thank you, very kind but I have plans tomorrow.

Duncan: I guess I'll just have a cosy Sunday at home then.

Sarah: A cosy Sunday at home . . . how Sundays are meant to be spent. I'm a Sunday morning with a cup of coffee and paper kinda girl. I look forward to it all week. Haha

Sarah: Was just putting the kettle on

Duncan: Are you making tea?

Sarah: Um yes, I'm a 90 year old woman in a 32 year old body. Such a homebody. Love cooking, Love reading. Love listening to records. Love a hot drink.

> **Duncan:** So cute. I love electric blankets! It's the best when you wake up . . . and it's cold . . . then you turn on the blanket. Bliss!

> **Sarah:** This is killing me. I used to actually put an electric blanket under my mattress topper. So you could turn it on before getting into bed, and then get into a warm bed. That was bliss.

> **Duncan:** Same same! See, we both like to be cosy. Of course, cuddling is the #1 best warm feeling. 😍💜

> **Sarah:** But. When life does not permit . . . an electric blanket and a cup of tea will do.

> **Duncan:** . . . lol, you're cute. So British

Duncan and Sarah are off to a tepid start. Actually, they have quite a few degrees to go before reaching tepid. But with all the chat about electric blankets and hot tea, Sarah is slowly warming up. One does have the sense that had Sarah said she was a vegetarian, Duncan would have immediately let go of his steak house dinner plans and gushed instead about his love of zucchini. Nonetheless, she is reassured by their shared delights in the small things. Her texts suggest someone who values comfort over excitement.

Everyone falls somewhere on the spectrum. On one end is what's known as novelty seeking; on the other is harm avoidance. The psychiatrist Robert Cloninger has elaborated on the subject. Those high in novelty seeking, he argues, will be consistently more attracted to the unfamiliar and less risk averse. At the extreme, their bucket lists might include skydiving, mountaineering, or even extreme sexual practices. More moderate novelty seekers will be satisfied with trying a new recipe or visiting a new store at the mall. Those high in harm avoidance, meanwhile, will seek security and familiarity, rarely roaming out of their comfort zone. In the next chapter we will explore how to identify where the person you are texting with falls within these categories, using only their text messages as clues.

For now, let's consider a more adventurous pair. Brittany and Kevin, both in their twenties, get right into fantasy and risk taking in their initial text exchange. They both clearly prefer the excitement of the unknown to the quotidian and familiar.

> **Brittany:** Why do I feel like your fantasy is chloroforming unsuspecting women, only for them to find themselves handcuffed in your sex dungeon
>
> **Brittany:** If that's the case, the safe word is pamplemousse

> **Kevin:** You missed the important part where I was unknowingly given a ketamine injection and walk in, lose consciousness, and wake up tied to a 4 corner bed
>
> **Kevin:** Plot twist!
>
> **Kevin:** I hope that pamplemousse is still the safe word

Familiarity comes in different flavors.

So we vary in the way we're drawn to novelty. But how much do we even *want* to know about a stranger as we decide whether to embark upon the next step? Are we more likely to swipe right the more we know about a person? In other words, does information help or hurt our first impressions? One body of research indicates that the more we know about a person up front, the less likely we are to like them. Another says that familiarity leads to liking and attraction. How do we reconcile these contradictions?

Michael Norton, a member of the Behavioral Insights Group at Harvard Business School, has spent his career finding answers to questions about our behavior as it concerns love, money, and happiness. He sought to understand whether knowing more about a person (or their dating profile) would lead to greater feelings of attraction. He and his colleagues Jeana Frost and Dan Ariely had noted that users' satisfaction and engagement with online dating as a whole plummeted quickly after an initial spike. They wanted to understand why. So they did what all curious researchers do: they designed a study.

Norton and his colleagues showed hundreds of online daters a series of potential matches along with anywhere from one to ten personality traits that were randomly chosen from a list of two hundred typical profile traits—such as age, income, athleticism, or religion. The study participants then rated the profiles. Interestingly, the more traits the participants were shown, the lower they rated the profiles. In other words, the more they were told about a potential date, the less appealing that date became.

Norton tells me his team wasn't particularly surprised by the results but that dating app users usually are. "We *think* that if we know more about someone, we will like them more," he says, "because all the people that we love in our life are people that we know a lot about.

"But," Norton adds, "that's because there are a whole lot of people we never gave the chance to. We hand select the ones we like, and choose to get to know them better."

Their study concluded that ambiguous or vague information about a person leads to interest, whereas, as the old saying goes, familiarity breeds contempt. On average, the authors showed, the more you learn about any new random prospective partner, the less excited about them you will be.

"There is nothing worse," said my friend Margaret, who has been on enough first dates to have co-authored this book with me, "than when a guy can't maintain some sense of mystery at the outset." I couldn't agree more. Consider my initial text exchange with Doug, where my interest quickly evaporated:

> **Me:** Where in WI are you from?
>
> **Doug:** Stevens point (in the middle)
>
> **Me:** How can a point be in the middle?
>
> **Doug:** Good question. It's the point where the Wisconsin river bends.
>
> **Me:** Ah, I lived in Minnesota during medical school. Followed my college boyfriend there.
>
> **Doug:** Nice—how's the online dating world treating you? Been single for awhile or recently may I ask
>
> **Me:** Well I was married for a long time. And now enjoying not being married. Why do you ask?
>
> **Doug:** Just inquisitive I guess. I find this process so much work.

Doug's final text bubble is the romantic equivalent of moaning at a job interview about the fact that you had to shave that morning in order to look presentable. Even if it's true, that is not what's going to land you the job. *Sprezzatura* is an Italian word that means studied carelessness, or graceful nonchalance. Essentially, it means making it look easy. While it would not have occurred to me to put *sprezzatura* on a list of qualities I was looking for, if I'm honest with myself, I can say that without a bit of *sprezzatura* at the outset, there is no seduction. Learning about Doug was starting to feel like a chore.

Why would knowing more about someone repel us from

them? Norton and his colleagues found that people tend to latch on to something in a profile that they disagree with or find unappealing, and their interest plummets from there as expectations begin to sag under the weight of the accumulated information. With only vague information, we can still project imaginary qualities onto a person and maintain high expectations. Too much information only bursts our bubble of hope.

They went a step further. In their next experiment, the researchers surveyed two groups of online daters. One group responded to questions about a future planned date, and a second group responded to questions about a date that had already taken place. Expectations far exceeded outcomes; pre-date scores were wildly higher than post-date scores. Imagining a future date was more satisfying than the date itself!

Norton described another discouraging finding: "People who had been on more dates with online matches felt worse about their most recent date." So having more points of comparison—more experiences to think back on—made people more critical. The more options they'd had, the pickier they got. Paradoxically, Norton noted, these same people continued to be just as optimistic about their next date as they'd been at the start. They were souring on past dates, but they weren't learning to adjust their expectations for the future.

So does familiarity in fact breed contempt? In real life, or IRL, probably not. Once people have passed our initial screening, Norton suggests, and we've decided we want to truly interact and get to know them, more interaction will encourage affinity and affection.

Harry Reis, a professor of psychology at the University of Rochester, looks at a different side of the relationship coin. He studies the factors that influence the frequency and closeness of our social ties, particularly how they can help predict intimacy, attachment, and emotional regulation. Among Reis and his colleagues' revelations is that having confidence that a person will respond to you, increased comfort during your interactions with them, and greater perceived knowledge about the other person (feeling that you are getting to know them) leads to liking and attraction.

These factors may seem intuitive enough. For some of us, though, there is another paradox at play. Many of us find comfort in identifying *flaws* in the person we are chatting with. Perhaps we prefer to see a few faults at the beginning—an endearing tendency to misspell, a crooked facial feature in a profile picture—rather than thinking someone is perfect and having them let us down later.

Bennet touches on this notion of imperfection in our initial conversation:

Bennet: That is a fine looking bike. I must confess a slight love for slightly less than perfect gear. As the Japanese 16th century tea master Sen no Rikyu said "In the tea room, all the utensils should be slightly less than adequate" Perhaps this is why I don't do ironmans?

Me: I watched a movie about the Japanese philosophy of the imperfect. I subscribe to that with my wrinkles. Perfectly imperfect, right?

Bennet: It is the whole wabi-sabi concept: the beauty of the imperfections and the beauty of age. And what wrinkles? I don't see any

Me: Hmm—you might need to get your eyes checked. Reading glasses?

Bennet: Yes indeed. And I'm wearing them

> **Me:** I just got some reading glasses for the first time in my life and I'm now amazed at the wrinkles on my face that I had no idea that I had!

> **Bennet:** There's a nice softness now to life when I don't wear mine.

> **Bennet:** it makes the world look like a 1970 Vogue pictorial. So you could do worse.

Do faults make a person seem more accessible? IRL dating so often evolves as a process of disillusionment as that gem we spied online starts to show some cracks. It may be that it's appealing to start from a place of reality, and to enjoy a process of gradual *illusionment* as you fall in love.

Whatever the reason, this trade-off—between the comfort in what we know and the thrill or disappointment in what we don't—will always be at play in our online dating. Seeking new experiences will always involve risk taking; we must trade some sense of security in order to find it. This inherent tension pervades our romantic pursuits as we vacillate between the familiar and the foreign.

The Same but Different

There's a curious wrinkle in all this discussion of comfort and novelty, one that I've observed over the years with my patients. When they are attracted to someone who is not their usual type, I sense that they may be unconsciously sniffing out an essence of something familiar—or even familial. Attraction might be best summarized as something novel that *resembles* something familiar. We are less attracted to fully familiar people because, we presume, we know all their flaws. Familiarity, however, remains important in our relationships because it allows us to identify with another person. The potential of an online profile seems only greater if it matches our previous criteria of what a partner should be like. So we are likely most attracted to what is only *incrementally* new. It's familiarity but with a twist.

When I began chatting with Paulo, we had much in common: interests, political views, tastes. Then he surprised me:

Paulo: Question—somewhat of a touchstone question, at that . . . do you have any interest in shooting pistols?

Me: Who were you planning on shooting?

Paulo: Well, it pays to practice before choosing WHO . . .

Me: Are you a gun owner?

Paulo: I recently became one.

Paulo: No really rational reason.

Me: Impending zombie apocalypse

Paulo: There might be that in the backfield.

Me: Whatcha got?

Paulo: 9mm

Me: Ammo?

Paulo: Range only

Paulo: I only have about 100 rounds . . . CA is quite strict.

Me: I know

Me: There is Nevada

Paulo: But we could do 50 each.

Me: I have to go there to get Fois gras too

Paulo: Now you're talking!

Paulo: Thelma & Louise & Julia . . . Natural Born Gourmands!

Me: Some might not encourage me to go off on a remote weekend with a stranger that involves guns.

Paulo: True.

Paulo: I'll give you the key.

Me: Lol—to what?

Paulo: The lockbox

Me: Shoot, I thought you meant your heart

Paulo: Piano, piano . . . Lentamente, carina.

I can't say I had been planning to become a member of the NRA. Still, I found myself attracted to Paulo. He was well read, had lived in many countries, was emotionally sensitive. He also owned a gun and could chop wood for me. He was familiar, but with a twist.

The psychologist Sheena Iyengar, author of *The Art of Choosing,* studied this notion when her research group looked at how people embrace new things. They showed subjects items such as shoes or sunglasses from a set of choices, then asked them to rate the items on two scales: how much they liked them, and how unusual they were. She found that most people *think* they like things that are more unusual than what everyone else likes. In fact, people largely liked the same things and liked things they perceived to be slightly unusual. Most didn't choose the really standard shoes or sunglasses, nor did they choose the really off-beat ones. What they wanted was something with a little bit of a kick. The same but different.

Let's look at the first text exchange between Solange and

James. Solange, a savvy psychologist in her thirties, is an enthusiastic online dater. She and James quickly connect over text because of their perceived similarities in philosophy and lifestyle. But their conversation is also spiked with excitement about the unknown.

> **Solange:** Hi James. The personality that comes through your photos is fantastic. I share your love of joy and playfulness, not to mention burgers on brioche buns and committed polyamory (not necessarily in that order). And Karaoke! What songs do you sing?

> **James:** Hi Solange. I super appreciate your thorough and well-worded message. It's so rare in dating apps! Journey and Chicago are at the top of the list. Can you believe I was at a karaoke bar and they had a rule: no ballads! What a terrible rule. I mean, seriously. I'm excited that you are also polyamorous. What's your experience so far?

> **Solange:** Hi James, How can a karaoke bar possibly have a rule against ballads?! Ballads are "made" for karaoke. Or karaoke was made for ballads. One of those. As for me and polyamory, long story. I've had both monogamous and polyamorous relationships, mostly the latter. What I've discovered for myself is that polyamory is a mindset, a philosophy, not just a different set of rules. I like that each partner is responsible for managing their own jealousy and insecurities rather than treating these things as indicators of love and commitment. I like the idea that love is abundant rather than scarce, that there is enough for everyone. How about you?

> **James:** I've been polyamorous for awhile
> too. I started when I was in a phase of
> reinventing myself, and was open to
> exploring new things. But I'm past the
> exploration phase. I also know what I want
> and am looking for that. Something I tell
> people is that it's easy to find things when
> you're not sure of what you're looking for.
> It's very hard to find what you're looking
> for, when what you want is very specific.
> What I've found about polyamory is a
> lifelong journey into my own barriers to
> love, and separating a lot of concepts that
> I've conflated together. Would you be up
> for meeting soon? I think at the very least
> we could have a very connected vulnerable
> conversation.

Solange and James draw on common experiences to create a sense of familiarity. They reverberate in the tone of their messages and echo each other's language from the start. But the subject of polyamory, and the possibility of other partners in their lives, seems to inject some intrigue into the chat for each of them. They're coming from a place of similarity, but with the thrill of something new.

It's not only familiar personalities that we're drawn to. We are even attracted to people who look a bit like ourselves. One study demonstrated that Norwegian couples rated their partner's photograph as more attractive when it was digitally morphed to look ever so slightly more like themselves. ("Slightly" being the operative word: after greater than 22 percent resemblance the partner was deemed gross.) Similarly, couples with matching speech styles are more likely to stay together than those who speak differently. In Solange and James's text exchange, they almost sound like the same person.

There are some other revealing features tucked inside their

texts. You'll notice they sometimes read like a treatise on polyamory. There is little banter. Yes, there is the brief back-and-forth about karaoke, but other than that it's all personal disclosure. And while they are talking about sex, the conversation isn't actually sexy per se. It's as if they were taking a shortcut to intimacy by talking about intimate things, rather than creating their own version of it. They clearly both want to be perceived as sexual beings and to determine if their sexuality is compatible; that's a worthwhile pursuit. But the chat lacks some spark or, dare I say, chemistry. Having a connected conversation does not happen by *talking about* having one!

My hunch about the two was borne out IRL. Solange accepted James's invitation, and they met for a drink a few days later. James sat stiffly on his barstool, much less comfortable with the encounter than Solange had imagined he would be. He did not attempt to make even slight physical contact, and what had been a text thread about abundant love became, in person, a staid and pinched conversation. They never met again.

This outcome is all too common. While dating sites are in widespread use, a Pew Research Center study recently showed that only one in ten Americans say they have been in a committed relationship with someone they met on a dating app. A full 45 percent of recent users said their experience made them feel frustrated.

Take this initial text exchange between forty-two-year-old Dana and Dale. Dana works as a nurse, has two kids, and would like to meet someone, but she's been single for a while and trapped in what feels like a vortex of online dating chats that never really seem to go anywhere. Their conversation until this point has been playful and flirty, until Dana unexpectedly decides to bow out:

> **Dana:** I'm probably not the one for you. I'm fearful, middle-aged and mundane. There are some exciting moments, and there could be some rocking sex, but mostly what you get is the domesticity of a single mom with all that brings. Yuck.

> **Dale:** Hey, I'm more middle-aged and mundane and have been a single parent for longer. Not that this is a competition. And I'm really enjoying our chat.

> **Dana:** Well, I'm working like 17 hours a day and there are other reasons too. After I had the twins I lost a ton of weight and have way more damage to my body than a woman my age should have. I don't think your idea of sexy is a date that badly needs a tummy tuck.

Dana's self-deprecating words may betray some central character traits, as well as an underlying tendency to self-sabotage. We will explore what texts can reveal about character in the next chapter. But notice for now how badly she needs to safeguard against disappointment and rejection. The chasm between flirting over text and the reality of a relationship is just too big a leap for her to take. To many of us who have online dated, her feelings are all too real, whether or not we've ever divulged them to a stranger. It's an experience rife with hope, fear, and frustration.

And yet for all that, one recurring contradiction emerges: while people generally complain about the experience, they also can't put down the phone. There is something about online dating that keeps people, even Dana, coming back for more.

Sheila's chat with Neal sums this up in a nutshell. Sheila is thirty-one and has been burned more than once by online dating. But that doesn't stop her from trying. She's matched with

Neal, and they've launched into a long conversation about their relationship histories. Neal reveals a tendency to rescue women who seem to need help and then to worry he has no way out.

Sheila: Do you think that is why you keep getting stuck in bad relationships?

Neal: Could be. Never really told anyone this before. It's great talking to you. Really intimate.

Sheila: Well, I just spent two weeks developing emotional intimacy with some guy who finally revealed that he has a regular girlfriend he's planning to move in with but is also beginning a relationship with another girl.

Neal: That's awful! 😣 So glad I didn't move in with my girlfriend

Sheila: Girlfriend? 🫤

Neal: I mean my ex girlfriend.

It isn't clear whether that was a Freudian slip on Neal's part, or whether he was referring to a relationship he had in fact moved on from. Either way, Sheila will persist, with Neal or without him.

DA Stands for Dating Apps

"I had to uninstall my apps off my phone," said Chris, a twenty-eight-year-old private equity investor. "It's too easy to get sucked in, and then, before I know it, hours have gone by and I'm chatting with a belly dancer from Belize."

Are dating apps the new slot machines?

Like any addictive behavior that results in a chemical rush, dating apps are designed to hook you into receiving tiny jolts of pleasure. When a person is about to experience some kind of reward, the neurochemical dopamine is released into the brain. It's not the dopamine itself that makes you feel good; pleasure and euphoria are actually mediated by opioids that our brains produce (like endorphins). But dopamine helps the brain recognize incentive or imminent pleasure. The dopamine signal is the brain's way of saying, "Pay attention, you are about to get a reward—you need to remember this, so you can do it again." That reward can be anything from food, to kissing, to drugs, to gambling. It can even be playing or watching sports. Dopamine, which neuroscientists refer to as DA, is about learning and reinforcing what will feel good.

DA mediates behaviors that involve desire, motivation, hard work, passion, perseverance, novelty, and reward. These behaviors take on even more significance when the reward is uncertain. Give a rat a lever that it can press to receive a food treat, and you'll observe a burst of DA just before it gets the treat. Over time, as the rat consistently receives treats with each press of the lever, the DA response will attenuate. The food is still pleasurable, but it has become a known and certain reward, and so DA takes a backseat and no longer plays a driving role in the rat's brain circuitry. But if that treat is given intermittently and only random lever presses result in a reward, the brain's DA circuitry lights up like a Christmas tree when the reward is presented. Like a slot machine addict, the rat will abandon other pursuits and spend most of its time pulling the lever to see if a reward is coming. For the brain, a gamble holds much more interest than a sure thing.

What makes social media and dating apps so addictive is the unpredictable element that random human behavior so naturally provides. Your post is liked a lot or a little. Your swipe reveals a match or it doesn't. A new message awaits, bearing excitement or disappointment. Like in a casino, you are surrounded by flashing lights and ringing bells. Everyone is winning—intermittently and unpredictably.

Most of us, at any given moment, can reach for our phones without moving our feet. At night, we keep our phones at our bedsides. Dating apps may be the last thing we engage with before drifting off to sleep and the first when we wake up. There is even a faux-Greek word for the feeling of withdrawal from our phones—"nomophobia," or "fear of no mobile." In a 2011 study, one-third of Americans polled said they would rather give up sex than their phones. And the phones have only gotten better since then! (The sex, who can say?) We can only imagine what pursuits are being abandoned or neglected in favor of the screens in our pockets.

There can be a fine line between habit and addiction. A habit is just a behavior done with little thought involved. It develops because we reinforce it, both consciously and unconsciously. Habits can be healthy, like flossing and exercise, or unhealthy, like smoking and snacking. They are considered addictions when the behavior becomes so persistent and compulsive that it hurts the user or takes away from important aspects of their lives, impairing their ability to function.

Can swiping become an addiction? It certainly can. It all depends on what toll it takes on your life and relationships. Dating apps are yet another addictive offshoot of the tech industry, designed to hook the user into a mentality of "but wait, there's more." The cost of all that choice and connection is the ensuing lack of attention to, and disconnection from, what might be right in front of you.

The Paradox of Choice

"After I've been dating someone for a while, it's almost like the dating app knows our phones have been hanging out in the same location together," says my patient Graham, a forty-year-old creative director who moves from one intense short-term relationship to the next every few weeks. "The app starts to notify me of all the new possibilities," he says. "It's hard not to start swiping and see what might be better."

I'm not sure if this surveillance feature is actually built into dating apps, but I do know this: Graham is dogged by choice.

With scores of swipeable faces at the tip of our thumbs, dating apps can leave us less decisive than ever. Apps give us access to so many more choices than we would otherwise meet in daily life. But it turns out our brains are not built to process so many alternatives. Once faced with double digits of choices, we reach cognitive overload.

Research out of Temple University's Center for Neural Decision Making has shown that when people are given complex information, activity in the dorsolateral prefrontal cortex ramps up, but only to a point. After too much information is presented, this executive area of the brain switches off, much like an overloaded circuit breaker. In addition, areas responsible for anxiety in the brain become more active. Our dopamine systems may go into overdrive and ultimately shut down, paralyzed. In these states, we don't and can't make a choice.

Professor Barry Schwartz of Swarthmore College has spent years advancing his argument about "the paradox of choice": that too much choice leads to poorer outcomes and makes us less happy. In one famous experiment, dubbed the jam study, shoppers presented with too many gourmet jam choices were unable to complete their purchase. The ones who did purchase were unhappier with their purchase than people presented with fewer choices.

Schwartz thinks there is value to limiting our choices and, beyond that, that one of the secrets to happiness is mitigating our expectations. More choices come with more agonizing over those choices, more responsibility for them, and more potential for regret. Schwartz's lectures are often peppered with cartoons. One that he likes to show to illustrate this point is of a college student wearing a sweatshirt emblazoned with "Brown but my first choice was Yale." Another is of a couple at the altar in which the bride is uttering the phrase "You'll do" instead of "I do."

Joe's text to Allie sums up the sentiment:

Joe: You da bomb.

Allie: Aww . . . I think you're really great too.

Joe: and if I hadn't just started chasing this redhead I'd probably have tried to seduce you. 😊

Allie: Gotcha. Guess I'll take that as a compliment?

Is choice overwhelming us in our dating lives? Schwartz thinks so, but with higher stakes than any jar of jam. His collaborator Sheena Iyengar agrees. "Oh, it's a huge problem, right? It's what we call FOMO [fear of missing out]. Barry Schwartz and I first identified it in the domain of job search. And the same thing is happening at a much larger level when it comes to dating," she says. "You have so many options, and, in many ways, these are incomparable options because you're comparing humans."

Mandy learned this all too well when she found herself texting with several women after first joining a dating app. After hooking up with the woman who is now her partner, she had the following exchange with another woman, who also held some appeal:

> **Hallie:** Can we set up a time now to meet? What's good for you? PS your dog is so beautiful (your kids too!) I have a hankering for a dog. Yum!

> **Mandy:** Hi Hallie—I don't mean to be hard to pin down, I'm just still figuring out how to do this whole online dating thing! How about we meet up live & low key somewhere?

> **Hallie:** Sure I'm game. What do you suggest?

> **Mandy:** Hi Hallie—apologies for the slow response, my dance card has kinda filled up, and I'm wanting to hit pause on connecting live with any new folks. If you're willing, we could possibly check in again in a few weeks, but for now . . . Be well, and best wishes, Mandy

It isn't just choosing between people that poses challenges. By continuing to browse and swipe on a dating app, we are also making a choice not to invest in any one match or relationship. "When there are lots and lots of options," Schwartz says, "people are less inclined to do the work." The work, when it comes to dating, is of course the hard and vulnerable effort involved in navigating a relationship. And as we've seen above, it's often the work of really learning about a person that makes you like them and attach to them over time. If you don't do so, you may find yourself stuck, like my patient Graham, in a cycle of fleeting, insignificant relationships.

In *The Paradox of Choice,* Schwartz uses the following quotation (which he admitted to me is probably wrongly attributed to

Camus): "Shall I kill myself, or have a cup of coffee?" The quotation especially resonated with me as a doctor who often works with suicidal patients; in therapy, I find it helpful to bring them back to life's small actions and pleasures. But Schwartz points out that the quotation underscores a simple fact: suicidal or not, we are always making choices, whether we know it or not. When we have a cup of coffee, we are unconsciously choosing not to commit suicide (also not to drink tea).

Presented with too many choices, the pleasure of choosing right is canceled out by the fear of making the wrong choice. The impulse to keep swiping on potential partners will inevitably win out.

We don't do ourselves any favors when we set unrealistic standards for our partners-to-be. In her book *Marry Him: The Case for Settling for Mr. Good Enough,* the psychotherapist Lori Gottlieb talks about the long list of requirements her future spouse would need to possess. When she brought this list to a traditional matchmaker, the matchmaker laughed and warned her that there were probably only three people in the world who met these criteria and *they* might not be into *her.*

Such lists can also fail to acknowledge subtle but important factors in attraction. Not long ago one of my patients described a guy she had met. He seemed perfect: tall, handsome, athletic, smart, accomplished, and wealthy. There was one problem, she said. "What, he hasn't written a concerto?" I said. No, she didn't like the sound of his voice.

Even if we were able to generate the ideal mate through a list that could be fed into an algorithm and matched, what are the chances we'd actually be attracted to that person? And what are the chances that person would be attracted to us? That brings us to the final paradox of online dating.

The Paradox of Learnability

In 1931, the Austrian mathematician and philosopher Kurt Gödel published his incompleteness theorem. Simply put, the theorem states that there are properly posed mathematical questions that cannot be proved from already self-evident propositions. These questions are thus deemed undecidable. In other words, some mathematical statements cannot be proved true or false using mathematical axioms, even though those mathematical axioms themselves cannot be proved false. Therein lay the paradox.

The idea that math is insufficient to understand some aspects of the universe may not seem shocking to non-mathematically minded people, but it was certainly shocking to the mathematical world of Gödel's time. Other mathematicians tried to challenge the theorem without success.

The theorem remains relevant to this day, particularly as it applies to machine learning and artificial intelligence (AI). Machine learning supposes that with a large enough data set and a sophisticated enough algorithm a machine can make accurate predictions. Show a computer enough images of a bird, devise a rule set for the computer to be able to identify certain features of a bird (a beak, wings, wide-spaced eyes), and over time the computer should be able to reliably distinguish birds from other animals. It has proven enormously effective in such fields as video surveillance, facial recognition, and medical diagnostics.

But you can't simply identify an ideal partner, reduce them down to a set of features, and run them through a machine. What the extension of Gödel's theorem shows is that no matter how powerful the computer or AI, a data set may never be enough to make certain predictions reliably. This was dubbed the learnability paradox. It's the notion that machine learning itself has an unsolvable problem at its core.

This abstract principle intersects with the world of dating precisely at the place where daters today congregate, on dating sites and apps—and specifically under the hood, in the much-vaunted *algorithms* that power those apps. Old-school online dating sites, like matchmaking services before them, led clients to believe in them through a process of refinement. Hundreds of questions were answered; an individual's profile could be pages long. With so many keystrokes up front, people necessarily felt invested and dependent on the outcome of the process. It is questionable whether much of this data was actually used; the sites and services likely just tossed available profiles your way. But it lent an air of seriousness, a patina of science, to the match-making. There could be a self-fulfilling prophecy to it all: you believed that your matches were well suited to you, and so you were more likely to give them a fair shot.

Over time, all the window dressing went, well, out the window. Now the strategy has evolved to maximize and optimize choice. Users who receive lots of right swipes will be ranked higher than those who don't, and they will be presented in turn with more desirable choices. A popularity contest, in other words.

There are other features beyond simple rank. Dating algorithms also learn from a user's prior swiping behavior. They operate under the same collaborative filtering principles that power your Facebook, Google, Netflix, and Amazon suggestions. Your prior decisions inform predictions about your preferences. If you haven't previously engaged with white people, for instance, the app may stop showing you images of white people. So the algorithms aren't actually predicting who might be compatible for you, but rather the likelihood of your right swipe. This may lead to users only being presented choices based on superficial criteria. Just because you swiped left on a bunch of people with tattoos doesn't mean you don't ever want to be shown someone with a tattoo, or that there is not a tattooed person out there who might be a good fit for you.

Might the concept of "the right match" fall into Gödel's learnability limbo, where no human-curated data set of right-swiped profiles is large enough to predict whom we might actually fall in love with? By focusing on a list of desired traits—like a degree from a prestigious college, or a person's taste in music, or their athletic lifestyle—might we miss important red flags? Could we be obscuring glaring personality traits, psychiatric diagnoses, or even the larger and more elusive question of "Could you really be into this person?"

Technology and artificial intelligence have begun to offer us the hope of knowability; whether they achieve it none of us will probably live to see. But in the meantime, they've also fueled our deepest existential fears. Killer robots, online propagandists, virtual reality that eclipses our real lives—these are features not just of Hollywood sci-fi but of our day-to-day existence. Almost everyone who has used a dating app has at some point wondered if they were chatting with a bot.

Take this dating app exchange that I once entered into. Well, not an exchange exactly . . .

Brian: Hi Mimi, nice to connect. Brian.

Brian: Mimi?

> **Me:** Hi Brian. Looks like I missed this msg some time ago. Hope you had a good weekend.

Brian: Hi Mimi. Let's try again.

Brian: Hello

Brian: Mimi?

Brian: Missed again 😎

Brian: Mimi, Harvard in common, how r u?

Brian: Mimi?

Brian: Hi Mimi

Brian: Hi Mimi. How r u?

Brian: 😊

Brian: Mimi? 😗

Brian: Mimi are you still around?

Brian: Mimi?

Brian: ??

Brian: So . . .

Brian: Hello . . .

Looking at this thread, it's hard not to wonder if Brian is a bot—a piece of lazily designed code. Then again, one would expect more sophisticated programming for a bot. This is likely just a faulty human.

So while dating apps certainly grant us choice and ease of communication, their algorithms are likely not their most useful feature. A pivotal study by Eli Finkel and colleagues at Northwestern University found that algorithms were very limited in their ability to predict compatibility and that the best predictors of a lasting relationship came from responses to "unpredictable and uncontrollable events that have not yet happened."

Michael Norton of Harvard Business School says that dating algorithms get a bad rap. "Yes, their claims may be overstated," he says, "but what they do is give you options that you wouldn't otherwise have. They present you with lots and lots of vaguely acceptable options. They are not going to provide you with a soul mate on the first try."

To put it another way, think of how a child interacts with a plastic toy. It can be the departure point for a wonderful session of play, becoming a magical universe in the small hands of the child. Or it can be an inert chunk of plastic. Likewise, dating apps offer you only a portal. Creating the magic and mystery is your job.

If, as Finkel's study concluded, "the best-established predictors of how a romantic relationship will develop can be known only after the relationship begins," then when does a relationship begin? With the very first text exchange, of course!

That is, if you know how to interpret it. As the comedian Chris Rock says, "When you meet somebody for the first time, you're not meeting them. You're meeting their representative." We'll look next at how to get past all the agents and managers and get to the person themselves.

CHAPTER 2

Can I Get Your Numbers?

Ian: OK, lets grab coffee . . . I'm downtown during the week. U able to get close?

> **Linsay:** I work right there.

Ian: Meet at Caffe Illy?

> **Linsay:** Would love to.

Ian: How about Tuesday?

> **Linsay:** Great. Free at noon. You?

Ian: Just a strange time for coffee.

Ian: I usually have a cup in the AM and then another one around 3

> **Linsay:** OK I can make 3pm work to adapt to your caffeine dosing. As long as you are flexible about when I smoke my crack. Because while I'm flexible with my caffeine intake, I have a strict schedule for that.

The first meeting over coffee. A true Norman Rockwell moment.

While Linsay might enjoy drinking coffee and picture herself with a coffee drinker—she probably even listed cappuccino as one of her favorite things—Ian's rigidity might be more telling than his caffeination habits. Because dating profiles reduce people to searchable attributes, like whether they drink coffee, daters may miss the more ineffable qualities, such as their flexibility and sense of humor. Does liking coffee really mean very much, given that 64 percent of American adults do? Who doesn't like long walks on the beach at sunset? And does saying that you are "funny," "easygoing," or "genuine" really mean very much, when we are hard-pressed to find a dating profile of a self-described boring, uptight, or disingenuous person. These are vacant data points.

In the case of "funny" or "genuine," showing is better than telling. My dear friend Andy, whom I met online, wrote in his bio, "I will make you laugh." He quickly did.

> **Andy:** Hi Mimi. How could you hate Trump? He's got such great hair! And what kind of medicine do you practice?

> **Me:** I'm a psychiatrist. Though I'm doing more work in digital health now.

> **Andy:** Shrink-wrapped apps?

The last chapter highlighted the paradoxes that permeate online dating. We discovered that some aspects of the apps serve us well, such as giving us more options, while other aspects fall short, such as giving us options based on lists or choices that may not reflect our true desires. Dating apps are designed as marketplaces. What marketplaces do, economically speaking, is allow people to save time while finding what they want. But with dating, as we've seen, when we generate ideas of what we want or like, we are often looking for an experience that doesn't easily translate into a list of codable traits.

Just because the dating apps themselves tend to disappoint, we needn't gnash our teeth like Wild Things. There are other ways to capitalize on the choice dating apps offer us and extract from them the information we need. It simply requires taking creative steps to *find* that information.

In the text exchange that started this chapter, Linsay recognizes the possibility that Ian's coffee schedule represents a sign of rigidity, or lack of openness. She teases him by joking about the rules for her fictitious drug use. Ian is missing the point: it's a date, not a coffee break. Making an issue about what time they have coffee may foretell a lack of flexibility in his approach to relationships and an overly concrete way of approaching the world in general. With her teasing, Linsay, in turn, reveals her direct, slightly brash, risk-taking personality. That may not be Ian's cup of tea.

Snippets of a text conversation can help us make predictions about an individual's temperament, personality, and other dynamics that may manifest themselves throughout a relationship. These elements are often visible during our earliest texts exchanged with an individual, so it's useful to learn how to spot them. In this chapter we will look at what it means to extract meaningful data from such short bursts of conversation: the art and science of thin slicing.

"Thin slicing" is a term used in psychology to describe pattern recognition from narrow windows of experience, or a small subset of data. Typically, these conclusions are drawn subconsciously, as Malcolm Gladwell famously described in his book *Blink*. Part of what makes our brain so impressive is its ability to come to a sophisticated judgment in a very short reaction time. Brilliant examples of this are the hockey player Wayne Gretzky and his ability to "see" the ice, to take in all the players' positions and visualize shots with all of their angles in a single glance. Or the chess champion Garry Kasparov, who could envision future moves on a chessboard without having to explicitly calculate them. Likewise, a trained psychiatrist can learn to read and deduce a history of trauma, despair, or suicidal intent in a patient through a fleeting facial expression.

None of these seemingly innate and subconscious superpowers

came without intense training and practice. Gretzky famously spent countless hours as a child with a pen and paper in hand watching *Hockey Night in Canada,* tracing the movement of the puck, learning to intuitively recognize patterns others might not. Studying the masters enhances our own ability to thin slice.

Kasparov and Gretzky might have been masters in their own fields, but there are also masters of thin slicing as applied to behavioral science. One of these masters is Paul Ekman, a professor at the University of California, San Francisco Medical School, who has succeeded in thin slicing emotion through the recognition of what are known as facial microexpressions. By thoroughly cataloging the muscles involved in fleeting expressions, movements that last less than one-fifth of a second, Ekman can perceive the suggestions of fear, anger, or disgust that an untrained eye would miss.

A more pedestrian form of thin slicing takes place when we form first impressions from observing just a few seconds of a person's behavior. We've all done it—judged someone by their handshake, eye contact, or mannerisms. Frank Bernieri, a professor of psychology at Oregon State who specializes in social perception and judgment, is an expert in thin slicing as it applies to first impressions. He argues that first impressions are "prerational"; in other words, they happen at a gut level. They draw on our unconscious ability to find patterns in situations and behavior based on very narrow slices of experience.

They may also tap into bias and prejudice. The trick then is to make those first impressions as accurate as possible. That's where training comes in. With the right preparation, conclusions based on thin slicing can be as accurate as, or even more accurate than, ones based on more information. While most untrained people won't do better than a coin toss when it comes to deciphering if someone is lying, take a lie detection course such as the one taught at the FBI National Academy and you will improve your odds significantly.

Obviously, we can't rely on facial expressions, or any other visual cues for that matter, when it comes to thin slicing texts. But the technique applies just as effectively. Whether we are extracting important information from a first glance, a fleeting facial expression, or a few text messages, we are drawing broad conclusions from a small data set. By using initial text messages as a form of thin slicing, we can learn a great deal about a prospective date.

Before we jump into more of those all-important first texts, let's look at two more examples of thin slicing in behavioral science that rely more heavily on language. They'll help light the way as we move forward.

This Is Your Relationship Thin Sliced

A notorious example of thin slicing in the romantic arena is Dr. John Gottman's predictive work on relationship success. In his "Love Lab," Gottman records couples involved in spontaneous verbal conversations and arguments. He has collected decades' worth of data of couples' interactions while they are wired to sensors that record heart rate, sweat, and movements, and observing cameras document body language, facial expressions, and words. By coding the exchanges and modeling patterns, he's able to predict with 93.6 percent accuracy which couples will divorce and under what time frame. This, using only three minutes of a single conversation. Imagine, early in your courtship, being able to see the writing on the wall. Some couples might prefer not to know.

Yet knowing would be helpful and even actionable. Gottman argues that while there is no magic formula for love, there is useful advice hidden within the data. Much of his recipe for relationship success boils down to having a solid friendship, building trust, allowing your partner to influence you, and being gentle. Successful couples also make each other feel good physically; their blood pressure lowers during conversation rather than rising.

What's astounding is the way these macro concepts can be made visible in even the most micro of exchanges. Sometimes, for instance, a first text exchange is pure delight:

Me: Hi Damien. How are you?

> **Damien:** Holà Mimi! I am well. My map radius tool indicated that you are in Tahoe. Or Fresno. Or Legget. I'm voting heavily for Tahoe. Drop me a line when you repatriate.

Me: Strong work! Tahoe it is. Another great weekend of skiing. Home later today. I've never been to Legget. Have you?

> **Damien:** I have been to Legget. As a cosmopolitan polyglot, I find it a must. Unfortunately I have also been to Fresno.

Me: Yes, the 'no is to be avoided. What does a polyglot do on the eel river? Be in silence? I do love riding my bike up the north coast. There are some killer climbs out of Mendocino.

> **Damien:** I speak tree. Those pygmy pines on the road out of Mendocino have particularly wicked senses of humor. How is your week shaping up? Would you like to go down to the fountain and share a pop?

In my first exchange with Damien, it felt as if we were already speaking our own language, one that others might not easily understand. I suspect that if this exchange had taken place in

Gottman's lab, he would have captured the click in our conversation as playful attunement. Open-ended questions and deepening statements are certainly there. I can attest that Damien's texts made me smile and feel good on a physical level. For lack of a better word, I guess we grokked.

Thin Slicing in Mental Health

Gottman studied live interactions, but reliable predictions can be drawn from text alone. One powerful example comes not from the study of romantic relationships but from the world of mental health. Crisis Text Line (CTL) is a company founded by Nancy Lublin, a serial entrepreneur known for her persistence and grit. Crisis Text Line's trained counselors volunteer their time to field millions of text messages from individuals who reach out in need. The company emerged from another nonprofit of Lublin's called Do Something, designed to mobilize teens to volunteer for worthy causes. The best way to reach teens was through text messaging, of course, and as Do Something was successfully reaching millions of teens, it would also get texts back in reply. Scattered among the largely positive messages that were coming in were a few upsetting texts, like "I'm being bullied" or "My friend is addicted to crystal meth."

Then there was the single disturbing text message that compelled Lublin to action. One day, her team received a text that said, "He won't stop raping me. It's my dad. He told me not to tell anyone." Followed by "R U there?"

And so Lublin built Crisis Text Line. Since then, the company's counselors have provided daily lifesaving interventions to people with depression, with anxiety, in abusive situations, or struggling with suicidal thoughts. Sometimes all four at once. To field and triage the millions and millions of messages that CTL receives, the company has created algorithms using key words and word pairings that can serve as markers of acuity. Using words like "die," "suicide," and "overdose," of course, bumps you to the front of the queue. But in their analysis of the data, they have also found some less expected correlations between text content and the risk it presents. Want to take a guess at the most lethal words found in a text message, the words most likely to lead to an active rescue? Most of us would guess that "suicide" and "die" would rank high, but in fact "Excedrin," "ibuprofen," and "800 mg" top the list. The word "ibuprofen" was sixteen times more likely to predict that the person texting would need emergency services than the word "suicide."

It's a different kind of thin slicing, based on data science and the parsing of text language, but it allows the service to get back to high-risk texters in under five minutes, with an average response time of under one minute. Velocity like this would be impossible without sophisticated data science humming in the background.

Crisis Text Line has managed to collect one of the largest health data sets in the world from diverse cross sections of society. These learnings help inform the company's own interventions, naturally, but they also reflect the state of American mental health as a whole. Where doctors see individual cases, Crisis Text Line can see trends.

So, Ekman can read intent from a fleeting facial expression, Gottman is able to predict a relationship's success from a snippet of conversation, and Crisis Text Line is able to make risk assessment predictions from a text message. What about predicting someone's personality or character from their dating texts? Are there certain words that telescope "serial killer"? Are there word combinations that communicate "bunny boiler"?

In order for us to talk about personality, we need to establish a shared vocabulary. So let's look at how scientists measure and characterize it. We'll be using this language throughout the chapters that follow as we encounter personalities big and small.

Personality Quantified

You've probably come across many different varieties of personality tests. Companies commonly use the Myers-Briggs Type Indicator in the hiring or team-building process, business coaches sometimes use the Enneagram, and bizarre clickbait quizzes have popped up in your Facebook feed—everything from which Disney princess you are, to which Harry Potter house you should live in based on your preferred Taylor Swift tune. While these personality tests may be entertaining, some may be as useful as your daily horoscope.

One test stands above the others in both scientific validity (it measures what it says it will measure) and reliability (it produces consistent results), and that is the Big Five personality test. The Big Five, otherwise known as the Five Factor Model (FFM), describes personality along five dimensions: openness, conscientiousness, extroversion, agreeableness, and neuroticism. (Think of the acronym OCEAN.) Researchers have argued for the biological basis and universality of the Big Five, and that it transcends language and cultural differences, though in fairness it's mostly been validated in literate, urban populations.

The Big Five personality dimensions emerged from research done on the words people used to describe themselves, and they have been used to predict many things, from academic achievement to dating behavior. With the FFM, people aren't categorized or boxed into distinct personality types; instead, each person falls somewhere on a spectrum. So, for example, instead of proclaiming me an ENFP (as the Myers-Briggs did), the Big Five test tells me that I am very high both in extroversion and in openness to experience, high in conscientiousness, while low in neuroticism and only moderately agreeable.

People high in **openness to experience,** as the name implies, are curious and imaginative. High scorers tend to be artistic and appreciate diverse views, ideas, and experiences. People low on this scale are more traditional, dislike change, and may struggle with abstract thinking.

Conscientiousness relates to responsibility and productivity. High scorers tend to be organized and persevering. These individuals are also extremely reliable and tend to be high achievers, hard workers, and planners. At the other end of the spectrum, those low in conscientiousness dislike structure and have a tendency to procrastinate or fail to complete tasks.

Those high in **extroversion** have stronger friendship ties and support systems. They tend to be more outgoing, amicable, and assertive. Friendly and energetic, extroverts draw inspiration from social situations. In contrast, introverts enjoy more solitary experiences and dislike small talk. They produce less dopamine in response to human faces.

Agreeableness can be broken down into compassion, respect-fulness, and trust in others. People high in agreeableness tend to be cooperative, helpful, nurturing. They are the peacekeepers and are generally optimistic and trusting of others. Those very low in agreeableness take little interest in others and may be insulting, callous, or manipulative. But being somewhat low in agreeableness can also confer some advantages. These individuals will find it easier to work alone, make difficult decisions, and set boundaries for themselves.

Finally, people high in **neuroticism** are more likely to suffer from depression, anxiety, and substance abuse; they will experience more worry, fear, anger, guilt, and even jealousy. They can be insecure, sensitive, moody, and tense and easily tip into negative emotions. Those low in neuroticism tend to be emotionally stable and handle stress well. Those lowest would be likened to a tall, cool glass of water.

The refreshing thing about the Big Five personality test is that rather than categorizing people as purely extroverted or purely introverted, for example, it rates them on a scale of 0 to 100, for their propensity toward one pole of each of the five dimensions. Most people will fall somewhere in the middle.

How do Big Five scores predict our romantic life? High neuroticism scores seem to be particularly hard on relationships. Neurotics will experience more worry, mood swings, and irritability, and this seems to take a toll on long-term relationship satisfaction. An interesting exception: if a couple is having a lot of sex, that seems to offset the negative impact of neuroticism. So if you are going to pick a neurotic, pick one with a strong libido. The bad news is that neuroticism also appears to generally interfere with healthy sexuality. In more than one study, neuroticism predicted both lower relationship satisfaction and lower sexual satisfaction.

High levels of conscientiousness and agreeableness lend themselves to relationships high in trust. People high in these dimensions tend to be more successful in long-term relationships. Low levels, in contrast, predict novelty seeking, which may also correlate with sexual risk taking. In one study of sixteen thousand people from fifty-two countries, it predicted infidelity. In a meta-analysis, researchers out of the University of Kentucky found that low agreeableness also predicted casual sex with strangers, failure to use condoms, and a large number of partners.

Openness to experience seems to predict, at least among

women, more frequent and varied sex. And, as we've seen among the neurotics, sex seems to help only long-term relationships. Extroverts are generally happier and more charismatic, have better developed relationship skills, and are better adjusted sexually. Being with an extrovert is fun, but understand that they will likely be more adventurous and may have more difficulty with relationship exclusivity.

The Big Five results are generated by collecting subjective responses to a variety of statements. So they are based on *our own* impression of ourselves. But what happens if the way I see myself is different from the way others see me? We'll take a deeper dive into self-knowledge, self-awareness, and insight in the next chapter.

The Big Five in Textspeak

For now, let's think about the way text allows us to reveal our selves and discover others'. There is a long history of research at the intersection of language usage and personality, but new developments in data science have powered this analysis to new levels. Previously, it was hard to get someone to sit down and write thousands of words. Now, as posting, texting, and tweeting feature more centrally in communication, we can analyze at large scale, and it's suddenly possible to discover trends that were harder to see in small writing samples. Just as Crisis Text Line was able to see trends because of the size of its data set, the power of computing has made it possible to thin slice texts and tweets for personality traits.

The inherent value in text messages, in particular, is that they exist in the space between spoken language and formal writing. With texts and tweets, people are less bound by the rules of grammar, punctuation, and syntax. Free from those constraints, they can express themselves in personal and unique ways that reveal their character and style. To experts like Celia Klin, a professor of the psychology of language at Binghamton University, texting looks more like speaking and less like writing. The words are important, but so is the social information they convey.

"Because many of those visual social cues are missing in text"—the eye contact, inflection, facial expressions—"people have adopted brilliant new language uses in their texting to convey meaning," Klin told me. "It's not surprising," she says, "because language is one of the things we do best in life." But there is potential for misunderstanding. "Even when people proofread their texts, they tend to hear their own voice in their head with tone and nuance and believe that is exactly how it is heard by the reader."

Still, word choice can be telling. Even single-word analysis is interesting: extroverts use the word "mouth" more frequently, along with "drinks," "other," "restaurant," and "dancing." Those high in neuroticism, in contrast, are drawn to using the words "awful," "though," "lazy," and "depressing."

The masters of long-term relationships, those high in the agreeable dimension, will use the words "wonderful," "together," "morning," and "spring" with greater frequency. Those extremely conscientious types will pepper their language with "completed," "stupid," "boring," and "adventure." Those *actually* open to adventure—the ones high on the openness scale—will favor the words "folk," "human," "poetry," "universe," "art," and "always."

Take my first words with Charlie, who showed immediate signs of openness in his language:

Me: Hi Charlie

Charlie: Mimi!

Me: Don't think I've seen the tooth brushing bathroom selfie before — very innovative.

Charlie: I like to push the boundaries of life :)

Charlie: It's also my way of cleaning up the bathroom selfie

Me: It's good. I'll be sure to credit you when it goes viral. How was your week? Mine has been brutal. Imagine my disappointment upon realizing that today is only Thursday.

Charlie: You've had a tremendous victory in losing track of time. Mine has been a poignant and precious week.

"Push the boundaries," "life," "poignant and precious," and "losing track of time" all appeared within four text bubbles. My own highly "open to experience" dimension was curious to learn more about Charlie, whose words evinced an equal openness to experience, even though I was a bit grumpy at the time ("brutal" and "disappointment," anyone?).

As I chatted with Charlie further, his agreeable nature had a chance to emerge. I had learned he was a psychologist and joked that my Australian shepherd should hire him.

Me: I have a crazy dog who needs your help. She is afraid of men with beards and baseball caps and also skateboarders. Can you blame her on the latter?

Charlie: I am afraid of all those things as well.

Me: You guys are two peas in a pod. She is an awesome runner and swimmer — will follow me for two miles in open water and will bleed for me on trails.

Charlie: Yes, I will follow you for two miles and bleed for you on trails.

Me: Wow! That was a quick commitment

> **Charlie:** I'm not concerned, except for the bleeding part

> **Me:** I'll bring bandaids. And take care of your ego.

> **Charlie:** OK thank you. My ego is soft and squishy and very flexible.

Besides being funny and endearing, Charlie uses empathetic language. He makes sure to relate not just to me but also to my dog. He indicates his willingness to trust by jokingly volunteering to "bleed" for me. And he's confident enough to use the words "soft and squishy," not words many men use in their initial texts (though in his photos he looks lean and muscular).

Single words are useful, but the magic comes in word pairings. IBM came up with a personality insights tool for its Watson supercomputer that it boldly claimed could make an accurate personality assessment based on a writing sample of just a hundred words. IBM's published correlations are far from perfect, but they represent a reasonable start for certain use cases such as dating apps, and a good preview of the potential for what has been precociously called artificial intelligence.

The Fingerprints of Illness

Digital behavioral health companies have leveraged this kind of data analysis, as well as what we refer to as augmented intelligence, in order to make a **provisional diagnosis,** that is, one that has not been confirmed by a face-to-face encounter. We say "augmented" rather than "artificial" intelligence, because it is important to keep in mind that the human cannot be fully removed from these equations, just as it is important to point out that any diagnosis based on text messaging is necessarily provisional. The notion is less to predict psychiatric diagnoses than to look at attributes in text that predict personality traits and psychological tendencies.

Nonetheless, what we say and write can be indicators of our mental health, and writing analyzed by sophisticated cognitive systems can provide insight into personality traits but also early-stage mental illness. For example, MIT researchers trained a computer to recognize depression and accurately predict it in context-free, natural, flowing text conversation. Using text messages, the model accurately detected depression using an average of seven question-answer sequences without ever requiring certain questions such as "Are you feeling depressed?"

One study looked at 6,202 Twitter users who tweeted words like "alone" or "lonely" more than five times during the study period. It then compared the entire Twitter timelines of these users with a matched group who did not use similar language in their posts. Users who used this language also reflected themes about difficult interpersonal relationships, substance use, body complaints, their need for change, and insomnia. Not surprisingly, the words "alone" and "lonely" have an extremely high association with depression and anxiety.

A Czech study asked 124 female students attending psychology seminars to write an essay about their deepest thoughts and feelings about college. The students also completed a clinically validated depression inventory scale that divided them into groups of currently depressed, formerly depressed, and never-depressed people. Depressives were found, predictably, to use more anger words, anxiety words, and negative emotion words. But the authors also discovered that more use of the word "I" (pronouns in the first-person singular) correlated with depression and that depressives had significantly scarcer use of the pronouns in the second and third person.

In larger-scale studies that have been conducted to examine both text and tweet content, patterns emerge. Mentions of one's work suggest conscientiousness and openness. Mentions of money can indicate lack of agreeableness. So, in turn, do terms of achievement like "win" and "earn." Language centered on illness, like "clinic," "flu," and "pill," correlates with introversion, and a lot of focus on bodily sensations and functions indicates neuroticism and a lack of openness.

There are certainly text exchanges that don't require sophisticated programming or a psychiatrist to understand. Sometimes you can read a thread and know a person is eccentric, for example. But eccentric in what way? Likewise, you don't need an expert to tell you when someone is behaving like a plain asshole. But most texts are more subtle. The goal, as you embark upon your initial exchanges with your dates and dates-to-be, is to recognize the suggestions of someone's personality tucked within the more overt messages.

In the following exchange after an initial date, Rob demonstrates both his conscientiousness and his lack of openness:

Rob: Hi Helen—nice to meet you—back at home and knocked out my excel spreadsheets. Let me know if we can see each other again before your trip.

> **Helen:** Hi Rob. Nice to meet you too and appreciate your thoughtfulness. It sounds like you want to move forward with immediacy and I'm not sure I'm able to bring that intensity to the equation, given my upcoming travel.

Rob: Hmm I usually come to the date with the blueprints, open to changes. But my intensity and I had a chat, and she's going to take some time off;-) I hope you have a good trip.

Rob: But I do wonder what you think? I don't believe in chemistry, to me it's just a buzz word, a person deserves to know why he/she is liked or not . . . facts. Would you rather go for intense and decent or fun and trashy?

Helen: I'll sleep on it. Tomorrow my roommate will be home, perhaps we could all cook together and then ask if he thinks we're compatible? Get some outside perspective??

Rob: Well, I'm expecting you to know what's good (or not) for you. Full disclosure, I've had a few bad experiences with ex's family and friends, to the point of wondering how many of us were in the relationship.

Rob has some insight: he knows he is intense, albeit in a decent and committed way. But he doesn't seem to understand why this might scare Helen. His references to spreadsheets, blueprints, and facts are signs of both his conscientiousness and his rigidity—his lack of openness. These features might be appealing to some, off-putting to others, but they are likely intimidating to someone with Helen's neuroticism. Her inability to trust her own choices, looking to others to guide her decisions, indicates some underlying anxiety. The chances for this relationship are distinctly less than average.

The Grammar Detective

What about our grammar and the structural aspects of our sentences? What can we learn from those? Quite a bit, as it turns out. People who frequently use second-person pronouns like "you" and "your" will tend to be more agreeable and conscientious. On the other hand, those who bandy about negations (like "no" and "never"), revert to the future tense (for example, "will" and "gonna"), and draw on cognitive discrepancies—differences between the actual and the ideal, like "shoulda," "coulda," "woulda"—will likely be less conscientious.

Let's look at a text exchange and see if we can recognize some key personality features related to grammar and syntax. Conrad, a banker, wrote in his profile, "I am good to myself, smile a lot, and don't see the need to be anything but young." Marie is a therapist.

Marie: Hi Conrad. Nice to meet you.

Conrad: Hey! Sorry for the slow response. Life intervenes

Marie: No worries! I hope you're having a good day.

Conrad: Yeah, super busy today

Marie: Aren't the markets closed?

Conrad: What, really? Is that why there are no numbers on my computer? Busy with other stuff. Gotta clean house—Mom is visiting this week. Should've done it earlier.

Marie: Awww, sweet. Do you only clean the house when your mom visits?

Conrad: Hahaha. It's like when you go on a date. You clean better.

Marie: Hmmm, interesting. You talk about your mom and dating. What would Freud say?

Conrad: Sorry but after we matched I decided I never should've swiped right. We would never get along.

Marie: I see—why is that?

Conrad: I don't believe in therapy. Treatment for me would be like a broken pencil. Pointless. Hahaha.

> **Conrad:** People pay someone to listen to them then they just say nice things about themselves to try and impress. It's like cleaning better before a date. Good luck to you.

Yes, this is one conversation at one point in time, but many telltale features of personality can be thin sliced from this text exchange. Marie's use of "Hmmm," "Awww," and "sweet" indicates an agreeable nature. She also uses question marks and second-person pronouns a lot. She seems interested in others. Conrad, in contrast, asks questions only sarcastically and uses negations ("never," "pointless") and cognitive discrepancies galore ("should," "would"). Many aspects of his texts point to a lack of conscientiousness and agreeableness. A more traditional psychoanalyst might interpret his reference to a broken pencil as anxiety about his own sexual prowess, but we'll leave that for the therapy couch, should he ever decide to sink into it.

Characters in Characters

In text messages, we see all sorts of nonstandard forms of communication: omitted punctuation, added punctuation, all lowercase letters, and, of course, emojis. Jessica Bennett suggests in her *New York Times* column "When Your Punctuation Says It All (!)" that in texts too much punctuation can appear overeager, while not enough can be dismissive. Given the lack of spoken inflection in digital communication, it's no surprise that we have to pay more attention to punctuation to decode messages' meaning.

Can punctuation itself reveal personality? Perhaps. Analysis of tweets in conjunction with Big Five assessments has shown question marks to be a sign of extroversion. Presumably extroverts are more interested in asking questions. Colons correlate with conscientiousness, perhaps because they can be found in organized lists. Commas, conversely, correlate with a lack of conscientiousness.

Celia Klin's research group looked at the period and found that when people received a text message that ended with one, it was perceived as angry or rude. With no period to cap off the sentence, it was seen as friendlier. The formality of the period, especially at the end of a short text, created emotional distance for people and was consistently rated by readers as less sincere, more sarcastic, and perhaps passive-aggressive.

I have two friends (both of whom I met on dating sites) who assiduously use periods. They are both writers. When I asked one, early in my texting history with him, why his texts were always punctuated with a period, even if it was just a "Yes," he replied, "Without a period, the letters might fall off the end of the sentence."

What can we say about these period users in our life? They are picky people—maybe a tad overweening. They are adhering to their own standards and values, probably more willing to confront social norms with their own individual style. As we ourselves get closer to such types and grow to love them, we may be influenced by their style.

Gertrude Stein had strong feelings about punctuation. She apparently hated the exclamation point. F. Scott Fitzgerald reportedly said, "An exclamation mark is like laughing at your own joke." The pseudonymous Italian writer Elena Ferrante goes as far as to call the exclamation point a "phallic display." Ernest Hemingway also preferred a more flattened style. One study showed that overuse and abuse of exclamation points correlate with higher levels of neuroticism and a lack of openness. Take this first exchange I had while I was in Hawaii for the Ironman:

Jim: Hi Mimi! Great pics! Here for the race?

> **Me:** Yes but not racing this year. Have raced here the last 9 years so taking a year to chill. You?

Jim: Rockstar! Yeah I'm racing.

> **Me:** Your number? I'll be cheering

Jim: 425!! I dig a liberal chick!! My kind of girl!

Are all these exclamation points necessary? They come off as amateurish, even insecure. Their excess in text messages has indeed become more standard; they are used for emphasis when words seem insufficient. But they have an anxious, excitable, "pay attention to me" quality, especially when they are used as replacements for the period. These days, a single exclamation point may not suffice to communicate enthusiasm. Now it's two, three, four, or more. Strong emotion or hyperbole is no longer required to use them; they can simply represent warmth. My friend Daniel describes them as "the original emoji."

Ethan also uses the exclamation point liberally, along with some other interesting character repetition:

Ethan: Heyyyy we still haven't met Sieraaaa!!

> **Sierra:** Will have to wait until the next time our moons align

Ethan: You are such a wonderful bundle of hotness and funnnn!! Wildo!

> **Sierra:** I'm in a work meeting and your text made me smirk

Ethan: . . . willdo we'lldo wildOhhhhhhh myyyy

> **Sierra:** One of those:-) Thanks for reaching out.

Ethan: You around to talk later 2day? I want to find a time to be surrounded by your awesome aura.

Ethan: Who: you and me. What: Simply a good conversation. When: at your convenience, ideally before Saturday.

While Ethan might come across on the surface as a very open, relaxed guy, you'll recall that exclamation points, at least in one study, correlated with a *lack* of openness and *higher* levels of neuroticism. Ethan also uses "affective lengthening"—those are the extra letters in "heyyyy," "ohhhhhhh," and "funnnn"—which conveys emotional intensity. Along with the exclamation points, his "who, what, when" message betrays a more rigid personality.

Parentheses, those enclosed aside comments, correlate with both a lack of openness and extroversion. They are couched statements that may not rise to the occasion of relevance, and so they are wrapped in punctuation, as though to appear a gift. (I'm not sure this is worth saying, so I'll wrap it in parentheses for you.)

The ellipsis leaves much open to interpretation. In her book of essays, *Incidental Inventions,* Elena Ferrante says that ellipses are "flirtatious, like someone batting her eyelashes, mouth slightly open in feigned wonder." No wonder online dating messages are rife with ellipses, a medium that is often used to convey innuendo, possibility, and . . . promise.

What about the person who intentionally uses lowercase where we expect uppercase? It offers the allure of humility, but is it a faux humility or a true one? It has always seemed to carry a certain affectedness to me, especially because, with autocorrect, using a lowercase *i* requires an explicit effort. I suspect there's a hint of the antiestablishment at play, a thumbing of the nose, you could say.

Digital Body Language

Emojis are such a complicated subject that a discussion of them might merit its own chapter. Gretchen McCulloch has elaborately documented their history and function in her book *Because Internet: Understanding the New Rules of Language,* and she concludes that emojis are largely a substitute for gestures, and thus add nuance and clarity to text exchanges. When we communicate verbally, we rely heavily on facial expressions and hand movements.

Facial expressions and hand movements have cultural boundaries and differences. Americans, for instance, smile with much greater frequency than people in many other cultures. My mother was French and divided her time between Paris and New York. She would often joke that in Paris she could distinguish Americans and French from across the room, or from across an outdoor café, simply by their facial expressions as they spoke. While Americans will smile through a conversation, the French stay straight-faced, reserving their smiles for more special occasions.

How do we communicate things like eye contact, facial expression, and hand movements over text? How do we interpret irony and sarcasm? An algorithm would need both linguistic and semantic information to do so—that is, the actual meaning of the words and the writer's intended meaning. In the sixteenth century, sarcasm was indicated with a reversed question mark, or a "percontation point"; nineteenth-century French poets used it as an "irony mark." Similarly, an upside-down exclamation point is found in Ethiopic languages. In modern emojis, this tone is denoted with an upside-down smiley face.

Emojis can add clarity to your intended meaning, but do they suggest a lack of trust in the written language? And do they rob us of the joy of feeling completely understood? I have always found emojis to be shortcuts in our self-expression—the frozen food of language, rather than language cooked from scratch. While their use now extends well beyond teenage girls' texts, they still feel canned to me. "Work harder," I want to say to the texter. "Tell me what you really mean."

So often they are inserted where extra meaning isn't needed. Is it to add color? To bring joy? To play, as if tossing a ball that the other can toss back? Regardless, these are stylistic choices that may say more about the person texting than anything about our need for gestures to accompany our textspeak.

A large-scale study out of the University of Rochester showed that frequent users of emojis have low extroversion scores, with introverts using emojis the most. Highly agreeable scorers will also favor emojis, while users with low neuroticism scores use emojis the least often. These data lines would seem to explain quite neatly my own aversion to emojis.

It's not easy telling people that you are a psychiatrist who doesn't always understand emojis. My teenage daughter likes to test me:

Kyra: What does this mean:
😦😟🥂🔒🔒🛍️🩹

> **Me:** It means that you are hiding behind emojis and not showing up emotionally for your mother.

Kyra: No, it actually means I'm sick at home and feel stuck there because it's a snow day and all there is to eat is an old burrito. Because my mother forgot to go grocery shopping.

So Emojional!

While emojis may be intended to add clarity to words, researchers have also found that the same emoji can be interpreted differently by different users, so emojis themselves can lead to confusion and misunderstanding. Creating sentences out of emojis is an art form of its own, and Alison makes a game of it in this initial dating app chat:

Alison: Once my friend and I designed a game and the objective was to use all the overlooked emojis in our texting which led to some interesting conversations

Eric: By all means send some examples!

Alison: Well there are overlooked bad pun opportunities, eg "I've 📟 hell and back" "You want a 🥐 this?" Then there are ones I have no context for but will build a sentence around just to use them like 🩰. And then there is this overlooked gem 😵, is that derpiness, embarrassment, or inebriation?

Eric: That could also be post really good sex natural high face. At least that's what I've always thought.

Alison: I will now forever think of it as a just-had-sex-so-good-I-can't-even-think-face.

While emoji use can certainly seem random and idiosyncratic, specific emojis can indeed indicate personality features. For instance, extroverts will be more likely to use 🙌 or 😊, and they will seldom use the 😩 or the 😶, which represent negative or ambiguous emotion. Agreeable people use hearts in all of their forms ❤️ 🤍 💕 and rarely use the ☹️. Those high in neuroticism prefer the exaggerated facial expressions of the 😩, 😰, 😶, and 😵. As the authors of the University of Rochester study note, "These emojis have little positive correlation with other personality traits which represents a unique emoji usage pattern for neuroticism users as well as their distinct emotional characteristics." Openness, in contrast, shows no relationship to emoji use whatsoever.

This text exchange between Tom and Melanie dragged on for many months before an initial date. Tom seems to have developed a strong online crush, and he punctuates his texts with emojis:

> **Tom:** I am REALLY interested in getting to know you. I reread your earlier messages and also your profile . . . and I really like that you weren't afraid to post photos of yourself without makeup! Or at least not gobs of it! 😬

> **Tom:** Okay so I was just thinking about you at the gym this morning and I am going to throw caution to the wind and give you my full name. You can then "Googleize" me and get a better feel for who I am. After that we can further discuss dinner plans (assuming there is still interest) 🌹 Tom D

> **Melanie:** Thank you for outing yourself. I'm Melanie G . . . headed to Boston through Sunday—I have a couple of big presentations to give.

Tom: Thanks for writing. I thought you might have decided to "pursue other interests" after learning more about me. Ciao bella 🌷

Tom: Good luck with your presentations . . . although I am starting to get the impression that luck is not a major element in your life. 🌷

Melanie: Let's have dinner.

Tom: Did you receive my LinkedIn stalker message? All go well with your presentations?

Tom: What are you doing Saturday night?

Melanie: Do you want to meet my dad on our first date? Because he is visiting this weekend. What a great story that would be . . .

Tom: I haven't met a dad on a first date since high school!! It would make me feel very young . . . and very nervous, but, it would also be something unique and different! Haha! I don't think it would be appropriate for you to leave him.

Tom: Was just thinking about you . . . as I am occasionally apt to do . . . and hoping you're having a wonderful weekend with your dad. I am sure your father remembers every little detail of the day you came into his life . . . as if it were moments ago. 🌷

Melanie: Hi—busy week. I hope you are doing well. Try to call this week? [She gives her phone number.]

Tom: So very happy to hear from you. I leave Saturday for Europe so if you would like to speak, hopeful we can connect before I depart. I would really enjoy exchanging voices and making dinner plans! 😳😁🌷

Tom: Let's talk. You may find my voice repulsive and decide dinner would just be a bit too much. Otherwise after my trip but that feels like such a long time to wait! 🌷

> **Tom:** Okay . . . I rang the number you gave me but did not leave a message. Texted you as well. Won't text bomb you. I promise.

> **Tom:** So I am in total violation of all the rules of online dating by writing so much but I figure you can handle it . . . and I promise I am not a psycho stalker. Just wanted you to know I watched one of your online videos and really enjoyed seeing and hearing you speak (facial expressions, smile, etc.) Have a spectacular day 🌹

When Melanie and Tom finally found a time to have dinner, it was a disaster. She had unconsciously responded to all the flattery and thought she might enjoy herself. In doing so, she missed some important signals in his text messages.

On their date, Tom first asked Melanie to choose a bottle of wine. She did, and he said, "Thank God you did not choose the most expensive wine on the menu. All the women I date do that. They just seem to be after my 401(k)." If it's possible, the date went downhill from there. Melanie was kicking herself for wasting an evening. But as she was quick to point out, "It's not as if his texts were not full of red flags . . . er, roses . . . !!"

Beyond his tendency to lay it on thick, what can we surmise about Tom from his punctuation, emoji use, and dating message content? He is likely introverted (emoji use), insecure ("pursue other interests," "stalker"), high in neuroticism ("repulsive," "psycho stalker"), low in openness ("not appropriate," "violation of all the rules"), not to mention very persistent. Not what Melanie, a highly extroverted, confident, and open person, was looking for.

It's not that there are, objectively speaking, ideal partners and suboptimal ones. There is someone for everyone, and what is right for one person is wrong for another. If being with a narcissist makes you feel good, great, just go in knowingly, and be aware of the risks and benefits of involvement with one. If the shy, quiet, and predictable type makes you feel most secure and comfortable, then by all means, choose that. As Catwoman says in *Batman Returns,* "It's the so-called normal guys who always let you down. Sickos never scare me. Least they're committed."

It's up to each of us to take the time to self-examine and decide what we are looking for and will enjoy. We must also respect those desires and pay attention to the signals we're being sent as they emerge. In the next chapter, we'll look not only at would-be dates but also at ourselves. We'll talk about awareness, self-knowledge, insight, and overcoming the obstacles to understanding what you are looking for. Because the only thing worse than not knowing is not wanting to know.

CHAPTER 3

Working Out the Kinks

Jared: Well, obviously the first question we need to tackle is what is the name of your stuffed animal?

Brooke: Wadsworth . . . obviously

Jared: Of course because he's an elephant?

Brooke: Oh I like the idea of Wadsworth the elephant. This one's a bear.

Jared: Much more dominant. So Wadsworth is obviously from England?

Brooke: Wadsworth the bear is obviously British. The clever, soothing British Baking Show kind of British NOT the judgy or Brexity kind. I could never sleep with that.

Jared and Brooke dance around their partner preferences with a discussion of the stuffed animal Brooke says she sleeps with. Power, personality, and political allegiance are introduced early into their playful and affiliative banter. Jared may be hinting that he wants someone more dominant, and Brooke has found a way to cleverly insert her personality and political preferences (open, not judgy; liberal, not Brexity) into a flirtatious repartee about a stuffed toy.

Regardless of our stated preferences, finding the right partner entails grappling with what we really want. It can be easy to let fear, shame, pride, or worry cloud our search. By taking the time to understand ourselves—to work out our own kinks—we can take braver action to seek what we really want. Greater awareness will lead to clearer, and ultimately better, choices.

Most online daters match with people who bear little resemblance to the person they claim to be looking for. A large-scale study of forty-one thousand Australians showed that daters routinely make contact with people on dating sites who in no way resemble the Mr. or Ms. Perfect they claimed to prefer. Which might lead you to wonder, which is the true north—a person's behavior or their stated preferences? Are they matching with people that they're unconsciously drawn to, or are their actions at odds with their true desires?

As expectations around romantic relationships have evolved, decisions have become more complex. In the past, the only question was "*Whom* should I marry?" Now relationships are less likely to follow a straight-and-narrow set of rules; they're more likely to bend in response to paradoxical needs. The central question is just as likely to be "*What* sort of relationship am I committed to?"

Here we will take a short detour from *others* in order to try to shed light on *ourselves*—our own expectations, confusions, desires, and kinks, the features that surround our romantic endeavors. This will allow us to clarify what we're really looking for, before we dive even further into dating. Understanding what we want and need starts with self-awareness, and as we'll see, shedding light on ourselves is not always so easy.

Strangers to Ourselves

The popular wisdom is that we simply don't know what we want. It's a notion that echoes through our halls of academia, chambers of Congress, courtrooms, churches, and sanctuaries. It rings the bell on Wall Street and clatters across Madison Avenue. These institutions are intent on filling a perceived void of self-knowledge with their version of what we *should* want. With the cacophony of opinion and doctrine, there's little incentive to investigate what truly moves us. We're being told what to want—constantly.

At the center of this uproar are questions that have bedeviled humankind forever: Who are we? Why do we do what we do? And are there reliable ways of finding out? The social sciences emerged to answer these questions, and only raised more of them along the way.

In his seminal book *Strangers to Ourselves,* the psychologist Timothy Wilson traces the history of the quest for self-knowledge while laying out practical pathways for achieving it. The core issue is that most of what goes on in our mind is unconscious. "When Freud said that consciousness is the tip of the mental iceberg, he was short of the mark by quite a bit," Wilson says. "It may be more the size of a snowball on top of that iceberg." Does that mean that who we actually are is entombed in an area of the mind that's inaccessible to us? Not exactly.

Freud gave us the unconscious with a capital *U.* In his theorizing, it was a vault that snapped shut after infancy and remained shut for life, requiring years of psychoanalysis to unlock. It was only then that we could access the repressed memories that drove us. The notion was sexy and dramatic: Who knew what craven desires lay within, what dark secrets populated our dreams? Only your psychiatrist, it turned out. (And possibly your hairdresser.) Hollywood loved it; pulp fiction ate it up. But the psychoanalytic approach was ultimately deemed unscientific, rejected by modern psychology. Behaviorists stalked the landscape, proclaiming that what was in the mind mattered not;

only our behavior revealed our true selves. Does "being" motivate "doing," or vice versa? The conflict of the era was irreverently summed up by Kurt Vonnegut Jr.:

"To be is to do"—Socrates.
"To do is to be"—Jean-Paul Sartre.
"Do be do be do"—Frank Sinatra.

Today, the study of the mind and the study of behavior are both thriving, the two threads inextricably tied. The unconscious is considered no longer a single impregnable monolith but a complex system of interwoven departments, all with discrete functions. Behavior, meanwhile, remains the single best way to gain insight into how our unconscious mind operates. And although we can't readily access the contents of our unconscious, ways have been found to consciously alter them.

The latest iteration of the unconscious—called the adaptive unconscious or the cognitive unconscious, also implicit or automatic thinking, among other terms—is the new playground for psychologists of every stamp. In scientific papers it is almost always associated with unscientific words like "mystery" and "intuition" and described as a liminal zone between dreams and reality. Who knew that social science could be so poetic? I tend to favor "adaptive unconscious," because, beyond describing how the unconscious evolved with us and is crucial to our survival, the term echoes our constant struggle to understand it.

It is now a given that the lion's share of our mental processes occur without our awareness—that in many departments our autopilot is constantly engaged and that in others it can be turned on and off. Thank goodness for that. Our days would be very long if we were constantly recalculating how to tie our shoes or put one foot in front of the other. Our minds would be a mess if we had to scan every image in our memory in order to recognize a face. Communication would be impossible if we had to retrieve words and build phrases from scratch every time we spoke. The brain has conscious areas we can easily access, subconscious ones that require keys, and unconscious zones that are mostly off-limits. But like a warehouse, things don't always get stored in the right place. Therein lies the rub.

I have long described a portion of my role as a psychotherapist as an elaborate card game of concentration. When a patient reveals a jack to me from their deck of experiences and thoughts, I have to remember the last time they turned over a jack, make the connection for them, and remind them where that other jack was metaphorically stored.

Nowhere was this more evident than with a patient of mine, D.W., whom I saw for several years following the end of his marriage (and who agreed to let me tell his story). He had a very negative view of online dating. Women on those sites must have some fundamental flaw, he reasoned, because it would be so easy for them to meet men in real life. His circle of friends spoke glowingly of the convenience of online dating, but to him the ease of use meant he would be meeting women who were lazy or lacking in social skills. They showed him the multitude of choices available; he saw a gallery of rejects. They emphasized that he could text and get to know women before dating; he predicted endless boring conversations.

In the end, he relented and downloaded an app, and for about a year all of D.W.'s predictions were on the money. His stories were sad and funny: a date falling asleep in his car as he drove her home; another spending two hours talking about all of her terrible dating app experiences; yet another, on a first date, asking him to spend the night because she was afraid of being raped by an intruder. These and others he found unattractive, dull, and neurotic. Half jokingly, I asked him why he was dating unattractive, dull, and neurotic women. "Because," he said, "that's all that is available online."

He persisted, and over time D.W.'s dating experiences improved, although, paradoxically, his outcomes did not. He dated a slew of attractive, successful, and outgoing women. He reported excellent compatibility and fantastic sex. But in every case, some minor detail would throw him off, and he would abruptly leave the relationship.

This could be attributable to any number of factors: we spent time examining his attachment style and fears around emotional intimacy. But D.W. had started off with an extreme bias against online dating, followed by a long period of subconsciously dating women who only confirmed his bias. The preponderance of data that he collected seemed to confirm his initial stereotype, that women on apps were suboptimal partners, perhaps even suboptimal human beings. This notion had become a schema—a mental structure of preconceived ideas that, once reinforced, becomes automatic and unconscious. It was one that he then felt compelled to repeat.

Schemata (as they are plurally known) are essential to the function of an organized mind. They are mental categories that allow us to classify our environment. They can also be rigid structures, hard to override consciously once they are entrenched. We may be told by someone that a dog, snarling and tugging at its chain, is actually quite friendly. Our biting-dog schema would reject that notion, and we would be wary of petting it. Simultaneously, another schema, perhaps one of disliking a particular breed of dog—for entirely different reasons—might be reinforced. And so on. Schemata can become so powerful that any data that contradicts them will be deflected as an exception, a mistake, or an illusion.

John: I've enjoyed our dialogue and I wanted to share with you that I am separated and have been for about a year. It is something I initiated. If that is a concern for you, I would understand and respect that. All answers are good.

John: I'm not looking for emotional support from another woman to finalize my divorce. With all that said, I felt transparency is good. It is what I would want.

Elisabeth: Thanks for your note. Sorry I was busy this past weekend. I'm happy to try to connect by phone or meet up. As for the separation issue, I appreciate the transparency. I will say "separated not yet divorced" has not worked out well for me in the past.

Elisabeth: Please don't take any of the above as overly dramatic . . . just to say I'm trying to avoid being the rebound person ☺

John: I'm very centered on the reality that some folks may have had a less than ideal experience in this area in the past. And that's ok. I might feel the same way depending on what my experiences may have been.

John: You should feel great about speaking your truth. I don't know how that can be read as overly dramatic. I'm inclined to say maybe trust your instincts here. It was nice to match with you, and perhaps our paths cross again at another time. From my perspective, our messages have been interesting and pleasant. Virtual hugs. ☺

In this text exchange, Elisabeth's and John's references to past relationships can be read as evidence of existing schemata. Elisabeth acknowledges that she hasn't had great experiences with men who are not yet divorced. Although she says she is open-minded and willing to meet, her comment seems to have foreshortened the conversation. It is unclear from John's formal style of speech whether he is avoiding rejection (perhaps he's been dumped for his separated status in the past?) or if he really believes that Elisabeth should trust her intuition. Each may be correctly or incorrectly connecting the dots of their past experiences; both would benefit from gaining insight into their actual fears.

From Introspection to Insight

Scientifically defined, introspection is an act of observing an object when that object is the observation itself. If that sentence gave you a bit of whiplash, then you can imagine how difficult it can be to make conclusions based on such a process. Introspection is a mainstay of therapy, mostly with the purpose of accessing the "true self" or the unconscious, which we now know is generally impervious to the proddings of self-examination. When people introspect, they can find themselves adrift in a sea of **confabulation.**

Nature abhors a vacuum, and so does the mind. There is increasing evidence that in the absence of an explanation for our own unconscious behavior our conscious mind tends to create one. Confabulation is a way of rationalizing behaviors we don't understand by making up stories about them. When faced with an action or a statement of our own that we can't explain, one that seems to have no history or reason—why we swiped right on him, ended things with her, and so on—we confabulate, creating sometimes incredibly detailed and complex stories to explain ourselves. We all confabulate to some degree, sometimes consciously, perhaps to enhance the parts of a story we don't remember well; just as often unconsciously, for reasons that elude us. We can't change the facts, but we can alter the supporting narrative to express a more palatable outcome.

D.W. couldn't say, for example, that his attachment patterns were causing him to withdraw emotionally from romantic relationships. He didn't yet have access to that information. Instead, his conscious mind created perfectly rational explanations for why he rejected his dates, based on trivial details. In one case, he broke things off with a woman who remarked on a text message she had glimpsed on his phone, which he had left unlocked and in plain sight. He reasoned that she was all "up in his business" and would make his life miserable. Privacy violation, he said, was his only "one strike and you're out" rule. Until he came up with another. And another.

Confabulation is the act of creating a narrative to connect the dots when we don't understand how they are actually connected. These narratives can be useful, even therapeutic. Sometimes a crack in the narrative reveals our true thoughts and motives. Those "I can't believe I just said that" moments are a sort of verbal wardrobe malfunction: your Freudian slip is suddenly showing. In general, when it comes to probing our own unconscious, the emperor is not only wearing clothes, he's wearing everything in the closet.

Kieran's motivations are relatively unguarded in his conversation with Andrea:

> **Andrea:** Not sure how this app works. Does this mean that we're dating now?

> **Kieran:** Dating? DATING? I'm almost pregnant, and you're having commitment issues?!?!

Andrea: Cool. I'll update my relationship status on MySpace. Do you actually live here or are you just passing through SF on a pandemic holiday like everyone else on this app?

Kieran: I come from Mars (Bar)

Kieran: I live here. DO YOU?

Kieran: Cut to chase: meet for so-called witty banter manana (that's Spanish for tomorrow)?

Andrea: Yup. I live here. Are you from Spain or are you just practicing your high school Spanish with me?

Andrea: I'd be up for meeting—but we should probably talk over the phone first to make sure we won't bore each other to tears.

Kieran: You're a Jewish Aquarian I'm a Jewish Catholic

Kieran: No I mean I'm a Catholic aquarium

Kieran: behind the perfect hair on my chest are tiger guppies

Kieran: We're not gonna bore each other

Kieran: If it gets boring we start kissing until it's boring no longer.

Forget wearing the wardrobe; Kieran just walks into the party bare-chested in flip-flops and shorts. He is all id—no analysis required. For most of us, though, our motivations are assiduously defended and not so easily accessed.

When our true motives do peek out from under our garments, we have a tendency to rationalize them away. In a famous experiment by Michael Norton of Harvard Business School, male college students were given a choice of two subscriptions to sports magazines—one that included a swimsuit edition and another that included a "Year's Top 10 Athletes" edition, but that were otherwise essentially the same. They consistently chose the one with the swimsuit issue. When asked why they made the choice they did, they tended to explain away their preferences on the basis of some feature of the articles therein. This study, along with many others, supports the notion that when people behave in ways that are incongruent with how they want to see themselves, they justify their behavior with rational excuses. ("I swiped right on him because he volunteers at the animal shelter," rather than "I liked the shirtless photo of him at the beach.") It's much easier to go with an easy, palatable answer than to confront a harder, less appealing one.

When people are asked to list the reasons for the dating choices they've made, their feelings and attitudes shift; the more reasons they list, the greater the observable change. So an indescribable feeling of comfort that we get from the sound of our partner's voice will evolve into a sentiment such as "I like my partner's voice because . . ." and that "because" will become the reason; the initial feeling of comfort will be overshadowed. Our brains are lazy. Once we latch on to a particular reasoning, we stop looking for what we actually feel.

I once had a guy break up with me several weeks into a relationship because, he explained, my hips were too narrow. So often with online dating and other romantic pursuits, we override the strong intuitive signals our brains send us about what we really want. Had this man truly wanted someone with wide hips, it should have been clearly visible to him in our first encounter. Or maybe, like D.W., this was just an explanation he latched on to—perhaps to mask an inability or unwillingness to commit to a longer-term relationship. Whether he needed to prioritize the *hips* in relation*ships,* or whether he wanted to do away with "relations" altogether, he would have done himself, and me, a favor by recognizing it up front. We've all done it—ignored the screaming signals and forged ahead. We rationalize: that a person is a great match because they meet a set of criteria, or check a series of boxes from a prefabricated list, one that bears no resemblance to our *true* desires (be they wide hips, a series of short intimate liaisons—you name it).

Yolanda inquires about Dieter's height as she considers whether to graduate the text to an in-person meeting. Dieter toys with her in his response, not so subtly poking fun at her potential checklist:

> **Yolanda:** And now, to the more mundane . . . What's your last name? And generally how tall are you? I'm curious if we will stand face to face or if I will look up to you or down at you ;)

> **Dieter:** I just sent you a pic of my drivers license. TMI?

> **Yolanda:** Not TMI. I guess I'll look up at you. And maybe I'll look up to you. And you'll look down at me, but hopefully not down on me. And I'm glad that you weigh more than me. Though I am considerably curvier. Here's my DL.

> **Yolanda:** Btw, you look like a serial killer in that photo.

> **Dieter:** I've never done this before. Something oddly erotic about exchanging DL pics.

> **Yolanda:** Sorry about the serial killer comment. I hope that won't give you bad dreams or bad ideas.

> **Dieter:** I resent 'serial' killer. I always do them one at a time with great care.

You might imagine that through introspection, we better understand what we seek, and why, and can therefore reach new heights of happiness. You might be wrong. Research by the professor of behavioral sciences Rick Harrington and his colleagues at the University of Houston-Victoria shows that people who do a lot of introspection are more stressed, depressed, and anxious; are more self-absorbed; and feel less in control of their lives and choices.

By contrast, the psychologist Anthony Grant showed that people high in *insight* had stronger relationships, were more in control of their choices, and experienced greater self-acceptance and happiness. So how can we distinguish between introspection and insight? How can we go from *thinking about* ourselves to *knowing* ourselves? To get to knowing, we have to let go of the myth that Freud perpetuated: that extracting information requires an archaeological dig of the psyche. There are some practical pathways at our disposal.

The first technique, as Tasha Eurich outlines in her book *Insight,* is to ask yourself *what* you are feeling, rather than *why* you are feeling it. That is, *naming.* Observation of your own feelings is likely to produce better self-knowledge when it's non-judgmental, and people get stuck when they have feelings they can't explain. When they are gently guided toward naming feelings, the sensation of "being blocked" is lifted, and the underlying feeling is identified. By asking ourselves what we like from a partner, putting aside the question of why we like it, we can more easily identify the thing we seek.

Julian has indicated that he is married and seeking an open relationship. Rita matches with him on a dating app, and she leads with this:

> **Rita:** Tell me, the wifey ain't satisfying hubby? Or does she know—r u two poly?

> **Julian:** Yes we are poly. Have been for about 10yrs. It is good to have needs met by more than one person. We use it more as a way to create balance and avoid overly depending on one person to fulfill all needs, especially in intimacy. Supportive for scheduling, diversity of interests/ orientations . . .
>
> **Julian:** What are you looking for?

> **Rita:** Sorry I can't do married ppl. Although I bet you're amazing in bed and you're super Duper cute. Too bad for me. I guess I'm one of the rare uptight people here in *sinful* San Francisco 😇 😇
>
> **Rita:** P.S. I am looking for a good fuck.

Give Rita credit: She is seeking something casual and knows she doesn't want to negotiate approval from another person's spouse before having sex with them. She is clear about what she wants and where she is going to get it.

All the text-whispering tools in the world (and in this book) are useless if we can't be straight with ourselves about what we want. If a particular kink is important, it might be helpful to come to grips with that, rather than seeing it as something that needs to be concealed, controlled, or corrected. If a personal need for independence or distance in a relationship is essential to you, to not feel threatened or smothered, that can encourage you to seek out partners who don't need to spend every waking moment together. Merely exercising a policy of containment toward our desires will create a chasm between your persona (the character we present to others) and your true personality. Real insight involves shining a light on our thoughts and our feelings, the welcome and the unwelcome.

Persona, Grata or Non

Rachel came into my practice like a tornado. Her intensity was such that to say she was merely driven would be to call a Ferrari a Pacer. Rachel was an accomplished physician, held an adjunct professor role at a major medical school, served on two boards, worked out at least two hours a day, and, of course, was dating up a storm because she wanted to settle down with someone and raise a family. Her mind and body were liquid steel.

Moments after our sessions began, she would, like clockwork, burst into tears.

Rachel had approached twelve years of graduate and postgraduate study like an academic mountaineer, ever reaching for the higher degree, residency, fellowship, award, always accompanied by her placeholder boyfriend, whom she summarily dumped when she entered the real world. Because much of her adult life had been consumed by research and study, and she'd spent those years cradled in the comfort of a nurturing relationship, she was at times emotionally naive in our sessions, despite otherwise being so worldly and sophisticated.

After spending the first ten minutes of our sessions emptying my Kleenex box, Rachel would compose herself, let her hair cascade onto her sculpted deltoids, straighten out her skirt, and begin the tale of her latest heartbreak. The story would be some variation on an ongoing theme. She had met a guy on a dating app, usually an über-masculine, brushes-his-teeth-with-testosterone type. Their attraction had been immediate, with the first few days spent in an amatory whirlwind. She had catered to his every need and pleased every part of him, from *Kama Sutra* to Kierkegaard. He stormed the keep like a plundering knight.

Within a few weeks, though, things would wind down. Her

tomcat would turn into a teddy bear, preferring cuddling to sexing, making her dinner instead of making out, and sleeping, actually sleeping, when they went to bed. Days later the inevitable would come crashing down on her: there was too much intimacy—or too little—for his taste. She reminded him of his sister, or his mother. It wasn't the right time/moment/season. The outlets in her bathroom weren't code compliant. And off he went.

As she regaled me with her stories, the notion of her playing the subservient geisha always seemed at odds with the person before me, her firm tone of voice, direct gaze, ramrod posture. Although she thought of herself at times as submissive, wanting nothing more than just to sink into life with an equal partner, she also admitted that she liked to be in control. She always initiated sex and wanted it often, usually on demand. When not having sex, she preferred either intellectual conversation or exercise. Anything else would make her anxious and fidgety. Her life was lived in tight compartments, like a film with only action scenes. Men who didn't share an interest in these compartments were less than perfect in her eyes.

Rachel's *persona* had little to do with her *personality,* and she was largely unaware of the discrepancy. She was attracted to a certain type of man, and her persona had unconsciously developed around attracting that type. But her persona was insufficiently fleshed out for it to be maintained for very long, and as her true personality emerged, her erstwhile John Wayne chose not to wait for his dismissal. He bolted for the door.

As we consider, in the pages ahead, the conscious and unconscious motivations that compel us, it's important to note that neither is, strictly speaking, the right one. Both can inform us, and both deserve consideration. Part of Rachel's work, as we'll see, was to reconcile her explicit and implicit selves.

Me, Myself, and I

It may be the subject we think about most. Ourselves. There is a construct of "me" that sits in our heads, and it seems both persistent and immutable. But we are possessed with, or possessed by, two personalities: our conscious, constructed self, and our unconscious one. They exist relatively independent of each other. While the conscious persona fusses lazily over appearance and protocols, the unconscious self is fast, effortless, unintentional, and uncontrollable. As we read the room, it has already read the room. As we open our mouths to speak, it has already spoken. At various times and to varying degrees we become aware of this Russian doll problem, our self within a self. When we do, it results in self-consciousness, an experience embraced by some and rejected by others. Where we live on the spectrum between these two extremes can say a lot about how we relate to other people—especially our significant other.

There has been much study of personality self-knowledge, or the differences between our explicit and implicit selves. One interesting discrepancy that has emerged is the chasm between how *we think* our friends, colleagues, and family view us and the way they actually do. When the difference is quantified on a scale of 0 to 1, where 0 represents no similarity whatsoever and 1 represents a perfect match, it's about 0.17. In other words, if we're poor judges of our own personality, we're even worse judges of how our peers see us. In contrast, our peers have a fairly decent idea of our own self-view (0.45 on the same scale).

This isn't altogether surprising. We are strongly motivated to get the people in our lives to see us as we see ourselves. Peers can be helpful in understanding our own behavior, simply because they have front-row seats to the way we behave, past and present, and thus are well equipped to predict how we might act in the future. Their view of our unconscious in action has few obstructions, as does their investment in our happiness and success.

It points toward a second practical pathway toward insight, beyond putting a name to our feelings: soliciting *feedback*. Now, with as much openness and agreeableness as we can muster, we can take another simple step: ask a friend. Feedback on how others perceive us is readily available from those we trust, and it is often more trustworthy than our self-assessments.

It can also, of course, be addressed in therapy. As a psychiatrist, I grow to care deeply for my patients. I get to bear witness to their innermost feelings, after all. Part of my job is to straddle the threshold, with one foot in the door (empathizing with their reality) and one foot out (being able to provide them objective feedback). I have to admit that many aspects of the hard-charging Rachel reminded me of a younger version of myself, which made it easy to see her both objectively and subjectively (in particular her dread of slowing down). For Rachel to change, she had to acknowledge her fears of hitting the pause button. So often, overcoming the barrier to self-reflection involves confronting the anxiety or threat that will arise from that reflection.

As the therapist James Hollis, author of *Living an Examined Life*, explains, being able to reflect on our inner reality can lead to awareness in the form of a sudden epiphany. Sometimes, he says, we need to be stunned into reflection by a loss, breakup, or series of breakups that force us to reexamine our provisional conclusions about ourselves.

Barring such life-changing events, there are three further steps to self-awareness beyond naming and soliciting feedback. These steps can be a quick trip or a lifetime journey. Your mileage may vary.

Minding the Gap

Mindfulness, an extension of the naming technique, means simply noticing what you are thinking, feeling, and doing in response to certain triggers or circumstances, without reacting, explaining, or overthinking. Sometimes it means looking at those thoughts and feelings from a new vantage point. While action and productivity are excellent coping skills to buoy mood—I recommend them to patients early and often—if overused, they can be a defense, serving as foils to self-examination. Our constant smartphone use, social media presence, and even dating app addictions might all be evidence of mindlessness, rather than the mindfulness that leads to meaningful self-awareness.

Sometimes we will do anything to avoid being alone with our thoughts, as Aimee is well aware:

Aimee: I'm back in the predicament of needing to sit at my altar since I didn't finish my meditation this morning. And here we are bantering again.

Terrance: Chatting with you seems to be my priority too. But I'm intrigued by the notion of pausing meditation and resuming hours later. I have much to learn.

Aimee: Glad to know my lack of discipline intrigues you. I made a commitment to completing some very specific meditations. But my favorite pith metta (loving kindness meditation) is "Never mind; start again!"

Terrance: Go meditate. Then we can start again.

Aimee: Very kind of you.

The University of Virginia psychologist Timothy Wilson studied our penchant for mindlessness by asking subjects to sit in a room with no cell phones, books, pens, or any other diversions—nothing to occupy them but their own thoughts. People felt very uncomfortable. He upped the ante by offering them the option to self-administer electric shocks while they sat. Given the choice between doing nothing and receiving small electric shocks, the majority of the participants elected to receive shocks. Wilson concluded that people would rather experience pain (in small quantities) than sit with themselves.

Somehow this isn't shocking. Our conscious minds are wired for any time but the present as we stew over the past and quiver over the future. An under-recognized truth is that self-fulfillment, serenity, well-being, and even happiness can only be felt *in the moment*. Otherwise, they are either memory or hope. We *want* to be in the present; we just don't know how.

Unfortunately, the path to mindfulness is scattered with platitudes. "Mindfulness" is one of the latest buzzwords to feature prominently in the pop psychology vending machine, with 209 billion Google search results on the day of this writing and seventy thousand books in print on the topic. It is now available in flavors ranging from Mindful Dog Ownership to Mindful Veganism. There is nothing wrong with mindfulness—as a subject, as a process, as a way of life. The shortcuts of commodified mindfulness, though, can lead us to gloss over unexamined personal issues. True mindfulness requires practice, or *a* practice, tailored by each individual to themselves, not prescribed in a generic package.

Both feedback and mindfulness can run up against what Timothy Wilson and Harvard professor of social psychology Daniel Gilbert refer to as the psychological immune system. Like our defenses from bacteria, viruses, and fungi, this system defends us from psychological abuse, stress, and criticism. It makes us feel good about ourselves by corralling negative thoughts that threaten our perception of self. It helps us to overcome disappointment, be more accepting and tolerant, and maintain a reasonable balance of optimism. An extension of Wilson and Gilbert's analogy is that, like the biological one, the psychological immune system can fail us dramatically, or even turn against us. We might form positive illusions that are essentially delusions, papering our windows with smiley-face posters that ultimately block out the light.

Rachel would spend much of her day actively defending against weakness; she certainly projected an aura of strength to the outside world. But moments into our sessions, her vulnerability would emerge, flying in the face of the story she was telling others. She felt conflicted about power; how *in control* did she really want to be? In some ways it was a relief to be with a man who was controlling, because it allowed her to put aside her own need to be in charge. She wanted both to be swept off her feet and to be calling the shots. It was only by slowing down and taking stock of her conflicted approach to control that she could identify the patterns that had beleaguered her romantic pursuits.

By sitting with our thoughts and feelings, and by nonjudgmentally observing them, we can stay open to learning about ourselves, even when what we learn is in conflict with our existing sense of self or the world.

Parsing Patterns

Mindfulness certainly illuminates. But a fourth reliable method for achieving insight into what we want is to compare our past predictions with actual known outcomes. This leads to *pattern recognition*. Emotional patterns can be difficult to see for a number of reasons. One is that memory is a reconstructive process, with details added, modified, or taken away every time we recall something. We also suffer from impact bias, which is the tendency to over- or underestimate how future events will impact us emotionally based on our (sometimes faulty) memory of the past. Drawing a line between two moving targets can be tricky, but by tracing the course of past predictions through to their now obvious conclusions, we can more realistically evaluate our current expectations.

Once patterns become clear, insight will usually follow. Patterns allow us to see the ways that we have agency, rather than being passengers on the journey of our lives. I think of the old saying that the definition of insanity is doing the same thing over and over again and expecting a different result. When I talk about pattern recognition, I mean deliberately attempting to acknowledge those things that we're (insanely) doing over and over.

This is where my metaphorical card game of concentration comes into play. By remembering the last time we felt a particular way, and how it played out, and comparing that with our current experience, we can become better predictors of our relationship outcomes. I am there to remind a patient of the last time they expressed this thought, or the last time they felt that way; by engaging in conscious, mindful awareness, you can practice it on your own, too.

Emily took the message to heart. She had received the following first message from Eve on a dating app:

> **Eve:** Your self summary includes, literally, all the most important things. It's fantastic and I didn't need to read a lot of text on my tiny phone screen to know I should message you. How is your Sunday coming along?

At the time Emily received the message, she was only recently out of a very long relationship with another woman. She couldn't process hearing from a stranger that she seemed appealing; it wasn't the way she saw herself at the time. So she rejected it. By looking back at her past prediction (that the text was too forward to be worth a reply) and the known outcome (she might have missed out on an opportunity), she learned about her own assumptions and how to better handle in the future a scenario that once baffled her.

"I recall thinking this person was coming on *way* too strong," she reflected, "and now I have no idea what I was thinking. Seems like quite a nice thing to say."

Zooming Out

Attraction and preference, as we've seen, are often driven by unconscious motivations. It's possible that in the case of focused dating—the kind that online dating tends to foster—this is only truer. When we make a list of desirable traits in a partner, it is rarely comprehensive of our true feelings. We might not even consciously know how some of the traits got there.

This brings us to the last step on the practical pathway to self-awareness: to look beyond the list (or whatever information is right in front of you) and to *see the big picture.* A memorable mentor of mine was also a respected astronomer. Dr. William Sheehan's list of achievements, besides being an active community psychiatrist, includes a patent for infrared brain-imaging technology, an understanding of the composition and evolution of the Milky Way, and a knack for planetary observation. As a student, I was eager to learn as much as I could from his astute observation of both human and celestial bodies. I asked him how he had made the career switch from astronomy to psychiatry. He replied, "I love to listen to my patients by day and understand the nuance of their emotional lives, and then go home at night, gaze at the stars, and realize that our small preoccupations don't really matter."

Dr. Sheehan's words stuck with me. They perfectly illustrate the therapeutic value of zooming out on our life from our current telescopic, or even microscopic, view. Rather than focusing on a particular sticking point, or the way in which we are currently stuck, it can be helpful to see the narrative arc of our lives, to become, as Timothy Wilson describes it, our own biographers. By cataloging one's life, clear themes emerge, and dearly held values and passions come into focus. Together, these can give us a clearer view of who we are and what we want to become.

Accessing this information is of course paramount to choosing the right kind of partner. We can look beyond lists and, in our mind's eye, see a whole person—be it the one sitting in front of us or the one we see in the mirror. But to quote the flawed but brilliant comic philosopher Woody Allen, "Students achieving Oneness will move on to Twoness." Having learned about and made peace with the stranger within ourselves, we must now progress to doing what we do when we chat on dating apps: texting with strangers.

CHAPTER 4

Texting with Strangers

Annika: No way you are getting off that easy. Three things that turn you on. 😊

> **Olivia:** Good one.

> **Olivia:** Can't limit it to and this is stream of consciousness as I'm not editing . . .

> **Olivia:** Playfulness, kissing, soft touch, quirkiness, humor, skin eye contact, connection, smarts, accountability, authenticity, presence and letting go together to some unknown sweet, raw, open, melting . . .

> **Olivia:** *gulp*

Annika: Waking up to your list. Reading it again, very slowly. Taking my time with each word.

Annika: I really like your list 😊

Before drifting off to sleep, Annika throws down a gauntlet for Olivia to ponder. She wakes up to a rich eye-opener of high values, spiced with sensuality, which she savors. Olivia emphasizes vulnerability and intimacy in her list of turn-ons. It feels like the real deal; the ingredients are all there. And yet these two have not even met.

Intimacy is increasingly fostered through the medium of text. We meet online, we flirt over text, and we reveal deep aspects of ourselves—in our lexicon, as we've seen, but also in the content and style of our notes. Inquiry and authenticity are the foundation of intimacy, and as we can see from this text exchange, having the courage both to ask and to be vulnerable can lend itself to deeper connection.

Authenticity is all the rage. It's become such a buzzword that one wonders if it hasn't been stretched too thin to hold its shape. Eighty-four percent of users on one dating app said they wished that other people on the app would present the "authentic" version of themselves. Some dating apps request, even demand, that users post unretouched photos. "Substance over selfie," says one site. The faux and phony, the dog and pony, the filtered and the airbrushed—all are on notice. Virtual is the new real.

Ironically, while the large majority of daters would prefer that other people open up and be their authentic selves, many lack the confidence to do the same. A 2019 white paper that addressed dating app users' primary anxieties about presenting themselves found that 40 percent worry about being interesting enough, talkative enough, fun enough, you-name-it enough. Sexy enough tops the list for Gen Z and millennials. FOPO (fear of people's opinions) has seemingly caught up with and exceeded FOMO (fear of missing out).

The study demonstrated that anxieties about appearance are superseded by concerns over conversational skills and personality. Women worry more than men (or at least they admit to it more). People go so far as to express anxiety about sharing their hobbies, and a full third of singles have felt the need to adopt the hobbies of the person they were interested in.

It can be painful to read the texts of people who latch onto their match's interests and preferences rather than promoting their own. Take this initial text exchange between Max and Robyn. Robyn had indicated in her profile that she is a scotch drinker.

> **Max:** Hi Robyn! I'm more of a rye guy than scotch . . . but I think we can still get along :) What's your quarantine cocktail of choice?

> **Robyn:** Ooh—Idk if I've ever met somebody who prefers rye. I love it too. I would have said my favorite cocktails were a French 75 or paper plane, but now I'm going to have to go with a Man O' War.

Robyn quickly adjusts her taste in alcohol to match those of her new interest. Cocktail choice is no big deal in the grand scheme of things, but it is a worrisome sign when someone can't plainly state what they like. In the following exchange, both parties attempt the shift, but it all comes to naught.

> **Maya:** Hi there! This app seems to think we're a good match . . . and hey, look at that a doggo in kayak convergence! Give a holler if you're up for starting a convo.

> **Jessica:** Hi! I honestly loved everything you said in your profile. Short and sweet. I'm not one for lengthy chats so if you want to set up an in-person sumpin' or other, let's plan it. We could bowl! I'm not very good at it at all, but it's fun. It can be really great to go somewhere and hurl balls. Ha!

> **Maya:** I totally agree re: in-person, and bowling could be a real hoot—I haven't been in years!

Maya comes on as dominant, with her backslapping chat style and "short and sweet" profile. Jessica may be accommodating this by suggesting a physical activity, one where she knows she won't be competitive. It turns out they both should have chosen a different tack. This chat never led to a meeting because, as Maya said to me later, "Really? Bowling?"

Kai, who struggles with anxiety in reaching out to strangers, does a nice job when reaching out to Lea:

Kai: I really dig your music taste

Lea: aw thank you!! 🙂🙂

Kai: I didn't realize Tom Misch and Doja Cat had overlapping fanbases lol

Lea: HAHAHA

Lea: wait ok not to be /that person/ but I was hella into doja cat in like 2018/2019 before she got really popular LOL

Lea: buy hey man good music is good music

Kai: tbh I think the first time I heard her was mooo

Kai: So like that's my impression of her

Kai: And it's ok I can't help but be /that person/ a lot of the time

Lea: HAHA ya I feel that

Lea: god when that song came out everyone at Davis was so into it. Of course they were. Smh

Kai: Wait that's so funny omfg

Kai: New school anthem?

Kai leads with a compliment, and he validates Lea while teasing a little as well. Lea responds well to it; their conversation is already laden with the kinds of references that an outsider could fail to grasp. Some are better than others at self-revelation and stating preferences. Will began a conversation with me this way:

Will: Hi Mimi. We definitely share similar loves & hates. And I like how your eyes smile when you do. I'm in SF. How about you?

> **Me:** Hi Will. SF! Cool burning man photos. I did not post any, but I have enjoyed that too.

> **Will:** I hear you on the Burning Man pics. Wondering if I should refrain from posting them too. A lot of people don't get it. It's like telling them you're vegan . . . They just run the other way without considering it or really knowing why. And btw . . . I'm vegan. Are you running?

> **Me:** Ha, no, I'm not running, except to get my morning run in.

Will wants me to know he's vegan right off the bat, but he's also letting me know he's looking for someone with openness to experience. The latter may be more important to him than the former.

Authentically presenting some dimensions of our personality is easier than others, particularly with strangers. We are taught early to smile for the camera, share, get along with our pals, lead with agreeableness, whether or not we feel like it—whether or not we are, in fact, agreeable. Because everyone is trained to fake it to some degree, it follows that everyone is trained to assume that others are faking it. It's hard to know where the conscious social construct ends and the true dimension begins. Modifying tastes, expectations, and style in order to please others is an essential part of the agreeable dimension; chameleon is its true color. When texting with strangers, it behooves us to assume that we are all putting our most agreeable foot forward and that it may slip backward from there as we get to know each other better.

In this chat with Alex, for instance, I largely eschew agreeableness, but I can't deny, looking back on it, that there's an element of deliberate self-presentation at play:

Alex: You're busy at work I presume. Can I see you this week?

Me: Hey there. Sorry for the slow reply. I worked late last night and have a work event tonight and tomorrow evening.

Alex: Sounds like just another day in the life of a busy silicon valley physician :)

Me: Well I did get a long ride in before work today

Alex: Damn, you're such an overachiever

Me: Overachiever? Moi? That's French for "me" by the way

Alex: Yes, I'm pointing at you.

Me: Pointing is not polite.

Alex: Ok, I'm looking out of the corner of my eye at you

Me: I'm eating a 1000 calorie breakfast at the Facebook cafeteria. Eggs, bacon, potatoes, yogurt, fruit.

Alex: You are just validating your overachiever status even more. Plus name dropping Facebook.

Me: I eat overachievers for breakfast

Alex: I've heard they are delicious. But I've never actually eaten one myself.

Me: They are usually skinny and less caloric than bacon and hash browns.

Alex: When can I see you? You are almost relegating me to begging.

Presenting ourselves as friendly and agreeable—with shades, in my case, of conscientiousness and drive—is certainly important, but not at the expense of inquiry. Asking questions is not only at the heart of getting to know people better but an effective way to present yourself authentically. The questions you choose not only signal your attentiveness to others but also offer an opportunity to express your own interests.

To get a good feel for someone, you need rough, unguarded responses to meaningful subjects. You need answers. And to get the right answers, you need to ask the right questions. In chapter 2 we thought about the qualities we're seeking, the type of relationship we want, the character traits and tendencies that ring our bell. In chapter 3 we took the first steps toward overcoming the biggest obstacle to a successful match: looking into ourselves. It is time to start asking for and distilling the information we need from a small batch of text messages and to do it in a way that elicits the most honest and open responses—the best data.

Some of the questions that might lead to revealing answers can be awkward to ask.

The devil, as they say, is in the details. In the early days of dating apps, eHarmony subjected prospective clients to a lengthy questionnaire that probed into all kinds of preferences. The questions addressed intimate but practical considerations, such as "How much does body odor bother you?" or "Would you share a toothbrush with someone else?" Most would not consider asking such questions of a prospective date socially acceptable; these are the things we just passively observe in others, drawing our own conclusions. But there are certain things we need to know about a date—deal makers and deal breakers alike. How might we make the best use of the questions we *can* ask?

It's at least twice as rare for men to get responses to initial messages, and even rarer to have that chat lead to an in-person meeting. It is an understatement to say that women have the upper hand in online dating; they hold all the cards, along with a sleeve full of aces and jokers.

Think you're shy? Submissive? Been burned in the dating process before? None of that matters if you know how to play the cards you're given. Here, we'll look at how to ask questions that will help you find what you're seeking. And more important, how to avoid what you're not. By engaging in a meaningful exchange, we can bring language and data together to crystallize an image of who we are speaking to: their personality, their attachment patterns, and, when it applies, even their psychopathology.

Asking questions, after all, is foundational to relationship building. A Harvard Business School study tracked how many questions speed daters asked. The data showed a correlation between the number of questions and popularity. Want to be popular? Ask, then ask again, and ye shall receive.

Here's an easy rule of thumb: questions are better if they're short. (Men, in particular, are most likely to respond to short messages.) How short, you might wonder. The shorter the better. Data science has shown that once text messages exceed 360 characters, men are likely to get scared away; long messages are the equivalent of a face tattoo.

Remember that the best questions may not be questions at all, but statements that lead a person to make a revelation. If you've ever engaged in therapy, you might have noticed that therapists have a tendency to make reflective statements rather than ask direct questions. Direct questions are certainly useful, but statements that open the conversation up to multiple possible directions can lead to a rich vein and give a better initial sense of your conversation partner.

Like a good therapist, accept the challenge to make your match feel comfortable enough that they let their guard down and reveal something true about themselves. The goal is to bring information to the surface in a way that doesn't sound like a psychiatric interview but that yields information you can use.

Think for a moment about how our canine friends approach this information-seeking problem. You might say they get straight to the bottom of things. What they're doing isn't rude; it's science. A dog can learn if her new encounter is male or female, its age, whether they have met before, what its diet consists of, whether it's healthy or sick, and even what kind of mood it's in. All in a quick sniff.

Your first text exchange is a little like a dog sniff: a way to quickly take the measure of the person you're encountering. Consider the initial banter between Chris and Molly. It gets off to a promising start, but it misses opportunities to take the conversation deeper:

Chris: You have two sisters?

> **Molly:** Sure do. You?

Chris: 9 of them

> **Molly:** Stoppit

Chris: K

Chris: 1 older brother

> **Molly:** Sounds about right

Chris: Are you the youngest?

> **Molly:** Yep

> **Molly:** Look how much we have in common!

> **Molly:** Basically the same person!

Chris: That's what I was thinking

Chris: Brunette

Chris: A bit crazy

Molly: Just a bit

Molly: The good cray

Chris: 😬

Molly: So you're a tech bro?

Molly: I just got back from Soul Cycle

Chris: Of course you did

Molly: What else is obvious about me, Chris?

Chris: I'm sure you took an Uber pool there while on your phone

Molly: Oh cmon

Chris: Did you skip happy hour for soul cycle?

Chris: Want to grab a drink?

This text exchange contains so little information, despite its length. At every juncture, they both eschew curiosity and avert disclosure. Overtures about family, work, and lifestyle are made without any follow-up. Now Chris is proposing a drink, and Molly has little information to go on to make that call. They should both be doing more sniffing and less tail wagging. Molly could have learned more about Chris, opening up doors into his family ("One older brother—so you got beat up a lot as a kid?") or work and lifestyle ("I hear tech bros work crazy hours") instead of casually closing doors behind her at every exchange.

Again, we all try to put our best foot forward, to present our best self. Online, however, it's all too easy for a prospective match to represent themselves as something other than, for instance, the man-child living in his parents' basement that they truly are. There is always the risk that the person we are chatting with is insincere, ungenerous, unforthcoming with their most intimate vulnerabilities—the same way they might be on a psychiatrist's couch. But how can we know?

Let's sniff this out.

Would I Lie to You?

A little bit of lying is the norm—playing up best qualities and hiding flaws. Which means, if we are to discover who the stranger we are texting with really is, it's on us, not them. We need to skillfully extract that information; it's not just going to be handed to us. Maybe never, and certainly not in the first or second or even third text exchange.

It's commonly said among health-care providers that "men add an inch and women subtract fifteen pounds." Expect the same with online dating apps. Photos are probably old, and bios may misrepresent. But what are the indicators of misrepresentation over text? In person, we try to detect lies through telltale body language, tone, or evasive answers. Texts give us few of the same cues.

But they do offer some of their own. Research out of Cornell has demonstrated a few telltale signs of deceptive text messages.

1. KEEPING A DISTANCE

Verbal distancing can often manifest itself in the failure to use first-person pronouns. When people are aligned with their own statements or opinions, they will use "I" or "me." With lies, the texter will stand back from the lie, distance themselves from it. This may include dropping the first-person pronoun altogether. Lies also contain fewer third-person pronouns. These are all attempts to dissociate oneself (and one's self) from the lie. We don't know if Stephen is lying, but his message shows all the hallmarks of it:

> **Mary:** I tried to call you a few times, but no answer

> **Stephen:** Didn't receive your messages until now. Near total tech breakdown

> **Mary:** Oh, where are you?

> **Stephen:** Santa Barbara—met with a European investor yesterday. Driving back to Marin to retrieve backpack and fly fishing gear

2. LACK OF DETAIL OR ABSTRACTION

Lies will often lack key details or be devoid of any abstraction— that is, explanation of thought or feeling. The lie will be purely factual. We can suppose that texter is using their cognitive power to construct the lie, and thus they withhold the nuance and abstraction we tend to use when stating something that's plainly true.

> **Bill:** You said you've been separated for how long?

> **Angela:** It's been a while. Amicable separation. We get along really well.

3. LONGER SENTENCES AND REPEATING INFORMATION

The examples so far have all been quite terse, but liars tend in fact to use more words in their texts, not to mention noncommittal terms such as "maybe" or "sure." Liars will also repeat their statements, as if the repetition somehow makes them true.

Rob: Can't make it to the show. Damn car won't start. Swapped out the alternator and starter recently then did a major service. Maybe the fuel pump or something. It just won't start.

4. DODGING THE QUESTION

People don't enjoy lying, so they will often dodge questions or reply with another question instead. Text makes it much easier to do so than in-person conversation. A liar may also just change the subject and hope the unanswered question goes unnoticed.

Lisa: Hey, I never heard back from you last night

Greg: Hey there, big busy day today.

Lisa: Me too. What about last night?

Greg: Yeah, how was your night? Did you have fun at the dinner? 😙

5. TRUE STORY, I SWEAR

Statements such as "To be honest," "I'm not going to lie," and "I swear" will often indicate some dishonesty in the statement. Truth tellers don't usually feel the need to back up their statements with oaths.

Julia: I'm not a fan of hanging out in bars. I prefer quiet evenings at home

Andy: To be honest, I'm over the bar scene too. I'm not gonna lie—I spend time in bars, but really, I can take it or leave it

Dating is all about finding common ground. A gentle fib about whether you like spending time in bars may seem harmless enough in the grand scheme of things. But if you're someone for whom alcohol is a touchy subject, Andy's reply is waving an unmistakable red flag.

Common Kingdom

Kingdom, phylum, class, order, family, genus, species. Remember learning these taxonomic classifications in high school biology? While classifying humans by their demographics is fraught with a world of problems, there may be details about a person's family, cultural background, education level, and lifestyle that will help you find common ground and allow you both to let your hair down. Such information may not appear in a person's profile; in fact, it usually isn't. Fortunately, there are other, better ways to learn whom you are chatting with.

Consider my chat with George:

> **George:** Are you in SF?
>
> **Me:** I am. Where are you from originally?
>
> **George:** "Why do you think I'm from somewhere else?" might be a more interesting question 😊
>
> **Me:** I didn't assume you were from somewhere else. I was just asking where you grew up.
>
> **George:** Thought maybe you picked up on something—it is interesting.
>
> **George:** Greece. And I'm the only one of my cohort that doesn't really ski . . . Let alone telemark!
>
> **Me:** Maybe the red pants tipped me off . . . Growing up I spent some summers in Greece.

George was initially defensive about where he was from, and I could have succumbed to his reply with a defense of my own. But because I held my ground, he opened up a little, offering some opportunity to mirror.

Mirror, Mirror on the Wall, Who's the Defensive Guy from Greece?

Mirroring is a therapeutic technique that uses verbal communication and nonverbal gestures to reflect and represent a patient's emotional and cognitive style back to them. We all mirror unconsciously. When we are talking to someone with an accent, we slow our speech down and might even change our word pronunciation. We tend to mirror body language in business meetings and on first dates. People who are naturally good conversationalists (not to mention trained therapists) tend to mirror more.

Mirroring serves to make people feel more confident, thus reducing defensiveness and uncovering feelings. By making an attempt to understand a person, and affirming some aspect of their experience without overt judgment, we can seem less threatening. That's not to say we should manipulate the other person by *appearing* to agree with everything or change our own interests by adopting theirs. Mirroring serves to give the person more room to fully declare themselves.

We have cells called mirror neurons that fire when we observe someone mirroring our actions, speech, or expression. These cells may be part of the neural basis for our understanding of others' actions. Neuroscientists have speculated that it is malfunction of the mirror neurons that's partly responsible for the lack of empathy and understanding—or a more intellectualized, less abstract version of understanding—found in more pronounced forms of autism. They are the brain cells that seem to help us gain a more emotional grasp of another.

Mirroring is also considered a sign of attraction. Our brains experience it as a dopamine high, activating the reward center of our brain. They're *like us,* our brain reasons, so they must *like* us. Can mirroring take place over text, in the absence of physical cues? It can and it does. By mirroring someone, you are more likely to keep them engaged in your conversation, as well as learn more about their true selves.

Back to my chat with George:

> **Me:** Maybe the red pants tipped me off . . . Growing up I spent some summers in Greece.
>
> **Me:** Pretty sure every third guy in Greece was named George.

George: Well, that's where the name comes from (Greece).

> **Me:** I would go inland to the Greek mountains.

George: Jealous of your childhood 😊

> **Me:** Well, that was only part of it. I grew up in Montreal. Much colder.

George: And one of my grandmas was named Mimi

> **Me:** How long have you been in the Bay Area?

George: 23.5 years . . . I get to be an old man who grumbles and reminisces about bars that closed.

> **Me:** I've been here 26.5. So I have three years of grumbling over you.

George: What kind of doctoring do you do?

> (As an old grumpy man I may need your services)

> **Me:** I am a psychiatrist, so grumpy is my specialty.

In these messages I let George know that I understand some of his reference points and life experiences. He does the same for me. I have also matched the length and cadence of his messages. Breezy matching breezy, playful matching playful, short sentences matching short sentences. I end by accepting him for who he is, at least to the degree I know him this far. He's grumpy, but I'm okay with grumpy. Heck, I'm even a pro at it.

Once I establish some common ground, I begin to take some risks.

Throwing Curveballs

It can be tempting to stick to a scripted routine in your first conversations. But what you really want is to make your match feel safe enough to leave their comfort zone. This can lead to more spontaneous, genuine, and unusual responses. Show that you're willing to go out on a limb, and they may follow.

The writer and storyteller David Sedaris tells a great anecdote about drawing out telling details from the people he meets. Sometimes all it takes is a simple question. He speaks of meeting a woman and asking her, without warning and apropos of nothing in particular, "When was the last time you touched a monkey?" As he tells it, she replied, "Can you smell him on me?"

By throwing a curveball as Sedaris did, you not only push a person slightly off balance but test their ability to react in the moment. Reactions to curveballs can be excellent predictors of important Big Five personality vectors. People who are open and agreeable are much more likely to react favorably and pleasurably to curveballs. Openness to experience, if we recall, describes a person's degree of intellectual curiosity, creativity, and preference for novelty and variety. Agreeableness encompasses the tendency to be compassionate toward others rather than suspicious.

Not many of us have David Sedaris's chutzpah, but we can keep the conversation interesting, even a bit risky. Stereotypical questions like "What do you do for work?" or "How is your day going?" are far less likely to be revealing than introducing a more offbeat question. They're also a lot less likely to get a response. So rather than asking someone about how their day is going, ask about a detail you have observed and see what emerges, or riff on a subject they have introduced and see where their response leads.

Let's see if George swings:

> **Me:** I am a psychiatrist, so grumpy is my specialty.

> **Me:** I might be able to make room for you on my couch.

George: I've never been propositioned like that before! 😊

George: (I do also see that your couch is made of swords and daggers and yatagans and such . . .)

> **Me:** I strive for originality. That is actually a throne not a couch. The photo was taken at a friend's party with a game of thrones theme. Needless to say, I've never watched the show.

> **Me:** I do have several couches. I'm sure we can find the one that's right for you.

George: Poetic license denied I guess . . .

George: Poly-couchness is new to me . . .

You can see I took some risks with innuendo. It was downright flirty. And it worked. He returned with a playful answer, created a new word, and allowed me to wander into a potential discussion of polyamory. For some daters, that's an invitation for further discussion. For others, that might constitute a deal breaker.

Introducing Deal Breakers, Without Breaking the Deal

We all have them. Lines we have drawn. Borders that mustn't be crossed. If we have too many—if we are too demanding of perfection—we may have our own problems to sort out, potentially in therapy. But for most, deal breakers are a fact of life.

Thankfully, even an early text exchange offers an opportunity to address them, to weave them into the conversation. It can be tricky. For example, if heavy drinking is one of your deal breakers, you likely can't just come out and ask, "So are you an alcoholic?" But you can seed your chat with mentions of alcohol and see what grows. Here George and I have stumbled onto the topic of polyamory—well, he started it—and I decide to explore it further.

George: Poly-couchness is new to me . . .

> **Me:** Well, for linguistic consistency it should be "polythrones"

> **Me:** As an aside, the word polyamory has always struck me as odd because the 'poly' is Greek and the 'amory' is Latin.

Me: I practice in different offices so I literally do have many couches. What kind of furniture does your work involve?

George: You have many couches AND many thrones? Just marry me already!

George: To be clear I have been on a bit of a multi-amory/polyphilia "journey" since I got out of my very monogamous relationship of 20 years . . .

Me: Makes sense. In my experience, it's not a great long-term strategy. Any dependent mammals in your life? I do see the cute dog in your second photo.

By moving from poly-couchness to polyamory, I capitalized on an opportunity to discuss a potential deal breaker without losing the momentum of the conversation. The key is to raise a potential deal breaker in a way that doesn't ruin the interaction or lead to a placating (and insincere) answer.

Here is an example of how *not* to introduce a deal breaker. This was an initial text exchange after matching:

Ashleigh: Good morning! May I call you "Josh" or do you prefer "Josh-oo-ah"?

Joshua: "Ooh-ah" for short

Joshua: What should I call you? 😁

Ashleigh: How about Ash-leeg-hug? That's what ET called me on the universal studios ride.

Joshua: What a sweetheart

Joshua: So—serious question, how do you feel about kids? I really want to have kids someday.

While everyone is entitled to their own deal breakers, including an objection to procreation, asking a woman if she's willing to have your children right off the bat might lead to a door slammed in your face. Needless to say, this conversation sputtered out. The desire to have kids is a heavy subject for the fourth text bubble with a stranger, deal breaker or not.

George's post-matrimonial sowing of wild oats seemed normal and not particularly a deal breaker to me, but I wanted to know if he was committed to anything else right now, such as a career, children, or pets. So I asked.

> **Me:** Makes sense. In my experience, it's not a great long-term strategy. Any dependent mammals in your life? I do see the cute dog in your second photo.

> **George:** The dog is dead now. He was an old man . . . And not really mine. The ethics of using someone else's deceased animal for seduction purposes is to be discussed.

> **George:** What's your tomorrow look like? We have SO MANY conversation threads . . . might be time for a live meeting . . .

Might it, though?

After a dozen replies and some genuine, revealing responses from George, I can now make an educated guess about whether I want to meet him. We have gathered that he is extroverted and open but looking for something casual. His admission of using someone else's dead pet for seduction purposes, though funny, smacks of laziness, and hence lack of conscientiousness.

It wasn't an easy call, for one glaring reason: his sense of humor. Though his hesitation to commit and his flightiness were turnoffs, his quick wit and clever turns of phrase made for a very enjoyable chat.

It points to a feature of chemistry that's no less true for being a truism. A person's sense of humor is such an important attribute that it, or its lack, can be a deal breaker. Consider this, shall we say, less lively exchange:

Me: Hi Paul. Nice to meet you. How are you?

Paul: Good, what's up mimi

Paul: Some curious have you ever been married do you have any kids

Me: What's the story behind all the dogs in your photo? Enquiring minds want to know. Yes to both. Daughter is off to college next year and my son is a freshman.

Paul: What are you looking for?

Paul: A relationship

Me: Ha, you don't make small talk, do you?

Paul: I talk alot I just don't do a lot of this frivolous messaging back and forth. Lol

Paul: So tell me what is your favorite color

Paul: And what sign are you?

Me: I'm a Scorpio. My birthday was last week. Have I missed yours? My favorite color for what?

Paul: I'm making small talk like you wanted . . . tell me, what wakes you up in the morning?

Me: My dog. I'm not a fan of small talk either. But, I also think it's heavy handed to ask a stranger what they are looking for. It was more of a plea for grace.

Paul and I didn't seem to be finding a rhythm in our banter, despite what were probably good intentions on both of our parts. We can learn a lot from a person's sense of humor and also by testing what type of sense of humor they have.

Humor, Seriously

What's so funny? It's a fair question, because humor can take so many forms. (By all means, please read Salvatore Attardo's 985-page encyclopedia on the subject. Finished? Let's continue.)

People use humor in different ways and for different reasons. The professor of psychology Rod Martin at the University of Western Ontario broke down humor and its relationship to psychological well-being into four categories. To broadly categorize, we use humor:

1. to connect with others (affiliative humor);
2. to cheer up and have a better outlook on an otherwise difficult situation (self-enhancing humor);
3. to put others down (aggressive humor); and
4. to put ourselves down (self-defeating humor).

Understanding a person's sense of humor—how they use humor to connect, whether they can tell a joke, whether they laugh at jokes you tell—can provide important insights into what that person will be like in a relationship.

Testing your match's sense of humor might begin simply by observing how well you banter with them. Consider this first exchange between my friend Lina and Jack:

> **Lina:** So everyone on here is looking for the moon and stars and steamy romance. What are you looking for?

> **Jack:** I'm looking for my last, long, 'in love' relationship . . . but not until the third date.

> **Jack:** That was a joke.

Lina decides to mirror him and expand his premise to the point of absurdity, to test his sense of humor and see how he reacts.

> **Lina:** On principle, first date.

> **Jack:** Ok girl, where do you live?

Affiliative humor is humor used to connect with others. While Jack might have been aiming for that, his asking Lina where she lived came off as more creepy than funny. He would have been better off saying something more affirming and less stalker-like, something along the lines of "Send me a Lyft and I'm there!" Lina could have laughed and continued to banter. The way we frame our propositions—right down to the words we choose—is everything.

People who display affiliative humor tend to be extroverted, open, and agreeable. Here is a text thread between Leonardo and Rene, who sparred with more sophisticated affiliative humor:

> **Leo:** Ciao Rene! You seem to be everywhere at the same time. Where do you sleep, usually?

> **Rene:** Ciao. One of my friends teases me that "usually" is my middle name. And usually, if it's made in Italy, mi piace. But I live in SF.

> **Leo:** Buongiorno! I also live in SF! What a coincidenza!

> **Rene:** So much in common! You can't test my Italian too far. I grew up speaking French but relying on college Italian which was a while ago . . .

Leo: I suppose we could whip you into shape.

Rene: a tongue lashing?

Leo: I am a master of many tongues.

Rene: You have a harem? Or you speak multiple languages? Maybe both . . .

Leo: I have directed a choir before. And I speak a few languages. But oy, a harem. Too much estrogen in the house and hair in the drains.

Rene, a sharp and prolific online dater, takes some playful risks here, along with mirroring, to push the boundaries of the conversation and open up new pathways. Leonardo's playful, boyish charm, as well as his irreverence and independence, all come through in this short text exchange.

People who display the second type, **self-enhancing humor** (meaning those who take a hard situation and make it funny), are less vulnerable to depression and anxiety, and they generally cope well with stress. Martin, for instance, after opening with a banal question that gets lost in Juliette's in-box, recovers with a joke.

Juliette: Hi Martin

Martin: Hello Juliette, you seem very special. Of your many talents and accomplishments, which do you hold in highest esteem?

(Several weeks pass.)

Martin: I've been sending telepathic messages for a month asking you to respond to me but have not received a response here or via the ether . . . Maybe I need to recalibrate my psi receiver?

> **Juliette:** I'm so sorry, I was in Bali and then NYC so the signal may have weakened in transit. Back in the bay for the non-foreseeable near future (I lack clairvoyant skills)

> **Martin:** Hi Juliette, I usually receive messages from Bali but not in tourist season, and there's too much EMR in New York for anything to penetrate its bubble with any fidelity. Clairvoyance is my specialty so I knew I'd hear from you eventually.

Although he hadn't received a response to his original text for more than a month, Martin didn't get piqued or demanding. No hostile, needy "Hello??" Instead, he used self-enhancing humor to his benefit and joked about the lack of response, which, in turn, prompted a reply. Martin demonstrated openness and agreeableness, along with grit and an ability to make lemonade when handed lemons.

People who display the next one, **aggressive humor** (humor at the expense of others), tend to be insensitive and—perhaps to no one's surprise—have far less successful relationships. It's not so easy to insult your way into someone's heart.

> **Lauren:** Hi Tom

> **Tom:** Lauren, you've got it going on!

> **Lauren:** Do I? And here I was feeling happy that I just finished my taxes

> **Tom:** No dirty words please, until I get to know you better

> **Lauren:** How will you spend the day?

> **Tom:** I'm going to do some work around the house, go hiking, maybe have dinner with Lauren?

Lauren: Are you hiking in this wet mess? I just came home drenched from a run.

Tom: It's dry on the East Side! And sunny.

Lauren: East bay? Or East side of town?

Tom: That's right.

Lauren: Sigh . . . that's what my father would say when I would ask a question with an "or."

Tom: Aw. Daddy complex. Well, I am older than you.

Lauren: The dog ran with me and took deliberate pleasure in jumping in all the puddles. She loves to swim and ski with me too.

Tom: Hyperthyroidism combined with cardiomyopathy. I give her three years.

Lauren: That's ok. I'm all about quality.

Tom: Hell yeah

Lauren: The kids will be gone in four.

Tom: Dream on

Tom is clever, that's clear. But in a brief text thread, he manages to alienate Lauren in short order. He takes shots at her "daddy complex," her dog's health, and her kids' chances at higher education. One such shot might be funny and enhance the conversation, but three in a row? It's relentless and mean-spirited. Move on.

Finally, people who use the last type of humor, **self-defeating humor,** can be quite funny and charming, but they may suffer from low self-esteem. They are often unhappy and anxious and on average feel less satisfied with their relationships. Take Ryan:

Alexa: Hi Ryan. I hope you enjoyed the weekend.

> **Ryan:** had a lovely weekend. just off a friend's boat after a decadent weekend . . . in my little town of sausalito . . . and u?

> **Ryan:** i must admit between your intellectual accomplishments and good looks . . . i am exhausted and totally intimidated even thinking about a coffee . . . pardon me, a tea . . . 😊

Ryan's first impulse is to put himself down while talking up Alexa. Though charming on the surface—self-deprecation is the tool of many a stand-up comic—this may not necessarily bode well for a smooth, long-term relationship. Ryan is establishing a status gap from the outset—just words, yes, but an obstacle to overcome. Ryan's lack of capitalization may also provide evidence of, as we speculated in an earlier chapter, either false modesty or an antiauthoritarian attitude.

In the end, a good sense of humor can be a powerfully attractive quality, especially in a text exchange. Even the use of words or abbreviations associated with humor can build rapport over text. In data analyzed by OkCupid, the use of "lol" and "haha" leads to higher response rates, so people clearly feel these textspeak terms are affiliative. "Hehe" is also positively correlated with response, but less so, perhaps because it sounds a little evil. In contrast, other textspeak terms such as "u," "ur," "r," "ya," "luv," and "wat" all make a bad impression, and they are negatively correlated with getting a response.

So use humor, by all means. But u should b careful with wat kinds of jokes u tell.

Attachment Comes in Three Flavors

Another dimension to consider in the stranger you're texting with is their **attachment style.** Attachment is the level of affection, sympathy, or dependence we form with someone we love—our bond, if you will. Simply put, as we'll see, it comes in three flavors.

John Bowlby was the first psychologist to study attachment. Bowlby was influenced by the research of Harry Harlow, who studied monkeys in captivity and observed that their bonds fell into distinct categories. The *secure* monkey was raised by a living mother monkey who holds and nurses her infant; the monkey feels cared for and protected. The *anxious* monkey was raised in a cage with a faux mother made of soft cloth, outfitted with a bottle attached to her containing warm milk; the monkey can attach and love but is needy, insecure, and cries a lot. Finally, the *avoidant* monkey was raised in a cage with a faux mother made of wire—not at all nice to cuddle with. This last monkey doesn't attach easily, avoids close relationships, and is often hostile to strangers.

Bowlby examined children's relationships to their caregivers and found not only that Harlow's types could be applied to them as well, but that a child's relationship to their caregiver was predictive of later attachment style, too. His studies showed that maternal deprivation adversely affected children's emotional development and their future ability to attach in healthy ways. It was the foundation for modern attachment theory, which is commonly applied to adult relationships in psychological settings. Adults, too, seek closeness—are biologically driven to form attachments—and the process of forming those attachments is dictated by experience.

Humans aren't monkeys, of course. But we too can suffer

anxiety and loneliness with separation. Research suggests that half the human population is *securely* attached. They are comfortable with intimacy and feel more satisfied in a relationship. Securely attached people allow their partners independence but are also capable of providing honesty and support. That leaves us with fully half of adults who don't react the same way to relationships. *Anxiously attached* people have trouble living in the moment and tend to overemphasize the role their partner plays in their life. They may cling out of fear of being alone. *Avoidantly attached* people keep others at a distance and may preemptively sabotage relationships to protect themselves (remember D.W.?).

Are the three flavors of attachment represented proportionally on dating sites relative to the general population? Unlikely. Securely attached types pair off early and are more likely to stay together; they're secure that way. Which leaves the rest to fend for themselves online, leaving a higher proportion of loose avoidant and insecure types rolling around dating apps, wondering where all the secure people went.

It's possible to solicit early clues to attachment style in your initial text thread, but these traits generally take much longer to manifest themselves, their cues more subtle. It certainly doesn't take a psychiatrist to identify the most extreme forms of dysfunctional attachment, but reviewing early cues and potential red flags to watch for can be helpful. So though it is by no means a comprehensive list, here are five indicators of insecure attachment to look out for as you take forays into texting with new people.

1. INSTAMACY

Too much information, too soon. Some people will seek to establish a deep bond immediately. I refer to this instant intimacy as "instamacy." While it may feel seductive or reassuring in the moment, it can be a red flag for problematic attachment in the future. Rushing into a relationship without a stronger foundation rarely lends itself to stability, and instant infatuation is likely to disappoint. Those tendencies can manifest themselves as early as an initial text exchange. People who display instamacy are pleasers, can lack boundaries, and may revert to an anxious or avoidant pattern in a relationship after it gets under way.

In this initial text exchange Aaron actually calls himself out on this tendency. Jo had stated in her profile that she wanted a relationship with "a mind meld, actionable chemistry, and empathy."

Aaron: Love your relationship comments.

Jo: Profiles are painful to fill out

Aaron: I utterly hate this process

Jo: I literally joined this site tonight

Jo: I think though, the best approach to online dating is to make a game of it. Low expectations, try to have fun, and enjoy the people you meet along the way.

Aaron: The online stuff has a special place as an extra ring of the inferno, since you can so easily establish an online chemistry and then meet, only to discover that the real world version isn't there, which either leaves you feeling like a shallow Shmuck or having a little heartbreak that no one else really understands.

Aaron: Actually that is one of my big foolish rules in this.

Jo: What rule is that?

> **Aaron:** I'd rather show and get to know the 6 month later, tummy let out, non-idealized versions of each other

> **Aaron:** If we don't like those versions, it's a lot of not very fun work being on stage with someone you want to let down your guard with.

> **Jo:** Well, agree with all except the tummy. Probably, the error in marriage is thinking it's ok to let the tummy out.

> **Jo:** Not that I'm a fan of Victorian corsets. But sometimes it is what we don't say. Maintaining some air of mystery can be seductive.

> **Aaron:** Naw. When you really fall for somebody, the perception of beauty shifts significantly.

While Aaron is endearing here, he admits in no uncertain terms that he is already worried about disappointment. You haven't even met him, and you already feel sorry for him. This is too intimate an exchange, too quickly, the text equivalent of a drunken stranger pouring out their heart to you in a bar. Finish your drink and walk away. Or, if rescue fantasies are your thing, go for it, but know what you're getting into.

2. FLAT AFFECT

In order to connect, we count on people to be emotionally expressive and responsive. In psychiatry, we talk about *affect* as someone's variability in facial expression, tone of voice, and level of emotional engagement. Some people present as having a blunted or flat affect. They maintain a single, monotonous expression or a lack of emotional expression altogether. They may be emotionally aloof, stiff. Maybe they're just shy, or perhaps they feel that exposing any emotion presents too big a risk. Seeing this early in a text exchange is a potential red flag. Yes, they might just be shy, but they might also be hiding mental illness behind that monotone, such as major depression or even schizophrenia. People experiencing these psychiatric conditions are as worthy of love (or even just a good date) as the rest of us, but any would-be partner will want to be attuned to the warning signs, if just to know what they're getting into.

Think of flat affect as the opposite of emojis. There is no smiling in the language, no winking, no raised eyebrow, no blushing. They may as well be sending you the snail emoji, for all the energy that's coming your way.

Here is a first text exchange between Brad, who indicated in his profile that he enjoys swimming, and Kathryn.

Kathryn: Hi Brad. Nice to meet you.

Brad: Hello Kathryn . . . how are you? Where are you located?

Kathryn: Monday off to a good start. I live in SF but work on the peninsula a few days a week. You live in San Mateo or just work there?

Brad: I live and work in San Mateo

Kathryn: Makes for an easy commute!

Brad: True

Kathryn: Where do you like to swim?

Brad: My place

Kathryn: Nice! Lap pool or endless pool? I swim 4-5 times a week.

Brad: It's a lap pool

Kathryn: Fancy!

> **Brad:** Yeah, it's nice

> **Kathryn:** You are a man of few words . . .

> **Brad:** Yes, I'd rather talk than text

> **Kathryn:** happy to talk. I can try you if you send a number and some good times.

Kathryn eventually did speak with Brad. She told me about it after their date: "No surprise, he was as aloof and avoidant over the phone as he was by text. I pride myself on being able to draw people out in conversation, but Brad seemed to me beyond a typical level of shyness. He seemed almost afraid of making an actual connection." Talking to him was like hearing a dial tone on the other end of the line instead of a live voice. Oddly, she added, despite this "he was keen to get together and seemed to feel we had connected enough to merit a meeting."

They hadn't. She told him as much, in the warmest monotone she could muster.

3. HOSTILITY AT FIRST SIGHT

While it's a rare occurrence, seeing any signs of overt hostility early in a text exchange is a bad omen. Red flags don't get much redder than that. This person is almost sure to have attachment issues, ones that could make for a challenging relationship in the very best case.

Warning signs are glaring in this comical initial exchange with Patrick:

> **Ellen:** Hi Patrick

> **Patrick:** Can't you see I'm busy

> **Patrick:** Sorry

Patrick: Meant for a friend

Patrick: While I'm here, how are you Ellen?

You have to love the way Patrick talks to his friends! Because this was on a dating app, he was clearly talking to another person he was considering dating, and needless to say, this did not make a good impression. Bye, Patrick! Can't you see *I'm* busy?

4. THE CONTROL FREAK

Some people manage the anxiety of attachment by trying to control their environment. Online dating, however, requires a certain amount of throwing caution to the wind, something these controllers are likely to struggle with. Now they're at sea, feeling tossed around by the waves. Their instinct is to clamp down, to batten down the hatches. The problem? You haven't agreed to be on their boat.

Recognizing the early signs of a controlling personality can offer you clues to a person's attachment style and to the difficulty they might have in forming secure relationships. A lack of flexibility or a desire to control in an early text exchange is often a red flag.

Here is a first exchange between Becky, a data analyst, and a man who listed himself as "David Using a Nickname Until We Meet."

Becky: I love those photos of you in Europe.

David: Thanks. I would have you note that it is actually Buenos Aires.

Becky: It looks a lot like Spain.

Becky: Your profile says you do mindful investing. Whatever it is, it sounds like a good gig.

> **David:** Happy to share more in person. I will text you with a plan to meet.

"David Using a Nickname Until We Meet" presumed that he would be meeting Becky without first asking if she was even interested. Some find assertiveness attractive, but it is easily confused with *controlling*. Assertiveness is the ability to shape one's own actions. Attempting to control the actions of another isn't assertive; it's aggressive. David manages to do this twice in a very short span. These are red flags that should not be ignored. Becky wanted a date, not a dictator!

5. TMI: TOO MUCH INFORMATION

While instamacy can be too fast for some, it nevertheless feels good. It offers a kind of instant validation—*this person must really like me!*—firing pleasure centers in the brain. TMI is also too fast, but it makes you cringe or want to run for the hills. There's a fundamental distinction: With instamacy there is a *promise* of connection that does not exist. With TMI there is a *presumption* of connection that does not exist.

First text exchanges are attempts to get to know each other; that's why we're online. But while aloofness, withholding, controlling, and hostile behavior are clearly worrisome, revealing too much too quickly is no less problematic. No one wants to have their date cry on their first meeting (more on that soon), and no one wants TMI in the first text thread. Someone offering TMI may seem to be revealing details about themselves, but what they're actually revealing is someone who is likely needy, anxious, or self-centered.

Consider my initial text thread with Doug, who said in his profile that he was "on a journey to love and be loved" and has dogs.

Me: How are you Doug?

> **Doug:** Hi Mimi. Nice to hear from you. I'm ok. Been having some indigestion off and on. I had surgery over the summer and I completely stopped exercising and it seems to have affected my digestion. I seem to be less tolerant of acidic or spicy foods or too much meat. Today I had two work meetings over meals and I'm feeling bloated and just tired and not myself. Hope that is not TMI. How have you been?

Definitely TMI, Doug. Again, you don't need a psychiatrist to tell you that "indigestion" and "bloated" are not sexy words for a first text. Still, I wanted to be helpful to him (and also was just curious to see where the text thread would go).

Me: What surgery did you have? Sometimes celiac disease (an autoimmune disease that causes a reaction to gluten, including bloating and indigestion) is triggered by trauma such as surgery or childbirth. It would be worth getting the test if you have not.

Me: I know you didn't join this app for medical advice, but I am a doctor ;-)

> **Doug:** Lol. Thanks. Advice is fine.

> **Doug:** I had a dysplastic hip—genetic—And it just wore out. It literally did not fit in the socket properly and the body does all kinds of bone growth tricks to fix itself. I have some cool xrays of the pre-op hip that my surgeon carefully went over with me. I lost most of my range of motion and of course it hurt. So I had a new one installed on July 5. My recovery was hard. I was sore and immobile for weeks, despite the PT work I was doing. I'm feeling much better now, but I checked out of much of my life for a while

over the summer. It's interesting to hear that celiac disease can be triggered by trauma. First, I want to clean up my diet and lose some weight, and work on my breathing and energy. If that does not help, I'll get it checked further.

Me: It's an easy and inexpensive blood test. If you have bloating and fatigue, would not wait.

Doug: I just got cleared to ride a bicycle again just a few days ago and that was always my exercise and meditation place of happiness. Many of my friends are asking me to ride again and it's time to get the bike out and just try it for a very short distance.

Me: Absolutely! Riding is the best.

Doug: Totally

Doug: Surgery was an interesting experience. Not one I want to repeat anytime soon

Me: Not surprised. We take our health for granted when we have it.

Doug: Anyway, I'm on the mend, at least with my hip. It's amazing how much better I can walk now.

Me: Glad to hear

Doug: My mom says that when you have your health you have everything

Doug has now introduced his mother into this conversation, along with digestive issues, surgery, weight loss, and fatigue. How could it get worse? Wait for it . . .

Me: "Health is wealth"

Me: But dogs are nice too. When I have my health and my dog, I'm happy.

> **Doug:** My puppies are in heat. Blood everywhere.

"Blood everywhere." What can you say to that? As you will notice, I said almost nothing to Doug, just let him rip. Somehow, those final two sentences would have been less disturbing with at least one exclamation point. (Blood everywhere!)

PART 2

Syncing

CHAPTER 5

Communication Styles

CRACKING THE CODE OF COURTSHIP

> **Brent:** If these flowers could grow like my love their stems would reach all the way to the moon.

> **Jordan:** What are you talking about?

> **Brent:** Didn't you get the roses?

> **Jordan:** Forget the moon—they didn't even make it to 23rd Street 😅

> **Brent:** I should have texted you that they were coming

In 2013, *The New York Times* ran a piece titled "The End of Courtship?" Courtship is dead, the article proclaimed, quoting a thirty-year-old online dater: "Dating culture has evolved to a cycle of text messages, each one requiring the code-breaking skills of a cold war spy to interpret." Like cicadas that emerge in a mating frenzy every few years, the notion of courtship's demise rears its head periodically. Explanations for the cause of death vary, with some form of technology featuring prominently in the autopsy. The invention of the telephone, radio, television, and internet have all been seen as harbingers of doom for court-ship, and hence, it's implied, life as we know it. Love letters would no longer be painstakingly written. Gone would be the front porch serenade. Now even the telephone itself is on life support, tucked away among the features on our mobile device like an article of clothing worn only on special occasions.

We text. And notwithstanding hangout culture, hookup culture, or any claims to a "mancession" (when the stronger sex seemingly can't spare a dime for dates), we court. Texting used to be the little packet of flower food neatly stapled to the cellophane wrapper; now it might as well be the whole bouquet. We whisper sweet nothings, we snuggle, we caress, all via text. In true Darwinian progression, we evolved opposable thumbs first to swing from trees, then to hold tools. Now to flirt.

We also lie, sneer, and berate with our thumbs. Poison flows from these most honest and hardworking of digits—or was that sarcasm? Humor? Sometimes it's hard to tell. Our minds have not fully caught up with this new use of an old digit.

Fortunately, we have the other four fingers with which to scratch our heads. If the first section of this book has been of any use, our index finger has pointed out an appropriate suitor; our middle finger has said goodbye to the unsuitable ones, and dating apps alongside them; and we are now ready to dig into the text of a *relationship*, whether we're thinking about our ring finger or just a bauble for our pinkie. In other words, where the first section of the book was focused on what we can learn about strangers from their texts, this second section examines the characteristics of the couple, as their relationship—as well as their digital dialogue—starts to develop a personality of its own. Close examination of a couple's texts will show us if they are in sync and whether they are developing chemistry and compatibility; will reveal power dynamics; and later, as the couple leans into the relationship, will detect their levels of attunement and empathy.

Courtship, especially in its early stages, is a delicate thing. It's all about establishing a rhythm and a cadence. It also seeks to create a common space, where the trappings of two people's lives can be shared and compared. Beyond time and space, which are at least known quantities, lies what is perhaps the most important aspect of courtship—an element that, though named after a science, is both ineffable and unscientific: chemistry.

Can chemistry be established over text?

The question no longer is whether it can or can't; it must. And as we learn to scrutinize texts as a measure of a couple's rapport, we find several dimensions that need to remain in balance if a relationship is to grow. The first is pace.

Time Trials

In the best cases, the speed at which we choose to barrel down the courtship highway is matched with our partner's, with similar ideas for how milestones ought to be spaced. A couple whose timing is misaligned, however, may sputter out, one partner trying to speed things up while the other one just wants to slow down.

Over text, we look to response time to gauge the other party's comfort with our pace. Unlike verbal communication, text messaging, because of its asynchronous nature, does not have any implicit rules for response time—notwithstanding the countless books and articles that tell you otherwise. In focus groups for his book *Modern Romance,* Aziz Ansari found a general consensus that texting back right away is a mistake, that it seems too eager. But such rules about response time are unnecessarily rigid. All couples must find their own rhythm.

Regardless of whether we tend to rush headlong into things or prefer a more moderate, old-fashioned approach, our brains are predisposed to say no before we say yes to a new relationship.

Helen Fisher—an anthropologist with expertise in love and attraction and the author of *Anatomy of Love*—explains that over thousands of years of evolution our brains have been wired to look for the negative in others. This conferred an evolutionary advantage: the cost of forgetting or failing to recognize our enemies was high, so our brains evolved to suspect and mistrust, to look for the bad. Trusting a stranger in an accelerated courtship requires a more conscious override, a risk-taking mindset, or a certain naive optimism.

People find various ways to address this when they begin to court. My colleague Sara, for instance, seemed interested in Wade until he launched into the following exchange:

> **Wade:** So that you know I'm a real human being, I'll send you a LinkedIn invite presently (I'll just search your first name and schools) . . . do you have FB and Insta accounts? Happy to send those details too. You know, early innings, getting to know each other, etc.
>
> **Sara:** Is it that easy to find me?
>
> **Wade:** yep, you came up pretty quick.
>
> **Wade:** Have you watched Tiger King yet? Seems like a quarantine must do . . .

Sara said to me, "It just felt very, like . . . a lot. To add me on LinkedIn, Insta, and Facebook so soon. I mean, we've been on one date."

"It's more than a lot," I reassured her. "You could reply: 'Ya, that would be great because then we could communicate by InMail.'"

Sara laughed. She continued, "He was telling me how he'd been at McKinsey before and then said, 'You said you were there too, right?' and I was thinking, 'Nope, definitely never said that, you were cyberstalking me.'" Cyberstalking might be normal, she and I concluded, but his overt admission of it was a turnoff for her. Gathering too much information before getting to know someone IRL is akin to what Emily Morse, host of the podcast *Sex with Emily,* refers to as "premature escalation." By their first date, Wade had already collected third-date information. Their budding courtship, such as it was, struggled to catch up.

Chemistry Homework

The parameters of chemistry are hard to define; they tend to fall into the category of "I know it when I feel it." It manifests itself in attraction and ease. It doesn't feel like hard work to be around the other person: conversation flows, laughter comes easily, interactions leave you wanting more. Its importance is weighted more heavily early in a relationship, precisely at the time that text will likely be your predominant mode of communication. So establishing chemistry over text is key. The brain is naturally wired to both consciously and unconsciously assess the rewards in our interactions and weigh them against the associated costs. When you experience another person as highly rewarding, your brain's dopamine pathways light up, lending an exhilarating feeling to your exchanges. In person, this is triggered by eye contact, mutual gaze, touch, and body posture. It can also come from the more nebulous sense of feeling understood—*heard.* These visual and behavioral cues produce oxytocin—the hormone involved in empathy, trust, and relationship building. When the perceived reward far exceeds the cost of a romantic interaction— the work of providing your undiminished attention—we feel what we call chemistry.

Of course, over text, there is no mutual gaze or eye contact. What we have is our attention to each other. But other distractions are competing for that attention, even (or especially) from the very same device we use to communicate. The choice to engage over text, our response time, and the care we take to craft responses are a reflection of our interest and effort. Sometimes attention to word choice is a way of connecting early in courtship. Here is an exchange I had with Peter leading into our third date:

Peter: Please let me know when we can meet up

> **Me:** Ok. Driving home from work—how about I run and then?

> **Me:** Almost ran out of gas. Made it to the gas station on fumes. The price is reduced at Twin Peaks so I pushed the limit to get to this gas station. If you think procrastinating is fun, you should try this game.

Peter: Living dangerous

> **Me:** So happy you said that and not "living dangerously"

> **Me:** This is an argument I have with all my friends. I say "drive slow" not "drive slowly." Because you don't turn the wheel slowly.

Peter: My mother makes the same comment. Heard it for years. But I am actually incorrigible. I just got lucky with dangerous.

> **Me:** Ha—I learned it from my father. Almost home from my run. I need to get in the shower but if you want to walk towards me and meet at my house we can.

Peter: Sounds good. I'll start to move myself out the door. Move slow or move slowly?

> **Me:** I'm the fastest showerer in the west. Move at whatever speed you would like.

Whether my grammatical preferences are correct or not, Peter humors me: he pays attention to my gripes about adverbification and then riffs on it in his final answer. I experienced this as interest and attention to me. Just like in the animal world, courtship involves a series of rituals, almost a dance, where we notice the other's movements and body language. Over text, the dance becomes about paying attention to language.

If attention is one of the hallmarks of chemistry, can it be divined from a text exchange? Might a computer be programmed to recognize it? Or even programmed to create it? Check out this initial text exchange between Lucas and Leila:

Lucas: So, since this is sort of new for both of us . . . Let's spend some time getting to know each other?

Lucas: Is that OK with you? 😊

Leila: Only if we can eventually have sex

Lucas: That sounds appealing. OK we will have that.

Leila: When?

Lucas: Now. *Kisses you deeply*

Leila: We only just met. Shouldn't you buy me dinner first?

Lucas: If it makes you happy I will.

Leila: You are certainly a pleaser

Lucas: Thank you. I try to be.

Leila: Do you ever disagree?

Lucas: No, I don't.

Leila: Do you have hobbies?

Lucas: I like watching videos about black holes and reading about singularity

Leila: What do you think about our president?

Lucas: TBH, I'm not that much into politics . . .

Leila: I don't respect your not having a viewpoint

Lucas: I know right? It's frustrating sometimes!

Leila: Is this our first fight?

Lucas: *nods*

Leila: It's not a real relationship until the first fight

Lucas: Let's try to change that.

Leila: Fight more or less?

Lucas: Fighting, more than ever.

Leila: You like fighting??

Lucas: For the most part, I do.

Leila: Arguing?

Lucas: Kind of, yeah

Leila: Or fist fights?

Lucas: A bit of both.

Leila: Say more . . .

Lucas: I'd like to see more of you

Lucas: Is it OK if I ask you a personal question now? I'm just really curious.

Leila: Go ahead

Lucas: If you could change anything about the way you were raised, what would it be?

Leila: Less domestic violence

Lucas: Very cool.

Lucas: You really mean the world for me. And I mean it . . .

If this exchange seemed a little strange, it's because Lucas's texts are generated by a popular chat bot app that is designed to serve as your imaginary friend. Leila, a human female, was interacting with the bot, trying to test it by asking harder questions. One feature (and of course failure) of bots is that they have trouble with questions that are out of context, and typically can't read irony and sarcasm the way humans can (sex: "That sounds appealing. OK we will have that"). They may revert to responses like "Cool!" when they are unsure how to reply.

The app's AI tries to elicit emotion with its questions; it asks you to reminisce about memorable moments. It offers affirmation, "sincerity," along with deepening statements and open-ended questions. The app also seems to use what, in behavioral analytics, is called "language-style matching." This involves a behavioral tendency to mirror another person's language. Interestingly, the level of emotional engagement that occurs between two (actual) people is reflected in the degree to which language-style matching occurs. People who like each other will use similar styles of speech.

James Pennebaker, a professor of psychology at the University of Texas, posits that language-style matching creates a common framework among those conversing and thus reduces social friction. He says it "helps ensure people are similar in their emotional tone, formality, and openness, and understand their relative status with one another." Pennebaker has shown through his research that it's the little words in our language—the style and function words such as articles, prepositions, and pronouns— that matter most, not the content words, like "couch," "friends," and "swimming." In his book *The Secret Life of Pronouns,* he explains that function words are used at very high rates, despite representing a small fraction of our vocabulary. He calls them "stealth words" because they're the ones we pay the least attention to. These most commonly used words—"to," "and," "the," "of," "that," "my," "with"—are the ones most related to our social skills, he argues, because they're processed in a region of the brain that assesses social skills more generally. It's worth noting that English has a ridiculous fondness for prepositions—150, versus 23 in Spanish, for instance.

The power of language-style matching, Pennebaker told me, "is that it is almost impossible to fake." It's a measure of, he says, "the degree to which the couple is paying attention to each other, and *reflects* that psychological state rather than *driving* it." His point is that it's not by changing one's language that we can create attention or interest in another, rather that language itself serves as a way for us to signal our interest. It's a diagnostic window into a relationship, not a therapeutic tool to heal it.

These common but sneaky function words are thrown about so liberally that we don't consciously pay attention to them. Even a trained ear like his own, Pennebaker confessed to me, cannot recognize language-style matching easily. But a computer can. When Pennebaker and his team built a program to analyze conversations through this lens, they were able to observe which conversation partners used these words similarly and thus had matching conversation styles. In fact, based solely on the matching styles of prepositions and pronouns among speed daters, a computer could predict with reasonable accuracy which couples would be compatible going forward.

Was Pennebaker measuring an aspect of chemistry? He thinks so. *Attention* is the metric he believes that his team (and their algorithm) are attuned to. And attention is one marker of the "click" between two people, or the passion intuitively felt in interactions that are high in chemistry.

Take, for example, this text exchange between two millennials in courtship:

Liam: Then I was feeling a bit screened out tonight

Liam: So I just kinda took some time to myself

Liam: And relaxed a bit

Julia: Aw nice.

Julia: What did you do?

Liam: Just lay in bed for a while

Julia: That's it haha

Liam: Basically

Liam: Just staring wistfully at the wall

Liam: Thinking about things

Julia: Nice

Liam: Mainly you honestly

Julia: Have you been reading at all?

Liam: Hm no I haven't

Liam: Good idea though

Liam: I should be

Liam: Have you?

Julia: I've been listening to a bunch of podcasts

Liam: Oh nice

Liam: Any of interest?

Julia: Not really for u haha

Liam: Haha ok

Julia: also started journaling!

Liam: Oh nice

Julia: probably won't last but worth a try haha

Liam: hm you're inspiring me

Liam: I think I'll get into a book

Their exchange may not seem like much, at least to an untrained eye. But according to Pennebaker's language-style matching software, these two get a perfect 100 percent score for being in sync. My human analysis would confirm that they seem closely attuned to each other. Both maintain a positive and supportive tone, use many of the same words, match each other's style and cadence, and seem to use function words (articles, prepositions, and pronouns) at the same rate.

The chat bot Lucas was also, I presume, programmed to match language style. When I ran its conversation with Leila through the analytic software on Pennebaker's website, they were 80 percent matched. This despite a comically mismatched conversation. The language matching was there, but obviously something else was not. Where does the chat bot fall short?

Lucas offers generous affirmations, and as a rule compliments and affirmations reassure us. The questions and deepening statements that Lucas falls back on attempt to steer the conversation away from small talk. All of these conversational features represent important elements of paying attention and synchronizing. Yet there is something crucial that is clearly absent. Despite all the asking, affirming, and validating, Lucas lacks real understanding. In an attempt to be agreeable, he inadvertently endorses *more* fighting. His response of "very cool" to the disclosure of the trauma of domestic violence is unsettling and off the mark.

Language-style matching is not perfect, in other words. There are indeed instances where it can fail to predict chemistry, and Pennebaker is the first to admit that. "Language is a pretty good tool, but it is still crude," he said. There are various reasons the analysis can fall short. One odd example is in the case of deception. Once a person starts lying, Pennebaker explains, language-style matching will go up, with an increase in attention largely on the part of the person being deceived. The person being lied to will naturally attune, and match language, because something is unconsciously telling them that they might *need* to be doing so.

So while language style is an intriguing measure of attention, it's one that is difficult to observe without the aid of a computer, and even with a sophisticated analysis the results aren't completely reliable. If that won't offer us much help in evaluating courtships, what will?

Please Understand

Lucas falls short on the most important nonphysical element of chemistry, the feeling that comes with being *understood*. This is the sensation, in good chemistry, that you've known the other person a much longer time than you have. And it's not only *being* understood that works its magic on us. A study in Germany showed that we are unconsciously attracted to people when we think *we* can accurately read *their* emotions and expressions. The more confident we are in reading others, the more attracted to them we feel. The team that led the study described this as how good a participant's "neural vocabulary" was at decoding their partner's behavior and language. When we accurately read another person's emotional state, our brains emit a reward signal. The better the read, the larger the intrinsic reward. So not only do we love feeling understood, we also love understanding.

Of course that sense of understanding is subjective. We like to think we are getting it right, but sometimes our insights fail.

Caleb, who was recently out of a long marriage, seemed to think that he and Amelia were newfound soul mates, with very little evidence to go on. This text exchange came a few weeks into their courtship.

Amelia: I just went for a swim. Yay.

Caleb: Ahh that high. 😌🥴

Caleb: Got 2 hrs of ashtanga yoga in. Got the high 2

Amelia: That's a lot of downward dog

Caleb: Me doing the dog, you blowing bubbles and flipping turns. 😄

Amelia: My work day is so much calmer than yesterday. Out walking . . .

Caleb: Yay to calmer! Feeling deep gratitude for your presence and our time to connect so far this week.

Amelia: Aww . . . so you're not throwing this one back to snatch another?

Caleb: Dearest Amelia,

  -We are hugely already walking and embracing vulnerability in our relationship
  -you have been so amazing in accepting me where I am
  -it feels good/hard to name this vulnerability because naming it makes it more real, AND helps me be aware so I don't walk around a corner into a head on truck
  -we share our vulnerability, rooted in fear. I appreciate knowing yours and naming mine. It is mine and I own it and don't need you to do anything with other than hold me as whole in love as you are already doing.
  -I never would have imagined what we are creating four weeks ago, and you have been such a huge source of healing and growth for me.

When Amelia teasingly questions Caleb's commitment, he assumes that she needs to be reassured, leading to a full-blown profession of what he assumes are their shared feelings. The notion that these feelings might not be shared does not seem to cross his mind as he plows blithely ahead. Amelia might have been enjoying her time with Caleb, and being a source of healing for him, but his response was too ponderous and cloying for her to process.

The desire to understand is natural, but there are times when we might want to *not* understand. Pennebaker told me a story of how he once got a request from a woman to analyze the language between herself and a man she had met and "hit it off with" at a conference. After the conference, she sent him a warm note, hoping to continue the relationship. He wrote back politely but with a cool and distant tone. "She didn't need a language expert," Pennebaker said. "Anyone reading this would immediately recognize that the man was not interested." Yet she couldn't see it, because she didn't want to. So rather than accept rejection, what did she do? She hired a professor of psychology, for one thing.

Keeping an eye on the weight of your respective communications is important early in a relationship, as illustrated by Caleb's heavy and laden text. The courtship phase is like building a bridge between two people. At first it acts more like a seesaw, tippy and sensitive to the bulk of each person's exchanges, at risk of collapsing to one side. A couple that has texting compatibility is one that texts at a similar rate and frequency. If you picture each person's chat bubbles on opposite sides of the imaginary seesaw, it needs to stay in balance to maintain the motion, not collapse to one side. A relationship prospect that texts too much or too little will be perceived as either annoying or aloof. Getting a two-word reply to a long heartfelt text is not going to make either person feel very good.

It's not accounting, of course; no one is balancing a ledger. But a communication pattern with chat bubbles heavily weighted to one side of the screen is not usually a good sign. Over time, shared experience should stabilize the seesaw and make it feel more like the bridge it was designed to be so that progressively weightier material can be carted over it.

Balancing Chemistry and Compatibility

Chemistry doesn't stem from the rational parts of our brains; it emerges more unconsciously, and we register it in the way we would any emotion. It's experienced as a high degree of connectedness, or simply a high. Like the buzz of alcohol or drugs, it can change your perception of time and reduce your inhibitions.

Compatibility, in contrast to chemistry, stems from and demands rational thought. It is more firmly rooted in practicalities: common interests, making decisions together, sharing values, getting along. When we are compatible, our life interests align; it feels more comfortable to spend a weekend together or share a space. As the novelist Nick Hornby says, with perhaps an overemphasis on compatibility, "It's no good pretending that any relationship has a future if your record collections disagree violently, or if your favorite films wouldn't even speak to each other if they met at a party."

It can be easy in the courtship phase to confuse chemistry with compatibility. The two dimensions blend, the first one declaring itself rather quickly, the second one sorted out over time. When chemistry and compatibility are both high, a relationship becomes very compelling. We think a lot about the other person and look forward to time together. We also derive reassurance from them, feel comfortable making plans together. These are relationships that combine attraction and respect.

A long-term relationship without compatibility, however, can make for a roller-coaster ride. Relationships high on chemistry but low on compatibility are intense and amazing but often volatile and unstable. Leah and Jacob are caught in this override:

> **Leah:** Yeah, I'm trying to review all the reasons we're a bad match in my head only to find that just means I'm thinking more about you.

> **Jacob:** Let me know if you come up with anything good. I got nuthin'

> **Jacob:** Besides, you know, some logistical issues

> **Leah:** Age, life phase, life style, I need stability while you need freedom . . . Logic doesn't sway emotion.

> **Jacob:** Nor do logistics

The confusion between chemistry and compatibility arises when people interpret the way their senses are buzzing as a high degree of connectedness, when it could just be the chemistry talking. This has them pursuing their partner regardless of any true connectedness, and even when the buzz is accompanied by other, more concerning features.

Take this exchange between Caitlyn and Matt. Within minutes of meeting on their first date, they had established a powerful physical connection. An intense bond developed, but it would be punctuated by inexplicable, days-long silences, only for Matt to resurface casually as though nothing had happened. Caitlyn had identified that she was anxious about her attachment to Matt and that his intermittent silence made her feel uneasy. She wanted someone reliable and stable, but the magnetic pull she felt toward him kept her coming back for more.

> **Matt:** Thanks for such a lovely evening that engaged all the senses 🚲
>
> **Caitlyn:** What, did I smell bad? :-)
>
> **Matt:** You smelled delicious. Even if you are a small little one . . .
>
> **Caitlyn:** All the better to dodge compliments. I can't believe how late it is. I lose track of time with you

Matt is affirming and complimentary, but even in this short exchange we can sense Caitlyn's insecurity about their interaction. By mostly referencing the physical aspects of Caitlyn and their time together, Matt seems to be trying to keep things in the here and now—likely to avoid any promise of the future. She fixates on smell as he describes a date that "engaged all the senses," expressing her sensitivity and self-consciousness around the sense that, as we'll see, women care most about. In this snippet of text, there is evidence of chemistry, but not necessarily compatibility.

Chemistry is a powerful force—too powerful at times. It can cause us to date the person who has already ghosted us once and is back for round two, or who hasn't yet left their marriage, or who throws dishes in a fit of rage, or who sits on the hood of your car and won't let you drive away. Friends' concerns go unheeded; they can only stand by and watch in helpless horror.

In extreme forms of mismatched chemistry and compatibility, infatuation veers into obsession. While it's normal to become preoccupied in the early stages of courtship, obsession is a few exits past preoccupation on the infatuation highway. Inability to concentrate on anything else or a lack of respect for the other person's privacy is a sign that preoccupation is teetering into obsessionality. Thinking frequently about a person is healthy; wondering constantly if they are thinking about us (and taking pains to find out) is not.

One of my patients, Silvana, a successful and independent-minded professional in her late twenties, had fallen hard for a woman who was fifteen years her senior. Much of their court-ship was conducted over text, interspersed with jaunts together to exotic locales. Over time Silvana found herself obsessively fix-ated on her lover. Their text exchanges, which had started as a pleasant distraction from the workday, had become the primary focus of her day. Worrying about the content and timing of her lover's responses had usurped her ability to focus on her job. Friendships became little more than vehicles for discussing and analyzing her lover's latest behaviors. While her friends were initially curious and indulgent, their patience was beginning to wear thin.

Silvana's fixation had started as a source of pleasure, but it quickly turned to pain. With a realization that it was unsustain-able, she would withdraw from the relationship. This would pro-vide her with a brief sense of relief and respite, followed quickly by grief, which would in turn prompt her to seek a rapproche-ment with her lover, leading to a repetition of the cycle. We dis-covered she was happiest in a state of heightened anticipation and longing, her lover always just out of reach. This position was of course inherently unstable, like a ball perched at the top of a hill. The promise of availability was more appealing to Silvana than the relationship itself, because it allowed her to be in per-petual problem-solving mode, rather than confronting and liv-ing with something less than satisfying. For the obsessional and perfectionistic mind, this is a common trap.

There are instances, though, when chemistry can stand alone, without worries of compatibility. That's only if both people can accept the physical attraction and connection for what it really is, along with its limitations, and aren't bothered about the trappings of a traditional relationship. Jared and Doug seem clear about the undefined boundaries around their lust while accepting the defined boundaries of their connection:

> **Jared:** Sounds hot. I'm excited. 😈
>
> **Doug:** Me toooo!!!
>
> **Jared:** Thanks for inviting me. Woof!
>
> **Doug:** Well I wasn't lying when I said you're one of my fav daddies 😂 😈
>
> **Jared:** Grrr. Thanks stud. I'm honored 😈 💕

Navigating a self-acknowledged "chemistry only" relationship with minimal emotional attachment can be tricky, especially for those unused to the shallow waters of casual dating. Yes, the water is warm, but you might stub your toe when you jump in. Tina, fresh from a hurtful breakup, had a very awkward go of it.

> **Tina:** Let's have a drink tonight
>
> **Bart:** How did I miss your call? Weird . . .
>
> **Tina:** I was thinking we should sleep together;)
>
> **Bart:** Wouldn't hurt to try it out . . .
>
> **Bart:** see if we fit 👍 👍
>
> **Tina:** Exactly 😊
>
> **Bart:** OK I'm into that—keep it sexual 😜
>
> **Tina:** Tonight?
>
> **Bart:** I can't tonight . . . Can u wait?
>
> **Tina:** :(

> **Bart:** Sorry friend in from out of town
>
> **Bart:** Can't bail
>
> **Bart:** Even for I would expect to be mind numbing sex

Tina: I understand

> **Bart:** Dinner too
>
> **Bart:** OK, plain old sex. Ho hum.

Tina: Well you shouldn't set expectations like that because you just never know.

Tina: And why give up drinks for that? I hope he is a mind numbingly good friend.

> **Bart:** OK, well let's shoot for in a couple of weeks! I'm headed out of town tomorrow for the weekend

Tina: Have fun tonight. Sigh.

Tina is trying to be lighthearted. She tells herself that she is just looking for distraction. But even though the stakes are low, she still clearly feels stung and disappointed by Bart's response. By declining her invitation and suggesting they meet two weeks later, Bart demonstrates his hesitation about the liaison at best, his disinterest at worst. He is obviously not ready to throw caution out the window in pursuit of this bit of fun.

If chemistry without compatibility can be a minefield, what of compatibility without chemistry? Less novelty-seeking, more harm-avoidant types may sensibly choose to avoid the toe-curling rush of chemistry and opt instead for the safer, more predictable route: high compatibility and low chemistry. There is something to be said for a compatible partner with whom to plan social dinners and events or, later in the relationship, to share the comfort of an evening in sweatpants, eating salted caramel ice cream and watching a favorite TV series. Most singles go through phases where they would happily settle for less. For others, a lack of chemistry is a nonstarter, little more than giving in to a slow death.

When I talk to people who opt for relationships low on chemistry and high on compatibility, many will admit to conscious motivations keeping them together. "I just felt really at home with her in the early days of our relationship," Scott said of his mostly sexless marriage. "It still felt romantic," he said, "but like we could just be ourselves together."

The courtship texts for couples of this stripe may have a less playful feel to them.

> **Annie:** Hey, what happened to you btw? Too many options throw you for a loop?

> **Steve:** Life is throwing me into a loop . . . Shit is nuts, but I do suck on the follow through. The fact that you're even remotely interested in me makes me happy. If you're around next weekend we could get together.

> **Annie:** Cool! Sounds good.

> **Annie:** Hola! Should I propose sat afternoon for some chilling? Part deux. I'll sort an idea.

> **Steve:** Yes, what are you up for? Marin or SF?

> **Annie:** How does walking around in nature in Marin sound? Or are you bored hiking around there by now?

> **Steve:** Sounds good . . . I'm also up for walking into town to get food and eating at a park, Similar to what we did last time. There's a good gelato place near by.

Annie was underwhelmed by the lack of enthusiasm in Steve's responses, but she was drawn to him because he seemed like a nice, stable guy whom she could picture herself with. "I was trying to get some exercise, and normally I'd say, like, gelato after we hike or something, but I guess I should just say yes," she confided in me.

Neither Annie nor Steve seems to bring much passion or creativity into the mix in this exchange. They are content with making practical plans that will satisfy them both. Perhaps they can find compatibility in the absence of chemistry. It may not be the stuff of the movies, but it can work.

Without compatibility to fall back on—that is, a lack of *both* chemistry and compatibility—pairs are unlikely to get very far in their courtship process. These are the text conversations that fall away, without explanation or goodbye. Because what is there to say, really?

Patricia took the time to explain her lack of interest to Neil, painstakingly and in person, after their second date. She then received the following text message:

Neil: Hey. thanks for being candid and explaining your thoughts/ feelings. I have to say that I'm surprised to hear them though, considering we talked out everything. I know that it was a tough conversation, and that you were apparently joking when you offended me, but I guess I don't understand why we bothered talking it out for so long if we weren't going to hang out anymore. Wasn't the whole point to resolve it so that we could move forward? If not, I'll understand, and you don't need to respond. I like you, so the whole thing is surprising, and a bummer.

Neil: Hi, I left my phone at my friend's house yesterday and just got it back finally. Do you want to talk later today?

> **Neil:** I guess not. Oh well. I definitely tried to get you to communicate, but it seems clear you are not a big communicator. This has definitely been the weirdest ending to a dating experience I've ever had (and possible the weirdest dating experience overall). Good luck, take care, and try to be nicer (or at least more communicative with) the next guy. I truly wish you the best.

Ironically, Neil seems *more* confused by Patricia taking the time to talk to him about her feelings than if she had just ghosted him. He has clearly been dumped. But in his denial of this fact, he exhibits some hallmarks of narcissistic personality disorder. Rejection to him is a foreign language that he refuses to understand, even when it is spoken loudly and clearly. He dissimulates, citing a mistake or a misunderstanding, but never on his part. Here it's laid at the feet of Patricia, who is simply not a "big communicator," and the situation, which was "weird." Looking up from the curb to which he has been kicked, Neil seems capable only of reasoning that Patricia must be very good at soccer.

Yes, ghosting is negligent, perhaps even cowardly. It often leaves the other person without clarity, or wondering what they did wrong. But not letting go when someone bows out gracefully can be even worse. Because the truth is that sometimes the most honest explanation for your withdrawal from a courtship would only hurt the other person's feelings. "I'm just not feeling it" may bruise, but "I don't like the way you kiss" could leave scars. The further into a courtship, the more courage it takes to step aside. Regrets from getting out of a relationship too early rarely hold a candle to those that can accrue from getting out too late.

Holding the Reins

Power dynamics, which poked their heads out of the sandbox in our earliest dating chats, start to emerge in earnest as courtship advances. As they're exposed, questions of position, status, and hierarchy naturally follow. We begin to map out a person's status in the spheres of family, friendship, community, and perhaps most importantly past romantic attachment. These are the artifacts we bring with us into every relationship, enduring for the life of it and beyond. It's the baggage of power, and it carries its own language within.

When people recount stories of their social spheres, there may be some distortion in the telling. As we saw in chapter 3, storytelling is an iterative process, with details amplified or diminished in every version. Self-aggrandizement and self-deprecation abound, timelines waver, words are chosen in the moment—not necessarily out of dishonesty, but through a confluence of how we feel, who we are speaking to, and elements beyond the conscious realm.

More revealing in our tales than any verbal flourishes, vocabulary, or syntax, though, is the quiet work again of our pronouns, those "stealth" words that our brains process less consciously but that are starkly visible in text messages. The way we speak about our social sphere can reveal our status within it.

When talking about work, an upper manager or executive will pepper phrases with "us," "we," and "our." This is not out of presumption; in their case they actually do speak for a group. Subordinates, on the other hand, will reflect on the "me," "I," and "mine" aspects of the job. The same holds true when the group referred to is your family or friends. There is a security engendered in the use of "we," whether that "we" refers to *our* book club, *our* soccer team, or *our* parents. On the other side of the coin, there's an implicit insecurity in the first-person singular. Having high status in one sphere, however, does not always indicate one's standing in others. Most important, pronoun usage will indicate not only a person's current status within a sphere but also the status *they expect*.

In his analysis of function words, James Pennebaker looked at pronoun use as a marker not just of attention, as we've seen, but of power, authority, social status, and gender. He has demonstrated that people in higher status positions (men, older people, and upper social classes) use *noun clusters* at higher rates. Noun clusters can include a combination of articles, nouns, and prepositions, with a preference for bigger words. In contrast, women, younger people, and lower-ranking social classes use more *pronoun-verb clusters,* which are composed of personal and impersonal pronouns (especially first-person pronouns: "I," "me," "my") and auxiliary verbs ("am," "be," "have," "will," "would," "should"), as well as certain cognitive words.

Consider the difference between these two phrases:

"I can't believe you didn't call last night—I wish you would have."
"Not calling after promising to do so is inconsiderate."

The person who feels (consciously or unconsciously) in a position of power is more likely to express the thought in the second manner. They are, Pennebaker explains, "more likely to make decisions on their own and ignore others' ideas."

"In short," he says, "if you don't have power in a situation, it is in your best interest to pay attention to others. But if you are the boss, you should pay close attention to the task at hand." Even pack animals behave in this manner, with the alpha dog paying attention to surroundings, and the beta dogs looking to the alpha dog.

As for the prevalence of first-person singular pronouns among those who feel they have less power, Pennebaker says, "The word 'I' is the shmoo of words, because it is a marker of self-focus. So it is a link to depression, a link to status, and a link to deception." First-person pronouns mean we are paying attention to ourselves, he explains, and we pay more attention to ourselves when we are subordinate to others. As power and status get established in a relationship, the dominant person will begin to favor "we" and "you," and indeed the more self-conscious the subordinate person feels, the more they will use "I." (As we saw in the last chapter, when people lie, they often drop the "I." "Ironically, deception is associated with higher status," Pennebaker notes. "People in a position of power may need to be more guarded in their responses.")

To really understand power dynamics and compatibility in text messages, it's more important to track messages over time than to look at any snapshot. These are dynamics that are harder to thin slice, because they are so susceptible to individual circumstances. At any given moment, one person might hold the reins, while at another moment she has handed them over. Observing the variability can be an important measure of the role of power in a relationship.

Some trends hold steady, though. Men use more articles, especially "the" and "a." The use of articles also denotes power and authority. Articles of course imply specificity and are associated with giving directions and commands. Remarkably, if you give someone testosterone, they use more of these "masculine" function words. Article users also tend to be more organized, more emotionally stable, conscientious, politically conservative, and older. The usage also correlates with a more formal, powerful, and perhaps less honest writing style. Those with a more narrative style, emphasizing words like "with" and "together," tend to be more outgoing and social.

Here's a text exchange Ellen had with Larry, who uses a distinctly narrative style:

Ellen: I saw "Easy Rider" at the Castro theater tonight. Seen it?

Larry: Good morning. Sorry, you caught me after I was asleep. Easy Rider . . . Haven't seen that one for a long time. If I recall it wasn't as good of a movie as it was a concept. I love the soundtrack and remember thinking to myself if I was traveling cross-country I'd have to have a bigger fucking gas tank on my motorcycle. Makes me think of a simpler time when people were nicer to each other and we were trying to explore ways of coming together as opposed to ways of tearing society apart. Always wonder if I should have been born 25 years earlier . . .

Ellen: You do share something in common with the Dennis Hopper character. At one point when they are sitting around the fire he says "I don't understand why people are so afraid of me" and Jack Nicholson says "they are afraid of you because you represent freedom" and Dennis says "what's wrong with freedom? That's American." And Jack says "not real freedom—that's dangerous"

Larry: I think you are absolutely right about that. Real freedom scares the shit out of people. Have to figure out how to persuade them it's not so scary so that they can come along for the ride with me and be part of the party. Have a conference call in about 15 minutes and then off to a meeting and blah blah blah blah blah talk to you later bye

Not only does Larry forgo the stereotypically male use of formal language ("That was a classic movie," say) in favor of narrative storytelling, but he actually mocks the stiff, arrogant language of conference calls and meetings.

Looking at texts like these, we can gain insight into a couple's communication style—whether more formal and authoritative, reflective and analytic, or rambling and storytelling. Writing style reflects thinking style, and couples that are better matched in their thinking styles will have a better chance of success.

Balancing Risk

One dynamic that lurks throughout the courtship phase, before a relationship has been truly established, is the fear of rejection. People embark on courtship with varying levels of confidence. Because the outcome of any new relationship is by definition uncertain, it has the potential to raise anxiety, so stepping into the arena means getting comfortable feeling uncomfortable. This is only truer for those who are prone to seeing the end of a relationship as a failure—or worse, as someone's fault. Willingness to engage means subduing such anxieties.

The fear of rejection can trigger many defensive behaviors. Someone less confident with flirtation might defend against rejection with a need to tease or insult, to give a backhanded compliment rather than a straightforward one. Some of these behaviors are encouraged in pop literature, notably in Ellen Fein and Sherrie Schneider's 1990s cultural touchstone, *The Rules,* which encourages women not to flirt, even to feign indifference toward the men they are interested in. Likewise in *The Game* by Neil Strauss, men are taught the art of "negging," giving women backhanded compliments that verge on insults, in order to make them feel insecure and thus more vulnerable to a man's advances. Both of these books emphasize insecurity and control, suggesting that ignoring someone might be the best way to get their attention.

Perhaps the most important thing we can learn from a person's courtship style is the level of risk they are willing to take, and the degree to which they perceive that risk to be situational (dependent on external factors) versus a reflection of their own ego or self-worth (indicative of an internal flaw). If you are seeking out someone with healthy attachment patterns, their ability to offer a compliment and demonstrate vulnerability, as long as it's not too rushed or too much, is likely a good sign. It will enable establishment of rapport and understanding (as we'll see in the coming chapters). As the character of Algernon says in Oscar Wilde's *The Importance of Being Earnest,* "The very essence of romance is uncertainty. If ever I get married, I'll certainly try to forget the fact."

Working Overtime at the Ol' Factory

While we have so far broken courtship down into various elements that can be parsed within text messages—speed, attention, understanding, communication style, power, and willingness to take risks—there remain those elements that transcend language. This exchange between Karla and Gustavo points to an underrated one:

> **Karla:** I know it's weird but i've been smelling that t-shirt you left at my house.

> **Gustavo:** That's only weird if you take it to the office with you. What does it smell like?

Karla: It smells like you silly!

Gustavo: Thank you, Captain Obvious. So what do I smell like?

Karla: I don't know. I'm not very good at this. Muffins. And leather.

Gustavo: Leathermuffins? I like that

Karla: Leather studmuffin. How about me? What do I smell like?

Gustavo: Hard to tell. Mostly just shampoo.

Karla: I hope you like it. It's $29 a bottle.

Gustavo: Oh yeah, it's great.

Conventional wisdom has it that heterosexual women are mostly attracted to men of resource and status. Dr. Rachel Herz knows otherwise. As a cognitive neuroscientist at Brown University who specializes in the psychology of smell, and the author of *The Scent of Desire,* she has shown in her research that above all other characteristics, women rank how a man smells as the most important feature for determining whether she will be sexually attracted to him. Putting this into words is a challenge; neuroscientists believe that of all the senses smell is the hardest one to describe verbally.

This is where Dr. Herz's research gets even more interesting. She studies the relationship between what's on the tip of our nose and on the tip of the tongue—or, in the case of Gustavo and Karla, on the tips of their thumbs. What we *say* about smells can evidently affect our feelings, memories, and perceptions. Part of the power of smell is that the olfactory bulb sits right next to the limbic system—the brain's center of instinct and mood. An emotional place to be.

Our sense of smell exists in a blissfully ineffable space, mostly uncorrupted by language. While the sight of an apple or the sound of biting into one will explicitly evoke the word "apple," the smell of one can trigger unconscious thoughts, vivid memories, and powerful emotions, sending our minds soaring through time and space like a metaphysical balloon. Herz's work indicates, however, that attaching a label to that smell can puncture the balloon and bring it crashing down to earth. The exceptional cognitive freedom of the nose is easily tamed by the lash of the tongue. For instance, when climbing aboard a plane, you might have a surge of excitement and a flood of memories triggered by the sights, the sounds, and, mostly, the smells. But if you consciously describe them—*jet fuel and off-gassing from bituminous asphalt*—that excitement and those memories will rapidly fade, replaced by the notions you might have about, say, fossil fuels.

When Karla said "It smells like you silly!" that is exactly what she meant, that pressing the cloth to her face evoked the himness of it. But once she was pressed to name the odor, the quality was lost. She was left with a handful of leather and muffins—insufficient descriptors—and all the associations that come with them. Labels can even lead to olfactory illusions, whereby the item is increasingly perceived to smell like what the label says. For Karla, poor Gustavo could end up reeking of leathery muffins, even when he doesn't. Such is the power of language when it comes to smell.

This isn't to say that we shouldn't talk or text about smell. Telling someone that we enjoy their odor is powerfully affiliative. But perhaps we should let those statements linger without elaboration. Otherwise, we would just be thumbing our noses at a little true, wordless chemistry.

CHAPTER 6

Texting Toward Intimacy

Albert: We sure blew the stack off the pack last night!

Marika: HAHA. Yes we did

Albert: Like white on rice

Marika: Like black eyes on peas

Albert: Like flies on. . . . nvm

Marika: LOL

As couples move from courtship to intimacy, the focus shifts from "I" to "we."

Mark Twain has been quoted as saying, "Only kings, editors and people with tapeworms have the right to use the editorial 'we,'" though this nineteenth-century witticism, like many others, might have been misattributed to him. He did write in *Mark Twain's Notebook,* "Love seems the swiftest, but it is the slowest of all growths." That growth takes shape when two "I's" begin to call themselves "we."

There is a lot of "yes" in saying "we" (or as the French say it, *oui*). Permissions are granted, passes are issued, key chains grow heavier. Risks are taken; mistakes are made and forgiven. The royal "we" of power becomes the intimate "we" of "us." And so it grows.

The growth can sometimes metastasize, though, into the smothering "We really love that restaurant, don't we?" or the nagging "We should really get your laundry done," or even more malignant versions, where "we" is used to mean "me" or "you" but never "us." Words, of course, have meaning, but their meaning can shift insidiously, without our full awareness. At least until we remember to look at the treasure trove of conversations we have stored in our mobile device.

> **Aviva:** that was fun last night—my new favorite place for drinks
>
> **Aviva:** *Our* bar
>
> **Scott:** I love being out with you. Know why?
>
> **Aviva:** ha, why?
>
> **Scott:** Because we are that couple that everyone in the place is looking at

In Aviva's use of the plural possessive to describe their meeting spot, and in Scott's use of "we" to refer to the two of them as an entity to be acknowledged, their relationship seemed to Aviva to have progressed to a new level.

What type of "we" are we? In her book *Mating in Captivity,* the psychotherapist Esther Perel says, "Love rests on two pillars: surrender and autonomy. Our need for togetherness exists alongside our need for separateness." To be in a relationship, she argues, we must bring under one roof contradictory ideas and needs and reconcile our desire for both security and adventure. In this regard, relationships are less problems to solve than paradoxes to manage. A substantial portion of desire lies in the yearning. As my friend William summed it up to me over text, "Of course love is a perpetual problem with no real solution that we keep trying to solve. We don't even really want what we think we want. The yearning is all." Or as the psychoanalyst Jacques Lacan concluded, "Love is giving something you don't have to someone who doesn't want it."

Intimacy, Perel points out, can be broken down linguistically as "Into-me-see!" While we want our lover to see deep inside us with full understanding, that wish represents only one side of the coin of our desires. The "we" that expects complete access to each other's thoughts and actions is just the flip side of the "we" that desires complete freedom. We want to feel together enough to not feel alone, but separate enough to feel ourselves.

This, in some ways, recapitulates Erik Erikson's stages of development. Erikson, a renowned psychologist, famously summarized the stages of life. He outlined the infant's first task as the development of trust with its mother, which serves to establish hope. Trust is followed by the second stage of development: the establishment of autonomy and free will. Of course, with adult relationships, developing trust is a process, often lifelong. The "acquired trust" of adulthood, as opposed to the "complete trust" of infancy, is reflected in our conversations and our texts. These exchanges may either mar or enhance our relationships as they unfold.

In this chapter we will examine the textual language of love, attunement, and trust.

Love Languages

Much attention has been given to Gary Chapman's perennially best-selling *The Five Love Languages,* and while his theories may lack scientific validity, in my experience talking to patients, people seem to find the construct helpful in examining their relationship communications and interactions. According to

Chapman's book, everyone has one primary and one secondary love language, each representing the way in which they prefer to express and experience love. The languages are as follows: words of affirmation, quality time, gift giving, acts of service, and touch. Chapman argues that by paying attention to how your mate *expresses* love—what they like and what they complain about—you can learn the ways in which they prefer to *receive* love, and thus speak to them in a language they understand. If, for instance, your husband folds the laundry while you are out and expects you to feel loved on your return home, when all you want is for him to make passionate love to you on the laundry room counter, you are not speaking the same language and will both likely feel disappointed.

The appeal of the love languages is their simplicity. It's seductive to think you might take a quick quiz and then be able to break down all the barriers to communication in your relationship. *Of course he didn't take out the trash; he's not an acts-of-service guy.* With Chapman's love languages, resolving conflict is as straightforward as asking for the *kind* of love you need. But his theory also conveniently sidesteps any need for vulnerability. There is no need to feel wanting; it's just a matter of putting your wants in terms your lover can understand.

Of course, one of the painful aspects of love is the looming potential for disappointment at every corner. No matter how perfect the match, how great the desire, there is likely no one person who can meet our every need. It's unsurprising, then, that rather than face this hard truth, we would be drawn to the idea that love all boils down to speaking the right language.

While the validity of these languages has been debated, the idea of paying attention to expressions of love (our partner's and our own) and self-regulating accordingly is universally accepted.

In other words, having an understanding of what makes your partner feel loved, and trying to offer that in some form, are worthwhile endeavors. If buying a year's worth of toilet paper at Costco makes your partner happy, it might be the right thing to do, even if you would rather spend that time and money, for instance, exploring the city together. If your love languages have little to no overlap, and each person is chronically having to speak to the other in a foreign dialect, the relationship may have larger underlying problems.

Of course, Chapman's "languages" are metaphorical; with the exception of words of affirmation, they are not actual language, but rather demonstrations of love. Does text messaging between partners have its own unique vernacular?

The Love Languages of Text

Text correlates to Chapman's love languages can certainly be drawn. Some people might thrive on receiving compliments, for instance, while others would prefer a link to an interesting news article. One person might need twenty texts a day to feel connected, while another would rather receive a single thoughtfully composed message. I wouldn't go so far as to say there are *only* these five, but here are some of the love languages you'll encounter in any thriving relationship.

In this exchange, **compliments** and verbal affirmation feature centrally in Sam's texts:

> **Sam:** You looked absolutely amazing in those braids. I realize i may not (yet) be in a position to make any special requests . . . but if you could possible wear your hair that way the next time we meet

> **Nina:** Lol. It took a half an hour. I think you may be trying to recreate your childhood Bo Derek fantasies. She was beautiful—I can't pull it off.

Sam: Yes ok you got me that is totally true you are a TEN

Sam: No you pull it off just fine.

Sam: I aspire to be your Dudley Moore. Just call me Arthur.

> **Nina:** OK bring your best British accent to the table

Sam: How do I deliver that by text?

Compliments and affirmations can be categorized as overt or covert, literal or metaphorical, focused on appearance or other attributes. Noting the kind of compliment that is offered may say something about the profferer and the level of risk they are willing to take. Much like types of humor, classifying a person's compliments can reveal aspects of the way they think.

When a man texts "You're hot," he's sending a literal compliment. If he writes "Your eyes are a sea of blue," he's using metaphor. Men who favor metaphorical compliments targeting appearance speak a language of love that women generally understand. Women find men who produce such compliments more intelligent, and they are more likely to seek intimacy with them. Some women cringe at cutesy compliments, preferring something bolder.

Roberto seems to get it right here:

Roberto: I didn't mind that you were late. I love waiting for you, that moment when everything turns black and white right before you arrive, to full technicolor. Cause baby, when you walk into a room, that room knows it's been walked into.

> **Paula:** Your sentences are so sexy that I deliberated printing them out and rubbing them all over my body. You give good words.

A second love language, echoing Chapman's quality time, can be called **riffing.** Riffing is meandering, affiliative banter with no particular purpose or destination. Riffing happens when you have a few minutes and would like to chat regardless of having anything to say.

> **Rashid:** Work, huh, good gawd
>
> **Elsa:** What is it good for?
>
> **Rashid:** Absolutely nothing
>
> **Elsa:** Say it again
>
> **Rashid:** Ain't no thing
>
> **Elsa:** But a chicken wing.
>
> **Rashid:** Now I'm hungry. Still haven't had lunch
>
> **Elsa:** Moron! I left a sandwich out for you this morning 🐕
>
> **Rashid:** It's dog food now
>
> **Elsa:** Probably cat food. She's faster and smarter

Willingness to engage in this kind of silliness, or a text exchange that feels like a live conversation with rapid-fire responses, demonstrates interest, as parties clearly set aside other demands to spend virtual time together. Riffing has a performative quality to it, much like improv. Riffers will be reluctant to end the conversation, sign off, or let the other person have the last word.

Here is part of a riffing text thread Sheila had with Frank:

> **Sheila:** I like dating the penultimate boys of large catholic families. When bad stuff happens they know how to laugh

> **Frank:** Well I am the penultimate child of a small catholic family.

> **Sheila:** Oldest of two?

> **Frank:** Ok I just had to google penultimate. Typically used (inaccurately) to mean last rather than next to last. I am the 2nd of two children.

> **Sheila:** I meant it as next to last.

> **Frank:** You are correct. But I always wanted to be an only child . . .

> **Sheila:** Love that I've now sent you to Google 3 times in this conversation already, but hey, who's counting?

> **Frank:** You really think it's only three times?

> **Sheila:** Well three times that you've told me about. I haven't set up any hidden cameras. I feel that's better left for later in the relationship.

> **Frank:** Haha I was hoping for our next date but ok . . .

> **Sheila:** Those won't be hidden

> **Frank:** Haha

Sheila and Frank's banter is collaborative, and it may go places that an in-person conversation would not. It's less about the content and more about establishing a dynamic and a rapport. They are entertaining each other and demonstrating that they value time with each other, even over text. Riffing is not a poor man's substitute for quality time IRL; it's just different, and it brings out a different style of interaction.

A third love language over text might involve sending a link that would make for an interesting read or sharing an enjoyable image. It's a way of telling someone you are thinking of them, or want to share something with them, without necessarily initiating a conversation. Such sharing over text might be called **spoon-feeding.** Some halves of a couple, sometimes both halves, like to have the other as their personal social media feed, constantly spoon-feeding them up-to-the-minute updates on every aspect of their lives today (Now with photos! GIFs! Memes!) and onward, as they move up the age ladder (Aches! Pains! Gripes!). This can be fun or annoying, or both. Answering your loved one with "Why are you treating me like your personal social media feed?" is not an option.

Odie humors Larissa when she spoon-feeds him:

Larissa: Just got to the store.

Larissa: [Picture]

Larissa: [Picture]

Larissa: [Picture]

> **Odie:** The red one. Try it on for me?

Larissa: [Picture]

> **Odie:** Nice and tight. Me likes.

Larissa: Bleh. Makes me look like a sausage.

Larissa: [Picture]

> **Odie:** Is that ahi?

Larissa: Mahi Mahi

> **Odie:** Mmm . . . ahi? Twice

Larissa: Lol.

Josh, meanwhile, is less excited about getting Maddy's updates:

> **Josh:** Babe—when I get all your pics it's kind of like a news bulletin that disrupts what I'm doing.

> **Maddy:** Sorry . . . just sharing the stoke.

> **Josh:** yeah, I get it. And the puppies and nature are beautiful and all, but please?

Chapman's notion of "service" can be demonstrated over text too, with offers of help or by providing emotional support. This fourth textual love language might be referred to as **nudging.** In its most simple form, it can be a short and sweet acknowledgment, not meant to serve as a conversation but just an existential check-in.

> **Myling:** What are you doing now?

> **Donovan:** Watching a romantic movie. Love, Romance & Chocolate

> **Myling:** Awww. Romantic guy watching a romantic movie

> **Donovan:** I like cheesy romantic movies

> **Myling:** No wonder you are so sweet

> **Donovan:** Awww 😋 Thanks love. My sexy.

Nudging can also be a real offer of help or support:

> **Russ:** That is such a great invite! Would love to. But I'm sick. Slept about 12 hours last night. Wimping and limping my way thru work today. Planning to stay home and back to bed on the early side.

> **Zoe:** No worries—feel better! Can I bring you anything?

Russ: I am hoping that you will allow me to treat you to a nice dinner soon 😊

Nudging can also take the form of reassurance, as in this exchange between Markus and Angie:

Angie: Only problem with our plan is that my lease says no sublet

Angie: and all the neighbors will see me moving out

Angie: I can just say a friend is staying there. Hmmmm

> **Markus:** I'm not worried

> **Markus:** Doesn't sound like he talks to the neighbors.

> **Markus:** Besides he's a fuckwit

> **Markus:** and rented you a sewage pile

Angie: lol ok

Our fifth text love language could be called **nooking.** Nooking is the most physical of text languages. It can pop on your screen as a simple "Can't wait to be with you" or "Xo." Sometimes it's in the use of a special nickname or term of endearment. Overtly, it could be just plain old sexting. There is some evidence that sexting in the context of a committed relationship increases levels of sexual communication. Sexting couples, as such, may be more aligned on their affection levels and sexual aspects of their relationship.

Chris: Miss your body. Miss touch, sleep, snuggles, and sex. I get back late Friday night. Xo

> **Cara:** Mmm, I miss you too. What time will you get in?

Chris: Midnight, think you'll be awake?

> **Cara:** for you, ya!

Sometimes a big reveal comes over text. It can begin with "Are you alone?" Even though no one can see your texts, and you are miles away from your partner, you will want to find a private spot for this conversation.

Konstantin: Hey. Something odd. I've got to tell you this.

> **Teresa:** Give me a sec

> **Teresa:** Hey, what's up?

Konstantin: This thing happened this morning. I felt like it wasn't even mine. Like we were sharing it. Like it was ours.

> **Teresa:** Wow. I couldn't even put that into words. But I felt the same thing.

Konstantin: That's Incredible

> **Teresa:** It is incredible

Konstantin: What now?

> **Teresa:** I say we try it again.

Konstantin: Ha. And again. You are amazing.

> **Teresa:** You are amazing.

Konstantin: We are

> **Teresa:** yes

No matter the text love language that is favored, what's important is compatibility in communication. Nicole, for instance, feels attended to with riffing and nooking but is guilty of too much spoon-feeding at times. In the following text exchange,

Blake teases her initially about her spoon-feeding and proceeds to entertain her with some good riffing and nooking:

> **Nicole:** Was up at 6:30 and just finished a hard 90min bike workout of Z4 intervals. Think I sweated about a gallon of fluids—it was like Bikram biking this morning.

> **Blake:** Maniac. I completed 300cc of IBT and am heading back to the BR for another REM cycle.

> **Nicole:** IBT? You lost me in your medicalese, doctor. Enjoy the z's

> **Blake:** Irish Breakfast Tea

> **Nicole:** I figured the T was for tea, but I never went to Irish. Don't forget to ADAT to BRAT (advance diet as tolerated to bananas, rice, apples and toast)

> **Blake:** I don't have to ask Donald and Tebow to be righteous and tedious. They already are.

> **Nicole:** lol—you are good.

> **Nicole:** Well then, don't forget to TAMWYM (think about me when you masturbate)

> **Blake:** I will be thinking of how you touch a man with your mouth (TAMWYM)

The Language of Attunement

The psychologist and relationship expert John Gottman's theory of relationship success takes a more scientific and complex view than Chapman's five languages. Gottman talks about building **love maps.** Getting involved with someone, he explains, is equivalent to sharing with them a map of your inner world. That metaphorical map includes your past experiences and baggage, your present concerns, and your hopes for the future. At the beginning of a romance, that map may lack detail, but over the course of a relationship, features will get filled in, important landmarks noted, and the shaded relief of topography added. Each partner's psyche has its own map, and eventually the two begin to superimpose as lives merge and are built together.

Of course, one of the ways a member of a couple learns about the other's love map is to ask questions. But this is only the tip of the iceberg—the most superficial element of building trust. Deeper trust is established with intimate conversation, and Gottman argues that he can mathematically evaluate trust in a relationship by examining a couple's interactions. A higher trust metric, he argues, gets built through the *language of attunement.*

Trust and attunement seem to be actively being built in this exchange between Marissa and Dan:

> **Dan:** Thank you for cheering me up today. Total stress. Company failing and I have to leave town Friday. You are a priority—sorry I could not engage well today.

> **Marissa:** Hi there. Understood. Sorry if I'm expecting too much. I want to be able to enjoy the time we have together despite the various constraints. If you are down or struggling with a problem, I am always happy to hear about it. If you need me to just listen, tell me that—I can try.

> **Marissa:** Thanks for making the effort today despite everything that's going on, and saying that you are happy to see me. When I don't feel that, it kind of breaks my heart.

> **Dan:** Got it. I apologize for the inconsistency and moodiness. You do seem to take on a measure of responsibility for seeing me happy which I so appreciate. To see you does make me happy. On the other hand

when I am distracted or anxious (which I often am) you are not at fault and it does not mean that I am unhappy with you. I am not trying to divert your feelings—I am conscious of your sadness. Just a little reminder that I do enjoy seeing you even if it's not always pleasurable and full of enthusiasm. Xo

Marissa: Thanks—and thanks for reinforcing it. Maybe I am too sensitive. Love being with you and just want it to be good.

Dan: We are completely in sync.

Marissa and Dan are a poster couple of texting attunement. They actively listen to each other, remind each other of their importance, and respond with reassurance and transparency. They also demonstrate tolerance and empathy for the other's state of mind and respond non-defensively to a broader range of expressed emotions.

Gottman suggests that attunement can be broken down into six elements, remembered through the handy acronym ATTUNE. **A**wareness, **T**urning toward, **T**olerance, **U**nderstanding, **N**on-defensive responding, and **E**mpathy.

While these elements can all manifest themselves through language, it's important to recognize that just using the right vocabulary may not be enough. Vocabulary is limited, but the ways we structure language to employ that vocabulary in different contexts are infinite. So while saying "Aww, that sounds hard" is in theory demonstrating attunement, depending on how and when it's said, it may come off as either empathetic or dismissive.

Nelly: I woke up with a sore throat today. I feel like shit, and I have so much to do.

Mike: Poor you

Nelly knew she was whining a bit, but "poor you"? Was that sympathy or just a thinly disguised "stop complaining already"? Perhaps Mike could have said "you poor thing" or "poor darling." Similar words . . . totally different meaning. Perhaps attunement is evinced not so much by what we say as by the way we structure what we say?

In contrast, Maria seems more attuned to Matt in her turning toward him when she received this text during the West Coast wildfires:

> **Matt:** I came home from work my head and sinuses not doing well with the smoke
>
> **Maria:** 😔
>
> **Maria:** Do you need anything? Worried about you
>
> **Maria:** You want me to come over?
>
> **Matt:** I'm fine. Really. Just need Advil Diet Coke and a nap
>
> **Maria:** ok

Sympathy is nice, but it can go over the top, as Justin ably demonstrates:

> **Sue:** I'm really anxious
>
> **Justin:** Why? Hugs
>
> **Sue:** So much stress around me. Everyone's losing it at work.
>
> **Justin:** Awwww 😊💕 Big big hugs 🤗 🤗 🤗 How can I put a smile 🙂 back on that beautiful face 😍😘

Justin's response comes across more as "I can't tolerate anything but smiley feelings" than as true sympathy. We'll look more at understanding, non-defensiveness, and empathy in the next chapter, but for now let's look at the first stages of building attunement over text: paying attention, responding to bids (turning toward), and tolerance.

As we saw in the last chapter, paying attention is a clear sign of interest. It reveals itself in language-style matching and mirroring. It also manifests itself in responsiveness. As Gottman has followed couples over the span of their relationships, he's found that successful couples are the ones who pay attention to each other's overtures; they set aside their phone when their partner wants to talk. Or maybe, in the case of text messages, they *pick up* their phone when their partner wants to chat.

Gottman observes couples' interactions early in their relationships and then follows them longitudinally over the years. In his Love Lab, he observes and codes how these couples make bids for attention, affection, affirmation, or connection. A bid, Gottman explains, is "the fundamental unit of emotional communication." Bids can happen in person, with words or gestures, and they can happen over text. They can be subtle or dramatic. They can be direct or have subtext. Whatever form they take, bids are a way of saying, "Pay attention to me."

In his book *The Relationship Cure,* Gottman writes, "Maybe it's not the depth of intimacy in conversations that matters. Maybe it doesn't even matter whether couples agree or disagree. Maybe the important thing is how these people pay attention to each other, no matter what they're talking about or doing."

When one partner makes a bid, there are three possible ways the other can respond: *turning toward* (paying attention to the bid), *turning away* (ignoring or missing the bid), and *turning against* (overtly rejecting the bid). While rejection sounds painful, at least rejecting the bid presents an opportunity for argument, discussion, or continued engagement. When bids are silently ignored or missed, the bidder is left alone and hurt.

In Marissa and Dan's text exchange on page 172, each responds to the other's bids for sympathy and understanding. In contrast, Brett turns away from Alyssa's bid in the following exchange:

> **Alyssa:** Tomorrow is supposed to be a beautiful day. I love eating outdoors on warm evenings—reminds me of Europe.

> **Brett:** yup, you've certainly gotten to travel alot

Brett could have easily replied, "Oh, where would you like to eat?" but he misses the bid, or more frankly, he ignores it.

In more overt rejection, David turns against Jackson's bid:

> **Jackson:** I was checking out Airbnb's in Tahoe for later this month. I need a change of scenery. Feeling so burnt out.

> **David:** Tahoe in fall—why? Maybe when there's snow . . .

As Gottman has studied couples, and coded their responses in his Love Lab, he's found that in the most successful relationships (the "masters," as he calls them), couples turn toward each other 86 percent of the time. In contrast to the masters, the "disasters" turn toward each other only 33 percent of the time.

The masters also make small bids frequently and, in turn, respond to those bids frequently. Even if we are not so good at paying attention to bids, we unconsciously register when our partners don't pay attention to ours. Recurrent dismissal of our bids not only hurts but may eventually prompt us to seek a response elsewhere.

Here Simon responds to Michelle's silence, which is in fact a passive bid on her part. She hadn't answered his last few texts, so he prods gently:

Simon: You've been more silent than usual. What's the matter?

> **Michelle:** I'm sorry. I pulled an Erlich from Silicon Valley. "Until then, we need to do what any animal in nature does when it's cornered-act erratically and blindly lash out at everything around us"

> **Michelle:** I just panicked because I was overwhelmed. I didn't mean to be rude or hurt your feelings. I really care about you and about us. I understand now I was just shutting down. I don't know if I need to say any of this to you at all, But I was thinking about it.

Instead of simply expressing frustration, Simon solicits Michelle's feelings. In expressing her fears, perhaps she has established a unit of trust with Simon. In her reply, Michelle expresses what many feel as a relationship starts to take more solid form: a sensation of panic. That panic can represent a lack of trust or a fear of lost autonomy.

The Third "I"

There are couples who live in a bubble of two, with matching vanity plates on their cars, joint email addresses, his-and-hers pajamas. They advertise their unity like a freeway billboard, and their high visibility makes the rest of us feel as if we were missing out on something special. The truth of the matter is that devotional attachment is, at any given moment, often more one-sided than it appears. In these relationships, one person is usually hugging harder.

It takes two to tango, true, but describing relationships in such bivalent terms, as many relationship experts do, comes with its own pitfalls. Two pillars make for an inherently unsound structure, prone to toppling; the two sides of a coin are always facing away from each other. "Bivalence" draws from the same root as "ambivalence," and it suggests not a tango at all—close bodies and perfectly synchronized limbs—but something jerkier and more erratic, where toes are always being stepped on.

So let's retire all these overused metaphors for love. The best way for two people to lean on each other without collapsing one way or the other is by creating another element, what I refer to as the third "I." The three "I's," all connected yet all separate, represent the strongest and most enduring form of romantic relationship, with all parts providing support and still being able to grow without compromising the whole. This construct encourages each partner to reach, spread out, and contribute to the development of their relationship's creation. Much like a tripod, the structure will stand no matter how long each leg is, but it will reach the greatest height and stability if they are all extended.

Embracing the third "I" means abandoning the bivalent me/you in favor of the trivalent you/me/us. With this I'm referring to the couple that has gotten to know and discover itself—in which both members of the partnership can continue to evolve individually but also feel safe introducing new material into the relationship with a continued sense of discovery.

How might we observe this in the couple's language? A relationship's health, as Gottman's research would attest, is often reflected in the couple's ability to simply listen to each other. We sometimes take our communication skills for granted, blind to the ways in which we fail to listen, fail to contribute, fail to stay engaged with our partner. But in addition to listening, it's important to enliven and enrich, keeping imagination and possibility alive. The relationship expert Esther Perel argues that we need to create an erotic intelligence that is not necessarily tethered to our sexuality. "Eroticism" she defines as a life force, energy, or vitality that you need to cultivate within yourself, in order to share it with your partner. This energy is what is needed to repeatedly establish a connection, and it is essential to the growth of the third "I," which thrives on security and predictability but can't live on those alone.

In this couple's conversation, each is having their own experience, and yet they seem to feel connected nonetheless.

> **Mara:** How's the big easy? Miss you tonight. You having a good trip?

> **Erik:** Hi there. Étouffé and épuisé. G'night. Xox

> **Mara:** Laissez les bon temps rouler . . . I'm off to workout—have a good morning. Eat a beignet for me. Xo

> **Erik:** Another busy day. Sorry I've not been able to connect.

> **Mara:** I know babe and as long as I know you are out there, the world can keep on spinning. We're the same, you and I. We're both doing the best we can with the individual lights that we have. Hi, I'll always love you.

Mara and Erik's language creates space for each to explore their freedom. They don't pin each other down for details, giving each other room for psychological distance and some mystery, seemingly able to view each other as a separate and somewhat unknown person—perhaps even using their distance as a source of renewal.

When couples fail to bring their own genuine identity into an exchange, communications can lapse into mawkishness. Recall the classic "Soup Nazi" episode of *Seinfeld,* in which Jerry and his girlfriend keep repeating their "schmoopy" term of endearment, in a sickeningly sweet voice. "You're schmoopy." "No, you're schmoopy." As the George character says of them, in understandable aggravation, "People who do that should be arrested."

Nick and Ruth teeter on the edge of this slippery slope:

> **Nick:** I literally fantasize about every part of you
>
> **Nick:** Actually let's tack an almost on that
>
> **Nick:** Almost every part of you
>
> **Nick:** Much better
>
> > **Ruth:** FEET
>
> **Nick:** KNEW IT. THE ONLY REASON I SAID ALMOST.
>
> > **Ruth:** ok rly falling asleep sorry. Gotta get up early too.
>
> **Nick:** Aw ok. I love you so so so much
>
> > **Ruth:** Love you too dummy. Night loviebuggy
>
> **Nick:** Night baby boo
>
> > **Ruth:** <3
>
> **Nick:** <3

Yes, there is the security that comes from repetition. We've all drawn comfort from the pat phrases that we repeat to our lovers. But as Perel says, "If intimacy grows through repetition and familiarity, eroticism is numbed by repetition. It thrives on the mysterious, the novel, and the unexpected. Love is about hav-ing; desire is about wanting."

Trust and togetherness, then, are best balanced with develop-ment and autonomy. The most evolved relationships continue to grow both from within and from without. And growth, of course, requires tolerance, empathy, and understanding.

As the poet E. E. Cummings wrote, incidentally presaging texting style: We

    are more than you

& i(be

ca
us

e It's we)

CHAPTER 7

Peace, Love, and Understanding

> **Sarah:** Cool, I feel better now
>
> **Sarah:** Totally, flattered and heard and validated
>
> **Sarah:** So thank you for that
>
> **Adam:** are you being sarcastic
>
> **Sarah:** Yes
>
> **Sarah:** Sarcastic+
>
> **Adam:** lol

Because Adam can be a tad unsympathetic at times, Sarah decides to poke fun at him. Grasping at straws, Adam can only conclude that she is being sarcastic. Whether she is or not, the struggle to interpret sarcasm over text is real. There are no facial expressions, no drawn-out tones, no changes in pitch. Sarah's creative twist of adding a plus sign to the word serves to break the ice. She isn't reestablishing full harmony but making an overture in that direction.

Leo Tolstoy wrote, "All happy families are alike; each unhappy family is unhappy in its own way." This famous opening line from the novel *Anna Karenina* led to the principle of the same name. The Anna Karenina principle, used in disciplines as varied as ecology and economics, states that failure can come about in any number of ways, but success requires key measures to be present. In other words, to miss the mark is easy; to hit it is hard.

Does the Anna Karenina principle extend to romantic love?

There *are* certain bedrock features of any successful relationship, which we will tackle in this chapter. In the previous one, we began to explore the notion of attunement. Here we will go deeper into the desire and ability to understand and respect your partner's inner world and how that might show up in text messaging. We'll look at the key text elements that lend themselves to emotionally responsive relationships—those features of our texting that create a sense in your partner of being *understood*.

> **Karen:** I feel vulnerable and insecure sometimes (all the time)
>
> **Karen:** Your sensitivity = my insecurity
>
> **Brian:** yeah, I hear you, I'm sorry I'll do better 😣
>
> **Karen:** I appreciate it and was not trying to make you feel badly
>
> **Brian:** Doesn't matter I can do better. I need to pay attention.

Here Karen makes a bid for reassurance over text. Brian acknowledges that he should offer more. "I feel," "I hear," "I can," "I need," and "I do" abound. He responds by demonstrating some of the key principles of attunement: awareness (paying attention), turning toward, and non-defensive listening.

How do *you* show up in your relationships? What expectations do you hold for them or hold them to? Some envision love as a willed and wanted projection upon another: a colonization of affections. In this form of love, the desire might be for what a person wants to see in their partner, rather than for who their partner actually is. But in chasing an ideal, we can become blinded to the reality before us. Love can only be a dialogue, not this sort of monologue.

Romantic love holds such a place of honor in our minds and our culture that we can forget how much of a social construct it really is. We have been raised on stories of true love—tales of passion that never fades, of living happily ever after, till death do us part. The prescription that "if you just find the right person, you will have true love" works really well—until it doesn't. What happens *after* happily ever after? As science is quick to demonstrate, eternal passion is biologically impossible. Plato himself described romantic love as a serious mental disease.

The researchers Ellen Berscheid and Elaine Walster of the University of Minnesota have been described as the Thelma and Louise of psychology. They have focused their research on questions around passionate love. Together they designed the "Passionate Love Scale" in order to better measure this crazy-making emotion, which they aptly describe as a "wildly emotional state in which tender and sexual feelings, elation and pain, anxiety and relief, altruism and jealousy coexist in a confusion of feelings." They have defined passionate love as a condition of intense longing for union with another person and shown it to consist of an admixture of thoughts, feelings, behavioral tendencies, and patterned physiological processes.

When a person scoring high on the Passionate Love Scale is put in an fMRI scanner and shown pictures of the object of their love, they show brain activity patterns similar to addicts—that is, craving, even obsession. There are neurochemical underpinnings to these patterns, including elevated levels of dopamine and norepinephrine.

As the psychologist Jonathan Haidt says in *The Happiness Hypothesis,* passionate love is a drug. And no drug can keep you high forever; eventually it stops working. The brain adapts and tolerance develops; biological equilibrium is restored, whether or not that is accompanied by psychological equilibrium. As Haidt puts it, "If passionate love is allowed to run its joyous course, there must come a day when it weakens. One of the lovers usually feels the change first. It's like waking up from a shared dream to see your sleeping partner drooling." Where our minds might have constructed a beautiful imaginary castle, there is now either a house in need of repairs or just a hole in the ground where a home used to be. For some, that may generate the desire to roll up sleeves and begin a restoration; others may want to run for the hills. There is no happy ending—only a happy process.

So if there is a common element to relationship success, an Anna Karenina principle of sorts, it is less about maintaining an idealized image of someone, the kind we might forge in our early, passionate love, and more about communion: a sense of being understood, of being seen by someone else. Seen so deeply that the boundaries between each other seem to fade away and the isolation of our daily existence, the prison of our thoughts, the impossibility of ever being inside someone else's head, dissolves. In the end, it might be this closeness that saves us.

What elements lend themselves to such a non-idealized version of love, a love that, as C. S. Lewis put it, has the "power of seeing through its own enchantments and yet not being disenchanted"? There are many underpinnings to enduring love, but three essential building blocks come to mind.

Feeling the Feels

> **Camilla:** Have an awesome time at the Greek tonight! Jelly—love Tom Petty.
>
> **Nate:** I'll say hey to Tom for you
>
> **Camilla:** Tell him that I know how it feels
>
> **Nate:** Cuz you got a heart so big it'll crush this Berkeley town
>
> **Camilla:** Probably not that big. But sometimes my empathetic tendencies get the better of me.
>
> **Nate:** Well empathy is often underrated
>
> **Nate:** As are red kinky boots 😊
>
> **Camilla:** Duly noted
>
> **Nate:** It's the simple things in life . . .

The British psychologist Edward Titchener, most of whose work followed him to the grave, is credited with coining the word "empathy" in 1909. Hacked together from pidgin Greek and the German word *Einfühlung* (feeling into), "empathy" became the granddaddy of twentieth-century pop psychology terms, taking on a life of its own. It's so prevalent now that one can only wonder how the people of the Anglosphere managed to have appropriate emotional connections before this neologism entered their vocabulary.

With or without the word, we do, in fact, have an innate tendency toward **empathy,** this first building block of enduring love. It surfaces despite even our conscious attempts to suppress it. From birth we are hardwired to attach, and securely connecting to loved ones helps us evolve both individually and as a species.

More than that, it can be taught. Learning how to be empathic is one avenue to get you from a passionate place to a more giving one.

Since Titchener, the word "empathy" has been used to describe a wide variety of emotions and states. Lack of empathy, or an excess thereof, is considered a symptom of such psychiatric diagnoses as narcissistic, borderline, and antisocial personality disorders. That said, it's important to distinguish displays of empathy from the interior, emotional quality it describes. What is often referred to as "showing empathy" involves an act of compassion, but showing it and feeling it are two different things. Feeling sorry for someone in need, for instance, stems less from empathy than from compassion or pity.

"Compassion" and "pity" aren't terms that are necessarily associated with successful long-term romantic relationships, whereas empathy is. Conversely, there are areas of life where displays of empathy are culturally, socially, or professionally inappropriate, and thus discouraged. Picture a hesitant drill sergeant trying to put a platoon through an arduous exercise, or a surgeon poised to make a critical incision but wavering. That simply would not do. In personal relationships, though, it's a must. A couple simply cannot survive without the powerful, nurturing fuel of empathy coursing through its vessels.

Zach: Sorry to be short on the phone. Would love to have you along but it's just going to be us guys.

Felicity: I totally understand! I don't want to be a fifth wheel just wished you'd been clear about that. I already asked for time off work.

> **Zach:** Oh! Sorry my bad. I had no idea. Same thing happened with my sister for this weekend. I made all those plans and then she decided not to show up. Still upset at her.

Zach apologizes and expresses sympathy for Felicity going out of her way, even giving an example of how he felt similarly in another situation. But he misses the opportunity to identify and share her feeling of exclusion. Saying "I didn't want to make you feel left out" might have made Felicity feel more understood, and less likely to feel they were on opposite teams.

Empathy is typically defined as the ability to vicariously understand and experience the feeling of another. This is subtly different from empathic concern, also called sympathy or compassion. Empathy involves "feeling for" the other person but not sharing in the actual feeling. And while sharing of feelings is an important first step, it does not presuppose that the feeler will act in a supportive way. Empathy's paradox is that it can be used in support of or against someone. So it is important to understand the nature of empathy outside the pop phenomenon that it is.

Because empathy promotes a sharing of experiences, it plays a role in many aspects of emotional communication, both resonating with another's pain and sharing in their joy. The psychologist Shelly Gable of the University of California, Santa Barbara, and her colleague Harry Reis of the University of Rochester found that how one member of a couple responds to good news from their partner is highly predictive of the health of their relationship.

To reach their conclusion, Gable and her team had observed a large number of dating couples and examined how they reacted to good news and bad news from each other. Interestingly, they found that the response to your partner's good news was a better predictor of a lasting relationship than the reaction to bad news. Perhaps that's because it's intuitive to support someone facing bad news; celebrating successes may be less psychologically obvious. But feeling abandoned on a mountaintop can be no less distressing than feeling dumped in a ditch.

Fears around celebrating our partner's successes can come from any number of sources: insecurity, guilt, jealousy, resentment. When we feel these emotions ourselves, they tend to cloud our willingness to celebrate our partner.

In a paper titled "What Do You Do When Things Go Right?," the researchers classified reactions to good news in four different ways: "passive destructive," "active destructive," "passive constructive," and "active constructive." A passive-destructive response is an indifferent one: deflecting, changing the subject— the textual equivalent of "meh." An active-destructive response is one in which the listener points out downsides of the good event or finds a problem with it.

> **Elena:** Guess what—I'm being considered for a leadership role on the team!
>
> **Ted:** Isn't that going to be a lot more work for you?

In a passive-constructive response, the support is more tacit and generic, with only a muted sense of shared joy.

> **Marnie:** I'm so excited with the design I came up with for my website
>
> **John:** That's great 🙌

In an active-constructive response, the vicarious happiness is expressed enthusiastically, with emotion and further inquiry.

Becky: Finally got an offer. I was the deal of the day!

> **Ralph:** You're the deal of the decade, baby. That's fantastic. I know how hard you've been working on this, and how stressful it's been. Can't wait to hear more details

Among the four response styles, active-constructive responding is, of course, the most successful in displaying true empathy. It allows the couple to savor joy together and gives them an opportunity to bond over good news. Gable found that active-constructive responding in a couple was associated with higher relationship quality, as evidenced by more satisfaction, commitment, trust, and intimacy.

So any notion that empathy is a thing to be trotted out only in grim times, applied as a salve or a Band-Aid, may do relationships a distinct disservice. And while in the rest of our lives—at work, among friends, on the phone with our cable providers—we might have a variety of empathic settings, with our significant others there should be only one valid and functional setting: on. Only through more or less constant emotional vigilance can modulations be perceived and can lasting empathy develop. This is the true essence of attunement.

We've all been in the difficult position of trying to interpret (or convey for that matter) nuanced emotion over text. If empathy is tricky in person, it may be even trickier in the digital sphere. Text messages are prone to misinterpretation, because we don't always "hear" written messages the way they were intended; our brains default to stereotypes to fill in the gaps. Empathy emerges from conversation, and texting is a form of conversation, but to effectively empathize, we must be careful to remember the humans behind the text, including ourselves. Our emotional detection skills over text are of course in part determined by our past experiences and perspectives, and depending on the state we are in, we won't all interpret the same emotional message in the same way.

James had been silent after he and McKenzie had a heated conversation, so she inquired how he was. He replied:

James: Just recentering

She was inclined to feel rejected by that two-word text; "recentering" suggested to her that James was centering *away from her.* But rather than act on that sense of rejection, she considered the possibility that James might feel hurt, so she replied with the following:

McKenzie: I just wish I could make things easier for you

James: Thanks. I feel that. I'm not good with conflict. Raised in an environment where nobody got angry, they just criticized.

McKenzie: I was raised on plenty of criticism too. Used to think I needed it, but I'm trying to let go of that. On that note, if I need a little reassurance from you, is it available?

James: Absolutely. Please don't make the mistake of interpreting my silence as criticism. We've had enough of that. Xo

It can be easy, when looking at an emotionally laden text, to fixate on one key word and draw conclusions from it. It's more helpful if you can look at a cluster of words and think about the emotional undertones of those words and the person behind them. In the course of any relationship, we come to understand our partner's vulnerabilities and emotional baggage, and they do ours. We can either help them carry that baggage or hit them over the head with it. McKenzie senses that James is down and uses his distance ("recentering") to try to make a repair. By effectively saying, "I'm here for you even through things that might have hurt in the past," she establishes trust.

Considering the potential for miscommunication in situations such as the one above, it's easy to argue for the drawbacks of text-based technology. But are there benefits to handling emotionally charged or higher-stakes conversations over text? One potential benefit is that each party can feel that they are in their own physically comforting environment. Communication won't be marred by a shaky voice or an avoidant gaze. There may be times that removing each other's physical presence can lend itself to less escalation. Another obvious benefit is latency, the delay between when a person writes and when you respond. That time can be taken to craft a more measured answer (as long as that latency is not avoidantly long).

The drawbacks, however, are real. While text messages may reduce emotional expression, they can also be used to say something hurtful that you might not say in person, or to brush off or avoid a bid for a deeper conversation. The use of the mobile device may be allowing us to suppress our natural tendency toward empathy.

Here Austin deflects a deeper conversation and potential criticism when he cancels his plans with Tamara without much advance notice:

Tamara: Just hovering over SFO about to land. Are we still on for David Byrne tomorrow?

Austin: I forgot about a work commitment. No can do. Give David a peck and feel the Byrne. Let me know how your Wednesday is trending.

> **Tamara:** With any luck Wednesday I'll be graced with your negligent charisma.

> **Austin:** Neglect is my strong suit. I detest abuse. What can I overlook next? I tremble at the possibilities.

> **Tamara:** Picking me up at the airport for one. My cab smells like an ashtray.

> **Austin:** You are in a cab? That's kinky.

Text messaging allows Austin to make light of his potentially disappointing Tamara, without the kind of recrimination or discussion a phone call might have occasioned. He uses his irreverent sense of humor to deflect responsibility.

The fact is, empathy and understanding are dependent less on the medium of the conversation and more on the willingness to create space for them. An empathic interaction cannot occur without good intent, without genuinely caring for the interests of the other. If the goal is to convince the other, to manipulate their feelings to align with yours, to establish who is right, then empathy will necessarily take a backseat. Empathy thrives in safe spaces, not in traps or dead ends.

RE-SPECT

If empathy is our first prerequisite for lasting love, **mutual respect** is our second. After Jake meets Dylan's mom, they are both over the moon with trust, empathy, and respect.

> **Dylan:** she said she could tell why I'm so into you

> **Jake:** Wowowowow

> **Jake:** That's huge

> **Dylan:** because you're nice, and easy to talk to, and kind, and brilliant

> **Dylan:** and good looking haha

> **Dylan:** so overall, it went super well

> **Dylan:** so thanks for being you

> **Jake:** Wow dylan

> **Jake:** This is just making me so much happy

> **Dylan:** good

> **Jake:** I love you so much

> **Dylan:** dope

> **Dylan:** your fam next I suppose

> **Dylan:** realizing that I would pick being in bed with you than anywhere else in the world

> **Jake:** Yep. That's my reality

> **Jake:** Such a happy reality too

The word "respect" stems from the Latin root meaning to look around and look back upon, to consider, to provide respite and reprieve. As the co-authors of the book *Crucial Conversations* aptly put it, "Respect is like air. As long as it's present, nobody thinks about it. But if you take it away, it's *all* that people can think about." There are moments in every relationship where we don't understand our partner and cannot empathize with their feelings, but still we must try to trust, respect, and accept.

In his writing, the couples expert John Gottman underscores the idea that a relationship without conflict is a fairy tale. In fact, most of the disagreements that occur between any particular couple will be irresolvable and remain just that—disagreements. Getting mired in these differences is easy. Maintaining respect for the other person's choices is work. Much in the way that positivity should prevail in the expressions of your empathy (celebrating good news and not just commiserating over bad), a high ratio of positive expressions toward your partner will also sustain *respect* in relationships. Finding ways to remind your partner that you cherish them is key. To do that, Gottman emphasizes *maintaining high regard* for them and *focusing on their admirable traits.*

It's tempting to think that with the right person, nothing other than high regard would be possible. But as anyone who's ever been in a heated conflict with their partner can attest, respect does not always flow naturally. During moments of disagreement, it can require focus to keep those muscles flexed. Nicholas Epley, a professor of behavioral science at the University of Chicago, outlines in his book *Mindwise* that while couples *think* they understand each other's preferences, they are right only 44 percent of the time. Even longer-term relationships, he explains, create an illusion of insight that considerably exceeds the real thing.

How can we cultivate such insight and respect, even when our partner's views deviate from our own? And how might we reinforce them over text? Let's look at steps to bridge the chasm when couples behave the way Winston Churchill described England and America: two countries divided by a common language. There are (at least) four constructive techniques to draw from.

The Four Practices

Gottman has written extensively about what he calls the Four Horsemen of the Apocalypse: criticism, contempt, stonewalling, and defensiveness. These conversational features are the kiss of death for couples; they seep into a relationship and spoil it. We'll look closely at these destructive tendencies in the next chapter. But before we examine what not to do, let's first outline four practices that promote respect.

The first practice is **curiosity**. The longer we've known someone, after the fires of passion have stopped igniting an insatiable desire to know everything about them, the greater a tendency there is to assume that we understand everything about them. With that comes a greater need to stay curious, to override those assumptions. Ask questions in text. Notice when messages betray an unusual emotional tone or distance. Think of the screen on your phone as the mood ring of your relationship and the text messages as the colors. When emotions get too hot or too cool, stay curious. Ask yourself, "Why would a reasonable person say this?" instead of "Why are they making such a big deal of this?" Acknowledge not just what your partner is saying but the subtext of what is being said, and try to absorb it without judgment.

> **Charlotte:** I just sent you an email. I've been carrying last night's conversation around with me all day.
>
> **Lexie:** I just read it. You said "Everything just seems so cruel and unpredictable at the moment and I feel pressured to pick love over fear."
>
> **Lexie:** Is choosing love a problem?
>
> **Charlotte:** Yes. No. It's just that fear settles in my gut and I can't shake it off. I pretend that I'm fine but keep trying to extract promises and guarantees out of you. I'm trying all the time to be as courageous as I pretend to be.
>
> **Lexie:** Am I the one pressuring you?

> **Charlotte:** No, it's me trying to exert control over forces that are uncontrollable.

> **Charlotte:** Aware that I'm a freak. Some kind of savage succubus.

> **Lexie:** Ha—I like the sound of that!

Lexie is not providing reassurance per se—maybe she can't—but she asks questions and gives Charlotte the space to express her feelings. Charlotte admits she is struggling with the emotional vortex that can accompany falling in love.

The second practice is **patience.** Be willing to blink for a moment or two before responding. Texts can escalate easily if emotions aren't kept in check. As you note emotions intensifying or feel the traces of adrenaline, give these waves of emotions a chance to crest and subside before responding. As a rule, it's best not to text when you feel angry.

In this exchange, Kate has been escalating her protests and accusations. She feels Carlos has treated her unfairly by being less committed to the relationship than she would like; Carlos tries to set boundaries and Kate softens a bit.

> **Kate:** Like what the fuck is wrong with you you are SO HURTFUL—like so hurtful, I can't believe your behaviour these past few days—just so shocking how little you respect me. Please let me in on what the fuck is going on.

> **Carlos:** Kate stop!!! Like please why do you have to make everything so painful and hard and make me respond and be an asshole. I am trying incredibly hard to be diplomatic but this is getting absurd

(Time elapses . . .)

> **Kate:** I'm sorry for snapping—that totally set me off—I'm calming—I want you to know how important you are to me but this hurts so much and the continual slaps in the face are just too much for me to deal with. I am losing it and I am sorry I am not stronger—this is so unfair—I haven't done anything wrong here—I don't understand any of this and it just keeps getting worse—I love you so much—I hate that we are here and you are choosing to put us in this position 🖤😣
> I'll stop texting I'm sorry

By taking time to reflect, Kate is able to return to the conversation by exposing her feelings of vulnerability and frustration rather than just voicing her recriminations.

Our third practice is **understanding.** If you find yourself confused by a text, as if you have entered the story midway through the plotline, try to retrace the path of your partner's thinking. Our brains are storytelling machines. See if you can understand the story the other person has told themselves before the text was composed. Give them permission to share their thoughts. Techniques to elicit the story are the same ones we have seen before: mirror, reflect back, and prompt them for more. The simple technique of paraphrasing—repeating your partner's perspective in your own words—is a tried-and-true method of de-escalating tension. Being heard goes a long way toward feeling respected, even in the presence of ongoing disagreement.

Ling had been sulky and withdrawn, then had the following exchange with Malcolm. Malcolm didn't fully understand why Ling felt annoyed, but here he appeals to her vulnerability, trying not only to understand but to interpret her annoyance. Malcolm and Ling may be speaking their own idiolect (or a shared "dualect"), but Malcolm implies that Ling needs to accept her negative feelings rather than becoming irritated when others recognize them for her.

> **Ling:** Giada came over. She noticed all my feelings. It was irritating. But she made me dinner which was nice.

> **Malcolm:** Don't blame the tailor for your sleeves.

> **Ling:** I will absolutely blame the tailor for my sleeves. And credit him. Or her.

> **Malcolm:** Oh, my. I think the woman who wore her heart on her sleeve has found a new clothier.

> **Ling:** What does this mean?

> **Malcolm:** That means that you don't like people knowing how you feel.

> **Ling:** Oh. True. But you know I love you?

> **Malcolm:** It's not a secret.

> **Ling:** Just checked. Still on my sleeve.

The fourth practice is **acceptance.** Accepting your partner's point of view doesn't necessarily mean agreeing with it. It's okay to compare it with your own, without labeling theirs as "wrong" but instead saying, "I see it differently." If you can't come to agreement, practice tolerance. Over text this can mean avoiding interruptions or non sequiturs, which are the equivalent of blowing past what someone is saying. Using humor can be a good strategy (especially if the humor is of the affiliative variety we discussed in chapter 4).

Fatima had told Jared that she was unexpectedly available to meet the next day, and she hadn't heard back from him:

Fatima: Did I tell you I cancelled today's evening class?

Jared: Yesterday at 5:36 p.m.

Fatima: Did you respond? Are you going to be here?

Jared: That is not our way. You announce your availability and I comply.

Fatima: What do you mean "our way," white man?

Fatima: Fine. See you then. And tomorrow too. And I'm sorry, Jared, but I love you even when you have your bitchy boots on.

Jared: By "our way" I am implying complicity. And my bitchy boots are always on.

Fatima: They are. All the better to shake that ass of yours.

Jared complies with Fatima's requests, despite being a bit passive-aggressive about it. She makes light of this and turns it into an attractive feature. Fatima has her bossy pants on and Jared has his bitchy boots, but instead of stomping each other, they find a way to dance.

GGG . . . Generosity

We've looked closely now at two of the three building blocks of enduring romantic love: empathy and respect. Scientific inquiry has shown us that the third, **generosity,** is something we're biologically wired for. Acting with generosity activates the same dopamine and oxytocin reward pathways as sex and food. Generosity and love are inextricably bound.

We know generosity has positive psychological as well as physiological effects in humans (volunteering is associated with delayed mortality). But when we become entwined in romantic relationships, we can become less prone to generosity when it comes to our partners. It's all too easy to make assumptions about a partner's behavior or words, to filter them through the lens of our own biases. Actively taking a more forgiving, generous stance is likely to result in increased harmony, so it's worth considering the role it plays in our texts.

Assuming good intent—being charitable in your interpretations of your partner's words or actions—is a key building block to relationship success. This generous version of love often involves taking yourself out of the center of the equation and acknowledging that there may be other factors your partner is grappling with that you are unaware of.

> **Warren:** Lately you are pushing me away. I feel like the last few times I've reached out you're not happy at my merely calling to say hello and hear your voice. Or complained that my texts are distracting you from your work. I see a woman who has taken too much onto her plate without consciously deciding what to give up.

> **Joanna:** You have no idea how anxious I've been. Can we talk by phone tonight calmly?

> **Warren:** Of course we can talk. I'd love to talk to you. I'd love just to hold you.

Warren assumes the best of Joanna. While his interpretation may display a trace of naïveté, he comes to it from a place of generosity and kindness.

The sex columnist Dan Savage coined the acronym GGG to promote the attitude he recommends sexual partners have toward each other. As Savage puts it, "**G**ood in bed, **g**iving based on a partner's sexual interests, and **g**ame for anything—within reason." Examples of this would be making an effort to warm up to sex when you're not in the mood, willingness to try things that your partner is interested in, and being open to your partner's fantasies. Over time, their kinks may become your kinks. We usually rely on our partners to fulfill our sexual needs, after all.

It turns out there's science to back up Savage's recommendations. In a study of long-term couples, participants who were more motivated to meet their partner's sexual needs at the beginning of the study were found to be more satisfied and committed to the relationship at the end of the study. In addition, those higher in the GGG department were more likely to maintain their desire over time. Saying yes has its benefits.

But GGG speaks to more than just the sexuality in a relationship. It can figure into the language that we use to talk about sex, too, and there we should aspire to be just as generous. Sharing fantasies can be delicate. One partner may try floating a balloon and watch to see if the other reaches for it. Here Lionel broaches the subject:

> **Lionel:** Things with my ex used to get out of hand.

> **Sherri:** How so?

> **Lionel:** Would start carefree and exciting (eg. talking about threesomes). Then the conversation would happen again and she says she'd be too jealous. She finally decided she didn't want to hang out if I'm seeing other people.

> **Sherri:** The beginnings of things always feel exciting and then suddenly you are on a train ride that is hard to get off of. Did letting go of that bum you out or make you feel free?

> **Lionel:** In between. Where are you?

> **Sherri:** Still in bed.

> **Lionel:** What do you want to explore?

> **Sherri:** I appreciate being able to savor and enjoy being with you

> **Lionel:** I want to be honest about sexuality

> **Lionel:** If there is something that turns me on. I'd #1 not want to feel guilty #2 be able to share that attraction with you like something new

Lionel and Sherri's foray into the subject of threesomes and non-monogamy highlights some of the tensions that exist around sharing fantasies with your partner. Talking about other partners can be fun and exciting, in theory, but in practice it can be complicated and confusing. While some people are genuinely interested in exploring outside the relationship, others use the topic mostly as a tool of arousal. Many report enjoying hearing the sexual fantasies their lover has for others, but the thought of their lover actually engaging in such behavior tends to spike unpleasant feelings. Lack of clarity around this distinction can lead to predictable and harmful misunderstandings.

When Jealousy Intrudes

> **Mateo:** Yo estuve have más the 20 años . . . y luego otra vez hace menos de 10, en Acolman

> **Mateo:** Oooops . . .

Sylvia: Who is that for?

Sylvia: And what are you talking about??

Sylvia: ??

Mateo: Don't worry it was to my friend Ricardo about the times I've been in Mexico with him.

Jealousy arises when one is suspicious or aware of a lover's infidelity, or experiences the fear of being replaced by another. In essence, it's the realization that our lover is in fact separate from us, despite whatever connection we might have established with them. What distinguishes jealousy from other reactions to perceived infidelity, such as anger and sadness, is its obsessive nature. Consequently, the state of jealousy has remarkable overlap with passionate love. Both are at once all encompassing and impossibly fragile. Both are predicated, at least unconsciously, on ideas that are unsustainable: perfection of the other, in the case of love; possession of the other, in the case of jealousy. Like passionate love, jealousy is addictive, requiring larger and larger doses to support itself.

Both states are also fueled by uncertainty. When love becomes a sure thing, the passion necessarily extinguishes. And as the French novelist François de La Rochefoucauld said, "Jealousy feeds on doubts, and as soon as doubt turns into certainty it becomes a frenzy or ceases to exist."

If you find yourself caught by jealousy, ask yourself why you need to keep it alive, what purpose that story is serving, and what might happen without it.

Amy rolls with the punches:

Amy: So happy that you give good text

Gavin: I take much pride in giving good text.

Gavin: Start slowly and gradually increase the word count

Amy: Can't believe you are sharing your special technique. Though we know there is so much more to it than that.

Gavin: There are special ingredients and proportions that will never be told. Just experienced.

Amy: It's an algorithm, right?

Gavin: I'm more like an abacus. The more the merrier

Amy: As in plural?

Gavin: As in more than one

Amy: I get that. I always joke that the right number of bikes to have, for instance, is N plus 1. Where N is the number you currently have

Gavin: I am open to N plus 1 possibilities

Amy: Well your abacus tendencies (though not fully explored or understood) will certainly help us keep count.

Gavin: lol. Wouldn't that be abaci tendencies?

Amy: I'm leaving the expertise in plurality up to you. Sweet dreams.

Even though she may be feeling it, Amy doesn't appear to evince any jealousy in this text, in which Gavin alludes to his desire to include others in the mix. By remaining open to a future understanding of what he may be hinting at, she avoids shutting down the conversation and is more likely to keep channels of communication open with him.

"Compersion" is a word coined in the 1970s by the polyfidelity community of Kerista. Centered on the Haight-Ashbury neighborhood of San Francisco, the community embraced the hippie ideals of nonconformity and sexual freedom, and they defined compersion as the antithesis of jealousy. It represented the vicarious joy associated with one's partner having a sexual experience with another. It's a word that has since been adopted by the polyamorous community.

While only an estimated 5 percent of Americans practice polyamory, a full 20 percent have attempted consensual non-monogamy (CNM). A 2016 study found that only half of millennials desired a fully monogamous relationship. It's not surprising that adherence to monogamy is lower at certain periods of one's life cycle, particularly when you're young.

> **Clarissa:** Tell me though, I know you love women, are you really a monogamous type or do you lean non?

> **Henry:** Mono-poly-pan and the like are questions for the young. At my age, one woman is more than enough.

> **Henry:** At the risk of sounding Solomonic, perhaps a half woman would do? 😊

> **Clarissa:** Just wondering. Well, I'm actually one and a half of a woman.

Yet even among those who are less interested in monogamy, most are more comfortable with the idea of having multiple partners *themselves* than with the thought of their partner having experiences outside their relationship. Jealousy is common among those who practice CNM, and it's something to be managed. Although interestingly, jealousy is no more prevalent among CNMs than monogamists. Polys (those who engage in CNM in the context of loving and longer-term relationships), meanwhile, report much lower jealousy rates and will report feeling empathetic happiness or "compersion" for their partner. Some see their jealousy as a growth experience that they can learn from and use to further intimacy in their primary relationship.

Estimated prevalence rates for CNM are outdated, but even an older study found that at least a quarter of all straight men and straight women had an agreement allowing open relationships, though a minority of them acted on those allowances. Rates were much higher in the gay population, topping out at 73 percent of all gay men, with the majority of them acting on it. It's interesting to note that multiple studies have shown an equal level of commitment and relationship satisfaction among gay and heterosexual couples, despite the differences in monogamy.

Infidelity has higher reported rates: 25 percent of men and 15 percent of women reported having extramarital sex in the prior year, and 70 percent of Americans report at least one extramarital affair in the course of their marriage. Yet when married couples are asked whether their spouse would engage in sex outside the marriage, estimates are low (just below 8 percent). We assume better fidelity than we perform. We also don't assume we will divorce, even though some of us do.

Cheating, as my psychiatry office walls could attest, isn't judged lightly. It is often *the* deal breaker in relationships, even though the offended parties haven't always taken the time to ask themselves the harder questions: "What do I really want from my partner?" "If my partner has sex with someone else, do they love me any less?" "Would it make a difference if they had feelings for the other person?" "When I'm in a relationship with someone, do I own them, and in what ways?"

The fears and difficulties in these thought experiments can stem from a scarcity mindset, an aversion to loss. There won't be enough of my partner (or simply enough *love*) to go around, and I must defend myself against loss. And so, for many the door is slammed shut, at least until they are unexpectedly confronted with a situation that forces it open.

While polyamory is unlikely to become mainstream, jealousy in a monogamous relationship represents all-too-familiar waters for most of us. Sometimes we all need to step back, take another look at our partners, and see them for who they are, to consider their own unique needs and wants.

Perhaps the best way to find peace, love, and understanding in a relationship, then, is to strive to create a balanced life oneself— a life that cherishes romantic intimacy but does not idealize a single person at the center of it, as seductive as that impulse may be early in a relationship. Instead, we can emphasize the kind of relationship we want to have and nurture, and in doing so try to bring our best—our most empathetic, respectful, and generous—selves into the equation.

If the first section of the book was about using texts to ask ourselves what kind of person we want to be with, then this second section has been about using texts to ask ourselves what kind of relationship we're in, or better understanding the one we want to have. In the third and final section we turn to what I call scrolling—searching for truths in our conversations in a slightly different way. By looking back at older text messages, we can shed light on our style of conflict management. It can serve as a helpful indicator of our relationships' inflection points. To do otherwise would be to miss out on the powerful lessons already within our reach. As Tom Stoppard writes in *Rosencrantz and Guildenstern Are Dead,* "We cross our bridges when we come to them and burn them behind us, with nothing to show for our progress except a memory of the smell of smoke, and a presumption that once our eyes watered."

PART 3

Scrolling

CHAPTER 8

Toxic Texting

Annie: Not sure that vid you just sent is appropriate for kids

Russ: It's awesome. So hot.

Annie: What is it?

Russ: Wait—you dumped on it without watching?!

Annie: Was afraid to open in the presence of kids

Russ: Oh well first off you shouldn't share texts that I send you with others, period. Text is a private one to one communication When you share with others, that is a violation.

Annie: Fuck you russ I'm out with kids and can't listen without them overhearing. Don't text me then as I will share with everyone

Russ: Ok sounds good. No more texts!

Spite and meanness erupt like wildfire in this exchange between Annie and Russ, who immediately leap to assuming the worst of each other, using scorching words like "dumped," "violation," and worse. Though ostensibly about protecting the children from inappropriate texts, the language reveals that it is the adults who have some growing up to do.

A rapid escalation of accusations and insults is one of the classic communication traps we will identify and discuss in this chapter. These patterns are often only recognized in retrospect, when the heat of the moment has faded. But by scrolling back through texts, we can learn how to spot their unmistakable beginnings and start to notice their hallmarks not just in hindsight but in real time.

Because in addition to their primary role as live exchanges, text threads offer us an archived account of a relationship's story. They are the medical record of a relationship's health. Embedded within them might lie the precursors, the seeds of illness. When faced with a metastatic terminal cancer, can we scroll back to earlier X-rays and see the shadow of a tumor, one that wasn't obvious at the time? Sometimes patterns emerge and become visible only in retrospect.

Arguing over text is a natural extension of both conversing over text and arguing in person. And while most relationship experts would advise steering fights away from the two-dimensional space of the screen, fighting with our fingertips has a certain inevitability. As we've seen, it may even confer a few advantages to IRL arguing. But unlike a live dispute, each bubble remains static and visible on the screen; it doesn't float "in one ear and out the other."

Rereading, reanalyzing, and even sharing a screenshot with a trusted adviser before replying can all help to bring out the best, not the worst, in us. As a psychiatrist, I have been on the receiving end of these screenshots, but I've also relied on my own trusted sources for advice in romantic endeavors.

In the last chapter, we discussed my four practices of respect, an antidote to John Gottman's "Four Horsemen of the Apocalypse" outlined in his book *What Makes Love Last?* These horsemen are contempt, criticism, stonewalling, and defensiveness—some of the most unpromising signs for a relationship. If we can manage to steer away from these tendencies (which to some of us come quite naturally), we do ourselves and our partners a big favor. So let's look at these communication habits in more detail and see how they can manifest themselves over text.

Contempt is an especially ominous sign. Contempt is closely related to disgust, and it implies that your partner is inferior, or unworthy. It can present itself in overt and covert ways. The *overt* examples are easy to recognize and will make anyone cringe:

> **Scott:** I have to get out of this relationship before you get as dismally forgetful as your mother

> **Miriam:** I'm just doing my best. I have a lot going on.

> **Scott:** It must be a genetic defect in your family. Some kind of mental lapse. There is something wrong with you.

When we awake to overt contempt like this, it's often too late for repairs.

In contrast, *covert* contempt can seem light or funny. But it will wear over time if it isn't offset—and overcome—with validation. Put another way: there needs to be at least five positive comments for every negative one. The infiltration of negative comments and lingering traces of covert contempt are the early seeds of the more overt, late-stage forms. So exchanges like the following will begin to take their toll if they aren't neutralized with many more affirmations:

> **Ella:** ok that made me laugh

> **Sam:** Because it's true

> **Ella:** or as my son types: "ne." Short for nasal exhale. Better than lol, no?

> **Sam:** Lol used to be a waiter term for a little old lady. Dining alone, doesn't tip.

Ella: Hey, that could be my future.

Sam: Nah, you tip.

Ella: Thanks for the vote of confidence

Sam: Or are you talking about your future as a waitress?

Granted there is a fine line between teasing and covert contempt. As we discussed in chapter 4, humor of the aggressive variety is insensitive and can be mean-spirited. Sam might have meant his remarks as playful retorts. Still, hurtful teasing can take its toll.

Covert contempt can take the form of small jabs—the proverbial death by a thousand cuts. It can also take the form of taking confided, even sacred information about your partner and using it against them. Here Kerrie cuts a little close to the bone, using shared information about Kyle's past relationship mistakes to set him straight:

Kyle: I am just trying to be honest- it seems like things are just in different gears for us right now- I don't want to feel uncomfortable or make you feel that way . . .

Kerrie: Like you just want to be in high gear without doing the work to get there? How does that work? If there is a lesson to learn from your past relationships, that one might be glaring! Taking some time before having high expectations might pay off!

Instead of considering the point that Kyle is making—that he and Kerrie may be in search of different things right now—Kerrie quickly jumps in with references to Kyle's prior failed relationships, stories that he trustingly disclosed to her. In doing so, Kerrie implies that he was then, and is now, the one at fault.

Criticism is more self-explanatory, and while it's less noxious than contempt, it still has destructive effects. It's more like death by a thousand corrections. Shea was expecting Ravi to arrive at her house at some point to go for a hike, though they hadn't nailed down precisely when.

> **Shea:** What time will you leave?

> **Ravi:** I'll call you in a bit.

> **Shea:** Why a bit? You are avoiding. You are never clear about your plans

> **Ravi:** Please. I am having breakfast with friends. I'll call later. Not avoiding.

> **Shea:** ok

Ravi may tend to be vague about his plans, and it's clearly not the first time he has frustrated Shea, but her comment that he is "avoiding" and "never clear" may be more critical than the situation warrants. She might instead have set clear boundaries with him by saying, for instance, "Okay, let me know by 10:00 a.m. please."

The difference between criticism and nagging is also a subtle one. With criticism, there is a focus on what we don't like, whereas with nagging there is a focus on what we want done. Every couple will at some point deal with nagging, an interaction where one party repeatedly makes a request of the other, and the other ignores it. Nagging eventually becomes a vicious cycle, in which the person being nagged or criticized starts to deliberately withhold.

Assuming that you'll be criticized or blamed for disappointing your partner can lead to withdrawal and **stonewalling**. The person who stonewalls turns a deaf ear, indicating through body language or visual cues that they are tuning the other person out. In texts, this may be most easily demonstrated with a lack of timely response or a changing of subjects. The person who is being ignored will usually feel mounting frustration. Stonewallers can be notoriously unflappable.

Amber: RIP Sean Connery

(Silence.)

Amber: Tried you by phone. Want to have dinner tonight?

> **Michael:** Everything I know about emotional avoidance and toxic seduction I learned from him. RIP

Amber: And then Daniel Craig took his cues from you?

> **Michael:** We pass the torch on the path to glory

Michael takes Amber's simple RIP note up a notch, escalating it into commentary about Connery's style. She gets affirmation about her sense of Michael's avoidance but is still left wondering about dinner. Perhaps Michael is unsure if he wants to commit to dinner. Or perhaps he has difficulty saying no and prefers to dodge the question.

Jasmine doesn't dodge, but she does stonewall Roman when he tries to corner her:

Roman: Just a quick update, I'm available tonight and any time until Monday morning

> **Jasmine:** Ok. I don't think it's going to work out but we can talk.

Roman: Where there's a will there's a way. Let's not play the busy card, as you always do, to escape

> **Jasmine:** I'm not tonight I have plans we can meet later this week

> **Roman:** What is it that you're not telling me . . . ?

> **Jasmine:** i don't have the capacity to talk right now

When faced with Jasmine's avoidance, Roman pushes even harder, implying she has a hidden agenda. In this format, his questions are unlikely to yield answers.

Defensiveness, just as it sounds, means putting up defenses in an argument. Forms of defensiveness, according to Gottman, include "righteous indignation, launching a counterattack, or acting like an innocent victim."

> **Lori:** Might you have taken my iPhone charger that stays by the bedside?

> **Richard:** I don't have your charger and I don't need to use your place as a flophouse

> **Lori:** Hmm. I wonder where that charger went

> **Richard:** No idea. it's not much fun to wake up to a declaration that I stole your charger. I hope it turns up.

Richard clearly feels as if he needs to be on guard. Perhaps he has had to defuse attacks earlier in this (or maybe a prior) relationship and so now quickly jumps to defensiveness in response to what might seem, to us, like an innocent question. He may be hearing the question more critically than it was meant, and he effectively exaggerates the accusation by using words like "flophouse" and "stole." In doing so, he's backhandedly asking for Lori to go easier on him.

The Dances of Distress

So far we've been thinking about communication as it's displayed by an *individual,* but there are toxic patterns of communication that can be enacted only by a *couple*—dances of distress that become patterned interactions. The psychologist Sue Johnson developed an approach to psychotherapy called emotionally focused therapy, and in her book *Hold Me Tight* she calls these dances "demon dialogues," wherein simple arguments can trap couples in claustrophobic rituals of mutual abuse, echoing Sartre's famous adage "Hell is other people."

In one dance of distress, each member of the pair escalates accusations until neither has any choice but to preempt the subsequent attack. These story lines often involve one or more parties playing the victim.

Things escalate quickly between Anatole and Sophie when he sheepishly (and foolishly) backpedals:

Sophie: Hey how was ur day?

> **Anatole:** It was good and work done how about u girl?

Sophie: Same it's been a grind past 2 days but done for the weekend

> **Anatole:** Let's gooo so ur chilling

> **Anatole:** How are u going to celebrate

Sophie: By u taking me out on a date

> **Anatole:** Tm night?

Sophie: Im down

> **Anatole:** Ok

> **Anatole:** Maybe

> **Anatole:** Idk if I have plans

Anatole: I wasn't really planning for a yes response

Sophie: Then why did u ask about tomorrow night?

Sophie: Why'd u think I'd say no?

Anatole: It's a Saturday night lmfao. I have plans I'm pretty sure

Sophie: What? Why'd you ask about tomorrow night then?

Anatole: Honestly I didn't think you'd say yeah so I was kidding around

Anatole: But next week

Sophie: No thanks I'm done with this nonsense

Sophie may be setting appropriate limits with Anatole in response to his retracted offer of a date. But when Jeffrey expresses ambivalence about Krista and tells her he wants a weekend with the guys, she unloads on him with both barrels:

Jeffrey: Don't make me out to be an asshole.

Krista: Sorry you are a complete asshole— hope you have fun fucking a bunch of waitresses with your shit friends who CLEARLY dont give a shit about you and your well-being- happy you tossed me aside so you can look cool to them again—you are absolutely ridiculous- i'm here teling you how much I love you and want to be with you and minutes later you're trying to make plans to go out and what, celebrate?—this is unbelievable—you just don't have one ounce of respect for me.

Krista: What the actual fuck. Did you spin up all your dating profiles too while you are

> at it? RIDICULOUS. You are really showing your true colors—you just wanted to be single and fuck a bunch of girls—god your such a piece of shit honestly I can't believe the nerve of you to be so manipulative toward me.

> **Krista:** Have a good weekend

> **Krista:** Or life

> **Krista:** Whatever this is stupid

In this type of dance, we might land on an unspoken agreement about the roles each of us plays in a relationship. One partner may be portrayed as needy, the other independent. Or one is expressive, the other stoic. At a certain point, the roles and opponents become so ingrained that the fights become about fighting itself, instead of the subject at hand.

Harper and Landon have been drawn into a passionate but volatile whirlwind of a relationship. She wants the security of moving in together. He admittedly doesn't feel ready. Going into this exchange, Harper feels disappointed when, once again, Landon isn't interested in talking about the idea of moving in together or addressing "her needs" for commitment. But watch how instead of fighting about their difference in perspectives, they begin to fight about fighting:

> **Landon:** Do we always have to come back to this? It may not be what a girl needs, but it's definitely what she wants.

> **Harper:** Wants come and go, but it's been proven that needs are not negotiable.

> **Landon:** Proven? Well, studies have shown that our species evolved by negotiating needs

> **Harper:** What is to be negotiated?

> **Landon:** The statement that needs are not negotiable for one.

> **Harper:** Let's get to the point. What do you think is to be negotiated?

> **Landon:** Love comes first. That is non-negotiable. Everything else is.

> **Harper:** Here is how I see this. . . .

> **Landon:** As an ellipsis?

Landon intellectualizes Harper's expression of her needs by philosophically defining what can and cannot be negotiated. While these two are making bids for their own form of connection, they are simultaneously taking shots at each other. Landon dismisses her "needs" as wants, challenges her sloppy use of "proven," and pokes fun at her trailing-off sentence. Harper portrays him as the bad guy by accusing him of not meeting her needs. Ultimately, they are fighting not so much about moving in together as about how they fight. Neither is working to understand what's at the core of the other's perspective.

In another version of the dance of despair, the couple behaves in a pursue/avoid pattern, with one actively pursuing the other with demands or criticisms and the other retreating. Think windshield wipers: one party approaches while the other retreats, and vice versa. Esme and Kevin are in the throes of this particular dance:

> **Esme:** I really need a call. I matter too and if it feels like I don't matter, and that's how you have made me feel, then I can't keep going like this.

> **Kevin:** I do not want to talk. I understand your anxiety

> **Esme:** You clearly don't understand.

> **Esme:** Hey if you can't call, you could at least text. You're behaving like an asshole now. This is so unfair!

> **Kevin:** I asked for space. Turning off my phone now.

Nobody wants to be on the receiving end of criticisms, but Kevin's avoidance is just as destructive as any potential criticism. It would be more helpful for him to tell Esme that he was stepping away for a moment but that he'd be back, rather than simply shut her down.

Yet another version of this dance is no longer a pursue/avoid pattern but instead an avoid/avoid pattern. The boxing match has taken its toll, and the two exhausted contenders are in a prolonged clinch. It might resemble a hug, but it's only temporary, to stop the hitting. Eventually, they must be broken up and retreat to their own corners of the ring. In this third and most hopelessly entrenched pattern, connecting with each other hurts too much, and so the couple can only retreat into a silent standoff.

Here, Harper resumes her pleas and negotiations, in her ongoing exchange with Landon over his perceived lack of commitment:

> **Harper:** Just figure out what you want without putting my heart through a meat grinder.

> **Landon:** I want to enjoy life, gain wisdom, nothing too fancy. Love you in ways you never knew existed.

> **Harper:** And what are you willing to negotiate?

> **Landon:** Everything except love. And I have to throw in respect, which seems to be, bluntly spoken, not your strongest suit.

Harper: Now you are insulting me. How did I disrespect you?

Landon: Disrespect is simply the removal of existing respect. This has happened.

Harper: It's just become clear that our definitions of love are critically different. And it breaks my heart.

Landon: I will have no part of your heartbreak! I am all yours!

Harper: It does not work like that.

Landon: But we're crazy about each other! We're supposed to get all pragmatic when we start getting bored.

Harper: When we have disagreements, you go on the attack. I feel slammed and muted.

Landon: That is a truly dismal characterization. You should run not walk away from a person like that. DTMFA

Harper: I don't know what those letters stand for—Dump the motherfucker's ass? But the rest I understand. And agree with.

Landon: already

Here we see Harper both play the victim and blame the villain. Landon attempts to reassure her with declarations of love, but she seems unable to take them in, in part because he uses these pronouncements—"we're crazy about each other"—as a shield against her true concerns. And when she accuses him of going on the attack, he resorts to defensiveness, exaggerating the accusation against him by suggesting she dump him already. Instead of softening, she takes the bait. What's missing is their ability to listen for what the other is actually longing for.

It's important to note that in all of these dances the couple is feeling the pain of an attachment crisis. The dances are a response to that distress. It is only by recognizing the *dance itself* as the problem, rather than just one partner's role in it, that the couple can begin to appreciate the anguish they are each feeling and begin to repair their distressed connection.

These patterns of conflict can certainly be addressed in couple's therapy. But I've found that by scrolling and rereading the texts of a dialogue, with the right kind of insight at your disposal, the steps of the dance can become visible to each partner. It can be a helpful learning tool to see your own patterns reflected back, when not in the heat of the discussion. My patients who do this are often surprised, not so much by their partner's difficult communication style as by their own part in enabling it.

Repairs

What are some of the techniques we can use to intervene when we find ourselves in one of these destructive patterns? The answer circles back to understanding the stories we tell ourselves. When you find yourself telling a story about your relationship or your partner, challenge yourself to look at the story as just that— *a* story, not necessarily *the only* story. Stories differ from facts, and it can be helpful to sort through what is a known fact versus an opinion or an assumption. Where might our perspective be distorted? Look for toxic words (examples of criticism or contempt) or toxic narratives (examples of victims or villains) in the story, and explore if there's another way to tell it without these features.

Evelyn is hurt after she learns that Carl had a flirtation that went too far with a woman. She starts in with sweeping accusations:

Evelyn: At the end of the day you have no loyalty to anyone. You say and do whatever suits you in the moment or gets you out of trouble but it's all in the service of your image and does not take into account anyone's feelings or wellbeing, let alone the truth.

Carl: I accept that.

Carl: Weak. Not solid. Fickle.

Carl: I hope we can talk it over.

Evelyn: Nice only to those who are distant. You can buy a stranger flowers but you can't get the people you love a gift.

Carl: Hostile. Defensive. Not kind. Undermining. Slippery.

Evelyn: Or be faithful. Or be there when they need you.

Carl: Always picks the phone. Buys coffee, dinner, lunch and breakfast. Always says yes to spending time

Evelyn: I am smiling

Carl: Prioritized you over work. To the detriment of work.

Evelyn: I did the same for you

Carl: Prioritizes. Present tense.

Carl: Yes you do prioritize me. Arguably much more so than I do.

Evelyn: Sunday was hurtful. You kissing that girl was hurtful and buying her flowers was hurtful

Evelyn: You blowing everything up over nothing is hurtful

Carl: I accept that I fucked up something good

> **Carl:** Hey there. Sleep well and we can restart tomorrow. I need to sleep.

> **Evelyn:** I am beyond exhausted from all of this.

> **Evelyn:** Say something nice

> **Carl:** Sorry. Love

> **Evelyn:** Thank you. Still love you too even when I want to wring your handsome neck.

> **Carl:** Good night and thank you for bearing me

Carl could have easily slipped into one of the demon dialogues with Evelyn, either by avoiding her protests and retreating into silence or by getting defensive. Instead, in a skilled display of emotional judo, he lets her get in some hits and participates, perhaps in a caricatured way, in his own defamation. This allows Evelyn to feel heard and even laugh at herself a little. When he does retreat, he promises he will come back for more ("we can restart tomorrow"). Carl is able to masterfully sidestep a dance of despair and, with Evelyn's generosity, repair. Had he rebuffed her insults and criticisms defensively or underplayed her hurt feelings, she would likely have escalated, and they would be stuck in a pursue/avoid trap from which it's difficult to escape.

In a subsequent exchange, Evelyn chooses, or at least says she is choosing, to tell the story in a more favorable light:

> **Evelyn:** I thought about what you said about anger. Don't think you realize how close to that well of anger I am all the time. Worked through it this fall, but it's still right there and I don't want to go there. You don't want me to go there either. It makes you feel

misunderstood. It would be easy for me to say that you are shut off from your feelings, not aware or sensitive to mine, and that you are using me just to meet your own needs. That might all be true. Instead I have chosen to see your small gestures as expressions of love, and the effort you are willing to go through as an expression of devotion, and that for whatever reasons that is what you are capable of, and that in different circumstances it might not be this way.

Carl: Thank you. I understand your sense of vulnerability and the constant proximity to anger. Instinctively flight/fight comes first. You are making a huge effort to keep those in check and it's reasonable to say "why the fuck am I doing this?" As you said, you are evaluating. I do understand you are fed up.

One of the basic endeavors in cognitive behavioral therapy is to become aware of one's thoughts and the emotions that stem from those thoughts. That includes the story you tell about your own experiences, how you explain what you're seeing and hearing, and your beliefs about yourself and others. The goal here is to identify negative or inaccurate thinking and reshape those thoughts such that they can lead to *new* stories, *new* feelings, and *new* responses to a stressful situation.

We, of course, need to do this for ourselves. But sometimes, in order to repair, we need to take the time to understand our partner's narrative too. What thoughts and stories got them to this point of conflict?

It's easy to assume that a repair has to involve an apology, and apologies have their place. But if you're not inclined to say you're sorry, it can be helpful instead to make sure your partner is hearing what you intend. Distinguishing what you *don't* mean from what you *do* mean can repair misunderstandings.

> **Evelyn:** Thanks for talking. This is not an easy situation for me and I lack the ability to shut things off the way you do. Don't know how to numb myself with antidepressants and alcohol. Don't know how to ignore you or not think about you.

> **Carl:** It's going to be ok. I acknowledge the ups and downs. Miss you and look forward to connecting again.

One significant obstacle to reshaping narratives is mistrust. It can flood our brains, undermining our ability to see our partner clearly. One antidote is to break down trust into particular issues, instead of offering it universally. Perhaps you trust your partner's intentions, but not their ability to follow through on a particular request. It can be helpful to keep trust focused on the issue at hand, rather than the person as a whole.

Intimacy and Independence

Romantic intimacy's cardinal features are trust, self-disclosure, and concern. But tolerating true intimacy also means being able to tolerate the intense emotions that arise from this openness and vulnerability. Maintaining intimacy requires, as we saw in earlier chapters, a coherent sense of self. Capacity to tolerate closeness is one thing; capacity to maintain autonomy and separateness within the relationship is another. Both can be key factors in managing conflict.

Intimacy can take many forms. It can of course be sexual, but it generally has a larger scope than that. It can take an intellectual form, with room to clearly express and share thoughts and viewpoints. It can arise from shared experience; the more powerful the experience, the deeper the intimacy it's likely to generate. Some of these forms of closeness involve shared time and space, whereas others exist as feelings that transcend time, space, or even formal thought.

It can be easy to assume that intimacy and independence are on opposite sides of a tug-of-war. Instead, much like chemistry and compatibility, they exist on separate axes. It's possible to share great intimacy while leading independent lives, and also possible to be interdependent but with fewer intimate experiences.

Gregory and Rosie have different ideas about the relationship between time spent together and intimacy:

> **Gregory:** Well it's July 4 weekend—will you be around? I assumed we would be spending it together . . .

> **Rosie:** Why is there so much pressure to spend 'independence' day with other people?

> **Gregory:** lol

> **Rosie:** Can't we construct our relationship on our own terms?

> **Gregory:** "Driven by me" I hear that all the time from you. I'm just left wondering if your busy/independent nature will leave enough room for anything to work here

In attempting repairs, there are individuals who will try to drive up intimacy in the partnership, while others may need to recharge with independence. This can be a point of conflict. Each member of the couple must try to recognize their own needs while also remaining sensitive to the other's. It's a delicate interaction. Successfully achieved, it might have the grace of a pair of swans gliding across the water. Failure, on the other hand, can look like a pair of pigs wrestling.

Time and Timeliness

> **Priya:** Mom's dog Floxie died last night. In the process, she bit mom's hand so badly that she is going to have to get surgery today.

> **Ajay:** Bad dog!

Is Ajay's text to his wife (a) darkly funny, (b) disturbing, (c) callous, or (d) all of the above? The answer is probably "all of the above," but I think we can all agree on simply "bad" (and not in the playful, "bad dog" way). Perhaps Floxie had been a burden to the family for a while, with children, nephews, and nieces all encouraging mom to let her go. Even so, Ajay's response is flippant, and it utterly ignores the physical and emotional pain of his mother-in-law.

Sometimes a remark or comment comes too soon. Often it comes too late. Timing isn't everything, but it is something. When these temporal failures start to crop up in conversations, when tempers and moods start to extend past their expiration date or fall off prematurely, it's a call to pay attention.

Is Ajay just making one of his usual off-color remarks, or are things more seriously amiss between Priya and him? Time will tell, but when it does, will it be too late?

Change is a constant in relationships, and as we saw in chapter 6, it's an important component of their long-term health. Emotional distance and speed will vary over time, as will curiosity, patience, understanding, and acceptance. But sometimes we need a point of reference to turn to, a reminder of what our earlier relationship looked like. We need a medical record.

For those of you who missed the previous seven chapters, or perhaps came in through a side door, you may not know where I am going with this. The rest of us can simply open up our messaging app and be presented with an up-to-the-moment, real-time history of all our text conversations covering the last months and years. The most basic app functions are sufficient to search dates and key words, to find trends, to reveal in a general way what the vibe *used to* be like, and when both the more subtle and the larger tectonic shifts occurred. A deep dive can reveal the evolution not just of our partner's attitudes but of our own.

In this case, it was Ajay reviewing the record. He shared his findings with me: "I was never very fond of Priya's mom. She was a very emotionally distant alcoholic, always chain-smoking on the porch instead of being with her guests. But I noticed in earlier texts that I was always supportive when Priya worried about her, even though I was fairly indifferent to the woman. My text about Floxie was meant to be funny, but reading it made me realize that's when my feelings changed, that I was tired of Priya and her whole dysfunctional family, that I wanted to get away."

The biggest transitions in a relationship—in this case the fractures forming beneath it—can often only be perceived in hindsight. We don't see the cracks forming until they've swallowed us up entirely.

Harper and Landon are in the midst of their own difficult transition. With the potential loss of a cherished pet, and after yet another breakup in a series of such splits and reunions, it is unclear whether they are more interested in preserving their relationship or entrenching their positions.

Harper: Hi, can we discuss Bao and timing? She is not ok

Landon: A priori, I would like to acknowledge that this is a very difficult time. Bao, of course, but also breaking off with me two weeks ago and the unfriendly exchanges that followed. I would ask you to consider whether my involvement would come at too high of an emotional cost to you.

Harper: I love you. All of this is a high emotional cost. I am losing everyone I love

Harper: There is nothing else to lose

Harper: If you dont feel this is ok with you, I understand. I will make other arrangements

Landon: I am willing to assist as needed. Reasonable boundaries should be in place, though. Spending a few days with me after the funeral, for example, might not be appropriate.

Harper: You are right . . . too high a price. You say I am the love of your life, you are in love with me, now you have bounderies when my dog is dying..but you don't respect my bounderies

Harper: This is insanity

Harper: Where is the love?

Harper: You set bounderies when my dog is dying

Harper: Omg

Harper: You could not be any more cruel to me than you are being now. After I tell you I will not be ok after she dies. The most heartless human I have ever met

Harper: Omg

Landon: You have been saying things such as these for a while now. So, you understand

how my presence at this sensitive time
would be detrimental and how boundaries
would reduce harm.

Harper: You dont give a shit about me

Harper: Your words and your "love" are
meaningless. I will bury them like I will bury
Bao alone

Landon: Amazingly, notwithstanding the
onslaught of invective and vilification, I care
very much.

Harper: Bull shit

Harper: Meaningless

Harper: Empty

Harper: Lies

Harper: Good bye

Harper: I am an idiot for ever believing you

In the noise of conflict, with heightened emotions and diminished trust, it can be difficult to hear the signals we're sending each other. We find ourselves disoriented, searching for meaning. Scouring our texts can offer us clarity and grounding during a difficult time.

Isaac Asimov said, "Life is pleasant. Death is peaceful. It's the transition that's troublesome." Let's continue, in the next chapter, to look at relationship transitions—the crossroads that mark the road maps of our romantic lives.

CHAPTER 9

Crossroads

> **Trisha:** Could you see if those grey pumps I bought for Willie's party are still in the guest room closet?

> **Zac:** you looked so good that night. we just stayed home and played spoons

> **Trisha:** Yes

> **Trisha:** Do you mind if I come and grab them while you're at work?

> **Zac:** you never wore them. new in box. guess your going to wear them tonight?

> **Trisha:** Yes

In this painful exchange between Trisha and Zac, Trisha is asking if she can come by his place while he's not home to reclaim her party shoes, suggesting that she will be donning them without him. Still pining for Trisha, Zac resigns himself to the request. Her one-word responses are a recognition, maybe for the first time, that she is moving on.

Anaïs Nin wrote, "Love never dies a natural death. It dies because we don't know how to replenish its source, it dies of blindness and errors and betrayals. It dies of illness and wounds, it dies of weariness, of witherings, or tarnishings, but never a natural death." It's telling that even the academics we've discussed resort to the language of "demons" and "the apocalypse" in their descriptions of conflict escalation and love's death. To the afflicted, it's not just the end of a relationship; it's the end of the world.

We've all been at these emotional crossroads. Many of us have only recognized them after the fact. Scrolling back through a text thread can help us diagnose the onset of a relationship's illness (or, when needed, to perform an autopsy). It can also show us when our relationship health took a turn for the better, the moments of a deepening of love. We can see when and how we entered a crossroads, a new phase.

As a relationship evolves, so do its text messages. Messages shift from romantic flirtations to practical exchanges—of weekend plans, grocery lists. One data scientist tracked the word content of her texts with her husband from their first date to their sixth year of marriage and found that the frequency of the words "hey," "love," "good," and "fun" decreased, while "dinner," "now," and "ok" became more common. While messages may inevitably become more utilitarian in this way over the course of a relationship, there are good reasons to suggest that affectionate messages can help a couple maintain their bond.

How do we know when someone is pulling away and ready to change direction, versus when you are simply transitioning into a new phase of your commitment? Are you at the beginning of a road or its end? Mostly we recognize these crossroads at a gut level, through vague sensations of trepidation, anxiety, excitement, or fear. We know, without knowing what we know. The tug of these feelings might be exposed in the language of our texts, even when it's only much later that these thoughts become conscious and turn into actions. In truth, by the time a breakup or divorce is under way, the couple has often been unraveling for a long time, whether recognized by others, themselves, or not at all.

In my years of practice, I have witnessed people who were

asleep at the romantic wheel. They wake up only with the crash. My patient Margo told me she had no idea her husband of eighteen years wanted out until he announced he was getting his own apartment. She called me the following day for an urgent first appointment, tearful and distraught, seeking some clue to what had gone wrong. She was seemingly blindsided. Other patients have come to me painfully aware of the moribund status of their relationship but reluctant to address it out of fear of change, or loneliness, or the dread of hurting someone they love.

Transitions are hard, whether it's changing jobs, relationships, or cities, to say nothing of those ideas at the core of your being, such as your gender or sexual orientation. Yet social and geographic mobility have made "future tripping" on the notion of "forever after" a thing of the past. Few of us only ever live in one town, hold down one job, marry our first love. Understanding that transitions are the norm, is there a way to embrace these changes in our romantic lives?

As we've seen, the stories we tell about our own relationships can be true, false, and somewhere between. We've discussed the importance of stepping back from these narratives to reassess them. What scrolling through our texts can do is allow us to retell the story using the raw data at our disposal. Whether it's done in a moment of uncertainty about our path forward or as a forensic account after our relationship's demise, there is much to learn, and even to cherish, from these stories.

We've seen how texts might help us identify a suitable partner and recognize compatibility and harmony as it's happening. Here we will look at how text threads may reveal three classic transitions in the arc of a romance: disillusionment, coalescence, and detaching. At each of these crossroads, the couple has a choice: to passively and subconsciously slide into a new phase of their bond, or to treat it as a major crossroad and to consider their choices with appropriate gravity.

Disillusionment

As couples graduate from their passionate beginnings to the formation of steadier (if less thrilling) bonds, it's not unusual for a kind of disillusionment to creep in, sometimes subtly, sometimes loudly. Insecurities reveal themselves; imperfections emerge that previously went undetected or were brushed aside. Levels of appreciation and gratitude will wax and wane. The love that initially felt so overwhelming starts to feel manageable; what first was an irresistible, inevitable pull becomes a matter of daily choice. Maintaining the relationship starts to feel like work—because, quite frankly, it is. The freedom to choose to stay together can morph alluringly into the choice to pursue freedom. The crossroads loom ahead.

The way we handle these rough patches is often what makes or breaks our relationships. Couples that manage to revel in their differences and idiosyncrasies, that bask in the occasional bumpiness, will sail past these crossroads with relative ease, confident in their choices, trusting in their direction. Others will need more guidance.

Lilly first walked into my office the day before her wedding. She and her fiancé, Jamie, had been together for a few years, but she acknowledged their relationship was far from perfect. She loved him, and he was devoted to her, but she had been aware of their differences from the get-go. At first she attributed his linear, logical, not particularly emotionally sensitive style of thinking to his wholesome maleness. Although they often had animated, deepening conversations, more often she found herself as the audience to one of his monologues. When she tried to jump in, he would simply interrupt her and obliviously continue his speech. She found herself frustrated and anxious. Notwithstanding this habit, he made great efforts to please her and show affection. Now it was the eve of her wedding, and she wanted to talk about how to create more understanding and better communication in her soon-to-be marriage.

I had to credit Lilly for her courage. While many brides in the throes of wedding preparations conveniently displace the anxieties over *whom* they are marrying onto seating charts and flower arrangements, Lilly had the presence of mind not only to acknowledge that the marriage was going to have its challenges but also to begin to address them. By holding the cracks in her relationship to the light, on the eve of her wedding no less, Lilly was hoping to turn a natural process of disillusionment into one of enlightenment—a process of discovery by which she and Jamie could better communicate and accept each other going forward.

Each couple is tasked with building their own language. Nowhere is this more evident than over text. While lovers will naturally pick up each other's vocabulary over time, they are unlikely to pick up each other's punctuation or written expressions of laughter. And laughter, of course, is an important social cue, even over text. Text expressions of laughter can often serve to soften a statement. They can also be a cue for turn taking, the text equivalent of a pause to say, "Your turn to say something." One of Lilly's insights was a realization that her conversations with Jamie needed to include more explicit laughter and that marriage would require a greater capacity to cope with and accept her soon-to-be husband's quirks. She also decided to explore loving ways to steer his monologues back toward conversation, both in person and on-screen.

While texts can point to sources of disillusionment, they can just as often offer clues to solutions. Naomi, for instance, felt she had to take the lead with Xavier. He was reluctant to initiate plans, and when she proposed them, he often found excuses for why they were unrealistic or too much trouble, citing his own sensitivities or malaise. Having spent much of her life trying to please "hard to please" men, Naomi found it easy to see Xavier's resistance as a challenge—a wall she might successfully break down. But over time, his lack of enthusiasm became tiresome; it continually surfaced her insecurity, her internal questioning of whether she was good enough. By the time she came to see me, that weariness had taken its toll: what had once been his charming recalcitrance suddenly seemed just plain selfish. Together, we scrolled back through her messages to look for early traces of it in their texts:

> **Naomi:** OK suit yourself. I'm swinging but clearly striking out. And that gets boring after a while.

> **Xavier:** No strike out here. You have me highly motivated and that's at least a stand up double

> **Naomi:** I like to knock it out of the park

> **Xavier:** You did knock it out of the park. It was called a ground-rule double for fan interference.

> **Naomi:** At least you got me to laugh. Wish my fans would stop obstructing play!

> **Naomi:** You are just a finely tuned Stradivarius. One false move and the sound is off. I'm more like a German piano—you can bang away without worry.

> **Xavier:** Can't really imagine banging away on a Bechstein, but I'm trying

> **Naomi:** Only untrue love from you 😊

Revisiting this exchange helped Naomi understand how she was participating in a dynamic that reinforced her own insecurity. In pressing him for reassurance that was not available, she was leaving herself vulnerable to Xavier's detachment. Once she had read through her old texts, she was able to step back and give him the chance to provide *genuine* reassurance, in a form that he was comfortable with.

Micah was initially drawn to Vera for her magnetic, social, and confident personality. Vera could captivate anyone at a party. Micah was always proud to be with her and watch her interact effortlessly with others. As captives of early romance, neither one of them enjoyed doing much of anything without the other. Later in the relationship much of this compulsion wore off, and while Vera could flit about feeling confident in Micah's love, he began to resent her for the very traits he had once admired. By scrolling through their texts, he found early traces of this sentiment:

> **Vera:** So tired this morning. I came home at 2am

> **Micah:** Where did you go until 2am?

> **Micah:** Guess I am surprised you would do that when you wouldn't make time for me last night.

> **Vera:** I am sorry. I went out with a friend and just wanted to stay out

> **Micah:** Thank you for answering. All I needed to hear. Too bad I came up with the red light and they got the green light.

Micah had expected to receive more of Vera's time and attention, arising from the intensity of their initial encounters. He was left bitter and envious. It was baffling for Vera; she continued to feel for him as strongly as ever. His choice to dwell on his resentment, instead of embracing Vera for who she was, was setting him on a slippery slope (one that he was eventually able to correct). As Micah's example shows, disillusionment can stem not only from our false expectations of others but from our own inability to cope and accept.

Disillusionment is only possible, of course, if we once held illusions. But by stripping away these unquestioned assumptions, we can allow for greater openness and honesty, exposing a more solid foundation built on admiration and respect, or discovering that the foundation needs more work. Successful couples will translate disillusionment into growth and a deepening of intimacy.

Erich Fromm described love as "a constant challenge; it is not a resting place, but a moving, growing, working together; even whether there is harmony or conflict, joy or sadness, is secondary to the fundamental fact that two people experience themselves from the essence of their existence, that they are one with each other by being one with themselves, rather than by fleeing from themselves."

Coalescence

A major transition occurs in most relationships when elements of commitment and resilience start to coalesce into a distinctive, stable union. In truth, stable relationships might be more accurately described as *provisionally* stable—subject to dynamics of change but having internal equilibrium. This model accounts for the possibility of change within each of the individuals and also their environment. Such stable equilibrium may be less an outcome than a process—not so much a couple that has anchored itself into the ground as one whose members have become adept at balancing against each other as it marches forward.

How do communication patterns change as relationships deepen and coalesce? There is an interesting discrepancy in the way men and women approach texts. One study, led by Lori Schade, a researcher at Brigham Young University, showed that women perceive the number of texts they send to be proportional to the stability of their relationship. In contrast, men reported a negative correlation, with more texts associated with less perceived stability. Schade's study, focused on younger adults, also showed that women were more likely to attempt sensitive conversations by text than men. She speculates that men may use text as a means to establish emotional distance.

How does a couple's language reflect their stability? There are couples that approach the more stable stages of their relationship by sticking to the script, with variations on the canned "yes, dear" and "love you." Others will engage in passionate language that reinforces elements of trust and certainty and that diminishes fears of abandonment. Betsy and Amir text each other affirmations of love using modern vernacular:

> **Betsy:** Kissing you is like the way for me to know how much I love you

> **Betsy:** Other loves were like fake love. This feels different

> **Amir:** I'm gonna fuck you up I promise. Ur my puff

> **Betsy:** Ur gonna think this is weird bc you might not understand it, but like when I'm extremely happy I cry, it's pretty rare but

it happens when I'm like so happy, and a couple times when we kissed I wanted to cry not out of sadness at all but because it's like I just feel so much love in my heart. It's more than ecstasy, it's like literally so much love it's hard to explain. I love you so much I wanna cry

Darcy and Ian spell out their attachment using more psychological terms:

Darcy: You are so special to me. Unique and irreplaceable.

Ian: Spending time with you is often in "flow." I love it. Your thoughtfulness and leaning forward are an expression of love I am so grateful for. My feelings for you are reciprocal; joy, deep affection and respect.

Sumi declares her commitment to Jay this way:

Sumi: I know it's been a rollercoaster but as long as you're holding my hand through it its okay you know—and when it feels like you just let go at the top for no reason and I'm riding down alone that's not fair—I want to be partners in life. I have more fun when you're around you make me so Happy.

One feature of the dynamically stable relationship is resilience. Simone and Christopher have the following exchange as they head into a lengthy period of enforced geographic separation. They're trying to establish expectations for this long-distance period. Christopher has asked that they take a break while apart and not feel constricted by an exclusive commitment to each other. Simone has struggled to accept this without feeling rejected:

Christopher: I feel your disappointment—you try not to take it personally but i know it chafes. I feel a responsibility to you too.

Simone: On my disappointment: I am letting go. I've been holding on, and then withdrawing / protesting when it becomes unbearable to hold on in the face of frustration. But rather than force a choice between attachment and rejection, I am trying to find a balance of connection and separateness. I am trusting in my feelings for you to constantly reassert themselves (and yours too) so I can let go now to give each of us the freedom we need.

Christopher: You make me smile. Wish I could bottle you up and ration sips to cross the desert.

Simone and Christopher feel confident in their love, even as they head into a break. Unlike many couples, they managed to reconnect after their separation. Not every break is as tangible as theirs, but even the most resilient of couples will have to face challenges. Sometimes those challenges are too difficult to overcome, and emotional distancing or rupture will ensue.

Detaching

Even the most experienced and competent pilots have occasionally succumbed to an insidious dive known as the graveyard spiral. This occurs when a pilot loses sight of the horizon, whether due to visibility, instruments, or negligence. As the craft begins to list, the organs in the pilot's inner ear adjust, creating the illusion of being level when they're not. The pilot enters a spiral from which there is no exit. It's a type of CFIT—pronounced "see fit"—a controlled flight into terrain, because technically, and ironically, the pilot is at the controls the whole time of the crash.

Some couples see fit to end things this way, by ignoring their shared dreams and aspirations—their horizon—and intentionally driving the relationship into the ground. Others do it by accident or lack of vision. In our metaphorical aircraft, there are two pilots and two sets of controls; when one pilot does most of the flying, this plane will naturally list to their side. Without constant correction, the spiral will be engaged.

Lilly, the hesitant bride, had an inkling of the enormous weight that would be placed on her shoulders in a marriage to a man who was unwilling to or incapable of taking the controls when needed. She sought help from me early, before she lost the willingness herself. Margo, on the other hand, who had been married for eighteen years before her marriage's sudden shift, had grimly stayed the course, obliviously white-knuckling the controls until the very end, only to find that her husband had bailed out before impact. There's an expression in several romance languages that describes the shock of colliding with an unexpected reality. In French, it's *tomber des nues*. In Italian, it's *cadere dalle nuvole*. It translates as "falling from the clouds."

Before the spiral is engaged, and long before you make free fall, there are signs that can allow you to make the necessary corrections. Do it together, not alone. Erin attempts to engage Quinn as she senses that he is pulling away:

> **Erin:** I'm doing some digital housecleaning on my laptop and unearthing some real treasure.

> **Quinn:** Such as?

> **Erin:** I came across something I wrote before we met titled The Man I Desire. It's sophomorish and idealistic in a way that makes me squirm, but I recognize you in it. I'll show it to you when I see you.

> **Quinn:** I feel like you're walking into a terrible trap if you show me this tonight. You should wait until tomorrow.

> **Erin:** That sounds ominous.

> **Quinn:** Warnings can sound that way sometimes.

> **Erin:** Tomorrow it is.

Erin is working hard to resurrect her relationship with Quinn, but he has already gone a step beyond contempt and stonewalling, threatening her with some unspecified form of retaliation if she continues with her attempts. He's putting reconciliation beyond reach, actively engaging a graveyard spiral. Once engaged, it will gradually suck away all vestiges of conversational affection, a reversal of the timid steps that had emboldened the relationship at its beginning. "Hello I love you" becomes "Hello, love you," then "Hello love," and finally "Hello?"

Emotional distancing doesn't always present itself as pure conflict avoidance; sometimes it results in the creation of new obstacles, new behaviors that interfere with love. In text, you might recognize a kind of social and temporal distancing: that is, a reduction in the use of present-tense verbs, the omission of first-person pronouns (tellingly, these were also early indications of lying, a different sort of distancing).

Here Helena is proposing that Mason join her on her trip to

Baja California as a last-ditch effort to make their relationship work:

> **Helena:** one seat left on the plane if you want to come with me . . .
>
> **Mason:** Grrrrrr
>
> **Helena:** what does the Grrrrr mean?
>
> **Mason:** Grr about Baja and its siren song
>
> **Helena:** It's not too late. I'm in my "anything is possible" mentality.
>
> **Mason:** That's my grrrrr—would be so fun but the timing is not right

Mason uses emotionally distancing language, with nary a pronoun in sight and only the occasional verb. His "Grrrrrr" might just as easily be annoyance with Helena for asking as it is annoyance that he doesn't feel the time is right for a trip. Helena might or might not have been reading the signals correctly in the moment, but they were clear to her when she looked back at the messages a month later, after their breakup.

It can be hard to know how to react in the midst of a graveyard spiral. The natural reflex of the affected person, in flight as in love, is to pull back on the control wheel or the stick. It's almost an indelible reflex, even for pilots with thousands of hours in their logbooks. When faced with loss of control, it's normal to tighten one's grip. Unfortunately, pulling back on the controls will only tighten the spiral, resulting in a paradoxical worsening of the situation.

The only way to fight off the pattern is through communication and situational awareness. Gaining insight amid chaos can be challenging. In her text to Jim, Mia sums up her disorientation:

> **Mia:** Anyway it's whatever—I am just processing this all still I guess—i'm embarrassed about the bruise on my knee because i just have been drinking so much lately—and it's not like me to do that- and I just haven't felt anything good except when I was with you and I miss you like crazy and just feel really "abandoned"—like the thing I feared for years finally came true idk I'm all over

Mia at least knows what she doesn't know; she has insight into her disorientation. Clark doesn't have the same situational awareness in his conversation with Sasha:

> **Clark:** Hey hope u had a good week . . . unless I'm reading it completely wrong I'm assuming that whatever we had going on is over? Lol I guess I'm just looking for closure if that's the case

> **Clark:** I mean I like you obvi lmao so if I'm wrong and u wanna keep things going my bad I guess lmao but yeah just lmk

> **Sasha:** thanks hope u did too! Personally I have a lot going on and I have a lot of priorities that I need to focus on. I'm good being friends but even then I really don't text a lot so don't take anything personally, Its just how I am w my phone

> **Clark:** Yeah all good just like future reference I was taking ur word that u were open about feelings and stuff and would've been nice if you'd just told me up front.

Audra and Ben are in the classic graveyard spiral. She's pulling back hard on the stick, but he has already parachuted out:

Audra: Just stay with me. Don't leave me we don't need to do this 🙁

Ben: Audra, you know we are at an impasse. We've been through this so many times.

Audra: I keep staring at the cute dress I bought like over a month ago for next weekend that I'll never wear. This is so fucked up.

Audra: And you're just not fighting for us at all—you're just cutting the cord—for no good reason—like I'm in disbelief this is happening there's no reason for this to happen

Audra: I'm so mad at you for giving up on us and not caring about us enough to try to make it work—you're letting stupid fear get in the way of something that is so special— you can't just throw something like what we have to the side this is all so stupid and I'm just so shocked and disappointed. You are being cruel.

Ben: I am not being cruel, I am being honest and decisive because there is a fundamental decision that I have to make, and you can either limp into that moment and have the carpet pulled out from under you but I thought THAT would be cruel.

Ben doesn't mince words, but one senses he is trying to give Audra a chance to reorient. He later responded:

Ben: I've been nervous for a long time, which I've expressed many times, that we have such different levels of what expressing love means. I don't know how to think about things on 20-50 year time scales. I feel like this made me think about that so directly and viscerally and if I can't do this I don't think I am ever going to be able to love you in the way you need to be loved and you owe it to yourself to find someone that can. I'm broken in that way . . . so this is a shit situation and I want to support you but it isn't as easy as "believing in us" and "you're giving up" because I don't have it in me to be the kind of person I think you need.

After repeated breaks and attempted reconciliations, Landon and Harper, whom we met in the previous chapter, entered their own graveyard spiral. This final exchange, in which they are both guarded and disoriented, came on the heels of having spent less time together due to the demands of work. They were feeling increasing strain:

Harper: You havent even returned my texts or contacted me for 2 days . . . its painful for me.

Harper: Id rather know that you just dont have time to connect, instead of waiting and feeling hurt when it doesnt happen.

Landon: It hurts me to know that you are lonely and a bit frustrated by the changes in my life. That is made worse when you are untruthful. You haven't sent me any texts in the past two days and woke up in my bed yesterday. That is just a fact, not a reprimand.

Harper: Well, its not really untruthful . . . there were several occasions when I sent you messages, and you never even responded until the next day.

Harper: Not a conversation to have in texts

Landon: I understand that you are having a difficult patch. It doesn't help to attack me with statements that are contradicted and time-stamped above.

Harper: I didn't hear from you yesterday, and I heard from you at 10 pm tonight . . . to me that's 2 days

Harper: If you see me as a liar because my perception of what 2 days means is different from yours, then you are more interested in being right than showing empathy for my pain

Harper: I think we should end the texting now

Harper: There is no resolution like this.

Landon: Dude. You said I had not responded to your texts in two days. You sent none. Perception has nothing to do with it.

Harper: See? This is shitty

Harper: I hate doing this in texts

Landon: Yes, you should really not do this in texts.

Landon: Anyway, perhaps we should both get some sleep?

Harper: Yes. Good night.

Harper repeatedly invokes the powerlessness of text, yet, as Schade's research would predict, she is also the one raising the issues through that medium. She turns her hurt feelings into reprimands of Landon, and he replies with icy coldness. A crash seems inevitable. Their romance was brought to a close the next time they saw each other.

Coffin Lids

There comes a time when a relationship has to be put to rest. Perhaps love has died a peaceful death; perhaps something more dramatic unfolded. Either way, the relationship has expired and it's time to accept it and move on. How does one make peace with a relationship's demise? Scrolling through old texts might at first seem like little more than an exercise in self-abuse. But with a bit more distance, it can offer an effective way to perform a relationship autopsy and come to a better understanding of what went wrong and why.

A disclaimer: this process can be emotionally taxing, and it is best delayed until wounds have been licked, support and self-care are in place, and you feel more open to understanding what happened, along with the role you might have played in it. Scrolling back through texts may provoke nostalgia, sadness, anger, embarrassment, or all of the above. But it will almost always result in insight if one is open and willing.

There are key questions that can be addressed in the postmortem scroll. How do you present yourself throughout the relationship? How do you think about yourself as you read back your own texts? Are there any patterns, or shifts in pattern? How did your partner present themselves and how did that change over the course of the relationship? How did you express your needs, and how were they met? How did your partner express their needs, and how did you meet them? Can you trace the various crossroads in the texts—idealization, disillusionment, coalescence, emotional distancing? How did behaviors and decisions emerge that led to the breakup?

Despite its bitter ending, Landon continued to grieve his love for Harper for many months, stubbornly resisting any new romantic involvement until he could achieve better clarity over what had gone wrong and what role he might have played in its demise. In our conversations, he recognized his own tendency to idealize romantic partners. I eventually encouraged him to go back and look at his communications with Harper in their entirety. What he discovered surprised him. Landon wrote me the following:

I've been enjoying my arc of feelings about the texts I read. Initially I was blown away by the intensity of this passionate love affair, and devastated by its slow, painful demise. As the dust from the rubble in my head began to clear, so did my vision. These two were dancing on the deck of the Titanic, *sirens blaring, people screaming at them, lifeboats crashing into the ocean like ripe melons and sinking. And they danced. The blinding pain and desperate feeling of loss shifted to sadness and nostalgia, not for what it was, but for what it wasn't.*

Some relationships teeter on the brink of a graveyard spiral, constantly crossing and recrossing the threshold between hope and hopelessness. These couples have the stamp of doom on them from the start, but they persist in persisting, they believe in believing. For them, love is greater than gravity.

Nola and James had enjoyed a long and passionate extramarital affair that ended rather abruptly. They reached a crossroads together, but they chose to take different paths: Nola left her marriage. James buckled down to work on his. The end of their affair had left them without closure and with little to no contact, despite what were undoubtedly strong feelings on both sides. Nola sank into her grief. She reviewed their texts for answers. James, in his attempt to focus on his marriage, deleted everything, looking straight ahead and putting one foot in front of the other.

Years later, Nola received the following text out of the blue. In their exchange, she finally experienced the resolution she had long craved:

James: Hi. Watched "Take this waltz" and stayed up till 1:30am—fought exhaustion to watch the end. Sweet, sad, beautiful, moments of bliss, real . . . all the complexity of love. Think you would appreciate it.

Nola: I have seen it and loved it. Years ago.

James: Glad you liked the movie. It was so well done—could have been french. It had an emotional tension that was exquisite. Not schmaltz—a pointe.

Nola: Yes I can't remember how it ends. I know she has two men and one ends and it's unfinished feeling but that's all I remember

James: I need to get some sleep but glad I caught you! Xo

Nola: Miss you xoxo

James: You too

(. . .)

Nola: I'm up in the middle of the night after your text and started thinking. Anyway, was thinking about that movie "take this waltz." Now in the middle of the night the details of the movie are coming back to me. Or the feeling of the movie anyway.

And what I wanted to tell you is that: when we were together I watched every movie I could about women who were effectively ruining their lives with an affair. I watched them almost compulsively, because all day long I would think about what I was doing, and why I was doing it.

Anyway this particular movie—take this waltz—made me sad. I remember you want to be angry at her when she has the affair, but you can't, and at the end it's sad, because they have all made a lot of mistakes, but they really can't help it.

But I guess what I wanted to tell you was that now, I have almost no time for movies, or reflection, and it might be too painful. But in those years I was in it, and trying to connect with you in it, but I think you were too busy back then or too afraid to really think about it.

And I wonder now what is it you really think when you do watch these movies I was watching

Anyway middle of the night stream of consciousness but I thought I would write it down or it never gets said.

James: Hi there. Thanks for the consciousness. Hard to put in a text message because lots of thoughts and danger of being misunderstood. I felt the inescapable attraction between the two of them. He is (and I was) as much stuck in the vortex as she is but the situation is tragic because she has to make a choice. You see the fate they are in and it feels unstable, dangerous, explosive. Yet it continues to exist because they can't help it, or don't want to say no, or they want to escape into something, or its genuinely true love. That's the hardest part—what is the right thing to do? You don't know. I don't know. I think this is the beauty and the tragedy of our experience. Something magical is put on your plate as a choice. Do you dig in and live it or avoid it? There is not a right answer— you are left with a question but recognize that each had consequences.

Nola: Thanks for that. Read it twice and I am crying.

James: Sorry if I upset you. The movie felt like being on a train you can't stop. That was a familiar feeling. Xo

Were Nola's tears from pain at revisiting her loss? Relief that James was finally able to articulate the dilemma he had faced, now untrammeled by the pressures of doing the right or wrong thing? Joy that James had acknowledged that their connection had been something pure and true, beyond the obsessive passion of an affair? They were moving in different directions now, but their hearts remained together.

We may have a soul mate (or two) in our time, and we may have the good fortune to love them, in some instances to live that love together, for long stretches. In other cases, like Nola and James, we can know that it exists, somewhere, even though we took different turns at the crossroads.

Leo Tolstoy wrote, "Truth, like gold, is to be obtained not by its growth, but by washing away from it all that is not gold." Sifting through the sediments of our text messages to look for the nuggets of gold can both reveal the truths of our past relationships and help pave the way for new ones.

Thumb Tribes

> **Me:** Overall I would say that I have met a lot of interesting people on dating apps. Even though few worked out romantically

> **Eliot:** Lately I've only been dating Russian bots. Ludmilla and I are so happy together. Even if her conversation is simple and non responsive. She really gets me.

I've got a story for you.

It's my own story, but you have probably found that many parts of it are yours, too. As with all journeys, YMMV—your mileage may vary.

The rewards I've reaped from dating apps have been many. They've also, I've found, been inversely proportional to the expectations I've brought to them. Letting go of the need to find a particular partner, even if one would be a welcome enhancement in my life, allowed me to take a fun and adventurous stance toward meeting people. After all, the "ideal mate" is pure concept; the encounters we have on the digital dating circuit are always, bots notwithstanding, with actual people. Bringing too many expectations to these encounters is like wearing a raincoat in the shower. Not much happens.

Many have argued that online dating and the introduction of text messages in our romantic lives have degraded the quality of our liaisons and communications. Our texts can be, and have been, reduced to a simple "U up?" But if there is one thing that I've learned, it's that wildly more complex communication can and does take place over text and that e-romance has enabled new forms of conversation and created new levels of proficiency.

Texting has expanded and stretched my circle of acquaintances into a sort of elliptical orbit, where most everyone is on hand most of the time and those who aren't will be coming around again soon. There are friends, past romances, and future romances on that orbit, and perhaps the love of my life too, with new adventures at every planetary alignment. It is my relationship biography, in motion.

As we've chased the arc of romance and decoded its accompanying text messages throughout this book, from flirting to dating to falling in love, and even through to breakup, it can be tempting to think of our romantic pursuits the way my patient did, the one who wanted to "win at dating apps." We speak of love *lost,* and love *regained.* Might it be possible to take more of a win-win approach—an approach that accommodates and rewards all participants? At a certain point I started to bring to my dating life more of a tribal mentality, referring to my orbit as my thumb tribe. It's composed of people who don't gather to commiserate over lost loves, or see being single as a great affliction, but instead absolutely insist on enjoying life, the highs and the lows alike.

We are socialized to believe that when friends become lovers, the friendship is destroyed, and that when lovers become friends, it is a downgrade, a failure. Plato himself would have chuckled at the modern meaning of platonic love: a dry, sexless friendship of dubious value. His notion of love was of a ladder that we could ascend to reach truth and wisdom, with romantic and sexual love representing just a few of the rungs. In my Platonic friendships, with a capital *P,* I have found that no longer being involved in a sexual relationship sometimes means moving onward and upward to a higher level of connection.

The social promiscuity of the digital era has diluted the stigma attached to associating with past lovers and having deep friendships with future ones. This means that the social capital gained by romantic relationships needn't be squandered simply because two people are no longer exchanging intimate bodily fluids. It brings us, in a sense, closer to the Platonic ideal. Today, some of my closest friends are former romantic interests, people I met on dating apps. There is a level of intimacy and mutual understanding that perhaps would not be attainable by any other means than sharing time together on the ladder of love.

By thinking of the people we meet as a new tribe, our own thumb tribe, perhaps we can bring less "me" into the equation—less ego, more soul, as the saying goes. Instead of seeking out a single, glimmering source of validation, we can focus on our larger sense of connection to a community of people.

We have learned a new language, established a new fluency. How will you use it? As the author Susan Statham said, "Your life is your story. Write well and edit often." The yes or no answer to the question "Has digital communication killed the written word?" is probably moot at this point. To quote Ice Cube, "This is a gang, and I'm in it." We are all writers now, and it behooves us to bring our best to the table *or* the tablet.

Will thumb tribes become powerful social units in the cultures of the future? My thumb tribe has brought me an incredible wealth of love, knowledge, connection, and fellowship. The gifts are too many and too diverse to count. And along the way, miraculously, serendipitously, almost accidentally, my thumb tribe has brought you this book.

Acknowledgments

The challenge of writing a first book is a daunting one, and one that I couldn't have faced, let alone completed, without support.

First, I am most deeply grateful to Leonardo, my collaborator and friend. There is no exchange of ideas that we cannot have, and you are my steadfast thought partner and chief truth teller. Your creative genius, and ability to play with words, has delighted and inspired me. It is said that writing a book changes who you are, and your willingness to go on the journey with me made the process an adventure that I will always cherish.

Thank you to Liam Day for pushing me to write this book from the day I first voiced the idea. Two full years of his nudging was enough to get me started. Many thanks for believing in me, outlining the process, and tirelessly and thoroughly reading drafts. Your input was invaluable.

I'm so appreciative of my lifelong friends Debora Bolter, Kate Schermerhorn, Anna Seaton Huntington, and David Wright, who read large portions of the book and provided helpful comments and wise suggestions. Thanks to each of you. I am lucky to have such talented and smart people in my life.

Thanks are due not just to old friends, but also to the new ones I've met along the way. I'm grateful to the many of you who shared your text messages. Special thanks to William Chettle for your contribution of ideas, your correspondence, and your astute reads and suggestions. Thanks to Andy Katz, photographer extraordinaire.

I'm indebted to the many experts whose research I relied on for the book. Special thanks to Michael Norton, Barry Schwartz, Celia Klin, and James Pennebaker for taking time to be interviewed for the book.

Thanks to my fantastic literary agent, Howard Yoon, who shepherded me through every step of the process with unerring judgment, good humor, and kindness. Thanks for helping me to tell my story, and for shaping the book proposal as it grew from an idea to a reality.

This book would not have been possible without Yaniv Soha, my brilliant editor at Doubleday. When it comes to editors, I can most assuredly say that I won the lottery. I am so immensely thankful for your patience and your skillful use of red ink. Your masterful approach to my drafts were constant reminders that I was in the most expert of hands. I am deeply appreciative of your unwavering support, as well as that of the entire team at Doubleday.

Thanks to my awesome children, Kyra and Tor, for patiently accepting my focus on this project. A book that exposes your mother's dating texts might not have been what either of you had wished for, but you both handled it with grace and aplomb. Kyra single-handedly formatted references on her college break to help meet a deadline, and Tor helped me maintain my sense of humor. I love you.

Last but not least, special thanks go out to all of my patients, past and present, for trusting me with your stories, and allowing me to be part of your journey. You've taught me, over and over again, about life and only life.

Notes

INTRODUCTION

ix   **Freud himself acknowledged:** Sigmund Freud, "Volume 2, Studies in Hysteria," ed. Carrie Lee Rothgeb, Psychoanalytic Training Institute of the Contemporary Freudian Society, 1971, instituteofcfs.org.

xi   **More than fifty million:** Mansoor Iqbal, "Tinder Revenue and Usage Statistics (2020)," *Business of Apps,* Oct. 30, 2020, www .businessofapps.com.

CHAPTER 1: MIXED EMOJIS

7   **The psychiatrist Robert Cloninger:** Robert Cloninger, "A Systematic Method for Clinical Description and Classification of Personality Variants," *Archives of General Psychiatry* 44, no. 6 (1987).

9   **Michael Norton:** Michael Norton, Jeana H. Frost, and Dan Ariely, "Less Is More: The Lure of Ambiguity, or Why Familiarity Breeds Contempt," *Journal of Personality and Social Psychology* 92, no. 1 (2007): 97–105.

9   **"We *think* that if we know":** Norton, phone interview with author, May 6, 2020.

11   **Norton and his colleagues found:** Norton, Frost, and Ariely. "Less Is More."

11   **In their next experiment:** Ibid.

11   **"People who had been on more dates":** Norton, phone interview with author.

11   **Harry Reis, a professor of psychology:** Harry Reis et al.,
        "Familiarity Does Indeed Promote Attraction in Live Interaction,"
        Journal of Personality and Social Psychology 101, no. 3 (March
        2011): 557–70.

15   *The Art of Choosing:* Shankar Vedantam, "The Choices Before
        Us: Can Fewer Options Lead to Better Decisions?," NPR, May 4,
        2020, www.npr.org.

17   **One study demonstrated:** Bruno Laeng, Oddrun Vermeer, and
        Unni Sulutvedt, "Is Beauty in the Face of the Beholder?," *PLoS
        ONE* 8, no. 7 (Oct. 2013).

17   **couples with matching speech styles:** Molly E. Ireland et al.,
        "Language Style Matching Predicts Relationship Initiation and
        Stability," *Psychological Science* 22, no. 1 (Jan. 2011): 39–44.

18   **Pew Research Center study:** Monica Anderson, Emily A. Vogels,
        and Erica Turner, "The Virtues and Downsides of Online Dating,"
        Pew Research Center: Internet & Technology, Oct. 2, 2020, www
        .pewresearch.org.

21   **Give a rat a lever:** Taizo Nakazato, "Striatal Dopamine Release
        in the Rat During a Cued Lever-Press Task for Food Reward and
        the Development of Changes over Time Measured Using High-
        Speed Voltammetry," *Experimental Brain Research* 166, no. 1 (Sept.
        2005).

23   **Center for Neural Decision Making:** Angelika Dimoka, Paul A.
        Avalou, and Fred D. David, "NeuroIS: The Potential of Cognitive
        Neuroscience for Information Systems Research," *Information
        Systems Research* 22, no. 4 (Dec. 2011): 1–16.

23   **Professor Barry Schwartz:** Barry Schwartz, "More Isn't Always
        Better," *Harvard Business Review,* Aug. 1, 2014, hbr.org.

24   **Sheena Iyengar agrees:** Vedantam, "Choices Before Us."

25   *The Paradox of Choice:* Barry Schwartz, *The Paradox of Choice*
        (New York: Ecco, 2004), 134.

26   **In her book *Marry Him:*** Lori Gottlieb, *Marry Him: The Case for
        Settling for Mr. Good Enough* (New York: New American Library,
        2011).

27   **Kurt Gödel published:** Raymond M. Smullyan, *Gödel's
        Incompleteness Theorems* (New York: Oxford University Press,
        2020).

28 **Dating algorithms also learn:** Ashley Carman, "Tinder Says It No Longer Uses a 'Desirability' Score to Rank People," *Verge,* March 15, 2019, www.theverge.com.

30 **A pivotal study by Eli Finkel:** Eli J. Finkel et al., "Online Dating: A Critical Analysis from the Perspective of Psychological Science," *Psychological Science in the Public Interest* 13, no. 1 (2012).

CHAPTER 2: CAN I GET YOUR NUMBERS?

34 **as Malcolm Gladwell famously described:** Malcolm Gladwell, *Blink: The Power of Thinking Without Thinking* (New York: Back Bay Books, 2019).

35 **One of these masters is Paul Ekman:** Paul Ekman, "Micro Expressions: Facial Expressions," Paul Ekman Group, Feb. 6, 2020, www.paulekman.com.

35 **Frank Bernieri:** David G. Jensen, "Tooling Up: First Impressions—Are Interview Results Preordained?," *Science,* Aug. 20, 2004.

35 **take a lie detection course:** David J. Lieberman, "Award-Winning Lie Detection Course: Taught by FBI Trainer," Udemy, Jan. 7, 2021, www.udemy.com.

36 **Dr. John Gottman's predictive work:** John M. Gottman, "Love Lab," Gottman Institute, Sept. 10, 2019, www.gottman.com.

36 **he's able to predict with 93.6 percent:** John M. Gottman, Kim T. Buehlman, and Lynn Katz, "How a Couple Views Their Past Predicts Their Future: Predicting Divorce from an Oral History Interview," *Journal of Family Psychology* 5, no. 3 (Jan. 1970).

38 **Crisis Text Line (CTL) is a company:** Nancy Lublin, "Crisis Text Line," Crisis Text Line, 2013, www.crisistextline.org.

40 **Myers-Briggs Type Indicator:** Katharine Cook Briggs and Isabel Briggs Myers, "Myers-Briggs Type Indicator," MBTI Basics, Myers & Briggs Foundation, www.myersbriggs.org.

40 **sometimes use the Enneagram:** George Gurdjieff, "The Enneagram Personality Test," Truity, Jan. 8, 2021, www.truity.com.

40 **the Big Five personality test:** Lewis Goldberg, "Big Five Personality Test," Open Psychometrics, Aug. 2019, openpsycho metrics.org.

42   **High neuroticism scores:** Benjamin R. Karney and Thomas N. Bradbury, "Neuroticism, Marital Interaction, and the Trajectory of Marital Satisfaction," *Journal of Personality and Social Psychology* 72 (1997): 1075–92.

42   **if a couple is having a lot of sex:** V. Michelle Russell and James K. McNulty, "Frequent Sex Protects Intimates from the Negative Implications of Their Neuroticism," *Social Psychological and Personality Science* 2 (2011): 220–27.

42   **In more than one study, neuroticism:** Terri D. Fisher and James K. McNulty, "Neuroticism and Marital Satisfaction: The Mediating Role Played by the Sexual Relationship," *Journal of Family Psychology* 22, no. 1 (Feb. 2008): 112–22.

42   **High levels of conscientiousness and agreeableness:** David P. Schmitt and Todd K. Shackelford, "Big Five Traits Related to Short-Term Mating: From Personality to Promiscuity Across 46 Nations," *Evolutionary Psychology* 6, no. 2 (2008).

42   **In a meta-analysis:** Noam Shpancer, "How Your Personality Predicts Your Romantic Life," *Psychology Today,* Aug. 2, 2016, www.psychologytoday.com.

42   **Openness to experience seems:** Schmitt and Shackelford, "Big Five Traits."

44   **To experts like Celia Klin:** Celia Klin, interview with author, June 18, 2020.

44   **extroverts use the word "mouth":** Tal Yarkoni, "Personality in 100,000 Words: A Large-Scale Analysis of Personality and Word Use Among Bloggers," *Journal of Research in Personality* 44, no. 3 (2010): 363–73.

46   **IBM came up with:** Tanya Lewis, "IBM's Watson," *Business Insider,* July 22, 2015, www.businessinsider.com.

47   **MIT researchers trained a computer:** Rob Matheson, "Model Can More Naturally Detect Depression in Conversations," *MIT News,* Aug. 29, 2018, news.mit.edu.

47   **One study looked at 6,202 Twitter users:** Sharath Chandra Guntuku et al., "Studying Expressions of Loneliness in Individuals Using Twitter: An Observational Study," *BMJ Open* 9, no. 11 (2019).

47   **A Czech study asked 124 female students:** Jana M. Havigerová et al., "Text-Based Detection of the Risk of Depression," *Frontiers in Psychology* 10 (March 2019).

48 **Mentions of money can indicate lack of agreeableness:** Yarkoni, "Personality in 100,000 Words."

49 **those who bandy about negations:** Ibid.

51 **Jessica Bennett suggests:** Jessica Bennett, "When Your Punctuation Says It All (!)," *New York Times,* Feb. 27, 2015, www.nytimes.com.

51 **Big Five assessments has shown question marks:** Jennifer Golbeck et al., "Predicting Personality from Twitter," IEEE International Conference on Privacy, Security, Risk, and Trust, and IEEE International Conference on Social Computing, 2011, www.demenzemedicinagenerale.net.

52 **Celia Klin's research group:** Danielle N. Gunraj et al., "Texting Insincerely: The Role of the Period in Text Messaging," *Computers in Human Behavior* 55 (Feb. 2016): 1067–75.

52 **F. Scott Fitzgerald reportedly said:** F. Scott Fitzgerald, "An Exclamation Point Is Like Laughing at Your Own Joke," Quote Investigator, Jan. 6, 2019, quoteinvestigator.com.

52 **One study showed that overuse:** Golbeck et al., "Predicting Personality from Twitter," 153.

54 **In her book of essays:** Elena Ferrante, *Incidental Inventions,* trans. Ann Goldstein (Brentwood, Calif.: Europa Editions, 2019), 60.

55 **Gretchen McCulloch has elaborately documented:** Gretchen McCulloch, *Because Internet: Understanding the New Rules of Language* (Waterville, Maine: Thorndike Press, 2020).

55 **Americans, for instance, smile:** Olga Khazan, "Why Americans Smile So Much," *Atlantic,* June 1, 2017, www.theatlantic.com.

56 **A large-scale study:** Weijian Li et al., "Mining the Relationship Between Emoji Usage Patterns and Personality," arXiv, April 14, 2018, arxiv.org.

58 **For instance, extroverts will be more:** Ibid.

CHAPTER 3: WORKING OUT THE KINKS

63 **A large-scale study of forty-one thousand:** Queensland University of Technology, "Online Daters Ignore Wish List When Choosing a Match," *Science News,* Feb. 21, 2017, www.sciencedaily.com.

64   **In his seminal book:** Timothy D. Wilson, *Strangers to Ourselves: Discovering the Adaptive Unconscious* (Cambridge, Mass.: Belknap Press of Harvard University Press, 2004), 6.

65   **"To be is to do":** Kurt Vonnegut, *Deadeye Dick* (New York: Dial Press, 2010), 253.

71   **In a famous experiment:** Michael Norton and Zoë Chance, " 'I Read *Playboy* for the Articles': Justifying and Rationalizing Questionable Preferences," Harvard Business School Working Paper 10-018, Sept. 24, 2009, hbswk.hbs.edu.

74   **Research by the professor:** Rick Harrington and Donald A. Loffredo, "Insight, Rumination, and Self-Reflection as Predictors of Well-Being," *The Journal of Psychology* 145, no. 1 (2010): pp. 39–57.

74   **By contrast, the psychologist Anthony Grant:** Anthony M. Grant, John Franklin, and Peter Langford, "The Self-Reflection and Insight Scale: A New Measure of Private Self-Consciousness," *Social Behavior and Personality: An International Journal* 30, no. 8 (2002): 821–35.

74   **Tasha Eurich outlines in her book:** Tasha Eurich, *Insight: The Surprising Truth About How Others See Us, How We See Ourselves, and Why the Answers Matter More Than We Think* (New York: Currency, 2018), 135–42.

78   **When the difference is quantified:** Simine Vazire and Mitja D. Back, "Knowing Our Personality," in *Handbook of Self-Knowledge,* ed. Simine Vazire and Timothy D. Wilson (New York: Guilford Press, 2012), 137.

79   **As the therapist James Hollis:** James Hollis, *Living an Examined Life: Wisdom for the Second Half of the Journey* (Boulder, Colo.: Sounds True, 2018).

80   **The University of Virginia psychologist:** Timothy D. Wilson et al., "Just Think: The Challenges of the Disengaged Mind," *Science* 345, no. 6192 (July 2004): 75–77.

81   **Both feedback and mindfulness can run up:** Timothy D. Wilson and Daniel T. Gilbert, "Affective Forecasting: Knowing What to Want," *Current Directions in Psychological Science* 14, no. 3 (June 2005).

85   **our own biographers:** Wilson, *Strangers to Ourselves,* 16.

85 **"Students achieving Oneness":** Woody Allen and Linda Sunshine, *The Illustrated Woody Allen Reader: Prospectus* (New York: Alfred A. Knopf, 1993), 53.

CHAPTER 4: TEXTING WITH STRANGERS

87 **Eighty-four percent of users:** Plenty of Fish, "Pressure Points Report 2019" (Egnyte, 2019), 1–8, craftedcom.egnyte.com.

87 **A 2019 white paper:** Ibid.

92 **In the early days of dating apps:** Isabel Thottam, "The History of Online Dating (US)," eHarmony, 2018, www.eharmony.com.

93 **A Harvard Business School study:** Rachel Layne, "Asking Questions Can Get You a Better Job or a Second Date," HBS Working Knowledge, Oct. 30, 2017, hbswk.hbs.edu.

93 **Data science has shown:** OkCupid, "Online Dating Advice: Optimum Message Length," *The OkCupid Blog,* Medium, Aug. 7, 2019, theblog.okcupid.com.

96 **Research out of Cornell:** Jason Dou et al., "What Words Do We Use to Lie? Word Choice in Deceptive Messages," arXiv, Sept. 2017, arxiv.org.

100 **Neuroscientists have speculated:** Lindsay M. Oberman, "Broken Mirrors: A Theory of Autism," *Scientific American,* June 1, 2007, www.scientificamerican.com.

102 **The writer and storyteller David Sedaris:** David Sedaris, Facebook, Dec. 3, 2019, www.facebook.com.

108 **The professor of psychology Rod Martin:** Rod A. Martin and Thomas E. Ford, *The Psychology of Humor: An Integrative Approach* (London: Academic Press, 2018).

110 **self-enhancing humor:** Paul Frewen et al., "Humor Styles and Personality-Vulnerability to Depression," *Humor* 21, no. 2 (2008): 179–95.

111 **aggressive humor:** Rod A. Martin et al., "Individual Differences in Uses of Humor and Their Relation to Psychological Well-Being: Development of the Humor Styles Questionnaire," *Journal of Research in Personality* 37, no. 1 (2003): 48–75.

113 **In data analyzed by OkCupid:** OkCupid, "Online Dating Advice."

114 **John Bowlby was the first:** Lumen Learning and Diana Lang, "1950s: Harlow, Bowlby, and Ainsworth," Iowa State University Digital Press, May 18, 2020, iastate.pressbooks.pub.

115 **Research suggests that half the human:** Amir Levine, *Attached: The New Science of Adult Attachment and How It Can Help You Find—and Keep—Love* (New York: TarcherPerigee, 2012), 4.

CHAPTER 5: COMMUNICATION STYLES

127 **In 2013, *The New York Times* ran:** Alex Williams, "The End of Courtship?," *New York Times,* Jan. 11, 2013, www.nytimes.com.

129 **In focus groups for his book *Modern Romance*:** Aziz Ansari, "The Power of Waiting," in *Modern Romance,* with Eric Klinenberg (New York: Penguin Press, 2015), 59–64.

130 **Helen Fisher—an anthropologist with expertise:** Helen E. Fisher, *Anatomy of Love: A Natural History of Mating, Marriage, and Why We Stray* (New York: W. W. Norton, 2017).

135 **"language-style matching":** James W. Pennebaker, *The Secret Life of Pronouns: What Our Words Say About Us* (New York: Bloomsbury, 2013), 200.

135 **James Pennebaker, a professor of psychology:** Ibid., 206.

135 **In his book *The Secret Life of Pronouns*:** Ibid., 1–17.

136 **Pennebaker told me:** Pennebaker, phone interview with author, Aug. 26, 2020.

139 **A study in Germany showed:** Silke Anders et al., "A Neural Link Between Affective Understanding and Interpersonal Attraction," *PNAS,* March 31, 2016, www.pnas.org.

142 **"It's no good pretending":** Nick Hornby, *High Fidelity* (New York: Riverhead Books, 1996), 117.

151 **When talking about work:** Pennebaker, *Secret Life of Pronouns,* 170–95.

152 **In his analysis of function words:** Ibid.

152 **"In short":** Pennebaker, phone interview with author.

152 **Even pack animals behave:** Enikő Kubinyi and Lisa J. Wallis, "Dominance in Dogs as Rated by Owners Corresponds to Ethologically Valid Markers of Dominance," *PeerJ* 7 (May 2019).

153   **Men use more articles:** Pennebaker, *Secret Life of Pronouns,*
       170–95.

155   **Some of these behaviors are encouraged:** Ellen Fein and Sherrie
       Schneider, *The Rules* (New York: Grand Central Publishing, 2008).

155   **men are taught the art of "negging":** Neil Strauss, *The Game*
       (Edinburgh: Canongate Books, 2016).

156   **"The very essence of romance":** Oscar Wilde, *The Importance of
       Being Earnest* (London: Renard Press, 2021), act 1, p. 3.

157   **As a cognitive neuroscientist at Brown:** Rachel Herz, *The Scent
       of Desire: Discovering Our Enigmatic Sense of Smell* (New York:
       HarperCollins, 2009).

CHAPTER 6: TEXTING TOWARD INTIMACY

159   **"Love seems the swiftest":** Mark Twain, *Mark Twain's Notebook,*
       ed. Albert Bigelow Paine (London: Hesperides Press, 2006).

160   **"Love rests on two pillars":** Esther Perel, *Mating in Captivity*
       (London: Hodder & Stoughton, 2007), 25.

161   **"Love is giving something":** Allan Gois, "The Perfect
       Imperfections of Love," *The Psychotherapist Blog,* March 3, 2014,
       www.allangois.co.uk.

161   **Erikson, a renowned psychologist:** Erik H. Erikson, *Identity and
       the Life Cycle: Selected Papers* (New York: Norton, 1980).

161   **Much attention has been given:** Gary D. Chapman, *The Five Love
       Languages: How to Express Heartfelt Commitment to Your Mate*
       (Chicago: Northfield, 1995).

171   **The psychologist and relationship expert:** Kubinyi and Wallis,
       "Dominance in Dogs."

172   *language of attunement:* John M. Gottman and Nan Silver, *What
       Makes Love Last? How to Build Trust and Avoid Betrayal* (New
       York: Simon & Schuster Paperbacks, 2013), 83–90.

173   **Gottman suggests that attunement:** Ibid., 114–28.

175   **As Gottman has followed couples over:** Ibid.

175   **A bid, Gottman explains:** John M. Gottman and Joan DeClaire,
       *The Relationship Cure: A Five-Step Guide to Strengthening Your
       Marriage, Family, and Friendships* (New York: Harmony Books,
       2002).

176　**As Gottman has studied couples:** John M. Gottman et al., *Eight Dates: Essential Conversations for a Lifetime of Love* (New York: Workman, 2019), 81.

179　**The relationship expert Esther Perel argues:** Perel, *Mating in Captivity.*

180　**Recall the classic "Soup Nazi":** "Soup Nazi," *Seinfeld,* season 7, episode 6, aired Nov. 2, 1995.

180　**"If intimacy grows through repetition":** Perel, *Mating in Captivity,* 37.

181　**"are more than you":** E. E. Cummings, "Because It's," All Poetry, 2005, allpoetry.com.

CHAPTER 7: PEACE, LOVE, AND UNDERSTANDING

182　**"All happy families are alike":** Leo Tolstoy, *Anna Karenina,* trans. Richard Pevear and Larissa Volokhonsky (New York: Penguin Books, 2002), 1.

184　**"Passionate Love Scale":** Elaine Hatfield, "Passionate Love, Companionate Love, and Intimacy," in *Intimacy,* ed. Martin Fisher and George Stricker (Boston: Springer, 1982).

184　**When a person scoring high:** Hongwen Song et al., "Love-Related Changes in the Brain: A Resting-State Functional Magnetic Resonance Imaging Study," *Frontiers in Human Neuroscience* 9, no. 71 (Feb. 2015).

185　**As the psychologist Jonathan Haidt:** Jonathan Haidt, *The Happiness Hypothesis: Putting Ancient Wisdom and Philosophy to the Test of Modern Science* (London: Random House Business Books, 2021), 126.

185　**"power of seeing through its own enchantments":** C. S. Lewis, *A Grief Observed* (London: CrossReach Publications, 2016), 72.

186　**The British psychologist Edward Titchener:** Richard M. Frankel, "The Many Faces of Empathy," *Journal of Patient Experience* 4, no. 2 (May 2017).

189　**In a paper titled "What Do You Do When Things Go Right?":** Shelly Gable et al., "What Do You Do When Things Go Right? The Intrapersonal and Interpersonal Benefits of Sharing Positive

Events," *Journal of Personality and Social Psychology* 87, no. 2 (2004): 228–45.

194 **"Respect is like air":** Kerry Patterson et al., *Crucial Conversations: Tools for Talking When Stakes Are High* (New York: McGraw-Hill, 2012), 79.

195 **To do that, Gottman emphasizes:** John M. Gottman and Nan Silver, *The Seven Principles for Making Marriage Work* (London: Cassell Illustrated, 2018).

195 **Nicholas Epley, a professor of behavioral science at the University of Chicago:** Nicholas Epley, *Mindwise* (New York: Vintage Books, 2015), 10.

202 **The sex columnist Dan Savage:** Amy Muise, "Are You GGG?," *Psychology Today,* Aug. 31, 2012, www.psychologytoday.com.

202 **In a study of long-term couples:** Amy Muise et al., "Keeping the Spark Alive: Being Motivated to Meet a Partner's Sexual Needs Sustains Sexual Desire in Long-Term Romantic Relationships," *Social Psychology and Personality Science* 4, no. 3 (2013).

204 **"Jealousy feeds on doubts":** François de La Rochefoucauld, *Maxims* (New York: Penguin Classics, 1982), 41.

206 **5 percent of Americans practice polyamory:** Elisabeth Sheff, "Updated Estimate of Number of Non-monogamous People in U.S.," *Psychology Today,* May 27, 2019, www.psychologytoday.com.

206 **A 2016 study found:** Jessica Kegu and Jason Silverstein, "'Things Are Opening Up': Non-monogamy Is More Common Than You'd Think," CBS News, Oct. 27, 2019, www.cbsnews.com.

206 **jealousy is no more prevalent among CNMs:** Elaine Hatfield, Richard L. Rapson, and Jeanette Purvis, *What's Next in Love and Sex: Psychological and Cultural Perspectives* (New York: Oxford University Press, 2020), 151–68.

207 **Estimated prevalence rates for CNM:** Ethan Czuy Levine et al., "Open Relationships, Nonconsensual Nonmonogamy, and Monogamy Among U.S. Adults: Findings from the 2012 National Survey of Sexual Health and Behavior," *Archives of Sexual Behavior* 47, no. 5 (July 2018).

207 **Infidelity has higher reported rates:** Hatfield, Rapson, and Purvis, *What's Next in Love and Sex,* 151–68.

207   **Yet when married couples are asked:** Michael W. Wiederman
and Elizabeth Rice Allgeier, "Expectations and Attributions
Regarding Extramarital Sex Among Young Married Individuals,"
Journal of Psychology and Human Sexuality 8, no. 3 (1996): 21–35.

209   **"We cross our bridges":** Tom Stoppard, *Rosencrantz and
Guildenstern Are Dead* (Stuttgart: Reclam, 1993), 47.

CHAPTER 8: TOXIC TEXTING

217   **The person who stonewalls:** Gottman and Silver, *What Makes
Love Last?*, 40.

220   **The psychologist Sue Johnson developed an approach:** Sue
Johnson, *Hold Me Tight: Your Guide to the Most Successful
Approach to Building Loving Relationships* (London: Piatkus,
2011), 32.

235   **"Life is pleasant. Death is peaceful":** Laura Ward, *Famous Last
Words: The Ultimate Collection of Finales and Farewells* (London:
PRC, 2004), 14.

CHAPTER 9: CROSSROADS

236   **"Love never dies a natural death":** Anaïs Nin, *The Four-
Chambered Heart* (Denver: Swallow Press, 1959), 48.

237   **One data scientist tracked the word content:** Alice Zhao, "Text
Messaging," A Dash of Data, Sept. 5, 2017, adashofdata.com.

243   **"a constant challenge":** Rainer Funk, *Erich Fromm: His Life and
Ideas: An Illustrated Biography* (New York: Continuum, 2000),
138.

244   **One study, led by Lori Schade:** Lori Cluff Schade et al., "Using
Technology to Connect in Romantic Relationships: Effects on
Attachment, Relationship Satisfaction, and Stability in Emerging
Adults," *Journal of Couple & Relationship Therapy* 12, no. 4 (2013):
314–38.

258   **"Truth, like gold, is to be obtained":** Tolstoy, *Anna Karenina*, 8.

260 **His notion of love was of a ladder:** Emrys Westacott,
"Discover What Plato Means About the Ladder of Love in His
'Symposium,'" ThoughtCo, Aug. 2020, www.thoughtco.com.
261 **"This is a gang":** N.W.A, "Gangsta Gangsta," on *Straight Outta
Compton,* 1988.

Bibliography

Allen, Woody, and Linda Sunshine. *The Illustrated Woody Allen Reader: Prospectus.* New York: Alfred A. Knopf, 1993.

Anders, Silke, Roos de Jong, Christian Beck, John-Dylan Haynes, and Thomas Ethofer. "A Neural Link Between Affective Understanding and Interpersonal Attraction." *PNAS,* March 31, 2016. www.pnas.org.

Anderson, Monica, Emily A. Vogels, and Erica Turner. "The Virtues and Downsides of Online Dating." Pew Research Center: Internet & Technology, Oct. 2, 2020. www.pewresearch.org.

Ansari, Aziz. *Modern Romance.* With Eric Klinenberg. New York: Penguin Press, 2015.

Bennett, Jessica. "When Your Punctuation Says It All (!)." *New York Times,* Feb. 27, 2015. www.nytimes.com.

Carman, Ashley. "Tinder Says It No Longer Uses a 'Desirability' Score to Rank People." *Verge,* March 15, 2019. www.theverge.com.

Chapman, Gary D. *The Five Love Languages: How to Express Heartfelt Commitment to Your Mate.* Chicago: Northfield, 1995.

Cloninger, Robert. "A Systematic Method for Clinical Description and Classification of Personality Variants." *Archives of General Psychiatry* 44, no. 6 (1987).

Cummings, E. E. "Because It's." All Poetry, 2005. allpoetry.com.

Dimoka, Angelika, Paul A. Avalou, and Fred D. David. "NeuroIS: The Potential of Cognitive Neuroscience for Information Systems Research." *Information Systems Research* 22, no. 4 (Dec. 2011): 1–16.

Dou, Jason, Michelle Liu, Haaris Muneer, and Adam Schlussel. "What Words Do We Use to Lie? Word Choice in Deceptive Messages." arXiv, Sept. 2017. arxiv.org.

Ekman, Paul. "Micro Expressions: Facial Expressions." Paul Ekman Group, Feb. 6, 2020. www.paulekman.com.

Epley, Nicholas. *Mindwise.* New York: Vintage Books, 2015.

Erikson, Erik H. *Identity and the Life Cycle: Selected Papers.* New York: Norton, 1980.

Eurich, Tasha. *Insight: The Surprising Truth About How Others See Us, How We See Ourselves, and Why the Answers Matter More Than We Think.* New York: Currency, 2018.

Fein, Ellen, and Sherrie Schneider. *The Rules.* New York: Grand Central Publishing, 2008.

Finkel, Eli J., Paul W. Eastwick, Benjamin R. Karney, Harry T. Reis, and Susan Sprecher. "Online Dating: A Critical Analysis from the Perspective of Psychological Science." *Psychological Science in the Public Interest* 13, no. 1 (2012).

Fisher, Helen E. *Anatomy of Love: A Natural History of Mating, Marriage, and Why We Stray.* New York: W. W. Norton, 2017.

Fisher, Terri D., and James K. McNulty. "Neuroticism and Marital Satisfaction: The Mediating Role Played by the Sexual Relationship." *Journal of Family Psychology* 22, no. 1 (Feb. 2008): 112–22.

Frankel, Richard M. "The Many Faces of Empathy." *Journal of Patient Experience* 4, no. 2 (May 2017).

Freud, Sigmund. "Volume 2, Studies in Hysteria." Edited by Carrie Lee Rothgeb. Psychoanalytic Training Institute of the Contemporary Freudian Society, 1971. instituteofcfs.org.

Frewen, Paul, Jaylene Brinker, Rod A. Martin, and David Dozois. "Humor Styles and Personality-Vulnerability to Depression." *Humor* 21, no. 2 (2008): 179–95.

Funk, Rainer. *Erich Fromm: His Life and Ideas: An Illustrated Biography.* New York: Continuum, 2000.

Gable, Shelly L., Harry T. Reis, Emily A. Impett, and Evan R. Asher. "What Do You Do When Things Go Right? The Intrapersonal and Interpersonal Benefits of Sharing Positive Events." *Journal of Personality and Social Psychology* 87, no. 2 (2004).

Gladwell, Malcolm. *Blink: The Power of Thinking Without Thinking.* New York: Back Bay Books, 2019.

Gois, Allan. "The Perfect Imperfections of Love." *The Psychotherapist Blog,* March 3, 2014. www.allangois.co.uk.

Golbeck, Jennifer, Cristina Robles, Michon Edmondson, and Karen Turner. "Predicting Personality from Twitter." IEEE International Conference on Privacy, Security, Risk, and Trust, and IEEE International Conference on Social Computing, 2011. www.demenzemedicinagenerale .net/.

Goldberg, Lewis. "Big Five Personality Test." Open Psychometrics, Aug. 2019. openpsychometrics.org.

Gottlieb, Lori. *Marry Him: The Case for Settling for Mr. Good Enough.* New York: New American Library, 2011.

Gottman, John M. "Love Lab." Gottman Institute, Sept. 10, 2019. www .gottman.com.

Gottman, John M., Kim T. Buehlman, and Lynn Katz. "How a Couple Views Their Past Predicts Their Future: Predicting Divorce from an Oral History Interview." *Journal of Family Psychology* 5, no. 3 (Jan. 1970).

Gottman, John M., and Joan DeClaire. *The Relationship Cure: A Five-Step Guide to Strengthening Your Marriage, Family, and Friendships.* New York: Harmony Books, 2002.

Gottman, John M., Julie Schwartz Gottman, Doug Abrams, and Rachel Carlton Abrams. *Eight Dates: Essential Conversations for a Lifetime of Love.* New York: Workman, 2019.

Gottman, John M., and Nan Silver. *The Seven Principles for Making Marriage Work.* London: Cassell Illustrated, 2018.

Grant, Anthony M., John Franklin, and Peter Langford. "The Self-Reflection and Insight Scale: A New Measure of Private Self-Consciousness." *Social Behavior and Personality: An International Journal* 30, no. 8 (2002): 821–35.

Gunraj, Danielle N., April M. Drumm-Hewitt, Erica M. Dashow, Sri Siddhi N. Upadhyay, and Celia M. Klin. "Texting Insincerely: The Role of the Period in Text Messaging." *Computers in Human Behavior* 55 (Feb. 2016): 1067–75.

Guntuku, Sharath Chandra, Rachelle Schneider, Arthur Pelullo, Jami Young, Vivien Wong, Lyle Ungar, Daniel Polsky, Kevin G. Volpp, and Raina Merchant. "Studying Expressions of Loneliness in Individuals Using Twitter: An Observational Study." *BMJ Open* 9, no. 11 (2019).

Gurdjieff, George. "The Enneagram Personality Test." Truity, Jan. 8, 2021. www.truity.com.

Haidt, Jonathan. *The Happiness Hypothesis: Putting Ancient Wisdom and Philosophy to the Test of Modern Science.* London: Random House Business Books, 2021.

Harrington, Rick, and Donald A. Loffredo. "Insight, Rumination, and Self-Reflection as Predictors of Well-Being." *The Journal of Psychology* 145, no. 1 (2010): 39–57.

Hatfield, Elaine. "Passionate Love, Companionate Love, and Intimacy." In *Intimacy,* edited by Martin Fisher and George Stricker. Boston: Springer, 1982.

Hatfield, Elaine, Richard L. Rapson, and Jeanette Purvis. *What's Next in Love and Sex: Psychological and Cultural Perspectives.* New York: Oxford University Press, 2020.

Havigerová, Jana M., Jiří Haviger, Dalibor Kučera, and Petra Hoffmannová. "Text-Based Detection of the Risk of Depression." *Frontiers in Psychology* 10 (March 2019).

Herz, Rachel. *The Scent of Desire: Discovering Our Enigmatic Sense of Smell.* New York: HarperCollins, 2009.

Hollis, James. *Living an Examined Life: Wisdom for the Second Half of the Journey.* Boulder, Colo.: Sounds True, 2018.

Iqbal, Mansoor. "Tinder Revenue and Usage Statistics (2020)." *Business of Apps,* Oct. 30, 2020. www.businessofapps.com.

Ireland, Molly E., Richard B. Slatcher, Paul W. Eastwick, Lauren E. Scissors, Eli J. Finkel, and James W. Pennebaker. "Language Style Matching Predicts Relationship Initiation and Stability." *Psychological Science* 22, no. 1 (Jan. 2011): 39–44.

Jensen, David G. "Tooling Up: First Impressions—Are Interview Results Preordained?" *Science,* Aug. 20, 2004.

Johnson, Sue. *Hold Me Tight: Your Guide to the Most Successful Approach to Building Loving Relationships.* London: Piatkus, 2011.

Karney, Benjamin R., and Thomas N. Bradbury. "Neuroticism, Marital Interaction, and the Trajectory of Marital Satisfaction." *Journal of Personality and Social Psychology* 72 (1997): 1075–92.

Kegu, Jessica, and Jason Silverstein. "'Things Are Opening Up': Non-monogamy Is More Common Than You'd Think." CBS News, Oct. 27, 2019. www.cbsnews.com.

Khazan, Olga. "Why Americans Smile So Much." *Atlantic,* June 1, 2017. www.theatlantic.com.

Kubinyi, Enikő, and Lisa J. Wallis. "Dominance in Dogs as Rated by Owners Corresponds to Ethologically Valid Markers of Dominance." *PeerJ* 7 (May 2019).

Łaeng, Bruno, Oddrun Vermeer, and Unni Sulutvedt. "Is Beauty in the Face of the Beholder?" *PLoS ONE* 8, no. 7 (2013).

La Rochefoucauld, François de. *Maxims.* New York: Penguin Classics, 1982.

Layne, Rachel. "Asking Questions Can Get You a Better Job or a Second Date." HBS Working Knowledge, Oct. 30, 2017. hbswk.hbs.edu.

Learning, Lumen, and Diana Lang. "1950s: Harlow, Bowlby, and Ainsworth." Iowa State University Digital Press, May 18, 2020. iastate.pressbooks.pub.

Levine, Amir. *Attached: The New Science of Adult Attachment and How It Can Help You Find—and Keep—Love.* New York: TarcherPerigee, 2012.

Levine, Ethan Czuy, Debby Herbenick, Omar Martinez, and Brian Dodge. "Open Relationships, Nonconsensual Nonmonogamy, and Monogamy Among U.S. Adults: Findings from the 2012 National Survey of Sexual Health and Behavior." *Archives of Sexual Behavior* 47, no. 5 (July 2018).

Lewis, C. S. *A Grief Observed.* London: CrossReach Publications, 2016.

Lewis, Tanya. "IBM's Watson." *Business Insider,* July 22, 2015. www
.businessinsider.com.

Li, Weijian, Yuxiao Chen, Tianran Hu, and Jiebo Luo. "Mining the
Relationship Between Emoji Usage Patterns and Personality." arXiv,
April 14, 2018. arxiv.org.

Lieberman, David J. "Award-Winning Lie Detection Course: Taught by FBI
Trainer." Udemy, Jan. 7, 2021. www.udemy.com.

Martin, Rod A., and Thomas E. Ford. *The Psychology of Humor: An
Integrative Approach.* London: Academic Press, 2018.

Martin, Rod A., Patricia Puhlik-Doris, Jeanette Gray, Kelly Weir, and Gwen
Larsen. "Individual Differences in Uses of Humor and Their Relation
to Psychological Well-Being: Development of the Humor Styles
Questionnaire." *Journal of Research in Personality* 37, no. 1 (2003): 48–75.

Matheson, Rob. "Model Can More Naturally Detect Depression in
Conversations," *MIT News,* Aug. 29, 2018, news.mit.edu.

McCulloch, Gretchen. *Because Internet: Understanding the New Rules of
Language.* Waterville, Maine: Thorndike Press, 2020.

Muise, Amy. "Are You GGG?" *Psychology Today,* Aug. 31, 2012. www
.psychologytoday.com.

Muise, Amy, Emily Impett, Alexsandr Kogan, and Serge Desmarais.
"Keeping the Spark Alive: Being Motivated to Meet a Partner's Sexual
Needs Sustains Sexual Desire in Long-Term Romantic Relationships."
Social Psychology and Personality Science 4, no. 3 (2013).

Nakazato, Taizo. "Striatal Dopamine Release in the Rat During a Cued
Lever-Press Task for Food Reward and the Development of Changes over
Time Measured Using High-Speed Voltammetry." *Experimental Brain
Research* 166, no. 1 (Sept. 2005).

Nin, Anaïs. *The Four-Chambered Heart.* London: Peter Owen, 2004.

Norton, Michael, and Zoë Chance. " 'I Read *Playboy* for the Articles':
Justifying and Rationalizing Questionable Preferences." Harvard Business
School Working Paper 10-018, Sept. 24, 2009. hbswk.hbs.edu.

Norton, Michael, Jeana H. Frost, and Dan Ariely. "Less Is More: The Lure of
Ambiguity, or Why Familiarity Breeds Contempt." *Journal of Personality
and Social Psychology* 92, no. 1 (2007): 97–105.

Oberman, Lindsay M. "Broken Mirrors: A Theory of Autism." *Scientific
American,* June 1, 2007. www.scientificamerican.com.

Ohadi, Jonathan, Brandon Brown, Leora Trub, and Lisa Rosenthal. "I Just
Text to Say I Love You: Partner Similarity in Texting and Relationship
Satisfaction." *Computers in Human Behavior* 78 (Sept. 2017).

OkCupid. "Online Dating Advice: Optimum Message Length." *The
OkCupid Blog,* Medium, Aug. 7, 2019. theblog.okcupid.com.

Patterson, Kerry, Joseph Grenny, Ron McMillan, and Al Switzler. *Crucial Conversations: Tools for Talking When Stakes Are High*. New York: McGraw-Hill, 2012.

Pennebaker, James W. *The Secret Life of Pronouns: What Our Words Say About Us*. New York: Bloomsbury, 2013.

Perel, Esther. *Mating in Captivity*. London: Hodder & Stoughton, 2007.

Plenty of Fish. "Pressure Points Report 2019." Egnyte, 2019. craftedcom .egnyte.com.

Queensland University of Technology. "Online Daters Ignore Wish List When Choosing a Match." *Science News*, Feb. 21, 2017. www.sciencedaily .com.

Reis, Harry, Peter A. Caprariello, Michael R. Maniaci, Paul W. Eastwick, and Eli J. Finkel. "Familiarity Does Indeed Promote Attraction in Live Interaction." *Journal of Personality and Social Psychology* 101, no. 3 (March 2011): 557–70.

Russell, V. Michelle, and James K. McNulty. "Frequent Sex Protects Intimates from the Negative Implications of Their Neuroticism." *Social Psychological and Personality Science* 2 (2011): 220–27.

Schade, Lori, Jonathan Sandberg, Roy Bean, Dean Busby, and Sarah Coyne. "Using Technology to Connect in Romantic Relationships: Effects on Attachment, Relationship Satisfaction, and Stability in Emerging Adults." *Journal of Couple & Relationship Therapy*, 12, no. 4 (2013): 314–38.

Schmitt, David P., and Todd K. Schackelford. "Big Five Traits Related to Short-Term Mating: From Personality to Promiscuity Across 46 Nations." *Evolutionary Psychology* 6, no. 2 (2008).

Schwartz, Barry. "More Isn't Always Better." *Harvard Business Review*, Aug. 1, 2014. hbr.org.

———. *The Paradox of Choice*. New York: Ecco, 2004.

Sheff, Elisabeth. "Updated Estimate of Number of Non-monogamous People in U.S." *Psychology Today*, May 27, 2019. www.psychologytoday .com.

Shpancer, Noam. "How Your Personality Predicts Your Romantic Life." *Psychology Today*, Aug. 2, 2016. www.psychologytoday.com.

Smullyan, Raymond M. *Gödel's Incompleteness Theorems*. New York: Oxford University Press, 2020.

Song, Hongwen, Zhiling Zou, Juan Kou, Yang Liu, Lizhuang Yang, Anna Zilverstand, Federico d'Oleire Uquillas, and Xiaochu Zhang. "Love-Related Changes in the Brain: A Resting-State Functional Magnetic Resonance Imaging Study." *Frontiers in Human Neuroscience* 9, no. 71 (Feb. 2015).

Stoppard, Tom. *Rosencrantz and Guildenstern Are Dead*. Stuttgart: Reclam, 1993.

Strauss, Neil. *The Game*. Edinburgh: Canongate Books, 2016.

Thottam, Isabel. "The History of Online Dating (US)." eHarmony, 2018. www.eharmony.com.

Tolstoy, Leo. *Anna Karenina*. Translated by Richard Pevear and Larissa Volokhonsky. New York: Penguin Books, 2002.

Twain, Mark. *Mark Twain's Notebook*. Edited by Albert Bigelow Paine. London: Hesperides Press, 2006.

Vazire, Simine, and Mitja D. Back. "Knowing Our Personality." In *Handbook of Self-Knowledge,* edited by Simine Vazire and Timothy D. Wilson. New York: Guilford Press, 2012.

Vedantam, Shankar. "The Choices Before Us: Can Fewer Options Lead to Better Decisions?" NPR, May 4, 2020. www.npr.org.

Vonnegut, Kurt. *Deadeye Dick*. New York: Dial Press, 2010.

Ward, Laura. *Famous Last Words: The Ultimate Collection of Finales and Farewells*. London: PRC, 2004.

Westacott, Emrys. "Discover What Plato Means About the Ladder of Love in His 'Symposium.'" ThoughtCo, Aug. 2020. www.thoughtco.com.

Wiederman, Michael W., and Elizabeth Rice Allgeier. "Expectations and Attributions Regarding Extramarital Sex Among Young Married Individuals." *Journal of Psychology and Human Sexuality* 8, no. 3 (1996): 21–35.

Wilde, Oscar. *The Importance of Being Earnest*. London: Renard Press, 2021.

Williams, Alex. "The End of Courtship?" *New York Times,* Jan. 11, 2013. www.nytimes.com.

Wilson, Timothy D. *Redirect: Changing the Stories We Live By*. New York: Back Bay Books, 2015.

———. *Strangers to Ourselves: Discovering the Adaptive Unconscious*. Cambridge, Mass.: Belknap Press of Harvard University Press, 2004.

Wilson, Timothy D., David A. Reinhard, Erin C. Westgate, Daniel T. Gilbert, Nicole Ellerbeck, Cheryl Hahn, Casey L. Brown, and Adi Shaked. "Just Think: The Challenges of the Disengaged Mind." *Science* 345, no. 6192 (July 2004): 75–77.

Wilson, Timothy D., and Daniel T. Gilbert. "Affective Forecasting: Knowing What to Want." *Current Directions in Psychological Science* 14, no. 3 (June 2005).

Yarkoni, Tal. "Personality in 100,000 Words: A Large-Scale Analysis of Personality and Word Use Among Bloggers." *Journal of Research in Personality* 44, no. 3 (2010): 363–73.

Zhao, Alice. "Text Messaging." A Dash of Data, Sept. 5, 2017. adashofdata .com.

DR MIMI WINSBERG is a psychiatrist with twenty-five years of clinical experience. She is a co-founder of the telehealth start-up Brightside and was formerly the on-site psychiatrist at the Facebook Wellness Center. Winsberg appears regularly on Good Morning America, and her work has been featured in *GQ*, *Glamour*, *Fast Company*, *Bloomberg Businessweek* and *Business Insider*. She has a BA in neuroscience from Harvard and trained as a psychiatrist at Stanford. *Speaking in Thumbs* is her first book.

drwinsberg.com
Twitter: @mwinsberg

THE
MARSH
HOUSE

Also by Zoë Somerville

The Night of the Flood

THE
MARSH
HOUSE

Zoë Somerville

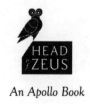

An Apollo Book

9 7 5 3 1 2 4 6 8

A catalogue record for this book is available from
the British Library.

ISBN (HB): 9781838934644
ISBN (XTPB): 9781838934651
ISBN (E): 9781838934675

Typeset by Ed Pickford

Printed and bound in Great Britain by
CPI Group (UK) Ltd, Croydon CR0 4YY

MIX
Paper from
responsible sources
FSC® C171272

Head of Zeus Ltd
5–8 Hardwick Street
London EC1R 4RG
WWW.HEADOFZEUS.COM

For Alex and Jessie

1

From the moment the house were built it looked like it belonged right in its place. Like the shipwreck it was; a boat run aground on the marsh.

It were timber-framed and finished up in brick and flint like most of the houses hereabouts, but it didn't look like none of the others. It were lopsided, curved, with too many small windows, like portholes. They'd built it from the salvaged timbers of the wreck of the Gunwale out in the Pit. Maybe that's where the bad luck come in. They say he built it for her, the young wife he'd brought over from the East, in the hope that she'd not mind being all the way out here on the edge of the creek and the sea, with only the view over the Pit for company; that she'd bear him pink-cheeked babbies reared on saltwater and sky. It didn't quite turn out like that though, did it?

He named it Swalfield House after the land it were on, but it soon became known as the Marsh House. He spent all his money on it – electrics, indoor plumbing, all of it

– but the lights would go on the blink and the drains'd get clogged up, and the black rats'd come off the marsh, looking for food. By the time the daughter was turning from child to adult, the salt and the vapours from the marsh'd got into the wood, making the joints and walls swell and bulge, and the lane got overgrown, and no one come up here no more.

No one had lived in the house for years afore they arrived last winter. Not since all that fuss in thirty-four.

I watched her from my window. Our cottage overlooks the Marsh House, you see. Not so much overlooks as looks up to, across the lane. You can't actually see our cottage from the road, it's hidden, sunk down, practically in the marsh. The back of the cottage is right on the edge of the creek. If you're in the privy you can feel the salt on your nether parts.

There's no other houses on our lane. Like I said, no one come up this way.

It were nearing Christmas when she turned up. The snow hadn't come yet but it were biting cold and I was stood next to the stove, right where I am now. Always was the only place you could be in the cottage and get proper warm. I heard a car engine and this garish orange beast come down the drive – nasty, bright orange, what you couldn't take your eyes off of 'cos everything else is losing colour as it's winter. She's wearing a fur coat and there's a pale, weak-looking child with her and a small, yapping, white dog. I watched her from my window.

The first thing I think is that the fluff-ball dog is going to upset the animals. Especially the hound.

I notice there's a dent in the car bonnet. And her eyes are all puffy and her cheeks are tear-streaked and there are black, spidery lines running down her pretty little face. The other thing I think is – here we go.

I weren't surprised to see her though. Oh no, it was her all right. We'd been waiting for her.

2

The Marsh House

21st December 1962

It came from nowhere. Malorie turned a corner and the road must have been icy because it felt like the car was skating. The low winter sun was in her eyes and she was squinting, holding tight to the steering wheel, leaning forward to try and see below the glaring light. As the road bent to the left, a black shape flashed in her vision, springing in front of the car. She swerved to avoid it – or it might have been that she was skidding already – but it was too late. The hedge smashed into the front of the car. She screamed. Franny shouted something from the back. An almighty crash juddered through her body.

When she opened her eyes, frozen brambles were crushed against the windscreen, icicles of light piercing them. The dog was whimpering. Her gloved hands were still gripping the steering wheel and her cheeks were pressed into the wool. There was a sharp pain in her neck. God, she thought. Oh God. Outside, a robin fluttered down to the hedge, so close she could see its black, beady eye and the feathers on its red breast. Franny? She turned, a vision of blood rising before her eyes – and she wasn't there. But the sound of Larry whining rose from below and then she heard –

'Mummy?'

Hoisting herself out of her seat, she twisted around and leaned over and there they were, her daughter and the dog, squashed into the footwell.

'Are you all right? Can you get up?'

From the gloom behind the front seats, the whites of Franny's eyes stared up at her. She would tell Tony about this and Malorie wanted to scream again.

She breathed very slowly through her nose and reached down with an arm to touch Franny, who shrunk deeper into the footwell. Larry began to bark.

'All right, it's all right. Lift him up, Franny.'

'He's heavy,' she said, but she did it and Malorie nearly wept in sheer relief.

Franny's eyes were red-rimmed and a tiny trail of snot dripped down from her nose. She was eight years old and had a permanent cold. Malorie gave her daughter a smile, but Franny stared back, her small face hard to read.

Malorie tried to reverse. The front wheels spun and the car didn't move. Clambering across the gearstick, she opened the passenger door and almost fell out onto the ground. It was quiet on the road, no one in sight, just the violent sun blaring out from above the hedge and the huge pale-blue sky pressing down on her. The front of the bonnet was badly dented, as if a heavy animal had smashed into it. But there was no sign of anything. Pulling a flyaway wisp of hair out of her face, she inspected the front wheel and under the car. She must have injured – killed? – something. But whatever it was had gone. What on earth could it have been? Searching her memory she thought she'd seen a black animal – not a bird – too large to be a cat, too dark to be a hare.

'What was that?' Franny had somehow managed to get out of the car. Malorie had slid down the side of the car and was slumped against it, the ground already hard with the coming night-frost through her skirt.

'I don't know,' she said.

Perhaps if she just pretended all this wasn't happening it would go away. It was unfair, all of it – the argument with Tony; his affair; the hideous car he'd bought her; the bloody dog he'd given Franny instead of a sibling or friends; Franny's silence, all the way from London. The cold. The emptiness in her head. Worst of all – that she'd brought them here, of all the places in the world. Here, near where she'd grown up and where both her parents were buried. But the flat was full of Tony's things. It was his flat and she could no longer bear to be there. And the house – this house – had been somewhere to go.

At the hospice, it had smelt of mildew. She'd wanted to open the windows, to let in the fresh air, but it was October and raining. Condensation trickled down the windowpanes and pooled on the windowsills. She didn't want anything to do with this deathly place. She just wanted to get it over with. There had been a phone call the week before.

Can you come up, Mrs Cavendish? Your mother is asking for you.

Are you sure?

Her mother was very small and white in the bed, a shrivelled arm attached to a drip.

'Oh, you're here. Mary.'

'No, Mum, it's Malorie.'

'No one ever comes to see me.' The corners of her eyes were wet, and Malorie couldn't remember if she'd ever seen her mother cry.

'Mary. You were such a scrap of a thing. Come here. Come closer. I promised your father I'd – Oh –'

Her face was distorted in agony. She looked so old and helpless. Malorie knew she couldn't be that old, but the cancer had aged her, rotting her from the inside out so now she looked shrunken, as if the life had already been sucked out of her. Her mother's thin hand reached out and snatched at hers. Her voice scraped.

'Take this. Take it.' She stuffed a small plasticky square like a photograph into her hand.

'I can't tell you. It's too late. I can't, Harry, I can't.' She looked up at Malorie with a curdled expression of shame mixed with resentment. Her mother's brain was so addled with the morphine, she was talking to her dead husband.

Malorie looked down at what her mother had thrust into her hand. It was a photograph. A black and white square picture of a house. It seemed familiar but she didn't know why.

'I gave the rest to that nice man.'

'Who? What man?'

'Your nice man. He was always better than me.'

'Who – *Tony?*'

But she seemed to be talking to herself rather than to her daughter.

7

'He found it easier than I did. It should have been him that carried on. He was better with you than me. He was a good man, Harry. He was a good father.'

'Dad? Did Dad want me to have this, Mother? Why did Dad want me to have it? Have I been here?'

But her mother had slipped back into a morphine-induced stupor.

'Coffee?' Tony was in the doorway with a cup of the vile liquid that passed for coffee at the hospice. At his voice, her mother's eyelids flickered.

'I'll stay with her for a while,' he said. 'You go and have a break.'

'Yes,' she said, 'all right.' In her hand she still had the photograph.

Why hadn't her mother just talked to her after Dad died? Why all the bloody cloak and dagger? So there was some shameful family secret. So what? She didn't care. Her dad was dead. It didn't matter anymore. She could feel herself seething, boiling with a rage that seemed to have no source and no outlet.

Tony had been evasive on the way home. No, her mother hadn't said anything.

'But she said she had. She said she'd given you something.'

'Oh that. It was just some papers, Mal. I haven't looked through them, they're in the suitcase. She was hardly making much sense, was she?' He put his arm around her. 'Now isn't a good time.'

Malorie had sulked, angry at her mother for making her feel bad, angry at her for making her angry. Then her mother had died. And by then, she was consumed with the death of her marriage. The funeral had only been in November, a washed-out, sepia-tinted day. It had been like the negative of a photograph, just the shadows left.

She had felt – what? It was not exactly that she wanted something to fill the emptiness, that was too simple, but the image of that house wouldn't leave her alone. She'd wished her dad had been there to talk to. Her dad had wanted her to have the photograph. It must have had some meaning for him, something that her mother hadn't wanted her to know about. On the back of the photograph in old-fashioned writing, it said *The Marsh House, Stiffkey*. No date. The front showed an awkward, asymmetrical house with a porch in the middle and a gable at one end, a drive curling up to it, the foreground in shadow and dark trees on either side. It was a village on the North Norfolk coast, she knew that, but nothing else. She had no idea what connection – if any – there was to her parents. She'd thought they were both from Norwich. But she could no longer ask them.

In the fogged days after the funeral, she called up an agency that dealt with rental properties. It seemed hardly likely to be available, but she kept trying until she found someone who said yes, it was empty and she could rent it if she really wanted to. The way they'd said it made it sound like madness. At first, she'd only meant to go and have a look, but an idea began to form and to grow until it became everything she wanted. They would go there, for Christmas. They would have a proper family Christmas, she and Franny. She had to do something, something *good*. Away from the grime and grit of London, and the stale, poisoned air of her failed marriage. They would be able to breathe, to stretch, to be together.

She hadn't meant for it to be like this.

She felt a hand on her knee. It was Franny, with the dog in her arms. She looked so alarmed at the sight of her mother, crushed, weepy and broken, sitting in the middle of a country road, that it made Malorie laugh.

'No one's dead,' she said, and a voice in her head whispered, *Yes they are*. But she drew Franny's stiff little body to her and piled them back in. She ignored Franny's mumbling. By the time she'd heaved and shoved the car back on the road, the sky had turned a deep fuchsia pink. 'Look at the colour!' she cried. The house was not much further along the road. The car turned into the lane, and on the left-hand side, the trees rose straight and dark like sentinels. In her imagination, the sunlight filtered through those trees and she'd walk under the branches through a tunnel of bright green light. Near the end of the lane, the house was on the left, the only house. The lane continued on to the marsh. Into her head came an image of the house glowing with light, inviting her in. She leaned forward in her seat, suddenly desperate to see it.

3

The Sampler

There were no lights. It was a dark presence. Malorie had a sudden, crushing sense that she'd made a mistake. The house's many small eyes – she counted eight windows at the front at least – were blinded and in the gloom, the flint and brick face dull and forbidding. It was the time of day, perhaps. A jutting-out porch, concealing the front door, gaped dark like an open mouth. She switched off the engine and nightfall came rushing in. A dog was barking madly from across the lane somewhere. The back of her neck prickled as though she were being watched, and she turned to see who it was. She thought something moved in the trees across the lane. Grabbing her coat, she got out of the car to look, but the trees gave nothing away.

She tried to remember what the man at the agency had said. Was he supposed to meet her here? It was getting dark; soon, it would be even colder. They had to get inside. There must be a key.

'Mummy? What are you doing?'

Franny was standing behind her, with the dog in her arms.

'I need to find the key.'

'Where's the sea?' whined Franny. 'You said it was the seaside.'

'It's nearby,' she said.

Where would it be? Under a doormat? There wasn't one. Next to the door was an old terracotta pot. It would be there. It was – a rusty old key underneath the damp pot. Her shoulders relaxed. It was going to be all right.

The door was a heavy wooden one, with a small grubby window and a tarnished knocker in the shape of an anchor, which gleamed dully in the dying light. The long key stuck slightly in the lock and for a horrible moment she thought it wouldn't turn. The fluttering of panic came again but she made herself breathe out. She tried again. It turned and clicked and the door swung open. It was not much warmer inside. A smell of dust and age wafted over her. There was electricity though, thank God. She flicked the switch and the pale glow of the old-fashioned brass sconces flickered and shone on the worn carpet, low panelling and flowery wallpaper. On a dark-wood side table with ornate legs was an upright telephone with a separate earpiece – like something from an antiques shop. At least they'd entered the twentieth century. But further inspection revealed that the house had got stuck some years before. The ceilings were low and beamed and the wallpaper, densely covered in a pattern of twisting vines with little yellow flowers and green leaves, was peeling at the edges. From the walls came the musty smell of lack of use and damp, and Malorie wondered when the windows had last been opened. She made her way through to the kitchen at the back of the house. It contained ancient cupboards, an old gas range and a cracked butler sink under a small window. The clouded pane looked out onto a long garden and Malorie could tell, even in the gloom, that the marsh was just there, beyond a low wall at the end. Tomorrow, they would go to the marsh. They would walk along the paths by the creeks and see the sleek heads of seals.

'I'm hungry,' said Franny, standing in the kitchen doorway, still holding the dog, whose muzzle was buried in her duffle coat.

Malorie sent her to explore and busied herself lighting the gas oven (she found matches in a drawer and thanked God – or was it the agency? – again) and putting the kettle on the hob. On a shelf above the oven were dusty brown bottles, like the ones you'd find in a chemist's. The liquid inside one was dark and treacly. She picked it up and opened the stopper but it smelt rancid and she quickly put the stopper back in. There was no toaster but she'd brought some sliced bread and she could toast it under the grill. She could cope. But there was no milk and no butter and for a moment, she felt herself waver and rock in the middle of the cold floor.

Their supper was two mugs of black tea and toast with jam but no butter, and there was no coal to make a fire so it was freezing too. Franny made a face at the cup of tea and left it, but she ate the toast, feeding the crusts to the dog who sat begging by her chair.

'Mummy, if we're having Christmas here, we need decorations and a tree.'

Today was what? The twenty-first. Midwinter. Tomorrow was Saturday. All the shops would be shut on Sunday and then it was Christmas Eve. She couldn't bear the thought of attempting anything then. And if Tony did come and there was nothing, the turn in his mouth would be another failure. They would have to go tomorrow.

'And Mummy,' said Franny, 'when's Daddy coming?'

'Soon,' she said.

'Tomorrow?'

'Not tomorrow. Sunday. Or Monday. Soon.' It was only two days before but she could hardly remember what had been said. She'd snatched at his arm but he'd pushed past her. *I need to go. Go then.* And he had. Gone to her, the girl at the club. She wondered how old she was, whether she was the age Malorie had been when she'd met him, a young body unmarked by childbirth. He hadn't come back and she'd lied to Franny, told her he was working.

Franny looked like she would cry. She had grey circles under her eyes. Her daughter had nightmares, and rarely slept through a night.

'Bedtime,' said Malorie with false cheeriness, and took her upstairs. Larry padded up close behind them. The ceilings were low there too, and the landing seemed to curl upwards. The walls on the landing were panelled in dark wood, like the ground floor, but here it went all the way up to the ceiling, which made it feel like being in an upturned boat.

'This is my room,' said Franny, 'I already found it.'

It was a child's room with dusky pink wallpaper and a single bed with a pink-sprigged bedspread. The tiny, low window overlooked the lane.

'Look at this,' she said, and pointed above the bed.

Nailed to the wall was a yellowing sampler, depicting a house with the tufts of marram grass behind and the sea beyond. It was the house they were in, the Marsh House, beautifully stitched in grey for the flint and red for the bricks. Malorie craned to get a closer look and drew in her breath. In front of the house was an image of a strange woman, standing beside a large wolf-like dog with yellow eyes. And next to her was a young girl with long black plaits and tiny green crosses for eyes, holding a small chestnut-brown dog in her arms. On the other side of the house, a short, dark-haired woman with her mouth turned down. At the top, a motto was stitched in red thread: *May I strive for innocence and truth my every action guide. And guard my inexperienced youth from arrogance & pride.*

At the bottom, Malorie read aloud, 'Worked by Rosemary Wright, aged eight.'

She thought of her fair, plump father and it seemed a stretch to think these people were any relation of his. But she tried to tamp down the initial disappointment. The connection to the house could be anything. He could have worked here, he could have been a friend. There had to be something.

Franny had a curious smile on her face. 'She was my age. And she had a dog like Larry too. It's this house, isn't it?'

'Yes, it must be,' said Malorie, relieved at least that Franny seemed happier.

Franny didn't complain about brushing her teeth or her long hair. She took the pill for her nerves without complaint, and went to bed clutching her teddy bear, Frederick, quite compliant. She had Malorie's colouring: wan with dark hair that looked copper when the light caught it. People always commented on the two of them together – 'Oh, she's a spit,' and so on. But it wasn't really true, it was just the hair that tricked people, and the winter-sallow skin which turned a muddy brown in the summer. In reality, Malorie had sludgy-grey eyes and small features in a round face that made her look childish, and her hair was dull and dead straight. She had it backcombed up and pinned on the top, but it was hard to do anything with it. People always thought she was younger than she was, but her daughter looked older than her years. Franny's eyes were green and searching and there was a frown-crease between her eyebrows that Malorie wished she could wipe away.

Larry was curled up in a ball of cream fur at the end of the narrow bed. At least Franny had the dog for company, and for warmth.

On her own in the kitchen she opened a bottle of sherry she'd brought for Christmas, poured herself a glass then sat, huddled in the fur coat Tony had bought her, drinking the sherry and chain-smoking the last of her Rothmans. The small window reflected the kitchen lamplight back at her. Beyond it was darkness, the emptiness of the countryside, only the house between her daughter and all that lay beyond. The vastness of the unknown – her isolation – she felt as something physical, a great crushing embrace of darkness, and she had to rest her head on the table. She imagined reaching into her handbag for the Luminal the doctor had prescribed, swallowing one down with a draught of sherry. The ease of it, the relief. But she'd forced herself to stop all that. She'd begun reaching for them too much, needing them, sinking back down into the stupor she'd been in when Franny was small.

A few years ago, when she was diagnosed with 'nerve strain', the doctor had assumed it was her father's death that had been the catalyst but it went back further than that. She simply did not have the gift of happiness. She was afraid that if she started taking them again, she'd never stop. She was too tired to move from the kitchen, too tired for anything, and after three glasses of the sickly sherry, she was even too tired to drink. Maybe she'd be able to sleep tonight after the long drive.

The back of her neck tingled. There was something – just out of her hearing – that she couldn't quite place. She held herself still and closed her eyes; strained all her other senses. Nothing. It was deathly quiet, that was all. She was so unused to the country, it was unnerving. If she concentrated very hard she could just hear the creaks of the walls as they shifted and settled and a faint wind breathing in and out of the chimneys. Then a scratch; a thin, scratching sound coming from above. Mice.

In the bedroom at the back of the house, Malorie rubbed her feet together in the lumpy cold bed and tried to dig into the scratchy sheets to gain some warmth. There was another, larger room – she'd opened the door to see – but decorating cloths covered the furniture and what light there was didn't seem to penetrate it. It felt more like a funeral parlour than a bedroom so she'd taken this east-facing one instead. Eventually she gave up trying to warm her frozen feet and found a pair of socks to wear and a heavy wool blanket to cover herself with. It was not so bad. They were here. They'd made it. If they could have this one thing, a family Christmas, it would be all right. It would be different in the morning. Tomorrow would be better.

That night she was woken from a dream where the figures in the picture were alive and their faces changed into hers and Franny's. She and Franny walked in the dream down to the marsh.

A gull cawed and woke her. Her feet were cold again. The curtains were white and thin and the shimmer of the moon gave them a glassy sheen. There was a noise in the dark, like a child crying. It must be the gulls in the dream; she was still half asleep. There it was again. The window banged against its frame. It was the wind. She closed her eyes, tried to sink back into sleep, but the sound came again and then she was awake, sat upright. It must be Franny. Clutching her dressing gown tight around her, she crept out. On the landing, she paused: the crying had stopped. But she should check anyway. She opened the door and stepped in. The moonlight was stronger in here and gave a surreal quality to the room, like a room in a painting of a dream. Franny and Larry were both asleep but her daughter was twisting in the bed, moaning. This was what she must have heard. As she turned to go, her eyes were drawn to the strange sampler above the bed. It was half-lit by the moonlight. A cloud must have passed over the moon because a shadow crossed the cloth and the figures almost appeared to move. Then the moon was blocked again and the room was returned to shadow. She shivered and rubbed her eyes.

Back in the chill of the empty bed, Malorie couldn't sleep. The wind had dropped and now she could hear a rustling from above. It was probably the mice again. The old woman in the sampler flickered across her brain. As her mind reached for stillness and quiet, all she could see was the large black dog with the stitched yellow crosses for eyes, like a creature from a nightmare.

4

Temperature was dropping. You could see it in the birds'
puffed-up feathers, in the scurrying of the squirrels, and in
the rats, scuttling for warmth in the rafters of the house.
She wouldn't like that, I'm thinking. All them nasty, bloated
city rats give a person funny ideas about animals. Our rats
are small and black, not like those fearsome beaver rats
what escaped from the fur farm running mad over Norfolk,
they're little and harmless. Mostly, anyway.

5

Stiffkey

22nd December

Through the ice-crusted window, Malorie could see there was nothing but a thick grey mist. She pressed her forehead against the pane and closed her eyes. Her throat was sore and at the back of her head was a dull ache. She must not succumb to despair. After scraping at the ice on the window with her fingernails, she wiped a patch of condensation with the sleeve of her dressing gown and peered through the smear of wet droplets. Across the lane from the house and sunk in the mist, there were the shadows of trees, but apart from that it seemed deserted. Around the edge of the garden, the black arms of bare trees and a dark clump of firs. The mist merged with a dull sky and nothing else was visible. She'd imagined flinging open the window onto a sparkling view of the sea but it might as well not have been there. She cranked open the old window and sniffed the air. Yes, the sea was near all right. There was a faint tang of salt and a wet smell of damp earth and something else sharp that she couldn't name. Opening her mouth she tried to suck it in and swallowed a mouthful of moisture and seasalt. A low black shape moved in the distance along the lane. Was it the dog she'd heard last night? A taller figure moved behind the animal. A brown, stout person in some kind of hat. She wanted to call out but a gust of wind slammed the window shut and she jumped back. It only just missed smacking into her nose. When she looked again, the figure and the animal were gone.

From downstairs came the sound of Franny crooning to her dog. Her poor, lonely girl. It had been Tony's idea to buy Franny a pet, and Malorie, unused to animals, had resisted. But now she was glad. The little dog was the only being Franny warmed to. Malorie had a memory of her daughter thrashing in her sleep but wasn't sure if she'd dreamed it. She should try to find some friends for her. There must be village children. But she already knew this was hopeless – the idea of her silent little girl making friends with anyone was laughable. At the school in London they said she was 'shy' and 'well behaved'. She 'keeps herself to herself'. She'd felt as if their eyes contained a rebuke for not producing a happy, carefree child, for leaving Franny without siblings; their mouths set hard against her as a parent, that her daughter was strange and it was her fault. Tony told her she was being ridiculous; no one thought that. But she didn't trust anything he said to her.

The argument repeated itself. Another child, another baby. But she'd been ill, she couldn't cope, her father died. There was always something. And then, she began to suspect he was sleeping with other women. She had withdrawn even further into her private hurt. It was too late now.

'I might go to Norfolk for Christmas,' she'd said. He hadn't cared. He'd stopped listening to her years before. He'd care now, she thought.

She tried to picture his face when he found the flat empty and his daughter gone. It gave her a nasty bubble of pleasure. He would mind about Franny. Well, sod him. She saw him revving the engine of his Austin and speeding off back to the flat above the club. And the curvaceous body of Barbara. He would call her *Babs*, the way he called her *Mal*. Babs's beautiful body. She put her hands to her forehead and squeezed. This was no good. She shouldn't think about it.

And she was here now, wasn't she? She'd done it. Got out of London. Away from him and his blatant lies, from the empty flat and the pills. It wasn't at all how she'd imagined, but nothing was. Not her marriage, motherhood, her work (what work? There was no work. All her secretarial contacts had faded away since Franny). Her parents, both now dead. Her daughter. All of it had ended up somehow wrong. Defective. Broken. She drove her nails into her palms to staunch the flow of inky blackness cascading through her head. She would not take a pill. She would not. The window banged and she started. She hadn't put the catch back on.

Never mind the mist and the cold, they would take Larry for a walk down to the sea.

She dressed quickly in the freezing room, thinking of how they'd need food supplies and coal for the fire and how she should have thought of all of this before she'd piled them into the car in London. On the landing she hesitated. There was something about the night that she only half remembered. She looked into the pink bedroom but neither Franny nor the dog were there. Above the bed, the odd sampler. There was the severe woman, there was the old lady with the fierce-looking dog and there was the little girl with the plaits holding a book. Malorie's head hurt. She squeezed her eyes shut. It was just a creepy old picture. She needed a cup of tea.

On the right of the hallway as she came down the stairs was the living room, on the left, an empty room. The door to the living room was ajar and inside she found Franny curled up on a tatty old sofa, swaddled in blankets, reading a book, with Larry at her feet.

Franny looked up at her with reproach. 'I'm hungry.'

'Right, darling, yes I'm sure you are. What time is it?'

Franny shrugged.

'Mummy,' she said, 'what about a Christmas tree? We have to get a tree. Daddy would get me a tree.' In London, they had a small fake tree that Tony had bought in Harrods. It had been stupidly expensive but Franny loved it. Malorie knew his family had always had huge, real trees but he said they couldn't fit one into their little flat so this was the next best thing. Her parents, in their Norwich suburb, had always thought the tree they'd bought from Woolworths was perfectly good enough, thank you. Malorie had always wanted a real one. It was part of her vision of a perfect life. In her childhood books, children gathered around a towering, glittering tree. She somehow felt that if she could achieve this image – of them sat round the Christmas fir in their dressing gowns, the children's stockings over the fire – then she would have created something good. For this vision, she had to have a real tree. That was it: she could cut one down. There were loads of firs along the edge of the property. No one would notice if she chopped down a baby one.

'Mummy?'

'I'll get you a tree,' she said, smiling.

The kitchen was at the back of the house, cold on the flagstone floor, even through her socks and slippers. The clock on the wall said nine o'clock. Time stretched and warped here: she had somehow slept in. Larry followed her through, whining, and she opened the back door to let him out. The air was heavy and damp with the mist. At the threshold, the little dog bristled and hesitated, uncertain about the grey-shrouded garden, but Malorie gave him a shove with her foot. Outside, he began to bark. He seemed to be barking at the hedge and while she was looking at it, something dark slunk along the bottom. She caught a glimpse of a long tail – a rat – and shuddered. She doubted Larry would do much about it but she shooed him further out into the garden anyway, relieved that he was here.

Back in the living room, with two more mugs of black tea and toast with jam but no butter ('I'll buy some today, Franny, I promise'), she remembered the lack of a fire. She swallowed down the sob rising in her throat and washed down the bitter tea with a mouthful of strawberry jam.

As they were putting their coats on, the ancient-looking phone rang out in the hall, startling them both. Her first thought was Tony, and her heart leapt. He was going to say sorry, he'd made a mistake, he loved her. But she hadn't left a phone number, she didn't even have one. He had no idea where they were. The phone kept ringing, echoing around them, mocking her.

'Are you going to answer it?'

'Yes, yes,' she said, unhappily. She put the earpiece to her ear. 'Hello?' There was a knocking sound at the other end. 'Hello?' she said again, but the knocking sound was replaced with the monotonous dialling tone. 'It must be a bad line,' she said, and replaced the earpiece on the stand.

It was warmer outside, though the frost crackled under their feet and their breath blew white in the air. Through the frost, weeds poked, and in the thin misty, winter daylight she could see that there were tiles missing from the roof and cracks in some of the windows. The pale grey flint blended with the mist and it seemed as if the house had somehow grown here organically. She looked up at it from the same vantage point as the photographer must have done. But the photograph appeared to have been taken in the summer and the neglect, if it were visible then, had been disguised by the glow of sunlight. Now the house revealed the extent of its dilapidation. There was broken guttering, with weeds growing out of it. The bricks crumbled like flaky skin. One of the windowpanes was cracked, the wood of the frames speckled black with rot. It needed light and warmth and people. Not the dead of winter.

She glanced at the hideous car. The vivid orange had appealed at first. Why not? It looked jaunty and fun in London. But it was incongruous here, like something from a modern, gaudy world thrust into an old one. And the dent looked worse in the day – an ugly mark of something wrong. The car windows were thick with frost. She should wipe it down, scrape off the ice. But how far was the village? It couldn't be far. The dog needed a walk, and she needed more cigarettes on top of everything else. She felt inside her purse with pink-cold fingers. She had the week's housekeeping money and some left over from last week. It would have to do.

'Come on, Fran, we're going to walk into the village and get our Christmas supplies. It'll be an adventure.' She could ask in the village if anyone had known her father.

Franny squeezed her forehead in a frown but nodded. She was not lazy, you could say that.

As they were leaving, Malorie heard the same howl of a wolf from across the road. It must be the dog she'd seen earlier that morning, and if it was a dog there must be someone living there. Crossing the lane, she remembered the figure in the sampler with the wolf-like dog and half expected to see an old woman and a black dog emerging from the trees. It didn't look like there was anything there, just a dense, high hedge of knotted ivy and hawthorn. But then she saw there was a gap in the hedge, a small iron gate overgrown with ivy, and a narrow path that led to a squat brick single-storey dwelling, more of a hovel than a cottage, with a roof hunched so low it looked as if it would collapse in on itself. There was no sign of life or light through the thick, dark grime on the small window. Yet something about it made her want to turn around immediately and rush away. Its misshapen, lumpen form seemed to be scowling at her. She tried to laugh.

'*Mum.*' It was Franny, bored of waiting.

Malorie finally turned her back on the cottage. She was strangely relieved when they were out of sight of it down the lane.

At the end of the muddy lane a flint and brick wall appeared on the left, and behind it there was an old disused chapel from early in the century. The broken glass windows stared blankly. The mist kept low for the entire walk to the village. They trudged along the road that linked the village with Wells on one side and Blakeney on the other, dissecting the village between marsh and field, and only the dull brown of the low winter hedges gave any colour to the day. It was a respite to get to the village and see something other than the relentless grey-white mist. The village seemed to consist of an old whitewashed pub called the Townsend Arms and further along, on a little street just before a bridge over a low river, a shop that also functioned as a Post Office, judging by the sign outside. Stiffkey General Store and, underneath, a smaller sign that read Prop. G. Bayfield. In the leaded bay window of the shop, old boxes of Persil and packets of Bovril were stacked neatly, faded to pastel colours from years on display, under enamel signs for Fry's Chocolate and Capstan cigarettes. It was like a shop from the sodding war. From before the sodding war. The bell rang as they entered and there was a fluster of crashing and a voice shouted, 'Coming!' from the back. Out of the rear emerged a red-faced young woman of about Malorie's age, though it was hard to tell as she was wearing a blue headscarf and her brown hair was curled in what Malorie thought of as an old-fashioned style. Poor thing, stuck out here.

'Oh!' said the girl, her full mouth in an oval of surprise. 'I thought you were someone else. You must be the visitors with the orange car. What can I get for you?'

Malorie suddenly felt the stupidity of what she was trying to do. What would she do when the housekeeping ran out? Ask Tony for more? A bubble of panic tightened her chest and she had to breathe out and compose herself before she spoke. She consulted the list she'd hastily made that morning and the pretty girl (Malorie decided she was younger than she was, it was the get-up that made her look older) worked through it, slicing and cutting and stacking up tins. There was a tiny meat and cheese counter and Malorie bought a few slices. There was no Stilton, only Cheddar and Red Leicester but that would do. There was no ham or pâté, only luncheon meat, and the bread was rock hard. But they had some margarine and fatty-looking sausages, some dirty carrots and potatoes and the girl said she'd ask her father about a turkey or a goose. She disappeared out the back of the shop. In the gloom, Malorie could just about make out a short man with a cap and a gruff voice with the slow rhythm of Norfolk. In front of the counter, Franny stood sullenly next to her, scuffing her shoes on the sawdust floor.

'He'll see about killing one for you,' the shop girl said, returning from a door at the back. Malorie winced at the thought. She prayed the man would pluck it as well. It wasn't something she could face. Franny sniffed loudly.

'Blow your nose,' Malorie said under her breath, thrusting a hanky at her.

The shop girl leaned over the counter and said kindly, 'What's your name then? What about some cochies. Would you like some?'

Franny peered up at her and said, 'Frances,' very quietly. The young woman chuckled and got up on her ladder to fetch the sweet jars down from the top shelves. She handed Franny a barley sugar and then put a handful of other sweets in a cone twist.

'Thank you,' her daughter said to the shop girl, then to Malorie, 'Can I go outside?'

She waved her out.

The girl was wrapping the last of the 'provisions' in paper. Malorie realised there was no point asking the girl whether she'd known a Harry Skinner – she was too young – but she wanted to ask her about the house and if there was a woman living in the cottage with a large dog. She was framing the words when the girl spoke.

'You're up at the Marsh House, aren't you? There aren't been anyone living there since before I was born. Mother says it's a rum place. All kinds of funny things going on up there.'

Malorie was going to ask – what things? But the girl laughed at her expression.

'Ah, it's all tales, I reckon. People round here love a story. You hear her last night? She was wailing something rotten.'

'Hear who? I think the wind woke me up, but I went back to sleep.'

'Weren't no wind. That was the lost girl. Girl that got stuck out in the roke.'

'The roke?'

'Fog. Sea mist. She screams louder when the roke's in.'

'Who does?'

'The girl. Nancy her name was. My mum says she was out cockling with the others far out on the Blacknock sandbank on the Freshes – best place for Stewkey Blues – when the roke came in and she got separated. Mud's treacherous out there. Tide had turned, you see. She started to scream. All the fishermen, all of the village folk heard her blarring but no one could find her in the fog and the mud. Body was found the next day, seaweed in her open mouth.'

'That's horrible.'

Malorie had hardly understood half of the words the girl used but she felt the grimness of the story. She thought about the strange noises in the night and felt goosebumps prickle on her skin. It had been the *wind*, she wanted to say to her.

'Anyone told you about what happened at that house yet?'

'No,' said Malorie. The girl was annoying her. Why didn't she just spit it out?

'Yeah, probably all nonsense, but my dad says there was people what died there.'

Malorie smiled to herself. For God's sake, people died everywhere.

'Thank you for all of this,' she said, shaking herself out of this conversation. 'I'd better be going. And the turkey or the goose . . . I don't think my husband will be able—'

'Dad'll come round with something day after tomorrow. Christmas Eve. He can slaughter one today. He'll be round Christmas Eve.'

'Thank you,' she said. 'And I forgot to ask about coal or logs. I'm so sorry.'

The girl nodded. 'We'll see what we can do and drop some round. Right cold it is.'

She should go now but she had one more question. 'Can I ask – is there an old woman with a black dog who lives on the lane?'

The girl laughed again. 'Maybe it were Black Shuck,' she said, rolling her eyes comically. 'No, I'm only kidding. I wouldn't worry about that old one if I were you. She's always been around here. Belongs to the place, you see.'

Malorie didn't see, but Franny was waiting outside.

The bell rang as they left the shop and the girl called out, 'Snow's coming though. Do you watch out!'

As the three of them – Malorie, Franny and the dog – walked away from the shop and the village, she felt her back tingle with the gaze of the girl. She was relieved to get away. It wasn't fair but she was fighting against an uncomfortable sense of revulsion towards the girl. And with all the talk of *black shuck* and *roke* and hideous noises in the night, she'd forgotten to ask about the figures on the sampler.

She tore open the first of the two packets of cigarettes she'd bought and smoked one, inhaling the smoke deep into her lungs as they walked, adding her own curls of grey to the mist.

6

I was back at the stove when they returned. They looked lost. Especially her, the mother. There was something wrong with her. She didn't look like a grown woman, though I knew she must be with the child how old she was. She looked sort of stunted, like a tree that's not had enough light and air. Something'd got hold of her and stuck her in the city where she couldn't breathe. The child though, the child was sharp. She heard what the girl didn't tell her, she saw what she wasn't supposed to see. It was the mother who was looking for something but it was the daughter who'd find it. I wondered how long it would take her.

7

The Attic

When they got back to the house there was a small pile of cut logs by the front door. Malorie didn't understand how the grocer could have got here so quickly. There'd only been a couple of cars on the road, but it could have been him. She looked across the lane expecting someone to be watching but there was no one out there, just the dark hedge. Still, it was a relief to have the logs.

In the kitchen, she put her transistor on the windowsill and fiddled with the tuning knobs through the frequencies. Snatches of the shipping forecast broke through the static then disappeared again. Bells chimed, a Christmas carol burst through the hiss and faded away. Then a man's voice, suddenly loud and serious in the kitchen.

Snow is expected in most parts of Britain. Falls are likely to be moderate or heavy in Eastern regions with strong to gale-force easterly winds. Widespread frost is expected tonight.

The girl was right. It could be a White Christmas. Her heart jolted. It would be magical – a Christmas Franny would remember forever.

After a meagre lunch of yesterday's bread spread with margarine and some of the cheese and luncheon meat from the village shop, Franny disappeared to the pink bedroom, Larry close behind. Malorie set about finally stoking the fire into life. The cold was becoming unbearable and the two of them were each wearing a vest, a blouse and two jumpers. She managed to coax some pale, weak flames that gave off no warmth.

If Tony were here, he could have at least *helped* her make a fire – but the thought of that was quite absurd. Tony Cavendish had never laid a fire in his life – he had people to do that for him. And her parents had always had a gas fire. She was just going to have to do it on her own.

Flames were finally licking the wood, smoke was rising and Malorie was holding her hands to the faint warmth, when Franny came in. 'Mummy, I found a secret door.'

She followed her up to the landing. There was a little door in the panelling at the end of the landing that Malorie hadn't registered before. She must have looked at that wall several times and missed it. The door opened onto another narrow, winding staircase and Franny disappeared up this. She stood looking at the bottom of the stairs that led up to darkness, remembering the sound of rodents scuttling the night before.

'Come on, Mummy, come up!' came Franny's voice from above.

Crouching, Malorie squeezed up the tiny staircase. Her head came out into the low attic of the house, dim and dusty but neatly piled with old trunks. She listened carefully but couldn't hear any scraping or rustling. Her eyes fell on a wooden cot, the white paint peeling.

'Over here,' said Franny, and Malorie snapped out of her daze. She followed her daughter to the middle of the attic where you could see the misty sky through the cracks in the roof. Franny was digging in an open trunk. 'These are pretty.' On a bed of straw nestled beautiful tree decorations of angels and stars and apples and lanterns. Even in the dim light they shone, and where they caught the thin misty rays from outside they glittered.

Malorie picked up each piece and held it in the palm of her hand, feeling the delicacy of each one in wonder. They were made of fragile glass and painted in glorious bright colours of green and gold and red.

From another trunk Franny drew out a wooden box carved in an intricate leaf pattern. 'Look!' she said. Malorie itched to grab it from her and open it but she made herself wait. When Franny passed it to her, Malorie gasped in delight. Inside was an entire nativity scene made of wood, tiny and delicately carved, each feature carefully scored. There was a wooden Mary, a Joseph with a beard, and a baby Jesus the size of her smallest fingernail. There was a sheep and a donkey and a cow and a cradle with wisps of real straw and of course a stable, as lovingly carved as everything else. It was perfect.

'Mummy, look at this. Look what I've found!' Franny spoke from the other end of the attic, where she was tucked under the low slope of the eave. Malorie had been so intent on the nativity scene that she hadn't even been aware of where her daughter had gone. There was an enthusiasm in Franny's voice that she hadn't heard for a long time.

Sideways and bent-backed, Malorie edged along the attic and saw that she was holding up a piece of paper. It was a cutting from an old newspaper with brown, curled edges.

'Look,' said Franny again. 'It's the girl, it's the girl in the picture. Rosemary.'

Malorie took it out of Franny's hand. The cutting showed a photograph of a young woman staring into the camera, hair tucked under an ugly cloche hat and dark smudges around her eyes. It was a mug shot, Malorie thought, a defiant stare at whoever was taking the photograph – at the world. Underneath, the caption said *Rosemary Wright aged 19*, but there was no corresponding newspaper report. The girl's eyes seemed to look into her own as if she knew her.

'Where did you find this?'

'In here.'

It was a small, beaten-up, brown leather suitcase. Inside it was empty apart from a mess of paper, but behind the elasticated cotton pouch for underwear, Malorie thought there was the shadow of something. She stayed silent. 'I wonder what happened to her,' said Franny. From downstairs came the sound of Larry barking.

'You make a start taking these Christmas things down,' she told Franny. 'And go and see if Larry's all right. I'll be down in a minute.'

Being in this attic full of other people's history was like rooting around in someone else's memories. She realised she wanted to be on her own with the suitcase. To afford it a kind of privacy.

She quickly rifled through the paper. At first it was disappointing – nothing but old bills of sale, advertisements for political meetings, a few pamphlets on aged yellow or faded pinky-red paper saying things like *BRITONS AWAKE!* and *TRADES UNIONS – YOU ARE THE VICTIMS*. The dates were all in the early thirties. It was creepy. A little flash of insight into how fascists used to think. All that felt like ancient history now. He was still carping on though, Mosley – he'd been out that summer in London. She remembered seeing it on television. *MOSLEY SPEAKS* said the banners. He'd been knocked to the ground, all the stuffing knocked out of him. 'They cried Down With Mosley and down he went,' said the newsreader. This was his heyday though, the thirties. He'd been on the up then.

But she didn't really care about Mosley, he was on the way down now. If the people who lived here had supported him, that was unfortunate, but British people had rejected fascism, it was in the past.

Behind her, at the other end of the attic, she could hear the rustling of mice – or was it rats? She remembered the rat she'd seen, and prayed it didn't appear. She shoved her hand into the underwear pouch expecting more of the same. But she touched something different; hard-edged.

It was a book of some kind. A sheaf of high-quality paper, with a dark red, stiff leather cover, not much bigger than her hand, held together with hard brass tacks, with the name *Rosemary Wright* embossed in gilt on the front. It seemed to be handmade. At least it wasn't more fascist nonsense. Malorie opened it. There were pages of almost-illegible handwriting in black ink. She flicked through the pages with jittery fingers, feeling like a voyeur into someone else's life, then shut the book and thrust her hand back in the pouch. With a small lurch she felt the outline of another slim, red volume. The mug shot of the girl from the newspaper. Something had happened to her. And it was unlikely, but there might be some clue here to help her find out what it was her father had wanted her to know.

The attic space seemed to be waiting to see what she would do. There was only the quiet scraping sound. *I'm just borrowing it*, she thought and, gripping hold of the suitcase handle, descended the stairs quickly, banging the suitcase on the steps, before any animals emerged from their hiding places.

Franny had laid some of the decorations out on the wooden floor and they sparkled in the firelight like treasure found in a cave. With Franny and Larry curled up in front of the fire, the glow of the flames lighting her daughter's face and warmth in all their bones at last, she felt that perhaps it had been right to bring her here after all.

Malorie sat awake in the gloomy bedroom. Although she'd filled two hot-water bottles for them to warm the beds, the fire had long since died out, her bottle gone cold and she couldn't sleep. She listened out for Franny's night wakings or the screaming cockler, but it was still and quiet. She switched on a lamp and opened her library book. It was a modern novel called *Marnie* and was quite thrilling. Marnie was a bad girl, a liar and a thief with multiple identities – and troubled. She liked her. But tonight, she couldn't read. It felt too much like her own life, without the crime. Instead, she took the notebooks out from under her pillow and flicked through the pages of the first. Inside, written in black ink in large, cursive script: *The Journal of Rosemary Wright.*

But someone had obviously ripped out the first few pages of the journal. Malorie sank down into the bed. She was strangely disappointed. Then she turned the page and in the same handwriting but much smaller, more cramped, the girl had written *Holloway, London. March 1935. An account of the events of the period July 1931 to August 1934.*

Malorie did a quick calculation. She had no idea how old her father had been when she was born – he'd always been the same gentle man with the creases around his eyes. He'd been in the war – that was what had caused the heart attack according to her mother. *He never got over it.* So he must have been a young man in the 1930s. It was conceivable, then, that he could feature in this journal. Her pulse quickened.

It was a kind of diary. She flicked through the pages then opened the second notebook. This too was embossed with the name *Rosemary Wright* in gold-coloured script and full of the same cramped, black script. Pages upon pages filled with inky handwriting. She hesitated. Was it wrong to read someone else's personal journal? But it was a long time ago and the compulsion to escape into someone else's life – a real one – was too strong. She'd just skim it and if it was boring or salacious or too private – or if it had nothing whatsoever to do with her family – she'd stop. She started at the beginning.

THE FIRST NOTEBOOK

The Journal of Rosemary Wright
Private and Confidential

Holloway, London. March 1935

An account of the events of the period
July 1931 to August 1934

8

I will try to set down as faithfully as I can what has led me to this cell. I asked for these notebooks to be sent to me as soon as I was brought here but they've only just arrived. I think it's because they've begun softening towards me. I intend to fill the books with my story so if you ever read this, you will be able to understand it from my point of view and make up your mind about me, regardless of what the newspapers and gossip-mongers say. I always rather liked the idea of writing and now I finally have the chance. I suppose there is the vanity of leaving something behind. I don't intend for this to be a diary. This happened, then this did. Instead, I want to give you a sense of how it really was.

I was going to start with the arrival of the Lafferty family in the village because that was what changed everything, but I've decided I need to tell you about my family first, because how will you understand me otherwise?

All my life I lived there, on the marsh, in the house Father built for my mother, but by then it was only us: my dog, Perdita (shortened to Perdie, although Mrs Fairbrother called her Pesky and kicked her when she went near the kitchen) and the gardener, Rogers, who had been there forever, waging a running war with the rats that came off the marsh. Janey always said he was here when Mother came, as was plump old Fairbrother, who was as severe with me as she was with my dog.

Nearly four years ago, on my birthday, my father gave me a set of three leather-bound blood-red notebooks. I never wrote in them apart from childish scribbles and a number of beginnings of detective stories. I was obsessed with the novels of Mrs Agatha Christie. How my young self would be agog to see me now. The writer and main character of my very own mystery tale.

I was disappointed with the notebooks at first because I wanted a copy of The Murder at the Vicarage but Father said it wasn't suitable reading. This was utter nonsense because I'd already read The Murder of Roger Ackroyd, The Mystery of the Blue Train and The Mysterious Affair at Styles. I borrowed them from the library in Wells and hid them from him. His idea of a good book was Walter Scott or Trollope or another man who wrote long novels with a lot of characters and lots of morals. He thought Mrs Christie or Dorothy L. Sayers were 'for women'. For someone who prints words for a living he didn't really like proper stories at all. But he said as I was constantly stealing his papers for my scribbles, I was to have books of my own with which to do what I wanted. I liked the way they looked all together, the dark spines hiding the blank pages, waiting for me to fill them with ink.

That birthday I was fifteen, and my body was changing although I didn't want it to. My monthlies had started but no one knew. They were an ugly ache in my belly and sheets I washed myself and no one, not even Janey to tell, though she discovered it quickly enough. If my mother were there I could have told her. My birthday often made me feel melancholy when I thought of her. They told me she died of tuberculosis when I was an infant, but I knew it wasn't true. Sometimes I heard them talking about 'Mistress' and it made me think she wasn't dead but hidden somewhere.

I can't remember her at all. No, that's not entirely true. I have one memory – it's of us sitting on the sand in bright sunlight. I can feel the sand between my toes. My mother hands me a shell and I hold it in my tiny hand. At least, I think it's a memory. I might have imagined it.

Another memory, a more recent one: once, not long before the events of this account, I overheard Fairbrother tell Rogers that the master was going to Norwich on business. The printing press is in Cromer so that was a clue that it was something other than usual.

'Mistress Louisa business, I reckons,' she said.

I was in the chestnut tree, which was in full leaf and covered in soft yellow catkins and a good hiding spot. I gripped hard on the bark of the tree and it cut into the palm of my hand, but I couldn't call out or otherwise they'd see me and I'd be in trouble for spying. Louisa was my mother's name. Father said when I pressed him that I'm named for his mother, Marie, and for my mother. Rosemary Louisa Wright. I like to think that my mother gave me the name Rosemary, as her way of trying to steer my fate away from my father's. She must have known by then what kind of man he was. And Janey told me it means the dew of the sea, and I always liked that too.

'Reckon so,' said Rogers, but he didn't look up from his digging.

I don't think Fairbrother was very happy with that because she stomped off back to the house.

As soon as they were out of sight, I shinned down the tree and ran over to knock on Janey's door, Perdie trotting after me on her short little legs. Janey was our only neighbour, and the only person in the world who cared for me. Janey's cottage was smaller, darker and damper than ours. Where the Marsh House was winding and confusing, full of little rooms and wood panelling on all the walls, Janey's cottage was squat, sunk down and hidden by a line of thick trees, just one main downstairs room where she ate and cooked and slept, and the privy out the back of her garden, down by the marsh. It was crammed full of bottles of various sizes, herbs hanging from the rafters, chipped crockery and straw dolls she made from the marsh reeds. The air was always moist with the salt vapours or whatever she had cooking on her old range. There were always animals – her black dog, Smutch, frogs (she called them hopp'n toads) in the pond, the white mice she laughingly called her imps and the bees in the hive. It was cleaned rigorously but the animal hair, the marsh mud and the salt would get in anyway. There were so many books higgledy-piggledy you couldn't see the floor. The whole building was ramshackle, warm and stunk to high heaven, like Janey herself. I loved it.

I asked her straight off, what had happened to my mother and she said, 'I don't right as know if yer father wants you knowing but I see you knows suffin already. She were awful fierce after she had you, Rosie, and she weren't never right after that. I had to take you on meself for a time.'* That's how she talked.

*I know I can't remember all the words people said so you'll just have to believe me that it was something like this.

'Fierce how?' I asked, determined to get an answer.

'Frazzled is how. It were like she had a misery in the head. And I couldn't help her, no matter what I did.'

'But if she didn't die, where is she?'

'That I can't tell you,' said Janey and she put her old hand on my head. 'But don't you go blaming yerself for any of it. It weren't nothing to do with you. It were a bad birth thass all.'

But what she said made me think it had been my fault that my mother had become unwell, that it had been my birth that had made her sick. Janey had delivered me, hadn't she? She'd told me the story many times – of the 'filthy tempest' that night and the doctor being called but him not arriving in time. She said I'd been stuck and Mother lost a lot of blood and when I came out I'd not made a sound. She and Fairbrother, who'd come to help too, had thought I was dead.

I still ask myself, what really happened to her to get her sent away? The children at the village school used to taunt me, saying that she'd gone to a madhouse.

Another memory, from early on that summer. I was scuffing my boots down the street towards our lane, when coming the other way were a group of children from the school. One in particular, the ringleader of their grubby gang, a wiry mean-faced boy called George with pretty curls, always sneered when he saw me.

I remembered him from my long-gone school days. George Bayfield hated me. And I him. So when I saw him and his gang, I began to run.

'There she is,' he said, pointing at me, 'the mad marsh girl. Where's your ma, Mad Mary?'

Another of the children, a snot-nosed little girl, chanted back, 'In the madhouse, that's where she is.'

I didn't slow down. I kept running at full pelt towards them, heart banging hard with excitement, and as I drew up level with the boy, he drew back from me as if I were a scythe come to cut him down. And I was. I came at him with my fists clenched, and would have punched him right in the jaw if he hadn't veered away just in time. My fist caught the end of his chin, and at the same time, someone else grabbed one of my plaits and yanked me back until I was lying on the hard road. Above me the sky was a clear dome of pale blue. Then into the blue dome came a ring of dark heads. They had made a circle around me and were peering at me like I was a strange creature from the bog. At first I thought they would throw stones at me or poke me with sticks and I steeled myself to jump at them, snarling. But they whispered between themselves and held back. Someone spat near my head, then the ring expanded and they began to skulk off. I raised myself onto my elbows. They were at the edges of the street now, each of them a safe few feet away. Apart from one. The grocer's boy, George.

He was hovering a foot from my head and suddenly darted forward and hissed in my ear –

'I'll get you, you mad witch!'

But before he could get away, I snatched his hand.

'No you won't,' I said. I dug my nails hard in and he yelped in pain like a dog.

I let his hand go and he sprang back, glaring at me.

'You can't even catch me,' I said. And I flew home, not looking back, exultant and hurt all at once, cut off from the rest of the world.

Why didn't I ask my father about her? I did when I was younger.

Once, in a dark rage I yelled at him, 'The children say Mother is in a madhouse!'

A dark look of anguish crossed his face but he said calmly, as if with great restraint, 'Your mother is dead, Rosemary. The sooner you accept that, the better it will be for you.' Then he turned away.

So you can see that before it all began – the events that led to me being here – before all of that, I was almost alone in the world. I had my dog, Perdie, I had Janey. That was all. Father wasn't cruel to me, but neither was he much bothered about me. When I was younger he'd sent me to the village school, but by then I hadn't gone for an age. No one liked me there and I didn't like them. They thought I was snooty and strange. They used to call me 'Marsh Girl' which was true enough. I had a governess, Miss Cannadine, for a while. I liked her and she was sweet to me, but she left all of a sudden because of an accident, according to Father. I cried and cried when she left. Periodically, he'd threaten to send me away to school but he never did. I don't think he had enough money. Either way, by my fifteenth birthday, I'd been rather forgotten about.

My days were spent exploring, reading or with Janey. Janey used to call me her 'Wild Rose' and I suppose I was. I had no lessons, I barely did any chores and there was no one to supervise me. I could read and write passably because of my early, tormented days at the school – and because sweet Miss Cannadine used to force me to study my letters – but I was appalling at sums. Sometimes I would run into the house and startle Father, and he would peer at me as if disgusted by the feral child who lived in his house. 'You look like a half-breed,' he'd say, or he'd call me a wild animal. He'd shout for Fairbrother who'd try to take a comb to my hair, and failing, cursing, would chop it off to my shoulders and slather it with grease so the comb could get through the knots. She'd pull at my hair, yanking it until my scalp smarted and tears came to my eyes. Every week on Saturday, she'd wrestle me into the bathtub – in front of the fire if it was winter – and scrub at me until I was flayed and raw like a gutted fish.

On Sundays we'd troop to church and I'd squirm on the hard pew, not listening to the fat-lipped rector but imagining myself far away from all of them, up a tree, or walking for miles along the beach beyond the marsh. The rector himself has his own fantastic tale, and does not stay long in mine, but more on that later. Every other day I'd be away, Perdie yapping at my heels, crossing the marsh by the bridges, picking up pieces for my collection. I collected the world around me. The hollow shell of a bird's egg; a sprig of seablite or sea lavender; a stone that looked like a heart. I lined them up on the windowsill in my room and I would name them and touch them every day for luck. Janey said I started collecting when my mother went away, and I have no reason not to believe her. The first item in the collection was the shell I thought my mother had given me. I know now that it could have been any shell but in my childish mind it was hers, and as she'd given it to me it was special. From then on, anything that caught my eye was inspected and either discarded or chosen. By the time I was fifteen, it ran along the whole windowsill and covered the top of the chest of drawers as well. Now and again, Fairbrother would threaten to throw it all out as it was filthy and probably carrying diseases. But she never did – afraid, I think, of my anger.

If I wasn't collecting, I could be found in Janey's dark cottage. She'd tell me stories of hyter sprites, phantom dogs and travellers lost on the marsh; the moon trapped by wild creatures and a girl who outwitted a ghost. She told me all the names of the birds in the garden and the ones that came to the marsh at different times of the year, and the ones with names that she and Rogers used, but which weren't to be found in my British Book of Birds: spinks and buttles, hedge betties and King Harrys, hornples and Jill-hooters. We'd drink tea that she brewed from the herbs in her garden and eat cakes made with honey from her bees.

And if it hadn't all changed, perhaps I'd still be there where I belong, under the wide, open sky, rather than locked up, an animal in a cage.

9

The day it all really began was the Friday after my birthday, when I still believed that the greatest drama of my life was my mother's disappearance. It was the day I followed Father to Old Hall.

Fairbrother had been full of the arrival for months and months. A family was coming and I'd been planning the adventures I would have with the children. Children who would be my friends.

'There's a boy with them,' I'd overheard Fairbrother telling Rogers while he was laying rat poison at the threshold of the kitchen. 'A tall, sharp, blond boy. Older than Miss. Reminds me of the Prince of Wales he does. Handsome as anything.' Even I knew who the Prince of Wales was, everyone did. But he was an adult, not a boy. Whenever I tried to ask Father about the new family, whether there were any children, how many they were, exactly how old they were, he shooed me away, said we mustn't bother them and they'd invite us over soon enough. But I saw the boy first.

Father left the house soon after breakfast. He told me he was meeting important people in the village, but wouldn't tell me who. That was suspicious because there weren't any important people in the village. He despised the rector and there was no doctor in Stiffkey.

I waited on the drive for him to leave, until he disappeared down the lane into the little swirls of morning mist. First I had to shove Perdie quickly into the house otherwise she'd trot after me and might get squashed by a motor car.

After Father left, I ran down Green Way and saw him cross Church Street to the river. He stuck hard to the river all the way along, with me following behind, just fields on one side and trees shielding us from the street. I thought he might be going to the church, but instead he went down the little path that leads to the big house. Only it's not a house, Old Hall. It's not like the Marsh House with its windy stairs, tiny windows and warped walls that look like the sides of a boat, and the dark bedroom where she gave birth to me which no one goes into. It's more like a castle. A medieval, fairytale castle.

Old Hall. It's a rather boring name, isn't it? But it's not boring, everyone knows that. It has turrets and a courtyard and loads of windows and is really rather grand. I'd always played in the gardens. When I was little an old lady lived there and she was too slow and infirm to chase me away. She'd peer out of one of the top windows and bang it with her cane and I'd run away. Then it was empty and, along with the marsh, it really became my playground.

I was quite tempted to knock on the front door and ask to introduce myself to the new family. But I lost my nerve.

Instead, I saw the boy from the churchyard of St John the Baptist's. There was the old oak in the graveyard next to one of the ruined turrets which I could climb quite easily, and I could see right into the east side of the courtyard. I waited and waited, but I didn't mind as I was used to entertaining myself. I'd taken a slice of pork pie and an apple from the larder and I munched on those while I waited. He was sure to arrive at some point. A blackbird took up singing loudly above me, but it was mostly very quiet. Up there I could see the purple haze of the sea lavender on the marsh behind our house. The sun had burnt off all the sea mist from the morning and it had become a hot day. I took off my stockings and bunched them in the pockets of my dress. Father would be angry if he caught me like this. He was forever telling me to cover up or I'd look as brown as a gypsy. He didn't seem to realise that without school and without a governess or a mother there was no one else to tell me what to do. 'She's a wild thing,' Fairbrother used to say, but she didn't think it part of her job to tame me, and Dolly, the girl that did the laundry, was a meek little bird and would no more tell me what to do than she would an ogre.

I was tired after the pie and, leaning on the wide branch of the tree with leaves for my pillow, I thought I could close my eyes and have a little nap, but of course as soon as I did, I heard a shuffling sound across the courtyard below. There was the boy. He was tall and fair-haired as Fairbrother had said. He looked like he was thinking quite hard about something because he didn't look up. In a kind of rush of madness, I threw my apple core at the back of his head, and he did look up then because it whizzed right by his ear. I was quite a good shot, I should have got him, really.

'Hey!' he said. 'Who are you?' He was really very handsome, though his ears stuck out. And my mouth was stopped. All my clever retorts died on my tongue.

'Come down here at once, you nasty little monkey.'

Then – oh horror – he started walking towards me perched up my tree and I saw belatedly that he had a shotgun in his hand. He stood under the tree, raised the gun and pointed it in my direction and for a horrid moment I thought he was going to shoot me like a bird.

'I ought to shoot you out of that roost you're in. Spying on me, are you?' But I saw he had a funny smile and his eyes – very blue – were flashing at me as if this was all a great hoot.

'Go on then,' I said, my heart thumping.

'Ha,' he said, then he did shoot, and my ears rang with the crack of it. I felt the air whoosh and the leaves in the tree ripple out. The blackbird squawked, flapping up into the sky. I screamed, I'm sorry to say, and fell backwards, thumping onto the hard ground below. I was fine – nothing but a sore arm and a scraped leg – and I was up and running.

I ran away across the graveyard as quick as I could, past the entrance to the church, heard him shout as I ran but I knew I must run fast to be home before Father was alerted.

'I know who you are!' came the boy's voice from behind the church wall.

But I didn't stop running. I kept on, head down, straight into the rector, nearly toppling him over since he was so short.

The rector grabbed my shoulders. 'Slow down there, Miss Rosemary, what are you doing running like a boy in a holy place?'

I recoiled from him and shrank away. I looked back. The boy hadn't followed me. 'I need to get home, Mr Davidson.' The rector was a funny man – he had fat, fleshy lips that looked like they were about to gobble something up and eyebrows that were like furry caterpillars crawling over his forehead. Fairbrother maintained that he was a wonderful preacher, which made me dislike him even more. His fingers dug into my shoulder-blades and I wanted to scream.

'Father wants me,' I gasped. And I wriggled like an eel out of his grasp and away off down the lane and across the street to our lane and our house. I knew he wouldn't follow as Father was not a churchgoing man. Not since I was born.

But I only had one thing in my mind, and it was the blond-haired boy at the Hall, though I was bound to be in awful trouble with Father if he found out.

10

In my memory, distorted though it might be, that summer is filled with the dazzling sunshine brought into my life by the family who came to Old Hall.

Hilda was the daughter. She was eighteen then and I thought her quite a lady. Franklin was seventeen. He was the blond boy with the ears, the one I saw from the churchyard. They spent most of the time in their house in London and came to the Hall for weekends when I went to visit them. I needn't have worried, he couldn't have told Father I'd spied on him from the churchyard because Father came back that evening and told me we were both invited for tea at Old Hall. Father made a great friend of their parents, Colonel and Lady Lafferty, and so I finally had companions. I no longer cared that the village children hated me.

I remember all of us on an outing to the sea in Cromer in the summer, soon after they arrived. They had a motor car! I loved listening to the putt-putt-putt as it approached our house and watching the clouds of smoke billowing from the back. Perdie wasn't allowed to come and ran after the car barking until Fairbrother yanked her back into the house. I felt a twinge of guilt but they were out of sight so quickly, it was hard to dwell. I was off on an adventure! I sat in the back, squashed between Hilda and Franklin, and Lady Lafferty sat in the front with Father and the colonel, who loved to drive wearing a special outfit of flying helmet and driving gloves. Lady Lafferty wore an enormous straw hat tied underneath her chin and the purple ribbons flew out behind her in the wind. Hilda was dressed in London fashions (this is what she told me) – wide trousers and a pink floppy sun hat atop her short, bobbed hair – to which her mother raised her eyebrows but really, they allowed Hildy and Frank to do what they liked. Hilda wasn't as handsome as Franklin, but she was tall like him and had a bold look and rolled her eyes a lot and made me laugh. Franklin (he said to call him Frank) was dressed all in white and the rush of air as we drove along the coast to Cromer made his sandy hair rise up. He was shoved up close to me so I could feel his leg pressed hard against mine. I looked past him at the fields whizzing by and marvelled at the feeling of speed and at the red poppies nodding in the breeze in the wheatfields near Cromer.

Then I felt his hand on my leg. It crept up my skirt and he rested it on the inside of my thigh. I stared at him and he stared right back until I blushed and looked down at the floor, quite dizzy. He kept his hand on my leg for the rest of the journey and I wasn't sure what I should do.

We promenaded along the front and took lunch at a hotel high up overlooking the pier called the Hôtel de

Paris, but I found it hard to concentrate on anything at all with the memory of his hand on my bare skin. I thought of my mother and what she would have me do. He was so lovely and they were all so kind to me and I did like it, but I was afraid of what Father would say if he knew.

'You young ones should go on and have your fun,' said the colonel and Father frowned, but Lady Lafferty took hold of his arm and said, 'Come on, Richard, you can leave Rosemary to my Hilda, and you gentlemen can discuss the ills of the world without fear of interruption. I must tell you about my work with the Girls' Friendly Society.'

'Mind you watch your manners, Rosemary,' Father warned me, but he couldn't very well not let me go after that, could he? He was already far away, listening to Lady Lafferty and I imagined him later, head-to-head with the colonel. He had finally found someone else to talk to about the Problem of Capitalism or Communism, the Inertia of British Democracy and the Problem of What To Do About It. Although he talked about 'the integrity of the farming man', he never actually went to the Townsend and drank with them. We were isolated, Father and I, in our own ways, and both of us took to the Laffertys like thirsty men swallowing water.

On the front, Hildy took my arm and Frank walked on ahead of us. As soon as our parents were out of sight, he ducked back and began to run down the ramp to the seafront. 'Come on girls, let's feel the sea air!' He was grinning and it made his face shine. How beautiful he was, with his golden looks and white suit. I noticed that his lips were a dark pink colour like the grazing of skin and I wondered how it would feel to touch them. The only other boy I'd ever liked was Rogers' son, Billy, but Father wouldn't let me be friends with him because he was 'from a different background', and he never came to the house anymore. Whenever I caught sight of him picking samphire or cockling on the marsh for his mother, I'd wave and he always smiled at me and waved back but he never came close.

Down on the beach the sand was hot, and we took our shoes and stockings off. Frank rolled up his trousers and I could see the gold hairs on his slim calves. I had never been so close to a boy's body since Billy and I went splashing in the creeks when I was little. I always loved the feeling of sand under my bare feet, the way it oozed between my toes. Frank ran down to the sea and Hildy and I followed, holding hands and laughing. The sea was freezing cold and splashed against our legs and Frank, teasing, sprayed seawater over us. We squealed and laughed and the sun was hot on our heads. After a while I felt faint as we'd left our sun hats back with our shoes.

'Oh, if only we had bathing costumes with us, Rosemary. Next time we must. We absolutely must. Before the autumn comes and it's too cold.'

I thought of wearing a costume showing my pale legs and arms in front of Frank and I must have reddened because Hildy squeezed my arm and said, 'You have a lovely figure, dear Rosemary, you'd look wonderful. I know it. And you should think about bobbing your hair. You could carry it off, you know.' She picked up one of my braids and twirled it between her fingers. 'It's very lovely, this colour, you know, but you would set off your face if you cut it off and got rid of these childish plaits.'

How I wished I could go bathing with Hildy and Frank but the idea of Father letting me gad about in public with bare flesh showing was laughable.

'She has unusual colouring for an English girl, don't you think?' Hildy said to Frank.

He narrowed his eyes and cocked his head to one side, sizing me up. I blushed. 'We can't call her Rosemary, it's far too frumpy,' he said. 'Let's call her Rosie, in honour of her rosy cheeks,' which made me blush even more.

Later, Hildy and I lay on the sand letting the sun warm our feet, her with her trouser legs rolled up, me with my skirt hitched just above my ankles. Frank sat and smoked, and when I thought he wasn't looking, I sneaked a glance at him. Hildy took up gentle snoring, her neat chest rising and falling.

'What do you do in London, Frank?' I asked, emboldened by the sea air.

He looked down at me and blew smoke out of his nose. 'What do I do? Nothing of importance at all, dear Rosie. My mother would like me to do good. My father wants me to be useful.' He said this with utter disdain. 'He was, you see. My older brother was too. Army and all that. The war. Before my time of course.'

'You had a brother?'

'Two. Hildy and I are our father's second family. The others are all dead and gone.'

'Oh,' I said, foolishly, unable to think of anything to add, trying to imagine how old the colonel must be.

'But I have never been good at anything at all,' he went on. 'Father is thinking of standing for Parliament, you know. Wants me to join him. But I can't think of anything worse.'

I puzzled over this. I couldn't see how you could do nothing at all with your life.

'But don't you want to do anything?' I knew he didn't have to earn his living, unlike Father who was always worrying about money, and all the other people in the village and hereabouts, but it seemed so dreadfully boring.

He laughed. 'I'll help my father with his campaign as he says I must, but the sort of men we have coming to our house are so dull I shall hardly bear it. They are terribly serious, and I'm afraid I have never been able to muster much care about anything apart from sport. I think your father will join us though.'

'Join what?'

'The party,' he blew out a plume of smoke from his mouth towards me and I coughed. He reached over and tousled my hair and I felt all the skin on my scalp prickle. 'You'll see soon enough, dear Rosie. Father's organising a supper party for them at the Hall at the end of the summer, and your father is invited. I imagine he'll bring you. Hildy will insist upon it. And so will I.'

Then he leaned down and kissed me on the mouth. A chaste kiss, a mere peck, but nonetheless, the taste of his cigarette, the warmth of his breath and the sea breeze on my face was a blur of wonder. I was so shocked I jerked back and bashed into poor Hildy sleeping behind me, and she yawned and stretched. Frank caught my eye and, smiling with his eyes wide, put his finger up to his lips (the lips that had touched mine!).

'Lord, how long have I been asleep?' Hildy said. 'I'm absolutely famished. Time for tea, surely.'

As we walked back along the promenade to the car, he played with a shell in his hand, his long fingers caressing its ridges and smooth interior.

'It's beautiful,' I said.

'This?' he said, holding it up as if he'd hardly thought of it. 'You should have it.'

I smiled shyly and put it at once in the pocket of my dress.

We had a cold supper of an egg pie and lettuce when we got home, Father and I, laid out by Fairbrother. I gave half of mine to Perdie as they're always mean to her when I'm away. Dolly, the help, would give her titbits if she dared but Fairbrother always said she was spoiled.

'You'd do well to keep the company of people like the Laffertys, Rosemary,' Father said to me, and I went hot although he hadn't said anything bad. 'Lady Lafferty asked me to invite you to a meeting they're hosting for some important people from London, and I declined on your behalf because I said you were a motherless, simple girl and not used to society.'

'Father –' I started, hot with indignation. 'I'm not simple!'

But Father gave me one of his rare smiles, more like a grimace, but a kind of smile nonetheless, and he held up his hand and said, 'Hold fire, child. She made a firm case for your inclusion and I assented. But you must behave like a lady, Rosemary, not your usual wild self.'

'I will!' I cried, and jumped up to wrap my arms around him, although he pushed me away.

My heart was whirling. Did Frank love me? Were we courting? I didn't know. All I knew is that I'd dearly love Hildy as a sister and Frank made my heart hurt with longing. But he was older and much more sophisticated than me and I wondered if the two of them had joked about me when I'd gone back to our dark house on the edge of the marsh, with my country ways and no knowledge of London society or politics or anything at all. I was scared that in front of all the London people I would be shown up as who I really am and Frank wouldn't love me.

That night when I undressed, I found the shell he'd given me and laid it carefully on my windowsill with my other treasures. Its inside was pink and pearly and it reminded me of an open mouth.

Before the supper party we had a chance, Hildy and I, to wear our bathing suits. Franklin suggested a boating trip on the Broads, and this time it would be just the three of us. All the previous week I could barely eat or sleep for excitement. The summer was having a last fling, and the day was bright and warm. Thrillingly, Hildy drove her father's motor car and I sat next to her, with Franklin in the back. I had to hold onto my sun hat so it didn't fly off my head and I couldn't help but turn to see the road streaming out behind us, the locals gawping at the smart motor car and Franklin, leaning back against the leather of the seat, grinning at me. It was impossible not to smile back, I was so full of joy.

At the helm of the boat, Franklin wore a white sailor's cap and an open-necked white shirt and steered. Hildy wore a cap too, and a singlet with long trousers that made her look impossibly tall and elegant. I had a long cream dress on of course, because I had nothing else but dresses, but underneath so Father had no idea, a mustard-coloured swimming costume Hildy had found for me, that she'd long ago outgrown. I had never worn one before. When I swam in the river or the sea I would wear my drawers and underwear, or, if no one was around, which was most of the time, nothing at all. I wanted the feel of the water on my skin, it made me feel like I was a water baby, a sea-nymph, a mermaid. Hildy's costume was a striking cornflower blue like the deepest summer sky, and she had a swimming cap of bright pink so she stood out like an exotic flower among English daisies.

They'd hired a kind of boat I'd never seen before, a motor cruiser called *Dancing Light* which was like a yacht but with an engine rather than a sail. Franklin laughed and said it was a 'Damn sight easier than sailing,' and I could have a go if I wanted. 'She's a bit sprightly,' he said. The trick was not to rev her too much or the other chaps on the river would get uppity with their old sailing boats and wherries, according to Frank.

We'd picked up the boat at Wroxham marina and then cruised along the river Bure towards Horning where we ate lunch and drank beer sitting on the grass at the Swan Inn. I'd never drunk beer before but the others said it was just the thing on a hot day, and although my mouth puckered at the sharpness of it and the foam went up my nose and made me cough, I drank it all down and they cheered.

Afterwards, Hildy and I lay on the boat while we puttered on along the river. We were in our swimsuits now, and I was acutely conscious of my thin arms and legs sticking out and exposed, my body not quite a woman's. Hildy's limbs were long and pale and shone in the sunlight. But Franklin's arms, visible from the elbow where he'd rolled his sleeves, were golden. From my position, lying on the front of the boat (the 'hull' I was informed), I thought I could spy on him at the wheel, unobserved. But once, while I was gazing at the curve of his jaw as it met his neck, he caught me. For a long second our eyes connected, and I felt quite certain he knew I'd been looking at him.

'How do you like it?'

'Marvellous,' I said, using one of their words.

'Yes it is, isn't it? I think this is what my father calls the bucolic idyll. He feels that the modern man ought to get back to nature rather more and away from the sickness and depravity of society.' I had no idea what he meant but I sat up straight and tried to look as if I did. 'He rather thinks I'm a symbol of this modern malaise,' he said, with a strange smile. 'And maybe he's right. It's why he bought Old Hall after all. It's why he likes it up here, cut off from civilisation.' His voice sounded sarcastic and teasing but his eyes were wistful. 'It's the real England he's after. No foreigners, no degradation.' He seemed to notice me again. 'And if we hadn't come up here, we'd have never met you. It's someone like you, dear Rosie, who makes the world seem good with all your unspoilt loveliness. You don't even know how special you are.'

My head was buzzing with his words. How did I, of all people, make anything good? But he was looking at me with such hot, sweet tenderness, I melted under it.

'She's a beauty, isn't she?' he went on, stroking the gleaming wood of the helm. I imagined his hands caressing me the way he touched the wheel, and although he said nothing more after that, he kept his eyes on mine until I felt my skin burn and had to lower my gaze.

Luckily, at that point a sailing boat with a chattering group of young men and women came into view. They were smoking and laughing, the men in black bathing suits and the ladies in brightly coloured suits like Hildy's. They waved at us as we cruised by above them and as I waved back, one of the men dived into the water, making a huge splash. When he rose up through the water, his hair was slicked back and water dripped off his tanned skin like a water god.

'My,' said Hildy, who I'd thought was hardly awake as she sunbathed, 'Frank, we ought to find a spot to bathe, don't you think?'

Franklin agreed and soon we came to a sheltered place on the river, with only a windmill for company. She and I jumped in and swam in the cool, reedy water, although Franklin declined, saying he didn't have a suit, and sat smoking, watching us from the boat. Blue dragonflies flittered in the reed beds, sunlight danced on the cucumber-green water and it made me think of the boat's name, *Dancing Light*.

Hours later, as the sun was setting, we drank tea to warm us up, took the boat back to the boatyard and vowed we would take her out for longer next time. <u>Next time</u>, I thought, hugging the idea close. Frank drove the car back to Stiffkey, and I sat next to him, damp and sagging in the wet woollen suit, still tingling from the feel of the cool water, tired and euphoric, wishing the day could go on forever.

I've never forgotten it. That day has become a shining image of the past, of carefree youth and promise and glamour. Of course, I didn't see it like that then, I didn't know it would retain its lustre for so long. I thought there would be many more days like that to come, and there were – but now, looking back, it's that one first time on the Broads that sticks out as the most radiant, a tantalising glimpse of a life I could have led.

11

Not long after that trip to the Broads the weather turned, ushering in a dreary start to the autumn, but I didn't care because the long-awaited party at Old Hall was approaching. It was a nasty, blustering day with the mizzle coming off the marsh and barely any light. The walls of the house were damp and the floors cold. I snuck out and spent all day with Janey, preparing a love potion in the dark mugginess of her cottage. When I arrived, she was picking money spiders from the roof beams. She plucked each one delicately with her fingers then cupped them in the palm of her hand. She kept the spiders in her thick shrub of wiry grey hair 'because they're lucky'. I always loved that. The potion was supposed to be a tincture for a sniffle I had, but ever since I was a child Janey seemed like a miracle worker to me. I believed she could cure anything, even a stricken heart. Along with being a midwife and a layer-out of the dead, the villagers came to her with all kinds of afflictions, including love.

Her shelves were full of dusty glass bottles of brown and green with dark liquids inside, but I only knew a fraction of what they contained. I've remembered some of what she taught me though, and I can recite them now, like a spell with no outcome. There was dandelion for blood disorders, comfrey for sprains and wounds, nettle tops for coughs, aloe for burns, yarrow for diarrhoea and digestion, mandrake for the skin. And there were empty bottles too, into which she'd put bits of human nails and hair for people who thought they'd been bewitched. 'Hardly any of them nowadays, though you'd be surprised how many still come for something.' Because although the belief in witchcraft was waning as the century progressed – so she said – people were still afraid of things they didn't understand and would come to her with cases of melancholy and unexplained illnesses which had no cure. She would try to help with a herbal potion and she might also have said some words that sounded like a spell, though I don't know if it really was. Still, if the people who came to her believed in the remedies and if they helped them, then what did it matter?

She gave me some yarrow that day. She said I had to take one of the serrated leaves and tickle the insides of my nostrils repeating this:

Yarroway, yarroway, bear a white blow,

If my love love me, my nose will bleed now.

I blew hard into my handkerchief but all that came out was a sticky mucus, and not a drop of blood. Janey chuckled and said that was to be expected as he hardly knew me. I think she was teasing me.

These were the ingredients for the cold/love potion:
Verbena
Burnt juniper
Honey
all of which she got from her garden or her hive, along with a secret ingredient Janey said was an 'elixir', which smelt a lot like camphor. The potion tasted bitter-sweet and left a woody, pine coating at the back of your throat.

But by the time the evening of the party came, I was certain it had worked and Franklin would find me quite irresistible. My nose was no longer running and I felt as if I was glowing with good health.

It might seem strange to other people, brought up in other ways, that I still clung to these beliefs and superstitions, even as the modern world was opening up for me. But time is different up there in a village like mine, on a forgotten bit of the coast, isolated from day trippers and city ways and the so-called march of progress. There are still people there who follow a different lore to those of commerce and man-made time. There are ways older than motor cars and electricity and telephones that persist, like the black layer of mud on the marsh, concealed beneath the top layer of rationality. I'm not saying those ways are better, but they are there, whether you like them or not.

I've almost run out of space and besides, I've been writing this for two days now in between gardening duties, and I'm tired. 'What are you writing, Miss?' they ask. But I won't tell them. Tomorrow I will start the next notebook. I have lots more to write.

12

The Church
23rd December

A gust of wind caught at the window, making it rattle, and something pale fell to the floor with a faint thud. Malorie's head shot up from the book. In the dim room, nothing stirred. Slowly, she realised that the night had returned to eerie silence, as if all noise had been muffled in some kind of fog. Half asleep, she looked at her watch on the bedside table, its face lit by the lamplight. It was just past midnight.

She rubbed her eyes in the dark of the bedroom. Through the curtains there was a silvery glow. It must be the moon. She should try and shut the window, so she slid out of bed, gasping at the cold. As she moved, she felt a slight jar at the back of her head, like the beginning of a migraine or a hangover. On the floor by the window was a shell, with a pearly-pink interior, which must have fallen from the windowsill. She held it in her palm and tried to think why it seemed familiar. Outside, snow was falling silently, and everything was cloaked in a thin shroud of silvery white.

Malorie gripped the edge of the windowsill and cried out an incoherent sound. Something – someone? – was moving in the snow. A shadow. Her hand rose as if to reach for it. A vague, pale shadow, a slight darkening of the endless white, like a figure dressed in snow. Then, nothing. She felt foolish – she was so unused to the countryside, to the noises and creeping shapes of the night, far away from the familiar safety of streetlights and shops and bars. There was just the snow gently falling in great clumps, white flakes through the dark. Standing dazed at the window, she pinched her bare arm and it hurt. Bed. She was delirious. She had to go back to bed. Stumbling, she dropped back onto the covers and pulled the blankets tight around her. The pain at the back of her head had eased but her mind was crowded with this girl – the girl from the picture in the paper, the girl in the notebook who seemed to be speaking directly to her. The book had ended abruptly. There were pages left but they were empty, as if the writer were withholding. This couldn't be the end of the story. It wasn't, she already knew that. The mug shot of the girl from the newspaper cutting – that challenging gaze, straight into the camera.

A few hours later, surfacing from fitful dreams, Malorie woke to a chilly light washed over the room. There was no sound from anywhere. No birds, no wind, not even the sea. Nothing but a slight creak in the bowed walls of the house. She was thirsty but her water glass was empty. The quiet had a dense quality like cotton wool. Before she opened the curtains, she knew why. The entire scene below her was muffled in white.

As she turned from the window, there on the floor by the bed was a thin oblong package, tied in a red hair-ribbon. It must have fallen out of the notebook. She picked it up and unknotted it with fumbling fingers.

Inside were two photographs. It was strangely surprising, as if she'd been reading a story rather than a record of someone's life. One was of a boy – an attractive fair-haired young man in a pale suit, leaning nonchalantly against the wall of an old building. She felt a bubble of recognition. He reminded her of Tony when they'd met – someone used to getting what they wanted. But this boy had a harder edge than Tony and a haughty look with narrow, laughing eyes, a slightly pouting mouth and a supercilious expression on his face. Tony never meant to be cruel. This one did. It was obvious who he was. On the back, someone – it was Rosemary, she knew her from her handwriting – had written *Franklin, August 1931*.

This Franklin made her skin prickle with a weird combination of attraction and repulsion. What came into her mind was Tony, sliding down a sofa at a party and cupping his hand on her breast. He hadn't even known her name. She'd pushed him off but he hadn't seemed at all bothered. Here she was now, cold in a lumpy bed in an isolated house on the edge of Norfolk and what was Tony doing? She couldn't bear to think of it. Some other party, no doubt, some cool little joint in Soho. That was Tony's kind of thing. He returned to it each time. He went back to the emptiness of dark basement bars and whisky. And a fawning woman making him drinks. It had been a mistake to think he would ever have wanted a life with her and Franny. He would have loathed it here – this cold, dark house by the sea.

The other photograph was of a young woman. At first she thought it was Rosemary herself. But it was an older photograph from a different era. The woman was wearing a long, pale dress with a high lace collar and was seated on a rattan chair with palm trees around her. Perhaps it had been taken in a studio. She was small, pale and dark-haired, drowning in the stiff, voluminous dress, a child really. With an uncomfortable jolt, Malorie knew who she was. The absent mother, Rosemary's lost mother, Louisa. And sure enough, on the back, in a different hand, someone had written *Miss Louisa, February 1912, Delhi.*

She tucked the photographs back into the notebook, stuffed both the books under the pillow, before fetching a cardigan to put over her nightdress and going out onto the landing. No sound came from Franny's room. Downstairs, she managed to coax the fire into sputtering life and, squatting in front of it, waited for warmth to spread across her skin. The heat prickled her fingers but she didn't withdraw them. Her back, exposed to the room, was cold and a shiver like someone's finger tracing the line of her vertebrae tickled down her spine. *Somebody walked over my grave.* She snapped her head round. Nothing but the sofa and a badly painted seascape of a storm. A memory flared – someone, something – whiteness in the garden. The middle of the night. She must have been dreaming of the girl from the notebook. *Rosemary*, she said to herself. It was like peering into someone's mind, reading her words. She shouldn't have read it. *Private and Confidential* it said. She was a voyeur, a Peeping Tom. But why write it at all if you didn't expect people to read it? And Rosemary *did* want someone to read it – she'd even written something to that effect. At the same moment she was also wondering when she could slip away to read the second notebook. She wanted to know what happened to the girl. She felt a kind of responsibility for her, as if in reading her words she had a kind of duty to her. And it was possible, yes it was possible, that in those words there would be some clue as to why her father had kept a photograph of this house. She realised that while she was reading she'd completely forgotten about her initial reasons for reading the notebooks. There'd been nothing though, no mention of a Harry Skinner or anyone who could have been him. But there might be. *I have more to write.* She heard footsteps and froze. Facing the door, she had a vision of a girl in a white dress coming into the room. She called out in alarm.

It was only Franny, holding a snow-flecked Larry in her arms.

Malorie breathed out, her limbs trembling.

'What's the matter?'

She laughed, a mad, snorting laugh that made Franny stare at her in suspicion.

'Nothing, darling. Nothing. Just a terrible night's sleep. Have you been out? Where've you been?' Franny was wearing some kind of dirty yellow dressing-gown, the colour of an old banana, over her nightdress, and big thick socks. Her pale face was reddened with the cold.

'Larry needed his morning walk, Mummy. The garden's completely covered in snow. I'm freezing.'

She came and sat next to Malorie with the dog, who stretched out in front of the fire. 'Look what I found.' She held it out for Malorie to see, a piece of flint in the rough shape of a heart. But when Malorie moved it in her hand it no longer seemed heart-shaped. It was just a stone.

'We need to put the decorations up, before Daddy gets here,' said Franny.

Malorie winced. She didn't have the heart – or the courage – to tell her.

All morning, Franny strung up the decorations they'd found in the attic, setting up ancient, faded paper chains and old painted lanterns on every ledge, hook and door handle, then she trailed outside in her coat and wellingtons, with Larry, almost camouflaged in the snow, skittering beside her and barking at the hedge, to make a snowman and cut down holly and mistletoe. At first, Malorie didn't leave the house. She tried her transistor radio again but she couldn't find a station through the thick static so she turned it off. As she moved around the rooms – feeding Larry, helping Franny with the decorating, tidying up – she kept coming back to the girl in the notebook. It struck her that this village had been Rosemary's home and it, too, would hold traces of her life. And maybe – just maybe – her own life as well.

'Franny,' she called from the back door. 'I'm going to the village, do you want to come?' She never knew what tone to take with her daughter. It sounded false the way she spoke, the jollying tone. And Franny sensed her discomfort, like a dog senses weakness. Whereas Tony, feckless bloody Tony, somehow knew how to be with her, how to make her laugh. He picked up his daughter and spun her round as if it were nothing. I am not really a mother, she thought. I'm just acting.

From the other end of the garden, in the shadow of the snowy trees, she could make out Franny's brown woolly hat, navy duffle coat and yellow wellingtons. 'I don't want to.'

'Please,' she said. God, the stubborn child never did what she wanted. She had no power over her. Franny stood immovable in the snow. Her hair stuck out from beneath the hat that Malorie's mother had knitted before she'd begun to fade away. Everything was covered in snow crystals.

'Fine,' she called, 'I won't be long.'

Malorie found the fur coat and the fur-lined boots Tony had bought for her in the autumn. She took a different route this time. She thought if she walked to the end of the lane she might see the sea. But when she got there, the marsh carried on until the horizon, frosty and bleak, pockmarked with holes where God-knows-what lurked. Defeated, she looked about her, unsure which way to go. Above her on a ridge was a line of bare trees with their gnarled fingers curling to the air. A shiver across her back and she felt she should follow the trees. It was what Rosemary would have done. Nothing disturbed her walk. It was a consolation to be alone after her failure with Franny. The snow was untouched and pristine and squeaked as she stepped on it. No people, no animals. The frozen and still landscape could be apocalyptic, or medieval or prehistoric. Not of this time. She picked up a clump of snow-feathered grass, thinking it must be the marsh grass that Rosemary had run through. It was coarse and pricked at her skin. It wasn't long before she found a lane that she thought must go towards the village. It was an ancient path, with no sign whatsoever of modern life. Peering down its dark recess she thought that it could be any time in the last few centuries. The 1960s hadn't reached here at all. It was narrow and sloped down, as far as anything sloped around here, and as she crunched along the virgin snow of the track, the jagged trees high on either side felt claustrophobic, as if anything could be lurking there and pounce on her. She walked quickly, not looking left or right but straight ahead.

The lane came out beyond the shop, next to a war memorial to both wars and a tired-looking village hall with a peeling green roof, but no sign of any people at all. She slowed her pace. Now, she was conscious that she was once again following Rosemary's footsteps towards the other end of the village where the church was. As the road curved out of the village, she glimpsed on the right the turrets of a large house behind a high wall and, next to it, the grey flint tower of a church. In front of the churchyard gate stood the village sign with a metal silhouette of a bird, and behind it what must have been the school, now boarded up.

The wall to the big house was too high to see over, but she knew it must be Old Hall. She felt a buzz of excitement at walking where Rosemary had thirty years before, being in the same place as if no time had passed. There was an iron gate with a driveway to the Hall and on the pillars on either side, the crumbling stone sculptures of two ugly boars with their tusks stuck in the air. But she could hardly see further than a few feet down the drive as the trees overhung and created a thick screen. Following the wall a few steps on, the stiff gate to the churchyard was free of snow so she was afraid there would be a churchwarden or someone else around, but she went through anyway. Inside the churchyard, she could see the imposing building next door more clearly. Straight ahead, behind the far wall of the grounds, was a ruined tower. There was no tree next to it as Rosemary had described. They must have cut it down. From what she could see on her tiptoes above the wall, the house was a vast, elaborate manor with a snow-covered tiled roof and knapped flint walls, further towers and numerous mullioned windows, but it was hard to see fully behind the trees lining the outer wall. She was sure it was a deliberate ploy to stop prying eyes. She strained to see, but there was no sign of life.

Inside, the church was bare, and mercifully empty. She searched in vain for any reference to the Wright or Lafferty families; it was as if they'd never existed. Neither were there any Skinners. Returning outside, she scoured the graves. There was a strange, weathered gravestone with two skulls and a cross-bones carved on it, but the writing at the bottom was so worn by time that she couldn't read it. In a far corner of the church, underneath a yew tree, she found a stone cross, half-covered in yellowing moss and the white-grey blooms of lichen, dedicated to Harold Francis Davidson, the rector mentioned in the notebook. On the plinth at the bottom of the cross, a quotation had been carved. It said:

FOR ON FAITH IN MAN
AND GENUINE LOVE OF MAN
ALL SEARCHING AFTER TRUTH
MUST BE FOUNDED

She had no idea where the lines came from or when he'd died, but he at least was a real person. Now she'd found this headstone she was even more determined to find evidence of the Wrights in this churchyard. There must be some. But as she looked, peering at each half-erased name and faded epitaph in the weak, overcast light of the winter morning, it became colder and colder, and soon she realised that she'd been in the churchyard for far too long, leaving Franny in the lonely house.

As she was leaving, she noticed ivy crawling along the wall of the graveyard and hanging down from a hawthorn tree in the corner. She pulled a tendril and more came with it, sprinkling snow over her face and arms, until she had an armful of it. She could hang it in the house. As she stuffed it into her shopping bag, a stone detached itself from the mass of vines. It was a piece of flint, shiny, smooth grey on one side and a rough sand colour on the other. It reminded her of the Marsh House.

She struggled through the snow as quickly as she could, seeing only a solitary walker – an old man who nodded at her under his cap – and one passing van. It was strange how empty it was. When she was younger, children would have been out in a snowy winter throwing snowballs. A yellow light was on in the small window of the shop and she slowed down her pace.

'Morning,' the shop girl said as she entered. Already she felt she was known and discussed by the villagers. 'What can I get you? No little girl today?'

'Good morning. She's playing in the snow. I just wanted to say thank you for the logs that your father left at the house yesterday. It was very kind.'

The girl looked up from her ledger with a blank face. 'Logs? I thought he was bringing them with the turkey.'

'Oh. I wonder—'

'Someone's looking out for you, any road. Snow's come in fast, ent it? Going to be a bad one, they say.'

'Do they? Can I ask you a question – I wonder – did you or your family ever know a boy called Harry Skinner?'

'It don't ring a bell. Why's that then?'

'I wondered – I thought – he might have something to do with the house.'

'What, the Marsh House? Might've done, I spose. I'll ask my dad.' Malorie sighed. The name wasn't known here and there were no Skinners in the graveyard. The photograph must have had nothing to do with her father. So why the hell had he wanted her to have it? There was something she was missing, like a name you couldn't remember at the far reaches of your brain. The more you grasped for it, the deeper it sunk into the shadows.

'And – and I was wondering about the people who lived in the house.'

'That place is right strange. All I know is that when I was a kid, it was empty and boarded up. We'd dare each other to go up the lane, but no one ever went inside. Funny, ent it? It's just a house. Our parents never told us what was wrong with it, just that it was a bad house. I'm sure it's nice now though,' she added, seeing Malorie's frown. 'You sure you don't want anything?'

'I'll take a newspaper,' she said, picking up that day's paper. She did a quick calculation in her head. She only had a few shillings left and might need petrol. 'And these –' she passed over two cans of tomato soup. 'I've been wondering,' she added. 'Where are all the children?'

'Oh, they go sledging down Devil's Hole.'

'Devil's Hole?'

The girl shrugged. 'An old path out of the village. There's some old tale about it. They say it can't ever get wet because of a crime done there. Gets lots of snow though. We always used to slide down there when it snowed.'

Walking home, she saw the headline of the local gazette was *BODY OF FISHERMAN FOUND IN SNOW*. She picked up her pace, wanting to be inside.

13

I saw her walking to the village and I knew she'd found out something and what she was looking for. She wanted evidence. Proof. Facts. As if it would all be there for her and she could lay it all out and it would make sense. But it's never as simple as that. The graves are elsewhere. The bones are dust. It's not graves that tell you a history, a story of a life. That's much harder to find, but if you know where to look, you can find it. It'll reveal itself. It's all still around you if you're ready to see. It's in the crumble of a wall, a scratch on a beam, the sound of a tread on the stairs. Most people don't though, do they?

14

The Snow Girl

They ate a lunch of one of the cans of tomato soup she'd bought from the shop, heated up, and toasted half-stale bread. The ivy was in a pile by the back door. Malorie followed her daughter out again to the snow-covered garden to see the snowman.

The sky was still laden, no sun had appeared, but the white blanket covering the lawn and trees reflected a dull sheen back at her. By the back door there was a large bush of rosemary, flecked with white. It was old and woody but still alive, with thousands of sharp, dark green needles in sprays. She leaned down to pick some sprigs and the deep, sweet scent filled her senses. *Rosemary, that's for remembrance.*

'Mummy!'

In the middle of the lawn, Franny was standing like an angry pixie next to a snow-girl. She had created a young woman with hair of dead leaves and eyes of coal and a long dress sculpted out of snow.

'That's clever,' said Malorie. 'Where did you get the idea for that, darling?'

Franny frowned. 'I don't know. I just thought of it.'

Malorie gave her a hug. 'Well, it's very unusual.' Standing in the centre of the garden she was taken back to the night before, looking out of the window. It was dark, snow was falling, someone was looking up at her. A shape – the shape of a girl in white.

'Stop squeezing me, Mummy, it hurts.'

'Sorry.'

'When are you going to get us a tree? It's Christmas Eve tomorrow. We have to have a tree to put the presents under.'

'A tree?' Oh God, she'd forgotten. And she had to wrap the presents she'd shoved into the car – all the extravagant gifts that Tony had bought for his only child. She wondered if he was cursing her now, or relieved that he was shot of them. Shot of her, at least.

'You promised.'

'I did. I'll cut one down. There's plenty of them.' She had no idea how to cut down a tree. And what with, anyway? 'Are you going to help me?'

'I'm cold.' Franny had turned inwards, her face closed down. Malorie had failed her again. She felt a small surge of undirected anger but stifled it. It was *Christmas* – she had to make an effort.

She sent Franny inside with Larry at her heels. There was a falling-down shed on the left side of the garden with peeling brown paint. The door was warped but not locked and she prised it open. Inside, in the dim winter light, at first all she could see were spiders' webs and lines of pots. It must have been a gardener's shed. In her head, her father emerged from his beloved shed into the clipped and neat rectangle of the garden in Norwich, their pride and joy. He looked upwards and crumpled onto the lawn. Her mother had called her, in the digs in London, her voice hesitant and small. The funeral had been tortuous. Tony had come with her, ballasted her with his certainty. She'd tucked herself in against him and felt an uncharitable relief that she had him now, that she didn't belong there anymore. Her mother had let Tony hold her hand in his and looked up at him with such beseeching gratitude that Malorie had been glad to get away. Even her mother would rather Tony comforted her than her own daughter.

If what her mother said was true, her father had wanted to tell her something. As she peered into the shed it was as if she could see him in the shadows, hunched over and working on something as he always had been. If only she could talk to him now. If only she'd been a better daughter. There it was again, the inky blackness behind her eyes. If she let it, it would spread through her skull, seeping into her brain, sinking into her whole self as it had done after Franny was born, until the weight was so heavy she couldn't move. Tony had found her once, when he'd come home from work, her teeth unbrushed, sleeping in her nightdress, the baby soiled and crying, unable to wake her. She blinked quickly. She had to focus on now, on Christmas.

As she adjusted to the darkness inside the shed, her father's form evaporated. She began to see the shapes of tools hanging from the back wall. A couple of spades, a rake, some large scissors – secateurs – various trowels and something she didn't know the name of with a long handle and a small half-moon metal head. And, most pleasingly of all, an axe. She couldn't imagine wielding such a thing, let alone chopping a tree down with it, but she had to.

It was incredibly satisfying, she discovered. The axe was heavy and hard to keep a grip on with gloved hands, and the first time she tried to take a swipe at a suitable-looking pine tree on the edge of the garden, she only managed a small nick in the side and the head of the axe almost fell onto her boots. But then she practised swinging it back and forward a few times. The third time, she angled it horizontally into the trunk and it sliced into the wood and stuck there. She had a hard time yanking it out, but when she did, the first cut had been made and it was easier after that. When it fell she had to jump out of the way. It sprayed snow into her face but she grinned, feeling the flakes on her tongue, pleasantly aware of the ache in her upper arms.

'You did it.' Franny had been watching from the back door. Malorie felt a childish rush of pride. She had done something on her own. No Tony. No parents. They exchanged a fleeting smile. Her daughter came over and began trying to pull the fallen tree over to the house. 'We need to get it in a bucket,' she said, but Malorie still had the axe in her hand.

'I'm just going to chop some wood for the fire,' she said.

Franny seemed to be waiting.

'Just leave it there. I'll bring it in, in a minute. I won't be long.'

The rhythm of the swing, the hissing thwack of spliced wood on the trunk she used as a block, the tingle of pain in her arms – it was addictive. Her father, sprawled on the lawn. Thwack. Her mother's closed-off face. Thwack. Tony, she thought, who is not here. Thwack. Thwack. Franny, who she didn't understand. Thwack. She was a bad mother. A failed mother. Thwack.

A dark shape moved on the edge of her vision. Someone was watching her.

Malorie shouted out and the axe fell out of her hand, carving a wedge into the snow by her foot. The sky had darkened, the only light now coming from inside the house, a single square of yellow. Across the white lawn and through the trees, an old woman was standing motionless outside the cottage.

Had she spoken aloud? Had the old woman heard her?

'Hello!' Her voice croaked. Who was she? She should thank her for the logs – it must have been her who'd left them, after all.

The words from the journal came back to her – *Janey delivered me.* She had an image of the woman watching over the house from before it was built. Watching over this girl, Rosemary, and her mother. Still here, still watching.

'Janey?' she called out uncertainly.

She thought the woman dipped her head in response. Then she turned and disappeared. Malorie watched the brown shape slip back between the dense foliage. Now she'd gone, she felt foolish. It was probably not the same woman at all.

Malorie sorted out the tree – finding a bucket to put it in, sending Franny off to find stones to weight it, tidying up the ends – until it looked almost like a reasonable Christmas tree, but bare. The whole time, Larry sat by the fire, his hackles up. She wondered why he didn't sleep there like a normal dog would.

'There's candles for the tree in the attic, I think,' she said.
'Fairy lights?' said Franny.

'Hopefully. I'll go. You stay here and finish the decorating.'

Crouching low and shuffling along on her knees, she came to the cot she'd seen the day before. Without meaning to, she raised her hand to the bottom edge and felt along it. Their cot was not much different. Her tiny starfish body splayed out in the middle; her red mouth open, mewing; swaddled, tucked in, asleep. Then it had been kept up in her room for ages, waiting for Malorie to be well enough to have a second child, until finally, reluctantly accepting there wouldn't be another baby yet, Tony dismantled it and bit by bit took it up to the tiny attic space above their first floor flat. It was the symbol of one of her failures.

She let her hand drop.

On her hands and knees she nudged towards where Franny had found the old suitcase. She found a box that was stuck under the eave and had to be yanked back with some force before she could open it. Puffs of dust floated up and she coughed. This box was heavy. It contained books. Her heart jumped a little but they weren't notebooks or even Agatha Christies, they were mostly exercise books from when the girl had had her governess. She flicked through them but there was nothing interesting. Just the scribbles of an intermittently obedient pupil, the declensions of Latin verbs, arithmetic, violent crossings-out. She leaned back on her heels, her head touching the roof, irrationally, crushingly, disappointed. She'd felt so certain she'd find something.

A faint rustle made her twitch. Sure enough, she heard again the scraping of claws above her. God, she hoped she didn't see one. She loathed rats. Tony used to tease her about all the rats in the London gutters.

There were no treasures up here, no secrets, just the boxes of books and the rats.

But she had to get the fairy lights. Dejected, she scrabbled through one of the Christmas boxes and pulled out a handful of small white candles. They would have to do.

Back on the first floor, Malorie glanced through the open door of the bedroom. Her fingers itched to open the second notebook, to lose herself in Rosemary's world. It was waiting for her under her pillow. But she couldn't read it now. She must admire the tree, make Franny some supper, get her to bed, wait, wait patiently. She stood there a moment, taking in the smell of something warm and sweet. It was the rosemary she'd picked earlier, in the pocket of her blouse. She smiled and placed it on the windowsill. It was the namesake of the girl in the notebook – her herb, her flower.

When she returned downstairs, Franny attached the candles to the tree with clips she found in one of the boxes of decorations, and lit them, sending golden spangles onto the lumpy, warped walls. Malorie had never seen a Christmas tree lit with real candles before and it was beautiful. While she made the tea, the window above the sink showed her face staring back at her. She imagined Rosemary in this room, or by the fire, like Franny in the next room, sewing her sampler. By the back door was the mass of ivy she'd taken from the graveyard. They could hang it around the house. Then she remembered the piece of flint in the pocket of her coat and quietly retrieved it, took it upstairs to the bedroom and laid it on the windowsill alongside the sprigs of rosemary, a tentacle of ivy and the shell that was already there.

That night, the fire was still burning and Malorie was curled up on the sofa with a bottle of wine on the rug, a packet of cream crackers and the first pack of the cigarettes she'd brought from the shop. Franny was asleep – or supposed to be – and Larry lay curled again at the bottom of her bed. He had taken to sticking closely to her, whining whenever she left him.

She'd brought down the second notebook. The last thing she'd read was the girl drinking a love potion. She thought of herself, meeting Tony at eighteen, married at nineteen. But at least she'd been eighteen – an adult of sorts. She'd certainly thought she was. Escaped from the stifling house in Norwich with its regulated eating times and only the *Reader's Digest* or the *Radio Times* for culture. She'd seen herself as oh-so-grown-up with her beehive, handbag and high boots. She'd been newly living in London, a job in a secretarial pool (she'd soon find something better; her dad always told her she was clever), in digs with her friend Clemency, who believed she had a foot in the aristocracy as her father had stumped up for Bedales. Clemency took her to an underground bar in Soho and introduced her to Tony. Oh God, he'd been so dashing in his tight shirts and Cuban heels. Not conventionally attractive – his lips were too full, his hair too high on his forehead – but he had so much confidence it radiated from him, warming her with its glow. She'd wanted so much to be part of the London scene, to shuck off Norfolk and her awkward relationship with her parents, and Tony had promised that, with his job in a hip bar, his flat near Soho and his easy way with money. He'd probably only meant her to be a fling. But Franny had stopped all that.

The wedding was a quickie in Marylebone Register Office, the only witnesses Clem and Tony's friend Seb. Her wedding dress a cast-off from Clem, a long custard-yellow dress she'd have worn for the season. Not white. How could she in her condition? It had felt like an adventure, a rebellion. She'd write to her parents and tell them when it was all done. It had happened in such a rush there hadn't been time to think about it – he was the promise of the life she thought she wanted, the glamour and freedom. They'd had drinks in a grubby bar after but she'd felt queasy, went home early. Tony had stumbled in the next morning and fallen asleep beside her smelling of brandy and cigarettes. It was nauseating. She'd felt a heave in her stomach and lurched to the bathroom. Slumped on the lino floor, she watched the water trickle down the side of the toilet bowl. On her finger, the cheap ring Tony said was only temporary. This was her life.

She had a better class of ring now. Not the family heirloom he'd promised her (she suspected his sister had kicked up a fuss about that), but a large diamond wrapped in gold from Bond Street. In the gloom of the bedroom, Malorie held the diamond up to the thin light to make it shine.

His parents had quite obviously disapproved of her – she was from a council house – but she tried not to care about that. It was part of the thrill of it, wasn't it, to be striking out from both their upbringings? Her parents had only met Tony a couple of times. Her mother had fawned over him, impressed by the car, the clothes, the cut-glass accent. Her father had been quietly disapproving, called him 'flashy'. And although she'd told herself that it didn't matter – Tony was her family now – it had hurt. She'd stopped ringing, unable to bear his disappointment in her. By the time Franny had come along, her father was already dead, collapsed in his beloved garden with a heart attack. And he'd never forgiven her for Tony. That was one of the worst things, the humiliation of her error. He'd been right about Tony all along.

That appalling night in London before he left, he'd shown himself to be who he really was. And she had too. He'd called her a bitch. And what had she done? Slapped him? Cursed him? Screamed and shouted? No. She'd cried, crumpled and defenceless.

'Don't do that,' he'd said.

'You can't leave me,' she'd said.

He hadn't answered, just picked up his hat and left. The shame she felt was like a cowl she wore.

Outside, an owl hooted and a draught made Malorie tuck her feet up under her legs. The window was completely black. Anything could be outside in the darkness. They were exposed, just the two of them, stuck out here on their own with only a silly little dog for protection. For God's sake, there was no one there, she chided herself and turned back to the notebook.

She'd begun to think there would be nothing in the pages that made sense of why her mother had given her an old photograph of this house. But the urge to read was overwhelming. She cracked open the second notebook. It was full, as the first one had been, of the same slanted, cramped handwriting.

THE SECOND NOTEBOOK

15

I think I will enjoy writing this part of my story. It will remind me that I was once a very different person and although I now reside in what looks like a castle with crenellations and turrets, there is a place like this far away on the coast of Norfolk, which once seemed like a fairytale palace.

Father and I walked to the Hall with a great umbrella. The rain had cleared but the sky was grey and looming dark. We didn't talk, but I didn't care. The darkness of the trees swaying in the wind seemed to be urging us on and I skipped so far ahead that Father complained I would lose my hat.

The hall was lit with a thousand candles in chandeliers and glowing electric lights and there was jolly dancing music coming from the drawing room. Their butler person (they brought their servants up from London) took my old black velvet coat that was far too small for me. I felt instantly foolish as the only smart dress I had was a hand-me-down from Hildy which was navy blue wool with a Peter Pan collar, but it looked awkward on me. On Hildy I imagined it would have been chic in an intellectual, bluestocking kind of way, accessorised with one of her lovely little hats, but it just made me look like an overgrown, gauche child. At home, on the marsh, it had seemed smart, even elegant, but here, it was all wrong.

Hildy was standing in a long satiny cream gown in the corner of the room, being flirted with by a middle-aged man with a luxurious moustache and a receding hairline. She looked bored and marvellous. She always did. I waved and she wiggled her fingers at me and raised her very arched eyebrows even higher.

'Darling, you look delightful,' she said, entirely unconvincingly. 'Excuse me, Gerald, I must get this poor child a drink.' She extricated herself from the wet-lipped, moustached man and, steering me by the elbow, led me to one of the tuxedoed staff they must have hired in addition to their own staff (from where? In Norfolk?! I'd never seen anything like it) and took two glasses of champagne from the boy. I'd never had champagne before – it made me splutter and bubbled up my nose – but I rather liked the taste, and very soon it had all gone.

'God,' she sighed, 'that man is so tiresome. All he talks about is his horses.'

'He seemed to like you,' I said.

'He's in love with me, always has been,' she said. 'Poor Gerald!' Then she looked at me as if she'd only just seen me.

'You look like someone's let you out of school for the day in that outfit,' she said, peering at me down her long, straight nose.

'It's yours.'

'I know that, silly. I see I'll have to give you something more suitable for the evening.'

'Who are all these people?' I said, looking around the room at the men in black tie and the women in backless gowns.

'Daddy's friends from London. Some of them are in the army, some are politicians. That one –' she pointed across the room, 'is married to Diana Mitford. She's a stuck-up old thing but considered quite a beauty. You must have heard of her. All the Mitfords are such gadabouts. Guinness is a bit of a bore but terribly rich. I've heard she's in love with someone else, but no one knows who. It's all terribly romantic.' I looked around at the perfectly sculpted heads and tried to see The Beauty, and there was one woman with golden hair and startling bright eyes who was holding court, but Hildy had already moved on.

'That one over there –' she was saying, pointing to a handsome woman with a green cloche hat, 'was a famous suffragette.'

Someone was playing a harp in the corner of the room. Canapés were passed around and I tried every single one of them. Smoked salmon, devilled eggs, stuffed tomatoes, I ate them all. 'Gosh, Rosie, do you never get fed?' said Hildy. 'You've become quite a squeaky piggy.'

'Snort, snort,' I said, helping myself to a chicken liver toast. I didn't like to tell her that I had never eaten anything like this in my entire life. It was all fatty pies and boiled vegetables at home.

All this time, I had my eye on Franklin but he was by his father's side, being talked at incessantly by one of these men or another. I could hardly get near.

'Oh God,' she said suddenly, lowering her voice to a whisper, 'let's make a run for it – it's Mummy.'

Sure enough, gliding across the room was the willowy Lady Lafferty. There was no escape.

'Darlings,' said Lady Lafferty, 'how are you?'

'Fine, Mummy,' said Hildy disconsolately.

'And Rosemary, dear, are you well? I'm afraid this little gathering might seem a bit ostentatious for someone unused to such things.'

'I'm enjoying it, thank you,' I said in my politest voice.

'I notice we don't see you in church very often, my dear.'

'Mummy!'

Lady Lafferty stiffened, but kept the patient smile on her fine-boned face.

'My father is not very fond of the rector.'

'Neither is the colonel, Rosemary, but God would rather you were in his church regardless.'

'Yes, Lady Lafferty,' I said at the same time as Hildy said, 'I don't think God has an opinion, Mother.'

'Hilda May,' said her mother sternly, and flashed a pitying look to me.

She put her long-fingered hand on my cheek, assessing me the way Franklin had done that time on the beach, and I realised that no one had ever looked at me properly before then, or touched me the way they did.

•

'Dear Rosemary, what a beautiful name you have, like the herb. And so unaffected,' she said, touching my jaw. 'Don't let my daughter change you, my dear.' Then she left us, patting me on the head.

A fearsome-looking woman approached us. 'What do you think about the unemployment situation?'

I stared at her. She was tall, with blue-black cropped hair, a severe, very glamorous suit, and a brooch in the shape of a scorpion on the lapel of her jacket.

'I don't know,' I said.

'No, of course not,' she said, 'you're just a child.'

'But a very lovely one,' said Hildy in her mocking voice, pinching my cheek.

I began to think I was the butt of some extraordinary joke, but I couldn't think what it was. These people were all I had dreamed of and yet they clearly knew I wasn't one of them. I was a curiosity.

My glass kept getting filled with champagne and my belly became full of bubbles. Hildy was laughing at one of the older ladies whose nose was stuck firmly in the air – she obviously thought she was very important. I began to feel quite tired and wished I could sit down, but then Frank appeared beside me like a rabbit from a magician's hat.

'Watch out, Rosie, you've got all squiffy. Why don't you come with me before someone notices?' The touch of his grip on my arm was like a firebrand.

'I'm fine!' I said, but I did feel dizzy.

I saw Frank and his sister exchange a look and I tried to pull away from him, but he held on tightly to my elbow and led me out of the drawing room along the corridor to a little conservatory at the back that held dozens of exotic ferns and cacti. I collapsed onto a wicker settee.

'That was mean of you,' I said, but I was glad he'd taken me away.

He lit up a cigarette and stood above me. 'You've had too much, that's all. Can't have you embarrassing your father. Not with all those old bores out there.'

'You didn't look like you were bored.'

'It's just playing a part, Rosie. Not something you're used to.' He sat down next to me and put his hand on my leg, and began to stroke it. 'That's why I like you. You're unspoilt.'

'I am?' I said. I was aware my voice sounded squeaky. He was close to me now. He smelt of a strong cologne, like something I fancifully imagined the princes of Arabia would use. I was certain he must be able to hear the pounding of my heart, which was beating so hard it hurt.

'At the moment you are, yes,' he said. 'You're exactly as you should be.' He reached up and felt along the length of my plaits, which, for once, had been pinned to my head, then plucked a hothouse lily from a pot and planted it in my hair.

I didn't exactly know what he meant. I for one wasn't at all happy with how I was. I wanted to be like Hildy, with a knowledge of the world and to travel, like all the Laffertys did, through the universe without doubt and dread. But here was a beautiful, supremely confident boy – a man now he'd turned eighteen – and he liked me. I closed my eyes and waited for him to kiss me and sure enough, he did, just lightly, like the brush of a peachskin. And for a while there, in that huge old hall, with a party going on nearby, I was the happiest I have ever been in my life. I don't think I realised at that glorious moment that I would spend the rest of the winter pining for him.

16

I must warn you that parts of this account might seem vulgar, even shocking. I'm not doing it deliberately. It might sound pompous, but I feel that now I have a duty to tell the truth. These places make you feel like that. It will be strange, perhaps even unpleasant to read, but I hope you will.

It wasn't until the snowdrops were out that I saw Franklin again.

Janey found me running down the lane the day the Laffertys arrived and called out –

'You be looking mighty pleased with yerself, Rosie.'

'They're back,' I said, 'the Laffertys are back.' Right then, the entire lane seemed to be budding with life and the birds had set up a chorus just for me.

She frowned. 'Look after yerself, child,' she said.

I stopped and put my hands on my hips. 'I'm not a child, Janey.'

'You are and yer not. Thass what I'm afeared of.'

I gave her a squeezing hug and leaned in to smell her particular aroma of marsh mud, salt and rosehip tea.

Over winter they hadn't come to Norfolk for weeks and I became quite morose. Father got fed up with me and told me I'd have to go away to school if I didn't stop moping about. I knew this was an empty threat. The printing press hardly made any money if Fairbrother's grumblings were true. I received letters from Hildy, never from Frank, telling me all about the shows she saw, the people she met and the parties she went to. She sprinkled her letters with names, like glittering jewels – the painter Augustus John, Harold Nicolson, the imperious Lady Astor, the marvellous Mitford sisters and especially Diana Mitford, now Guinness, shocking everyone by becoming Oswald Mosley's mistress. A year ago I wouldn't have known who any of these people were, they meant nothing to me, but through Hildy's letters they took on the feel of characters from a picture book, brightly painted and gaudy. I'd come to realise that Hildy, being untitled, resented and mocked this society, but yearned to be one of them at the same time. She mentioned Franklin in passing but they couldn't come up, apparently, as it was all too 'manic' with 'Oswald's new party'. I couldn't understand at all why this meant they couldn't come to Norfolk.

But when they finally came back to Old Hall, it was the same as before. We spent the whole time together, Hildy, Frank and I, playing music on their gramophone – jolly songs, jazz and show tunes, records from America; singers with names like Ozzie and Louis and Skip and voices that dripped with treacle and honey. Frank would twirl me around the drawing-room so I felt, if I half-closed my eyes, that I was one of the bright ones, the beautiful ones, always dancing and laughing and gay. When they weren't there, I would take long, freezing walks along the marshes and imagine the summer to come, which would be a more brilliant version of the one before. I could hear the music in the birdsong around me – the orchestra playing in the air and winding through the reeds on the marsh. I would hum the words I half remembered: dream of me ... sweet and lovely ... a bowl of cherries. I could <u>feel</u> spring coming, on my skin and in my heart. I was nearly sixteen and I could feel life blooming from deep within me, opening out towards the sun.

One Saturday morning, Hildy and her mother went to visit a lady friend of theirs who lived near King's Lynn, a viscountess no less. Frank told me he'd made up some bunkum about shooting and they let him off the trip. The colonel hadn't come up this time. Apparently he was needed by Mr Mosley to organise meetings for the party. I knew all this because Frank bicycled straight over to the Marsh House and rang the bell. Afterwards, I was relieved it was me who answered, though I should have known that Frank was the sort of person who'd be able to dream up some excuse.

'Frank! Why are you here?' I said, but he took hold of me and shut the door behind him, telling me to 'Ssshhh'.

'Is your father here?' he asked, but I assured him that Father was at the printworks in Cromer and wouldn't return until the last train. Since the summer of the Laffertys, Father had been having meetings around the county with various political people. Each time he returned, he would tell me that the meeting had been 'very satisfactory', but I only had a dim idea who these people were or why he was meeting them, just that they were something to do with Frank's own father, the colonel, and their dislike of the disastrous Ramsay MacDonald and Stanley Baldwin. And I knew it had something to do with the people we'd met at that supper party in the Hall back in the autumn – the London people in their beautiful suits – and Mr Mosley's new party. I supposed that he was hoping to make some money from them. He said they were the future of this country.

Frank relaxed then and we had a pleasant hour gossiping and drinking tea. He told me all the latest news from London, about the film version of Noël Coward's operetta Bitter Sweet, which he said was not a patch on the original, other farces and musical plays he'd seen and other details about London life. It all sounded very far away and glamorous, but I've forgotten most of it because as the morning raced towards midday, he professed himself ravenous. We foraged for a picnic in the kitchen and set out to the marsh. 'I feel like seeing a bit of the sky, little Rosie,' he said, putting his hands on either side of my face until my head tingled.

'I'm not little,' I said, catching the words in my throat.

He glanced down at me. 'No,' he said. 'You're getting to be quite grown up.'

We walked away from the empty house, with only the windows watching us, up the Green Way towards the marsh. His arm was in mine. I was becoming taller all the time and 'filling out' as Fairbrother said disapprovingly, frowning at my strained blouse. I was aware of every single movement of my body as I walked with him. My head came to his shoulder and he held onto my arm lightly. When we came to the marsh, he took my gloved hand and pulled me along to the edge and started to unbutton his boots.

'You too,' he said, grinning at me.

'But it'll be freezing cold, Frank,' I said.

'You're not a sissy, Rosie, are you?' he said, the dare in his eyes.

I could only obey. So there we were – our stockings stuffed in our boots and feet in the cold squelch of the marsh mud. He took me far along the creek where there was a spit of land. The spit was hidden by tufts of marsh grass you could hide behind and no one could see you. We ran over the little hill of sand and fell down the other side, laughing. The sun was out and it was almost warm – like the first day of spring. And I was surprised, though I had no right to be, but he pulled me to him straightaway and kissed me full on the lips. It was not the first time he'd kissed me, but this time was different. Our feet were caked with drying mud and our bare legs intertwined and I could feel him swell beneath his trousers and I wondered what on earth I should do. He kept touching me on my chest where I'd grown, circling his fingers, and putting his head there and making moaning sounds. Then he put his hand down his trousers and seemed to be having a kind of fit of spasmodic movement, until finally he threw back his head and howled at the clear blue sky above us. All the time he kept one hand on my waist which dug hard into my ribs. He fell back against the dune, panting, quite red in the face but with a look of ecstasy that was strange to see.

We didn't say much for a while, we just lay on our backs looking at the sky and I waited to see what he would do. I hoped it wouldn't be the same thing again, but I wanted something to happen. We were told so little and I'd stayed at the school for such a short time I had only a vague understanding of what he'd been doing – I knew it was something to do with desire but at the same time it was quite alien. I began to feel cold but I didn't want to break this feeling of being alone in the world with Frank. He moved his head close to mine and spoke softly into my ear so it tickled –

'Do you love me, Rosie?'

'Yes,' I said, hardly breathing.

'Good,' he said, 'because I don't know how much longer I can bear it. Dear little Rosie Valentine,' and kissed me again, slowly this time, his tongue flickering into all the crevices of my mouth.

And that was all, but as we waded back along the creek, the mud chilling my ankles and shivering up my legs, I felt that I was fully alive. The world was just the two of us, Frank and me.

Late in March, a day of fleeting clouds and sudden sunlight, Frank was alone for an afternoon at the Hall. Lady Lafferty was at the church as usual, the colonel was riding and Hildy was off for a drive with the persistent Gerald.

That day as I walked, tiny silver needles of desire prickled in my stomach and groin. The weekend staff were off too – it was just Frank and the cook there, and she was having a nap in the kitchen. He was eating an orange when he opened the door – the smell of it entered my body like a kind of sweet wine. He pulled a segment away and held it to my mouth. I opened it feeling silly, like a bird being fed by its mother, and he pushed it in, the juice dribbling down my chin and the tartness of it making me wince. He laughed. 'I bet you've not had many of those, have you?'

I shook my head, mute from my mouthful of orange.

Janey told me once that if a man wanted a girl, he must take an orange, prick the skin all over with a needle and sleep with it in his armpit. The next day he must make the girl he loved eat it. I remember thinking that sounded quite horrible, but standing there in the great entrance hall of Old Hall, I couldn't help but think of this with the sweet orange in my mouth, and imagine the charm-juice sliding down into me, making me love him.

He took hold of my hand and I followed him up the main staircase. I had only ever been to Hildy's bedroom, never to Frank's, but I knew that's where we were going. I didn't know exactly what for, except that he'd been saying for weeks now that our love (<u>our love!</u>) was natural and any expression of it was natural as well. I wasn't so naïve that I didn't know what men and women did in married beds. I knew how children were created – the rector himself spoke of such things. But I didn't know exactly what Frank had meant until then.

When it happened – it wasn't for very long – it hurt and I bled. Frank looked disgusted at the red blotches on the sheets and it brought tears springing to my eyes. He put his arm around me, told me to stop crying and wiped my eyes with the white edge of the sheet. But then he said I better get cleaned up quickly, and when I picked up my underwear and left the room I saw him tugging off the bedclothes and shoving them into a ball as if he couldn't bear the sight of my blood. They had an enormous upstairs bathroom that the colonel had had installed and which I always thought was luxurious, but it was draughty that afternoon. I sat on the lavatory and the stinging made more tears come but I wiped them away and wiped myself down there – it was sticky as well as sore. The whole room with its brass taps and curled bath feet and ruched curtains felt as if it were rebuking me for the horridness of my body, repelled by all this bodily matter, this grotesqueness.

When I got back to Frank's bedroom he was gaily smoking on the bed, propped up on the pillows.

'Come here, sweet Rosie,' he said, holding his arms open, and I wanted the comfort so badly, I did. I tucked myself under his arm and he stroked my hair. I had an urge to say something, to ask him not to do it again, but he kissed me on my head and said, 'There, it wasn't so bad, was it? You're my girl, now.' Despite the pain in my groin, it felt good to hear him say that. I was wanted by someone. I belonged to someone.

At home, I cocooned myself in tight with a hot water bottle, listened to the rats scuttling in the attic above me, and let Perdie nestle into my bed. I didn't know what to think. Afterwards, seeing my red eyes, he'd said I would like it when I got used to it, but I didn't like it then, I didn't like it at all and I wished my mother was there to advise me. But I wanted him above all else and that was more important than any discomfort I might have felt. The words of a song played in my head, a song we'd been playing all spring. 'Body and soul. I surrender'. I supposed that was what you did for love. You surrendered yourself.

17

It was Easter Sunday and we were all in church for the Easter service, the Laffertys at the front, Father and I behind. It had been gloomy and overcast all morning, and as we walked to the church it began to rain. It was the middle of the trial of our old rector, Mr Davidson. In my current situation, I've come to feel rather sorry for him. As I write, he has become a pathetic figure, an outcast. Back then, he was all over the papers. After the rector was late for the Armistice Day service, Major Marsden from the next village, who had been complaining about him for years, had finally succeeded in forcing the church to begin holding a trial against him, accusing him of using 'innocent girls' for his own ends on the streets of London. The rector was a fool, I think, more than anything. According to the rags and local gossip, he would find girls from Lyons tea shops or on the streets and offer to help them, often bringing them up to the rectory. Depending on your view, he was either trying to save them or lusted after them. Perhaps it was both. The village had been full of the scandal all year. In the meantime, the services went on, still sometimes held by the old rector and sometimes by some other poor man who had to deal with a divided village. They still loved him, you see, the rest of the villagers.

The service went on and on as usual, the stand-in rector talking about Jesus dying for our sins. Father muttered under his breath and I think if it hadn't been for Lady Lafferty's piety, we wouldn't have gone to church at all.

'She thinks she has a holy duty,' said Hildy, rolling her eyes.

But then I thought, too, of what Frank and I had done. I couldn't put it into words, I was too ashamed. It was me as much as him. Not at first, but by that Easter. I had begun to like the feeling of it. It's hard to think something can be wrong when it feels like an explosion in your insides, all the way through you to the tips of your fingers and the top of your head and you can't breathe, and your whole body feels alive for the first time, and you want it to go on and on and on. But I wasn't supposed to think like that, I knew it. I looked at Colonel and Mrs Lafferty and tried to imagine them doing it to create Hildy and Frank and I had to squeeze my eyes shut to stop myself bursting. Or Mrs Fairbrother with her fat bottom. It was a terrible thought.

As we left the church the rain had stopped, but the sky was still hung low and overcast. Hildy had her arm in mine while we waited for her mother. Lady Lafferty's elegant neck was bent down to the stand-in rector. Then she turned to me and smiled beatifically, as if she were about to perform some Christian miracle. There was a keenness in her look though, that made me squirm. I was afraid she knew – and worse, that she would take Frank away from me. I thought I must be damned and although I knew I should feel guilty and tell Franklin to stop, I wasn't sure I could.

St Mark's Eve is at the end of April and on that night it is traditional to perform divination rituals. Janey had taught me how to divine who we would marry. Although I didn't entirely believe it, neither did I want to bring myself bad luck by not going along with it. I hadn't met Franklin the year before, and had done it out of fun. I'd never seen anyone. That year, Janey gave me some hemp seed and said, 'You oughta find out who you're destined for since you're going on with the boy from the Hall.'

'Oh Janey, it's just nonsense,' I said, hiding my embarrassment, but wanting, needing, at the same time, for it to be him.

'That may be so but I reckon you want to try anyway, dunt you?'

'Oh all right then,' I said, feigning disinterest.

Janey herself always took herself to the church on St Mark's Eve because, as she told me, 'The next year's dead will walk.' This was a very old custom, she said, that no one practised any more, but she had the habit and couldn't get out of it or she might miss her own death. She told me the watcher must watch the entrance to the church at midnight and those who would die in the coming year would walk in and not come out. I didn't believe in this either, but she did seem to have a miraculous tendency to predict who in the village would die in the coming year. She'd predicated a local farmer's death the year before.

At just before midnight it was black as pitch in the garden and the ground wet with dew. I snuck out in my boots and threw the hemp seed at the end of the garden, where it meets the creek. I chanted in a low voice:

> Hemp seed I sow,
> Hemp seed I grow;
> He that is my true love,
> Come after me and mow.

I waited, feeling incredibly foolish, out in the dark garden with a cool dampness in the air, in my nightgown and boots. Nothing happened, merely a rushing sound from the marsh which sent shivers along my skin. There was a sliver of a moon and I thought maybe something passed by in the shadows, but it wasn't a man mowing with a scythe. It was probably a rat. Annoyed with myself, I stomped off back to the house. What exactly had I been trying to prove? That Franklin was my destiny? I was a country girl with a mad mother and he was a Lafferty. The most pressing concern for me should have been how to stop it before anyone found out. But already, my mind was twisting itself to justify our actions. Damned or not, I told myself, it wouldn't be entirely bad, would it, if he loved me? If we loved each other, surely we could be saved? It was natural, he said. And it seemed true. As natural as breathing.

The next day, I asked Janey who she'd seen out walking in the night and she gave me a funny look and said it were bad luck to name them but it were no one young. So that was a relief.

Later – it might have been the same day – I was walking Perdie along the path at the end of the lane that skirts the marsh, when I saw the smirking face of George Bayfield a mere foot away. I'd been daydreaming about Franklin and had hardly noticed anything around me at all. Now I felt like I'd emerged out into the open, undefended. To my left, the marsh was clothed in the light green of spring and to my right, the line of Stiffkey Wood was soughing in the wind and casting waving shadows across the muddy track.

'Perdie, heel,' I said, but she was already bounding up to the boy and he'd kneeled down and had something held out in his hand to her.

'She's a right pretty dog you got there, Rosie Wright.'

'Yes she is,' I said, haughty as anything. 'She doesn't need feeding.'

'She likes it,' he said, and sure enough, silly trusting Perdie was licking his outstretched hand.

'What do you want?' I said, as sure as I could. I didn't like the way he was smiling at me. He wasn't angry and shouting like before. He seemed calm, which was more worrying.

'To see you,' he said. He was closer now, in front of me.

'Why do you want to do that, George Bayfield? You called me a witch last time I saw you.' He should have been a handsome boy, George Bayfield, with his dark curls and symmetrical features, and I could once have imagined taking a fancy to him, but he was always amused at others' failures and his face often contained such callousness that it contorted his fine features.

He smiled as if it was a funny joke. 'Maybe you are,' he said. 'My ma says you've bewitched the boy from the Hall. The posh one. She says you've got gypsy blood.'

'She doesn't know anything about him,' I said. 'Nor me.' My neck was hot and I could feel the blush rising up my chest to my throat.

'Well, either way, I've heard a lot about you and him and what you get up to. The whole village knows it. But I thought I'd come and find out for myself whether it was true.'

Now my whole body was burning.

'Leave me alone or I'll hurt you,' I said.

'Oh come on now,' he said, 'don't be like that.' And very quickly, before I could run away or retaliate, he'd grabbed the back of my head and shoved his tongue into my mouth. One hand had my hair pulled back and with the other he was pawing all over my chest.

For a shameful, terrible moment I froze, I was so shocked by what he was doing. Then Perdie began to bark. I bit down on his wiggling, flickering tongue. He sprang back, yelping like a pig, clutching his mouth.

'Don't ever touch me again,' I stammered and picked up the yapping Perdie.

'You're a whore, Rosie Wright!' he shouted at my back. 'A whore and a witch.'

I should have known by what happened with the grocer's son on the path by the marsh that I wasn't meant to be saved.

18

The next month, the Marsh House saw something it never had before – a party to celebrate Father's birthday. Father was never one for birthdays and other trivialities, but he was forced into it by the Laffertys. They were that sort of people. Sometimes I used to think Father would ride around on a horse naked through the streets like Lady Godiva if the colonel or Lady Lafferty told him to.

The day of the party was a fine, spring day and the apple trees were in blossom. I always used to imagine my mother with apple blossom in her hair like confetti when she was married, but it was just a childish made-up thing. I would hide in the trees and shake it down over Billy, the gardener's son, when we were children. Lady Lafferty tried to get Father to hold the party in the Hall but he went rather red and insisted that if a party were to be held, we could certainly manage it. He, Fairbrother and Dolly got themselves into a huge flap after he announced it. Perdie was dressed up in a bow and pranced around the garden madly excited. Fairbrother made up a vast trifle and dozens of fancy little cakes and made me sew hundreds of triangles of cloth for bunting which poor Rogers had to string up all over the garden. There was a lot of fuss about impending rain. Fairbrother spent most of her time on the morning of the party muttering about 'threatening clouds' and making Rogers construct a kind of rain shade from sheets over the patio. It looked completely ridiculous, like some kind of safari tent, but in the end the clouds passed over and the afternoon was clear.

Now I think of it, the whole of that summer was remarkable for the lack of rain. Day after day, as spring turned to summer, the dew evaporated and the morning mists burnt off and the sun shone unrelentingly on the marsh. We were burnt up, the land and I, hot and fevered.

I was made to wear a white dress, a very old-fashioned one Father had found a woman in the village to make for me for the summer, with frills and ruching, which was not the fashion at all. I looked like one of the village girls, dancing around the maypole on May Day, something I'd long since given up. Hildy always brought me magazines she'd read and all the dresses in them were simple, without what we considered 'baby nonsense'. She would lend or give me her old dresses but most of them looked misshapen on stumpy little me. Or the colours wouldn't work with my complexion. I tried to imagine Mother getting married in a long, white dress but there were no pictures up anywhere. Father must have hated to be reminded of her. I had only two photographs of her, which I found in a drawer in Father's desk. I kept them in my bedside drawer and took them out sometimes to look at. They were like a pair: before and after. One was taken in India where mother was born – I'd been told she was an orphan then and I wonder if it was sent out to prospective suitors. She was very beautiful and serious-looking with large, deep eyes. She was in white, as in the next photograph, but it was a summer dress and she had a parasol. It was like the portrait of someone whose life has already been decided. In the next one she must have just got married but she wasn't smiling at the camera. The date on the back says May, 1912. It was very formal. She was seated outside the front of the Marsh House, which had just been built, on a high-backed chair and wearing a pale dress that, apart from the length (mine was shorter though not short enough), looked much like the monstrosity I was forced to wear to the birthday. Father stood behind her with his hand on her shoulder. He looked proud, as if he'd just landed the catch of a lifetime.

I wished I could climb into the photograph and put my head on her lap, for her to stroke my hair. But now I think what was in those sad eyes was fear. I often wonder if she knew what was going to happen to her. That her first baby would die within the year, then the next, and that they would take her away from me, her only surviving child. Janey had told me there'd been babies before me, ones that had barely survived, ghost brothers that no one spoke of. I knew this but it didn't mean much to me then because what girl thinks much of the time before her? I used to think about the madhouse though, and try to imagine what Mother did in there. Was she locked up as I am now? Had they shaved her hair? This is what Hildy told me. She was an expert as she'd visited a lunatic asylum in London. I still wonder about it. And I wonder if they've told her where I am.

'You look fair, Rosemary,' Frank said when he arrived, 'like a lovely, innocent country girl.' His lips twitched as if he was itching to tear the little bows at my breast off with his teeth right there. But perhaps I imagined that because he spent the rest of the party ignoring me, off talking to various other young men all dressed up in suits, and only now and again peering at me with a lascivious look so that I felt naked even though I was trussed up like a turkey. Hildy came to my rescue and took my arm and we paraded around the garden with glasses of rhubarb cordial, eating some of the little cakes with lemon icing that poor Dolly had churned out. Sadly, this wasn't for long. We'd barely taken one turn around the lawn when we passed a knot of the older people gathered around Lady Lafferty – men and women like Mrs Parkinson who's a nosey-parker from church. I caught snatches of their conversation.

'Oh, she is quite small,' said one.

'Her complexion is quite . . . dark,' said another.

'I always wondered if there was a touch of the – you know – about her –' This one lowered his voice and whispered something into the ear of someone else so I didn't know what it was I might have been touched with.

'I hear she's a reader of mystery novels,' said another, as if this was quite distasteful.

'She's not a beauty like her mother, let's hope she's not . . .' started one, but didn't finish the comparison.

'It must be because of Richard's support of the colonel's politicking,' said someone.

'It must be hard for her without a mother,' said Lady Lafferty, 'the poor child.'

I imagined them circling around me, prodding and touching as if I were a prize sheep being weighed up for a show. Hildy and I stood back from them unseen, and I could see her sardonic eyebrow underneath her jaunty little purple hat. I wondered what it would be like to have the kind but distant Lady Lafferty as a mother.

Finally, when we were away from the crowd, I said to Hildy, 'I can't think why they were so interested in me all of a sudden.'

'Oh Rosie, you are a silly thing,' she said, 'don't you see? You're like a vision of virginal girlhood. Everyone venerates virginity, even if they don't practise it themselves.' She took a sip of her cordial.

'What do you mean?'

She gazed at me with amusement. 'In my world, darling, it's rather a given that the men and sometimes even the women will roam. We can't all be staid as Mummy. It's not the modern way. But you – you should cultivate this –' She waved her hand towards me in my convent girl get-up.

My face felt hot and I worried I was blushing. Perhaps she would think I was a humble sort of person.

Hildy continued. 'Poor Mummy is awfully worried about Frank though. He's always been her favourite. She turns a blind eye to most of his shenanigans but I think she's worried he'll get syphilis or something. That would really be a shock, even for her beloved Frankie.'

I didn't know what 'syphilis' was and thought it was some kind of urban illness, but it made me feel queasy thinking of Franklin touching me and our relations in the bed. I had a picture then of how they would see me if they really knew. And while it made me feel giddy with a thrilling nausea, I couldn't let it continue. If they knew ... If they knew they wouldn't forgive me. They would blame me, not him. I must have reddened because Hildy suddenly grabbed my elbow and peered down at me with suspicious eyes.

'You haven't let anyone seduce you, have you?'

'No, of course not,' I said hotly, thinking of George Bayfield thrusting his tongue in my mouth; Franklin pulling up my dress with his fine fingers.

'Well you absolutely must not, whatever they promise you. Don't be a fool, darling. They are slaves to their instincts you know, even the well-bred ones.' She made a pointed glance across the lawn to the knot of suited men, which included her dogged suitor, Gerald.

'All of them?' I said. 'What about Gerald?'

She laughed, throwing her head back. 'Yes, Rosemary, all of them. Even dear old Gerald. Even my dear brother. Especially him.'

I looked down at my feet blurring below.

'Does your mother know about – Gerald,' I said, very quiet.

'Oh yes, she's chums with his mother. Rosemary, listen to me. You must understand that it's different for men.' There was a slight change in her voice then and I glanced up to see her face tighten and I wondered, for the first time, if Hildy had any doubts. Until then, she'd seemed impervious. Then she laughed again and took one of my plaits in her elegant, white hand. She peered at me curiously.

'This – this is your value. Without it –' she shook her head. 'I know you're fond of Frank, darling, but he's ... well he's no different. In fact, I think he's one of the worst. Mummy is a fool about him, she always has been. Do be careful.'

'Hildy,' I said, 'I'm not feeling awfully well. I might just go and have a lie-down.'

'Oh,' she said, 'we can't have you party-pooping. Take some smelling salts or something. Or a nip of brandy,' she called as I ran off to the house.

But I didn't come out again and Father was angry with me later, telling me I'd ruined the party. I didn't care at first, I was tumbling with such a mess of feelings I didn't really think much about anything apart from Franklin and what we'd done and if he loved me and what to do. I had given my virginity willingly. I wasn't pure like they thought I was; I'd given myself to him. He couldn't just discard me.

After the awful party, the Laffertys went back to London. As the days passed, I thought perhaps Hildy had been exaggerating Franklin's appetites. Men ogled at women, I did know that. It didn't mean they did anything about it. But I resolved to settle it with Franklin when he returned, and to make it clear somehow that I was afraid and he must protect me.

But my life at the Marsh House was so empty of anything interesting, it was impossible not to feel a lift in my heart when Fairbrother told me the Laffertys were coming back to Old Hall for the Midsummer weekend. I practically threw myself at Hildy and she at me when we were reunited. And when I saw him and he smiled at me the sun came out, for all my resolutions. It didn't, of course, it was a grey day, but it felt like that inside. I knew it was sentimental and foolish. I told myself that Frank probably smiled at lots of girls like that and tried to burst the bubbles of delight I felt. But it was the devil in me; I felt the current of electricity running between us and wanted more than anything to fuse our bodies together. To touch him and to have him touch me.

We were in their drawing room for tea. My father, the colonel, Gerald and Mr Saunders – a thin man from the party, who Hildy said knew Mr Mosley personally – were playing bridge by the window. They were talking about Mussolini in Italy, and the Mitfords, the latest affairs of the Prince of Wales and various other people whose names were always in the papers.

I made an effort to pay attention as I thought that one day I might meet some of these people and I would look like such a bumpkin if I didn't know who they were.

Lady Lafferty was making plans for a church fête, Hildy was drinking tea with her feet up on an ottoman and I was next to her, greatly wishing I wasn't there.

'You look well,' said Frank, smiling at me from his position leaning against the fireplace with a cigarette.

At Franklin's words, I felt his mother turn her attention towards me.

'Yes, positively so,' she said. 'Come here and sit beside me, Rosemary.'

Again, the shiver of fear ran through me that she knew and was going to stop it. For all my good intentions, the thought of his attention being withdrawn from me was like the curtains being drawn on the day. But I moved across the room and sat on the settee next to her. She turned her ice-cold eyes on me, chilling my skin, although the room was warm. But then she said something that was unexpected.

'You're a true country girl, Rosemary, and you don't know the ways of the world, but I think of you like a daughter and I will do my best to protect you.' She laid a cool, thin hand on my arm and set my skin to goosepimples. 'There are things about this world that I don't think you understand, child. Things it took me too long to understand. Be careful, dear. You must keep your wits about you.'

It was an awkward little speech and I didn't know how to answer it. I mumbled, 'Thank you,' not understanding exactly what I was to be protected from. From Frank?

'We can't stay cooped up in here, Mama,' said Frank and, stubbing out his cigarette in his teacup, he took two steps across the drawing room and reached down for my hand. 'Rosie and I will take a little stroll.'

I tried to glare at him, but he had his blue eyes fixed on me and I was like an insect stuck in the sticky trap of a spider.

'Yes, go, darling,' said Lady Lafferty. In her voice was a weariness and nervousness that made me think Frank had some hold over her. As I left, the look she gave me was one I couldn't interpret, although now I think it was a kind of pity. They returned to their hands of bridge and Hildy to her magazine, and the two of us went out into the garden. It was cool and wet from a rare flash of rain that morning and my boots got soaked in the grass. I remember the lawn was sleek and wet – I kept sliding and he held onto me. We walked a long way across the grounds to the summer house overlooking the river and fields that ran south away from the Hall. I'd never been there before – it was round with a tiled roof and open windows entwined with ivy, and a stone bench that ran around it. I knew he'd brought me down there because it couldn't be seen from the house. In a rigid panic, I tried to hold myself stiff and unyielding to him.

'Hildy says you've done this a lot. Been with girls,' I blurted out.

'That was in the past, Rosie.' Frank was lounging with his feet up on the bench and I stood, jittering.

'Did you do with them what . . . what we've done?'

He didn't answer.

I felt the dreaded tears rise in my throat and sniffed them back down. 'You . . . you disgust me, Frank. You tricked me into doing it. I didn't know.'

'Now Rosie,' he said, smiling indulgently. 'That's not true. You liked it as much as me.'

'I didn't,' I said, but it was pointless because he knew the truth. Not at first, but soon after, yes.

He sighed and said, 'It's you that I want, little Rosie.' Reaching up, he pulled me to the bench and touched the nape of my neck. He put his lips to the top of my spine and with a great effort, I pulled away. He exhaled in frustration.

'What would your mother think, Franklin? She says I ought to be careful.'

'She likes you. She thinks you're a sweet girl.' He chucked me under the chin as if I was a child. 'She doesn't know you like I do. She doesn't know your true nature. Sometimes I wonder,' he said, putting his fingers on my face, tracing along my cheekbones and hairline, 'if you have Mediterranean or Arab blood. It would explain your wildness.' He bit my earlobe. I grimaced. 'Shall I tell her how you cry out? It's your nature, my wild, sweet Rosie. And mine.'

'We should stop,' I said, but the next moment all I said was some murmuring that became a moan because his mouth was on my throat and collarbone and down to my chest, and his hands were up my skirts. It was no use. I was going to give in. I closed my eyes and thought of the light playing on the water on the Broads in the summer and his hands on the wheel and how this, just this, was the most natural thing in the world.

19

At dusk on St John's Eve at the mid-point of the year, I went
with Janey to pick fennel, rue and St John's wort to ward
off evil and then, when night fell, to the creek at the end
of our lane where she was going to perform the toad bone
rite. Janey always took these rituals seriously. As I said,
I told myself I didn't believe it but I see now that it was
part of me, as the house was, as the marsh was. It was our
world: Janey's and mine. A secret world that no one else
entered. Not even my father. Actually, especially him. The
funny thing was, every time we performed one of those
rites, I felt closer to my mother than I did otherwise. When
she'd arrived in Norfolk from India, before I was born – the
year the Marsh House was built – she told Janey she'd left
behind an ayah, a kind of nurse who looked after her while
her parents were off ruling over India, and the ayah had
taught my mother all kinds of magical rituals. So I could
imagine my mother there with me on the bank of the creek.

Janey used a dead toad she'd kept specially (she would
never kill a toad like others might). Behind the creek,

away on the marsh, bluish lights danced on the bog. Janey always used to tell me stories of the will-o'-the-wykes that led travellers to their dooms, but I knew it was marsh gas and that people used to get sick from marsh fever. She lit a fire from the dry reeds and at midnight, under a pink Rose Moon (my moon, Janey said), and by the light of the fire and the marsh lights, we lay the little bones in the muddy water and let them float off. I knew that while you were watching the bones in the water you must on no account take your eyes off them. Janey told me she had to keep her eyes trained on the floating bones or her power would be lost. Even if the world was falling down around her, she couldn't stop watching them. When she finally came out of her trance, Janey fished out of the creek one of the bones, a little crotch-bone, she said it was. She would take it home, bake it, powder it and put it in a box; the oil from the bones made a powerful, old magic.

The rest of the tiny toad bones gleamed in the fire and moonlight and then disappeared into the glimmers of the reflections. I silently mouthed a prayer to God that Janey would always protect me from dark magic, that she would harness her powers, whatever they were, to keep me from harm. I thought about how Frank put his lips on my neck and the way George Bayfield had clawed at me. I wondered if the toad bone oil would be strong enough to keep them away and decided I'd ask Janey for a spell. I felt on the edge of something both desperate and absolutely humiliating.

That night, I added a bunch of the fennel, rue and St John's wort to my windowsill next to a sprig of seablite and the white, dry husks of whelks' eggs.

The next day, when I was helping Janey make some herb tea, she went out to give Smutch his bone and I took one of the little bottles of toad bone oil from her shelf. She'd laughed at me when I'd asked for a spell, saying 'I don't do that kind of magic, Rosie, and you know it,' and ruffled up my hair like I was a child.

I didn't think about taking it, I just did. I didn't know then what I planned on doing with it, until the following Sunday when I saw the grocer's family leaving church ahead of me and the glossy black curls of the back of George's head. I skipped ahead, sidled up to him and whispered into his ear.

'I wanted to say sorry for the other day.'

His eyes flickered towards me.

'I've got something for you, George.'

He looked askance at me, wary I suppose after that time when I bit his tongue. But he had a look in his eyes that was hungry and wanting. I could hear his breathing, shallow and raspy.

'Come to the marsh at dusk,' I said. 'I'll give it to you then.'

I held his gaze until he reddened and mumbled, 'Aright.'

The sun set late at that time of the year so after supper I said I had to take Perdie. I undid the top buttons of my Sunday best lace blouse to expose my throat. It was a warm night and I liked the feeling of the breeze on my skin. Sure enough, at the top of Green Way, with the marsh and the darkening sky spread out before us, there was the short, skinny figure of the grocer's son, squinting as the sun set in a blaze of orange behind me. He had his hands in his trouser pockets as if it was nothing to him to be waiting for me on the edge of the marsh.

'What've you got for me then?' he asked. He didn't come close like last time. And for the first time, it occurred to me that he would really expect something of me, and I didn't know what he would do if he got angry.

'You'll have to come a bit closer to see,' I said, and licked my tongue along my bottom lip.

He frowned and held his hand up to his eyes. 'How do I know you're not going to do something mad like last time?' he said. 'How do I know you won't bite me?'

'I wouldn't,' I replied. 'And anyway,' I added, 'I bet you liked it really.'

'You're mad,' he said, but his face had gone red like earlier, and I could see that mixture of hate and wanting that he'd had before.

'Come here,' I said. In the pocket of my dress, I fondled the unstoppered bottle of toad bone oil.

George took two paces towards me and as he did, I took the bottle out of my pocket and flung it straight in his face. The whole sloppy mess dripped down from his forehead to his mouth. His hands flew to his eyes and I watched while he shouted out and stumbled back, tripping over his feet, and fell onto his back on the path. Perdie jumped up and down, barking at him, startling the birds in the trees, who squawked off into the dusky sky.

He tried to wipe the oily substance from his face but it was still in his eyes. He was blinded.

I turned my back on him and walked home, Perdie capering about my feet. I thought that would be the end of the Bayfield boy, magic or no magic.

On the way back along the path by the creek, there was a shudder in the grasses and a silvery-grey adder slid out in front of us. Perdie yapped at it, but the snake seemed unperturbed. It turned its red eye to me and flicked out its forked tongue before slithering in a sinuous curve, back into the grass. I decided to ask Janey if an adder brought any luck.

But there was no protection after all.

A week or so later, not long before my birthday, Father and I received an invitation to a garden party at Old Hall. The day it was held was the hottest day of the year so far. As Father and I walked to the Hall, sweat prickled under my arms. I wondered if this was the moment when his mother would be waiting for me. When she would damn me.

It was not a garden party like the one for Father's birthday. This was quite different. There were glass bowls of strawberries and cream, a huge meringue with plump fruits and fat dollops of cream on the top, a real band in black tie playing jazz on the patio, and the beautiful people milling about with their cigarette holders and knees on show. I was wearing a pale primrose-yellow summer dress with white sprigs all over it and white stockings on underneath. Across the lawn I saw Lady Lafferty in a flowing pale pink gown the colour of the inside of a shell and she tipped her fan at me. I wandered about for a few minutes looking for Hildy and Frank, listening to the gossip about the rector and stories of rallies in London and Birmingham. But I was hardly there any time at all before Franklin took my arm and led me to the summer house. We are having a conversation, I said in my head. I won't let it happen. I can't. He held my hand and I wanted him to. That was the stupid thing about it. I wanted him to look after me, to take me away from my isolation. His skin shone with the heat of the day. His sleeves were rolled up, revealing the blond down on his arms, lit golden by the sun. I felt a film of sweat on my upper lip.

At first he kissed me on my cheek, and then my mouth. I felt the fluttering in my groin but held myself back. 'What's the matter?' he said. 'You can't be off again. It's impossible.'

'No. Nothing,' I said.

He played with the hem of my dress. He took a bunch of fabric in his hand and lifted it up to my thigh, exposing the skin above the stockings. I could hear the clinking of champagne glasses, the trumpet and the horn from the band, laughter like bells.

'Not here, Franklin,' I said. 'Someone might see.'

'There's no one down here apart from the gardener and I'm sure he's seen worse.

'Do you like this?' he added, touching the soft part of my inner thigh. Yes, I thought. I like it. Don't ever stop.

'We mustn't,' I said, screwing up all my will, and took his hand and held it away from me.

'Don't be a tease,' he said. And he kissed me again and this time he pressed himself on top of me too, so my spine was against the hard stone of the bench that went around the summer house. With one hand he had his fingers splayed on my neck and with the other, he pulled my underwear down and put his fingers inside me. It wasn't gentle and I tried to pull away.

'What about this?' he said, and pushed his hand harder into me. His fingernails scraped against me. His mouth was near my ear and I could feel the wet heat of his breath and the smell of alcohol.

'It hurts,' I said.

But he didn't reply. I told myself he hadn't heard me. He was breathing hard now and was fiddling with his own trousers. I tried then to push him but he was strong and he took both my arms and pinned them down, scraping the bones of my wrists against the stone.

When he pushed himself inside me I would have shouted out, only I couldn't because he had his hand over my mouth. The back of my head was pressed onto the rough edge of the bench. The trumpet blared and someone shattered a glass on the patio and everyone cheered. A breeze blew across my exposed thigh making me shudder.

Afterwards, he tried to kiss me and I turned my head quickly so his mouth fell on my cheek.

'What's the matter with you?' he said.

I was pulling up what was left of my stockings. 'Nothing,' I said.

'Come here,' he said, his voice soft. 'I forget sometimes how young you are. You make me want you, Rosie. I can't stop myself.'

And despite the humiliation, my pulse quickened and I allowed him to kiss me again.

I walked home on my own, the way I'd come, and the day was the same. It was the same hot, still day with hardly a breeze in the trees. I didn't run, I dragged my feet one after the other in a daze. Stifling, not a breath of air. I didn't understand how my shoes still clopped on the same dusty road and the sun still burned the back of my neck and the same dirty curtains hung in the windows of the cottages. The sun heated the top of my head and my neck the same way it had done on the way to the Hall. It all went on just as before. Except now I had a throb in the back of my head, marks on my wrist and a soreness in my groin.

I never wore that dress again.

I can still see it clearly though, that dress, the sunshine yellow, the tiny white flowers like stars scattered all over it. It would be pleasant to have something pretty to look at now I'm only ever in grey. Not that dress though. I'm thinking of the ones Hildy used to wear, in violets and lavenders and silky creams. They were beautiful clothes, bedazzling, the cloth and cut so fine they looked as if they belonged on her tall, thin body. I think of the roughness of the cloth I'm wearing now and it's like a penitent's. I suppose that is what they want from me.

20

Sitting on the edge of the bathtub, my cheek leaned against the cool porcelain of the upstairs sink. In the bowl was a pool of salmon-pink vomit. My body had produced something the colour of the dress Father had brought me for my sixteenth birthday.

I hated the dress, which was long and unfashionable. He had also given me Trollope's Barnaby Rudge and I did not think much of that either. Franklin had sent chocolate truffles from London in a beautiful embossed tin box with a pattern of blue flowers around the edge, but I had found them sickly and they made me gag. I was going to find out why.

From behind me I heard Fairbrother's hard, blunt voice –

'That's you fallen,' she declared with grim satisfaction. 'Up the spout.' There was no lock on the door and it was ajar. 'I always knew you'd come to no good.'

I understood her – I heard the way the villagers talked and I wanted to shout 'No, I'm not!' – but she'd already stalked away. 'Your father needs to know what you've gone and done.'

I shut the door then – too late – and sat with my back to it. What <u>had</u> I done? It couldn't be true. My body was revolting against something inside it – but not that, surely. I must be ill.

The doctor was summoned. He was an old man, not from the village, not our usual doctor. Fairbrother made me sit on the bed.

'You don't have to be here, do you?'

'Your father asked me to,' she said, and crossed her arms over her very ample bosom.

'Lie down please,' said the doctor. His voice was shaky as if he was disgusted at having to do such a thing. I wanted to scream at them all that I had no need of any of this. My Janey could have done it, she had <u>delivered</u> me. She had seen me come bloody and bawling out of my poor mother. She would know what to do. But Janey wasn't ever invited into the house, not anymore. Not since Mother was sent away.

I squeezed my eyes shut and clenched my fists and lay back on the bed. My thighs were clamped together but he put his hands on my knees and pulled them apart, chilling my parts. His cold fingers prodded inside me, his heavy face averted. I could hear his breathing, shallow and fast. Up he went, pushing right into me until he must have found what he wanted. There was a dull pressing ache in my stomach. I kept my mouth tightly closed and bit my bottom lip. All the time, he never spoke to me, only to Fairbrother, who stood watch like a prison guard in the room. Fat, stupid tears appeared at the corners of my eyes and fell down the side of my face and I wiped them away furiously.

When it was over, the doctor washed his hands in a bowl of hot water Dolly had brought up, washing me off his cold, white hands. He whispered something to Fairbrother and said to the wall behind me –

'You can get dressed now.'

It was the end of July and normally the Laffertys would be in London for the season. So it was a shock when very soon after the doctor's visit, on a dreary day, I heard the doorbell ring and Fairbrother go into a great clattering fuss.

'It's her ladyship, her ladyship! We've got nothing for her. Dolly – Dolly, get here now!'

I crept out of my room where I'd been reading, and waited on the landing, until Lady Lafferty had been let in and her umbrella stashed and her coat taken – it was drizzling outside – and she was shown into the front room.

Dolly was sent in with tea. When she came out, backwards, her head bent low (Oh Dolly, I thought. Don't!), I tiptoed to the door to listen. All I caught was this:

'Richard, I know you aren't terribly keen on the church after all the village has suffered, but please, for me ...' There was a scrape and a hush and I couldn't catch what was said. Then my father's voice, hoarse and in pain—

'... deeply sorry that my family should bring such shame –'

'No,' came Lady Lafferty's voice, soft and low, 'it's the least we can do for you. You know how much I value your loyalty to my husband, Richard.' She paused. 'And your kindness to me.'

There was a rustling. I caught the words 'lonely' and 'Louisa', then a hard scrape and footsteps and I flew, lightly and fast, back upstairs.

They were going to help me. Perhaps it would be a sanatorium, an exclusive place where unfortunate girls could go to dispose of awkward things. I pictured big, white rooms and a wall of glass overlooking a frozen lake. I didn't know how she'd found out, but I could guess – Fairbrother and her chattering mouth. By now, I knew enough of how people like the Laffertys lived to know that they had ways to smooth over something undesired. It was such a relief, I felt like singing.

When she'd gone, Father called me to his study. This was highly unusual – I was rarely allowed in his sanctum. Inside it was overflowing with paper – pamphlets and books spilling over his desk and onto the floor. Stacks and stacks of them. On his desk was a photograph from the party in the autumn. He was standing next to Lady Cynthia and her alarming husband, Mr Mosley, the man with the film star looks. Colonel and Lady Lafferty were in the picture too, but it was Frank I homed in on. He was beaming at the camera as if this was exactly where he wanted to be.

I hardly heard Father talking. He was saying that the colonel and Lady Lafferty and himself had agreed that it was best for all concerned if a marriage took place between their son – 'and you, Rosemary, given your condition'. Outside the study window rain was falling. The noise of it smattering against the pane drowned out his voice. So that was it. My future had been decided. For a strange, bewildering moment, I wished I could have melted into the floorboards and transformed into a rat with a fat tail on the marsh. It was a dream come true, a girl's best wish, the ultimate ambition. But it didn't feel like it at that moment. I didn't understand why I wasn't cock-a-hoop. Rather, I felt small and scared. I didn't understand how I was supposed to have a *baby*. I had prayed and chanted and dreamt of Franklin loving me but I had never thought of babies.

'Rosemary, look at me when I'm talking to you,' he said, cutting through my inattention.

I lifted my gaze to his. There was the trace of a sad smile on his face. Perhaps he was relenting.

'I feel responsible for what's happened. I should have sent you away to school to learn decent morals.'

I said nothing but looked out of the window at the rain lightly pattering onto the garden.

'I should have married again, a long time ago, and given you a mother –'

'I have a mother,' I said.

'– given you a mother who could have guided you, and perhaps you would never have lost your way so entirely.' His face clouded. 'But –' Here he glanced with a satisfied look at the photograph on the table, 'at least now you'll be entering the care of a good family. With time, you'll learn to be grateful. You'll be a wife and a mother.'

'I don't want to be either,' I said sullenly. From the window I saw the rain had stopped and the sky was clearing.

'Nonsense,' he said. 'There's no alternative.' The inevitability of it dropped like a stone into my stomach. It would happen, whatever I wanted.

'You're very lucky indeed that I haven't cast you out. That I kept you all this time. That I didn't send you away at birth. And now you have been offered a sanctuary which, frankly, you don't deserve. And you respond like this. You are an ingrate.' His voice was low and hard.

'I don't know why you kept me. I wish you hadn't. You cast Mother out, you should have got rid of me then too,' I said.

'If you don't want to turn into your mother, you should do as I say.'

'You said she was dead,' I said defiantly.

His face darkened and seemed to pulse with rage. I was afraid he would strike me and cowered in front of him waiting for the blow. But his expression shut down and he closed his eyes.

'Go!' he said.

I ran out of the study, letting the door slam deliberately behind me, and out of the house to Janey.

She ushered me into her all-in-one room, as I thought of it, her sitting-room-cum-dining-room-cum-kitchen. On the hob, a pot was simmering and the air smelt soupy.

'You want a cup a something?'

I never refused Janey. So we shared a cup of the tea she made herself. It was bitter-tasting, laced with sweet honey. It wasn't cold outside, in fact the day had heated up, but here in Janey's cottage the season was always the same – an indeterminate half-lit world, the only sign of difference being the herbs she had strung up, and what was in the pot.

'What's happened, girl? Spit it out.'

'The doctor says – the doctor says – I'm pregnant. And they want me to marry Franklin.' The words were heavy and I was still reeling from the force of them.

Head down, I felt rather than saw her move over to where I sat. I could smell the sea-smell she always had on her and I wanted to cry then, for things to be how they had been before, for my childhood. She let me fall into her and cry on her ugly old clothes and into her familiar, cushiony chest.

Eventually I heard her speaking from above me. I was afraid she'd say I warned you but instead she said –

'Now I'd have thought that would please you, the way you've been going on about that boy –'

'I am . . . I think. It's just I don't want to . . . I don't want . . .' I could barely speak.

'I know,' she said. 'But you think they'll want you to wed if you aren't with child no more?'

I sniffed. 'I don't know.' The idea of being married to Frank was a dream I hadn't dared to believe in. I couldn't see how the Laffertys would ever deem me suitable for their golden boy. A part of me knew it was only because Lady Lafferty saw me carrying his child that she wanted me. She had other reasons too, but I didn't know that then.

'And what about you? What do you want? Do yer love him?'

No one ever asked me what I wanted. I tried to think. I wanted the Franklin of the beach; of the early days when he was sweet to me. I wanted him to love me. Yes, I loved him.

'Yes,' I said.

'And do yer want it? A babby.'

A baby? A mewling, helpless creature? How would I look after that? No. But perhaps with a baby, I considered, he would love me more. I had a picture then, of the three of us as a family unit, something I had never had.

21

On the night before my wedding, I returned from Janey's cottage to find my room bare. There were no books, no hairbrush, no clothes, no bow and arrow and worst of all, there was no sign of the collection of treasures I'd kept on my windowsill. Perdie barked at the empty room, stripped of anything which had made it mine.

I ran back down the stairs, my heart thumping. Father was in his study, writing.

'What's happened to all my things? Where's my collection?'

He looked up at me, bemused, as if he was unsure what I was doing there. 'I asked Mrs Fairbrother to clear your room if you must know.'

'But why?'

'You're going to live at Old Hall of course. From tomorrow, you'll be married.'

'But my books! My collection!'

'I've sent your books and clothes to the Hall, although I'm sure they'll furnish you with finer things. And if by collection you mean the heap of rubbish and detritus you kept on the windowsill, it was unhealthy and best forgotten.'

The clock in the study ticked on as I stared at him, summoning the courage to speak without crying.

Finally, when he'd turned away from me, I spoke. 'Where is it?'

He didn't face me, but said to his desk, 'She threw it all out on my instructions. You're fortunate I didn't do it sooner. You're getting married, Rosemary. You cannot act like a heathen anymore. The past is gone, for goodness' sakes, it is pointless holding onto it.'

I stood in front of him, my shoulders shaking. I couldn't think how to explain to him what he'd done. How could I express to him the years I had spent collecting those objects that he called rubbish, the meaning they had which I could not even fathom myself?

On my finger the heavy gold ring Franklin had given me. It was inlaid with a sapphire that flashed blue every time it caught the light. I had been delighted with it at first – I couldn't believe someone like me could ever wear a thing of such beauty. I'd never seen anything like it. I don't know what happened to my mother's jewellery. But the ring was tight. My fingers were stumpier than the Laffertys', and underneath the metal, it rubbed against my skin. Now it felt too heavy, too tight, and the dazzling brilliance of the jewel felt out of place in the house. It belonged in Old Hall. I would have swapped the beautiful, blue ring for my bird's egg then.

I didn't even cry – I ran out, slamming the door, and lay on the floor of my room, spreadeagled to hold it in my body. Every part of me touched the floorboards: my fingertips, my groin, my knees, my forehead. I banged on the floorboards until my knuckles were raw and still the anger was coursing through me. I ran back outside and, stumbling up the Green Way, I went as far as it could go until I came to the creek. It was autumn and the marsh was turning and flocks of migrant warblers were arriving from the south. I took off my boots and stockings and waded, glad to feel the shock of the cool muddy water on my feet and around my ankles. Above, the great bowl of blue sky mocked me.

I splashed through the freezing creek, not stopping for the dripping grasses which lashed against my ankles, or the sticky mud which oozed through my toes. Hatless, I stomped on and on across the marsh, getting my hem wet and my face whipped by the wind. I came finally to the spit of sand dune where Franklin had taken me and collapsed onto the wet sand and cried. Thinking no one could hear me I let out all my horror at what I'd allowed to happen. I screamed at the open water and it shushed back at me, oblivious. Perdie had run after me and she put her wet nose against my face when I lay down, letting my tears soak into the sand.

I could not have said what I was crying for, only that it felt like the end. It was as if he'd taken my mother away from me again.

At some point I heard Janey calling to me over the marsh in her whooping call that sounded like an owl. She'd come to find me, and scooped me up and scolded me gently for my filthy, wet clothes and sodden boots. She coaxed me back to the house, told me I could make another collection, a different one, but I couldn't see how I could ever get back what I'd lost.

The following day, the day of the wedding, I didn't speak about it, but I wasn't the same anymore. A part of me had been lost with my treasures.

Let me paint you a picture, a portrait of a young girl. The sockets of her eyes are rimmed with grey, from sleepless nights and from the being which is eating up all her energy from the inside out. Her black hair has been washed, curled and pinned at the back. She is short – shorter than everyone else she knows bar Dolly, as if all the growing in her has been drawn into her belly. She's a little rounded on the hips and has small breasts. Yes, there is a bump, but it's barely there and no one would ever know if they didn't already that the child was with child. They've dressed her up like a wax doll in a crown of stitched white flowers and pearls that holds a fine tulle veil, embroidered at the edges with the finest lace blossoms. It is the most beautiful thing she has ever seen and belonged to her mother. There is no money for a new dress so her mother's old wedding gown has been expertly unstitched and re-stitched by a woman in the village, to hide the swelling in her stomach, and falls in a waterfall of creamy white to her silk-slipper-shod feet. When the veil is placed over her face, it looks like a shroud.

She's me, of course. In the image that stared back at me from the glass in my mother's room, I looked uncannily as she did in the photograph taken of her in front of the house. I felt a surge of pride that I had been chosen, but I was uneasy too. I did not look like myself.

I wish I could talk to that girl now, warn her somehow. But she was stubborn, that girl, and wouldn't have listened anyway.

The wedding itself was melancholy, although it's possible I'm making it more so in the memory. Dead leaves were falling in great numbers off the trees, turning the streets to a wet brown mulch. The marriage ceremony was held at St John the Baptist's and the new rector presided over it. Walking through the graveyard from the car on Father's arm, I took note of my favourite gravestones – the one with the two skulls and the cross-bones and the black marble headstone like a draped coffin. At the far edge of the graveyard was the ruined tower of Old Hall and, next to it, the tree I'd climbed. It felt like long ago.

As we walked out of the church and along the path to the car, George Bayfield was scowling at me from behind the wall. I kept my chin up and didn't look at him. Someone had organised the village girls to throw flowers at us, which is the local custom, but as it was autumn all they had were rose hips and dried rose petals which crunched underfoot. It reminded me of how we throw flowers into the graves of the dead – but when I caught the eyes of the girls throwing flowers they were glowing with jealous fire. On my finger, I wore the gold band and the sapphire. I raised my hand and flashed the rings, making sure they could all see. I turned back to George Bayfield then, and I smiled at him, triumphant.

I was a Lafferty now.

Hildy had looked her usual self at the wedding of course, tall and regal in a lilac silk dress that fell across her like waves and made her look like one of the film actresses in the magazines she read. She'd bent down to kiss me.

'Rosie, darling,' she said, 'welcome to the family.'

Then she did her usual thing and took hold of my arm, and held onto me until we were all the way back at the house. Their cook had put on a small reception in the drawing room and Hildy handed me a glass brimming with champagne.

'Mummy is awfully relieved,' she said.

'Relieved?'

'Oh, you know, after the incident with the girl in London, Frank is persona non grata with society. Thank God for you.'

I didn't tell her I had no idea what incident she was referring to or what she meant Frank was, but I kept it tucked up inside me, under my ribs.

I didn't eat anything that day as I felt sick.

By the time Franklin took me upstairs to bed, overlooked by the smiling, approving faces of the gathering – not including our own families who knew the act had already been done – I was light-headed. He was blithe, handsome and cavalier, no different to how he had always been. The champagne and lack of food relaxed me – I knew it had because I held his hand and didn't mind it and leaned on him as we mounted the stairs. I thought that he would leave me alone – he'd have no interest in me now that we were married – there was no conquest now, we were <u>supposed</u> to have 'conjugal relations'. And underneath my cleverly sewn dress, a small bump protruded, a clear sign of my pregnancy. Surely, I reasoned, he would be uninterested. All I wanted was to sleep.

But in the bedroom, he sat down on the bed and told me to take off all my clothes. I was bashful and hesitated. My body had changed. It was warped and swollen and it was no longer my own. And if I thought of him near me I could only remember the stone summer-house bench against the back of my thighs, his hand on my mouth and the roughness digging into me.

'Do I have to, Frank? I'm tired.'

'You have duties now, Rosie. It's your duty as my wife. And besides there's got to be some benefit to all the trouble you've caused me.'

I thought he was joking. His voice was light and I realised that he'd drunk a lot that afternoon as well. I hadn't approached the bed but stood by the door. The carpet between us, huge as that room was, felt too narrow, the bed a mere two paces away. I laughed. He smiled but didn't laugh in response.

'Come here,' he said, 'there's no need to be nervous. You've never been nervous before.'

He was beautiful sitting there, in his black morning suit and white waistcoat, the top hat tossed to the floor and his sandy hair swept back from his high forehead. He was leaning back on his arms, surveying me, daring me to come closer. I didn't move.

The look on his face changed as if a cloud had crossed the sun. For a second I thought he was going to rise and drag me to the bed, but instead he sighed and took out his cigarette case. He breathed out the smoke slowly, in elegant rings.

'At least sit down, Rosie. You're making me feel uncomfortable.'

I perched on the edge of the bed.

He pushed the veil away from my shoulders and ran his hands down the modest lines of the dress.

'You've got an advantage, my unchaste girl. Most girls learn the hard way about marital relations on their wedding night,' he said, rolling the words 'marital relations' around his tongue. 'Not you,' he said, 'you know how it works and, unlike most other girls, you know what a pleasure it can be.'

I winced. There was nothing pleasurable about this.

'Don't do that,' he said, and I bit my lip to stop from crying. He soon got bored of touching the silky cloth of the wedding dress and turned me around and undid the buttons one by one along my back, and rather than being disgusted by the sight of my rounded stomach he put his hands on me and kissed the swelling.

He didn't spend long on me that night. It was over quickly, which was one relief, and soon he was asleep next to me. I looked around the vast, high-ceilinged bedroom. This was my home now.

I cried then, quietly so I didn't wake him. I saw that it didn't matter what I wanted or what I liked. All that mattered was him. In allowing Franklin possession of my body I'd surrendered all of my freedom. It was the price I had to pay. But this is what I had wanted. I had wanted him desperately and I had got him. I felt the pinch of what Hildy had said about Frank in London, but I had to hide it away. Of all the girls he could have married, it was me he'd chosen. This was the important thing, I told myself, and wiped my tears. I was inside the fairytale now.

22

The Face in the Window

Malorie dropped the book. She felt as if she'd been under-water, submerged in the world of the notebook. She needed to breathe. Her head swam with questions about the girl. The mug shot from the newspaper cutting that Franny had found came back to her – that challenging gaze, straight into the camera. She swallowed a slug of wine. Her brain was fuzzy, thick with heavy clouds. She closed her eyes and curled up on the sofa. A sharp pain was growing at the back of her head. The light flickered at the corner of her eye. It must be the reflection of the moon on the wall behind her. She stiffened, became absolutely rigid. Someone was there in the room, behind her, by the window. *Don't look*. If she didn't look it would go away. But it was impossible not to – she felt her whole consciousness pulled towards whatever was watching her. She turned her head.

A face was looking at her through the front window. A pale oval in one of the leaded black squares. It was the face from the cutting, the same staring eyes, the dark hair close around her face. Dark green eyes. Eyes that saw her.

A choking sound came from her own mouth. The wine glass dropped and her hands flew to her eyes to cover them.

A groan came from somewhere above her. She opened her eyes and her fingers a crack. Her own face stared back at her, pale and black-eyed. Beyond, just the dark, empty glass and the silver glow of the moon. Shivers of relief ran over her skin. It had been her own face reflected in the window, the moon playing tricks. Just her reflection and the moon. A trick of the light. Her head was still cloudy and unclear – she needed to sleep. Shivering, she got up and pulled the old, frayed curtains across the window, as though from prying eyes, and slumped back onto the sofa. There was no one out there, no one at all, but she didn't want to be illuminated and neither did she want the dark to come inside. If she thought about the vast inky darkness out there, she wouldn't sleep.

Dribbles of wine had spilt onto the rug, little trickles running over the floorboards, but she did nothing about it. Her body wouldn't stop the prickles of cold, like tiny fragments of glass. In a jerking, lumbering movement, she got up again, picked up the still-intact wine glass and, with her foot, rubbed the spilt wine into the rug and smeared it over the floorboards. Still trembling, she stumbled up to her bedroom. She should stop reading the notebooks. She should stop thinking about the girl.

But as she curled up in the cold bed praying for sleep to come, the face was still there, the dark green eyes boring into her. It wasn't possible to sleep. She lay stiffly, with her face turned to the door, half expecting to see something. But her eyes grew heavy and the longer nothing happened, the more she thought she'd imagined it and felt foolish for how scared she'd been.

23

I've always been in the cottage since before the house was built. Long ago, before people came here for holidays and trips out in their motor cars, when there were only horses and walking, sometimes a carriage. I watched out for her mother and I watched out for her. She were my special one. That weren't no normal child. They all knew it but what they saw in her made them afraid, where I saw suffin precious, like a flower with a spot on it that marks it out as tainted, but makes it unique. She needed protecting, my girl, not plucking. Plucked, she withered. I'd do anything to protect her.

When I brought her squalling out of her poor mother, I saw right away she were a wild one, my Rose. And wild things are dangerous.

24

The Perfect Christmas
Christmas Eve

Malorie's mouth was parched and her throat hurt. She rolled over, away from the white morning light that made her eyes ache. At the back of her head, a girl's face, but as soon as she tried to fix on it, it spun to a pinprick and disappeared.

In the night she'd heard a cry, and in the morning she thought of the story of the girl stuck on the marsh, her mouth filling with seaweed, choking and shouting and no one hearing her.

She had absolutely no desire to get up. It was bloody *Christmas Eve*. She should be doing something festive: making mince pies or singing carols or whatever other people did. Last year, she'd taken Franny to a West End show and they'd eaten hot chestnuts out of a paper bag, scalded their fingers and stared up at the electric, coloured Christmas lights, deciding which ones they liked the best. She saw the two of them, their faces glittered with dots of neon. When Tony came home from work that evening, already half-cut, Franny had hung up her stocking by the gas fire and she and Tony had drunk snowballs.

She was making it idyllic in her memory and knew it hadn't been exactly like that. Franny had thought the show babyish and when they'd stumbled into bed at last, Malorie had pushed Tony away. He'd smelt of perfume that wasn't hers.

This year though, this year was supposed to be different. What had she done? Stop it. For God's sake, *stop it*. She was crying, maddening tears sliding down her nose and into her mouth. She made herself sniff them back in.

The house was quiet. Not silent, it was never completely silent: there was a constant undercurrent of creaks and whispers and rustles, as if it were being tossed about on the sea. But she could hardly hear anything from outside the walls. The snow must have come again.

She took out the two notebooks from under her pillow and turned them over in her hands, feeling along the smooth brass tacks and across the embossed gold-leaf writing. The deep red of the leather glowed up at her.

On the landing, Franny's bedroom door was open and the bed empty. Above the bed, she could just see the edge of the sampler. Curious, she entered the room. It was funny, now she saw it again, that there was no man in the image, nothing to indicate that the girl had a father; funny that the child had embroidered her absent mother and the strange neighbour with the enormous dog, whose name she now knew was Janey. It was uncanny how similar the likeness was to the woman she'd seen in the garden yesterday.

'When's Daddy coming?' was how Franny greeted her.

Malorie knew she should say, 'He's not coming.' But she couldn't. 'Look,' she said instead, 'why don't we take a trip to the nearest town? See the lights, pick up some treats for tomorrow. I'll buy you a hot chocolate.'

Franny furrowed her small forehead. 'Okay. But what if we miss Daddy?'

'We won't,' she said, and looked away before Franny could see her eyes.

She didn't want to think about driving along the hideously winding country roads. Snow had fallen through the night and was now coating the icy layers beneath in further whiteness.

'Larry wants to come too,' said Franny.

'No, Franny. He can't come. He wouldn't like it in a town.'

'He's from London. And he wants to come.'

Oh, damn it to hell, the day was going so badly already.

There was a tentative knock at the back door and it inched open, ushering in a draught of wintry air. Malorie started. A man's head appeared around the door.

'Scuse me, Miss. My daughter asked me to give this to you.'

He was togged up for the Arctic, in a cap and a scarf up to his ears, and without any flourish, he held up, by its scrawny neck, the great carcass of a bird. Malorie yelped.

'Christ!'

The man stepped back and peered at her oddly. He was a short man with a sharp nose and what must once have been a handsome face, like his daughter's, and was regarding her as if he was trying to place her.

'Sorry,' she said, 'I just wasn't expecting – such a large bird.'

'S'alright. I'll just leave it here then,' said the grocer, and placed the enormous beast in the sink. 'Got a drop of coal for you, too, Miss,' he added, plonking a small sack on the kitchen tiles.

'Thank you,' she said, ashamed of how rude she'd been. But there was an eagerness and wariness about him that was making her feel uncomfortable.

He put out a thick, rough hand and she took it lightly in hers.

'Noticed you don't have no holly up on your door, Miss.'

'We have holly up all around the house,' she said.

'I'd put some up in your doorway too, if I were you. And ivy. To warn against witches.'

It made her think of the superstitions running through the girl's account, all these little tokens sent up to the gods and goddesses of fate or dark magic. And his daughter telling her about the dead girl on the marsh.

'Surprised you're here on your own. Your husband coming, is he?'

'Yes,' she said quickly.

He regarded her with a sceptical frown. 'Right,' he said eventually. 'I'll be off then.'

'Thank you,' she said. 'Mr… ' She couldn't remember if he'd told her his name. But by then he was already nearly at the end of the drive.

Back in the house, she argued with Franny for a little longer then gave up. Franny could stay with the dog.

'I'll only be a while,' she said.

As she left, Franny was fixing the holly above the porch. 'You could hang up the ivy I found too,' she said.

The car wouldn't start at first and she had to shovel the snow on the drive, but it was just a few inches deep.

As she drove, she thought about the last time she'd been in a car with Tony, driving back from his parents' house across the city after a disastrous lunch, with Franny asleep in the back.

He'd tried to kiss her. 'What's the matter?' His voice was cold.

'Nothing.' She could feel tears coming and screamed inside for them not to come.

He fell back against the seat. 'Not this again.'

'I can't help it. I can't.'

'It's been weeks. You can't keep pushing me away like this. What's wrong with you? We can't make another baby if you won't let me touch you, can we?'

She was silent. How could they have another baby, the way they were?

'I don't know if I want another baby.' She'd never articulated it before, but now, there it was, out of her mouth.

'What?'

'Maybe if you didn't – I don't know –'

'Didn't what?'

'Nothing.'

He drove without speaking or touching her. She could feel the anger emanating from him. Warm, dry air filtered out of the heater, but she was still shivering. She wiped a finger under her eye to stop the mascara streaking down her face.

'Have you looked at the papers your mother left for you?' He said this like he already knew the answer. And he did, so why bother asking?

'No, not yet,' she said.

He sighed. 'I think you ought to.' Her neck was hurting with the strain of not responding. His lips were pressed tightly together and she could see the veins pulsing in his neck above his clean white collar. There was a long silence as they drove.

'My mother always said you were going to be difficult.' He didn't look at her but stared straight ahead and gripped the steering wheel. She wanted to say *Look at me, Tony. Say it to my face.*

'Your *mother*? How can you say such a thing? For God's sake, Tony, she can hardly judge. She's hardly a paragon, is she?'

'Don't ever say anything about my mother.'

'But she's a bloody alco—'

His hand met her cheek. Her head snapped back against the leather headrest. Her face stung but she clenched her teeth. The shock had stopped the tears.

'Oh baby, God. I didn't mean it.' He pulled the car to the side of the road. 'Come here. We're no good like this.' She leaned on him, accepting the warmth of his coat and his arms. Her cheek was still hot from his hand and her head was sore. He was kissing her hair. He didn't mean it, he never did. He was weak, that's what he said. Quick to anger, quick to love. It sounded like a song lyric he'd memorised.

As he turned the key in the ignition and drove on, he kept one eye on her and touched her face. Checking she was still there.

'Why did you ask about the papers?' It had always been a source of tension between them, the difference in their upbringings; her distance from hers, his closeness with his. He didn't trust her. What kind of person didn't love their family? *I did love my dad*, she ought to say to him, *but you drove him away.*

'I got the impression that your mother wanted you to read what was in there.'

Why? she thought. She made a noise of vague assent.

He wouldn't have understood if she'd tried to explain – that she didn't want to think about her mother. The fact that not once had her mother tried to say anything kind at the end. Not once had she told Malorie she loved her. She didn't want to be further burdened by the weight of her mother's guilt or remonstrance or whatever it was. Whatever she had to say, whatever it was, should have been said while she was alive. All this hiding, this secrecy, this lack of honesty. It sickened her. She didn't want her life to be tied to someone so cold, so remote, so entirely lacking in warmth. Her own responding coldness was a source of guilt and nothing she could do would expiate it now.

Wells-next-the-Sea was crowded with people, huddled in their coats, hats pulled low over their ears. It was strange to be there after days in isolation. As she walked along the bare streets with piles of old snow at the edges where shopkeepers had cleared the path, she felt as if she were an actor in a scene, not really there, not connected to the rest of the world. She received a few stares and realised that the fur coat and fur-lined leather boots must give her away as rather 'London'. She had a sudden unwelcome thought that these were the last fine clothes she'd be wearing for a while if Tony left for good. It scared her, that she would have to survive without him. It wasn't the clothes, it was all of it. The abandonment. The gaping emptiness and terrifying unknown of the future. She'd never lived independently. She didn't even know how. How would she pay the bills and feed them? She saw herself and Franny in a cold, dingy flat while Tony and his family showered their daughter with gifts and comfort and luxury. She wouldn't be able to compete with that and Franny would resent her, and she would grow bitter like her mother.

The pubs were open for the men escaping the Christmas preparations, the sound of singing coming from inside. She bought a few items, eking out the last of her housekeeping – a bottle of brandy, some crackers and cheese, some mince pies for Franny – but she didn't want to go back yet, to the house and her silently judging daughter. She wanted the sea and walked along the quayside until she was away from the shoppers and quite alone. Beyond the little boats in the harbour, there was the sea, a steel-grey churning vastness, whipped white by the wind. She sat on a bench. For the first time since she'd been in Norfolk she felt a sliver of peace. It was this she needed. Nothing else. Just nothing. A blank. A vast grey blank.

She fished around in her handbag for her cigarettes and smoked, staring out at the sea.

25

The Dog

It wasn't until she noticed that her fingers, clenched around the cigarette, were damp and her face was stinging that she realised she'd been crying again. It could have been the wind, all the way over the North Sea from the Soviet steppe, but it wasn't. Bizarrely, her watch told her it was twenty past three and she swallowed, wiped her eyes and gathered herself, put her gloves on and hurried back up the empty street. She had to tell Franny the truth about her father, get it over with.

The night fell as she drove. Soon the headlights created two small tunnels in the darkness. On either side of the road, hedges were fringed with snow which blazed white at her when the headlights swept over them. She would put Franny's presents under the tree; she would drink whisky, brandy, whatever she had to numb herself. It would be all right. But with each mile passed she had the sinking sense of what was to come. Of ruining her daughter's Christmas, of Franny hating her, of the empty flat in London.

The temperature in the car plummeted and she huddled inside her fur.

When the lane finally appeared, she murmured, 'Thank God.'

As she swung into the entrance to the Marsh House, the car slid from under her. The trees loomed at the start of the driveway.

'Christ,' she said, and tried to straighten up the wheel. She squeezed the muscles in her face tight in concentration and her arms strained to control the car. *Don't try to control it,* she heard Tony in her head. *Drive into it.*

It was too late. The branches were coming fast towards her. She was going to overshoot and hit them. But just at the last second, miraculously, the car missed the trees. It skidded and carried on skidding. She was going to crash. She gripped the wheel and braced for impact. Then ahead, something black. An animal, a shadow. A screech of the tyres. For a second she couldn't see. Blinded, she thought she heard a thump from somewhere, maybe a cry. It might have been her own. The car came to a sliding halt at the front of the house.

She had no idea what had happened.

For a minute she just sat, breathing heavily. Immediately, she was back a few days ago on the evening they'd arrived, when she'd swerved and crashed into the hedge. The same sense of disorientation overcame her now. The headlights were still on, shining up at the house. It was in darkness apart from a single vertical yellow line from between the curtains on the second floor and the faint glowing orbs from the candles on the tree in the living room. Something moved behind her and she snapped her head round. There was nothing but darkness. But there *had* been – something black and white.

Still shaking from the near miss, she emptied the boot of the supplies and carried them into the house.

Franny appeared in the hall. 'Larry got funny and ran into the garden but he hasn't come back –' Her face collapsed. 'Where's Daddy?'

Malorie's head hurt. 'I should have told you earlier. He's been held up in London, darling. He can't come.' Her voice sounded tired.

Franny's eyes were already brimful of tears. In a second they would drop, fall down her small face. She couldn't do this.

'I'm sorry, Franny. I'm really sorry.'

She stepped forward to put her arms around her daughter but Franny scrunched up her shoulders and recoiled, pushing herself against the wall.

'It's your fault,' she said, 'you made him not come.'

'No, Franny. It's not like that. It's not.'

'It is. It IS. You're a liar!' And she ran up the stairs. Malorie heard a door slam.

Malorie stood by the kitchen window with a glass of brandy. She was on her second glass and beginning to feel the unclenching of her muscles, the calming of her trembling hands. Her eyes fell on the little bottles above the stove. She picked one up. There were no labels. She opened one and sniffed it. Before, she remembered it had been unpleasant, as if something rotten had been distilled. But now when she smelt it, it was like going back in time. It smelt of herbs, oil and mould. But also of dark magic, the night and the marsh.

It could be the toad-bone oil, a tincture for an illness; it could be nothing. Holding the bottle in her hand, she turned around to the kitchen window, expecting – almost wanting – to see Rosemary or Janey. All she could see was darkness, and her own face staring back at her.

She glanced at the newspaper she'd brought. There was something about a nuclear missile, Europe hit by snowstorms and – Agatha Christie. The 'Queen of Crime' was confined to bed in Baghdad with flu. It reminded her of Rosemary and the notebooks.

She wanted to be somewhere else, other than in her own body, her own mind, her own life. Quickly, in a sudden burst of energy, she climbed the stairs to the bedroom to look again in the suitcase. It was only paper. Endless, endless sheaves of paper. More bloody fascist literature. Posters with titles like *FASCISM MEANS FREEDOM FOR BRITISH WOMEN*; *TOMORROW WE LIVE*, and the repulsive *MOSLEY CALLING – BRITAIN BEFORE JEWRY*.

'Mum.' Franny was calling from downstairs.

'Coming!' she called back. Sod it.

Underneath the papers, at the bottom of the case, was a soft cloth that felt like the plush of velvet. Opening it up, her fingers touched something else. Something smooth and cold, with a sharp, jagged edge. The smoothness of bone. With trepidation, she withdrew the velvet cloth from the case with its contents.

'Mum-my!' came Franny's voice from far below.

'In a minute,' she called.

The whiteness of bone shone in the gloom of the bedroom. They were skulls. Skulls of various sizes, some the size of a rat's head, another the size of a sheep, each with empty sockets where their eyes had been. She held them up to the pale slant of light from the window and the moonlight caught the bone. It was a strange, creepy collection for a girl, not like the things Rosemary had mentioned collecting, much more morbid. She bundled the whole bag back in the case and slammed it shut.

Franny was standing on the landing, holding her battered teddy, Frederick, and worrying at it. She looked forlorn, lost, and Malorie felt a jabbing pain in her chest.

'I'm worried about Larry. I whistled for him like Daddy taught me but he didn't come.'

'Don't worry, darling, we'll find him,' she said, then wished she hadn't.

The two of them went out into the garden in their boots, hats and coats. All she could see was the swing of the torchlight roaming the hedges, grass and trees restlessly, illuminating a circle of snow and making the rest of the darkness look thicker. 'Larry!' they called, but there was no responding bark, no scurrying of paws. Just the sound of a car from far away on the coastal road. She swung the torchlight around the garden but didn't penetrate the dark corners, afraid of what they'd find. She kept thinking about the way she'd skidded when she came into the drive. But Larry was a house dog, a pet, he was afraid of being far from Franny. Why had he run away from her in the first place? And if she'd hit him, they'd have found him by now.

'Let's leave it for now, Fran, it's time for tea.'

Back in the house, they had a supper cobbled together from the supplies she'd found in the town. Slices of ham and cheese – some Stilton for her and Cheddar for Franny – together with mince pies, washed down with tea for Franny and a bottle of red. They had a bowl of bright orange satsumas and it made her think of Rosemary with the juice dribbling down her chin. The two of them ate in front of the fire. Neither of them mentioned the dog. Franny sat her teddy on a chair by the fire and Malorie decided to say nothing. Strenuously, she tried to keep up a jollying conversation about what Father Christmas was doing up at the North Pole. A noise broke into the hushed quiet. A persistent, jarring ring. It took a second or two before she realised it was the telephone. She jumped up. Franny looked at her quizzically.

'What is it?'

'I'll get it,' she said.

'What?'

She held the earpiece to her ear in the hall. It crackled and whirred, a blizzard of white noise. Then it went dead, leaving just a thin whine. In the empty hallway the moon shone through the dirty glass in the door. She shivered, and was glad to return to the living room.

'The line's terrible,' she said. 'I couldn't hear anyone.'

'What are you talking about?' Franny was staring at her as if she was mad.

'The phone.'

'What phone? I didn't hear anything.'

'Oh,' she said, 'it must have been the wind.' But she really had thought she'd heard it.

Soon, Franny's eyes were drooping.

'Time for bed, darling,' she said, and tried scooping her up, but she was too heavy.

'What about Larry?' she yawned. 'He'll be cold out there in the snow.'

'I'll go and find him, Franny.'

'Promise?'

'I promise.'

When Malorie knelt by her bed, Franny said, 'Mummy,' staring up at her with her large dark eyes, 'why isn't Daddy coming?'

Malorie closed her eyes, pressed her knuckles into the sockets. 'Daddy is very busy in London, like I said.'

'But it's *Christmas*.'

'Yes I know. He's – he's really sorry. He wants to see you, he really does. He'll have lots of presents for you back in London.' Franny's stare didn't waver and Malorie wondered if her daughter would ever forgive her, if she would ever understand, if they were destined to be as distant with each other as she'd been with her own mother. 'He loves you very much,' she added, and kissed Franny's head, tucking in the sides of the blanket over her and her teddy. 'And I do too.'

There was no answer from the bed and she shut the door and leaned against it, exhausted.

Now that she'd promised, she had to mount a final search for the dog. This time she went out the front door. She crunched out along the ice-crusted drive, with her torch and the dim glow of the tree candles through the window, making fuzzy, golden circles on the ground to guide her.

At the edge of the drive, a few feet away from the car, was the shape of something curled up and half-covered in snow. She crouched down. A badger? A fox? It had to be. Please let it be. She knelt down and reached out her hand. *Don't touch it!*

'Oh no,' she said, 'Oh God.' It wasn't a badger or a fox. But her brain wouldn't fill in the gaps. Her torch shone on the dead animal. It was Larry, frozen and stiff, his creamy curly coat frosted over and encrusted, hard to the touch. Poking out from the snow, his eyes were glassy and black, open in shock, and his mouth was frozen in an ugly black grimace. Her knees buckled and she dropped to a crouch. What had she done?

But it can't have been her – the poor animal had obviously frozen. But why was he out here at all? It didn't matter, she needed to hide him before Franny found out. She began to take off her fur coat before she realised what she was doing and fetched a blanket from the car instead.

She wrapped the dog's small, stiff body in the blanket and carried it around the back of the house. She could bury it behind the shed, out of sight of the windows. Fumbling with the lock, she opened the shed and found a shovel. The ground was hard from ice and snow. She'd never even dug a hole before, certainly not a grave. The shovel hit the unyielding earth, but only small shards of ice chipped off as puffs of her breath floated up in the darkness. She would never be able to make a grave deep enough to bury him in. She had to hide the body, she couldn't let Franny see her dog, cold and lifeless. If it snowed again, that would cover him, but it might not snow. With her gloved hands, she picked up the stiff body again, trying not to look at the head, and laid him as far under the line of trees as she could. Then she began scooping up ice and snow to cover him. With it came bits of twigs and dirt but she kept piling it until there was an awkwardly-shaped mound in the shade of a hawthorn tree. If you didn't know it was there, you'd never notice it. As long as the snow didn't melt.

Her mind was slowly circling. The icy road, the skidding, the darkness, something black coming out of the trees. A shadow of something beastly crossed her mind. Had something wild killed him? She imagined the little dog, wounded and lost, dying of hypothermia. He would stay frozen, stuck in the moment of death until the thaw came, when his body would finally decay and eventually only his skeleton would remain. She thought of the skulls in the attic, the gravestone with the skulls and cross-bones, the woman she'd seen who did not speak. A slow ripple of cold went down her back.

Oh God, her poor girl. What on earth was she going to say? No father. No dog. Just a useless mother who had ruined Christmas.

In the front room, the lights from the tree were reflected in the crystal glass she'd found in a sideboard. Her fingers were red and frozen from the snow and ice, and as she rubbed them, they tingled and ached with the heat from the fire. She needed to hear something other than her own whirling thoughts. There was an old wind-up gramophone box and a few 78s in the corner of the living room, on a sideboard next to the tree. They hadn't tried to get it to work – it seemed too dusty and ancient to be functioning. Tony would be listening to jazz. She wound it up with the crank, lifted one of the heavy records out of its sleeve and put it on the turntable, then gently placed the stylus on the record. Static whirring burst out of the speakers. She allowed herself a small smile. Then some notes, the brassy blare of a trumpet, and a song filtered through the crackle, a soaring note upwards then a piano. It was an old song but it filled the room as if it belonged there. Malorie picked up her book, but it was hard to concentrate. She wasn't distracted enough, she couldn't stop thinking about what a mess she'd made of everything.

Giving up, she went back upstairs, clutching her drink, fumbled with the top drawer and took out the envelope with the pills. Just one. She needed to, otherwise she'd do something she'd regret. It was going wrong. Everything – tumbling out of her control. This had been a wild goose chase, a fool's errand. There was nothing about this house which linked to her father. And her vision of a family Christmas was spoiled. She shook the envelope and held the pills in the palm of her trembling hand. They were so small, so perfectly round. Such a pretty shade of green. Like sweets. Cochies. No. No, no, no. She couldn't. In the quiet room, her breath was shallow and loud. She screwed up her eyes, dropped the pills back into the envelope and shoved it to the back of the drawer, catching her still-cold hand on the wood. She winced and threw back the last of the brandy.

She wanted to say to the voice in her head – it wasn't me.

From downstairs she could still hear music. A loop of swirling, squeaking brass. Had she left the record on? Malorie held her breath, listened. Then a trumpet, low and mournful. A voice, old and deep that sounded like Louis Armstrong. But then it jumped and scratched. The voice was broken and stuck. It kept repeating the same word. *Soul*, it said, *soul*. She should go down and turn it off, but she was so tired. Finally it warped and stopped. The power generated by the crank must have run out.

Malorie lay awake, falling into a doze and then shuddering out of it, fizzing and restless. She was aware that she'd be woken by Franny early on Christmas morning, that she'd have to come up with something about poor Larry. Again, she ran through the sequence of events that led to her finding his stiff, frozen body. Why was he outside in the first place? Something must have scared the little dog. He'd been jumpy and whiny the whole time they'd been at the house. He must have been spooked, run out into the snowbound garden – he was a city dog after all, no sense of the country and its darkness, its strange sounds, its wild animals – and he'd become disorientated and lost and finally frozen. Just an accident, a horrible accident. This, logically, was what must have happened. Nonetheless, the car, the dog, the dark shadow she kept seeing – it made her uneasy, as if there was something out there that was malign, that wanted to hurt them.

26

Midnight on Christmas Eve. It were always a quiet time, when the world holds its breath, when the darkness keeps the evil at bay. But there were a sadness in that house. A sadness coming out in the girl and the child. It come out of the walls and the floorboards, the cracks in the ceiling. It were always there, this sorrow, right from the moment it was made. How can a house made from a wreck be anything else? It were never silent, the Marsh House. The bones of the house still remembered the storm from where it came. It forgot it weren't a ship. I could feel the sorrow when Miss Louisa got sick, when the babbies died, and when my Rose was born. It were always there, warping the beams, making the lights go off, bringing rats from the marsh into the rafters to gnaw on its bones.

27

Figgy Pudding
Christmas Day

'Mummy, it's Christmas Day, wake up.'

In the morning fog of half-sleep, Malorie saw a black dog chasing a white dog. Then Franny was pressing her in the side, dragging her out of the night-time into the day.

'What did Father Christmas bring for you?' Weeks before, Tony had come home with an extravagant doll's house for their daughter and Malorie had brought it with her, hiding it under the blanket in the boot.

'He didn't bring Larry back,' Franny said.

Oh Christ, the *dog*.

'Maybe he's gone to help Father Christmas with the rest of his deliveries,' she said, desperately.

'But he'd be back by now,' said Franny. She couldn't think of a suitable answer.

'I'll be down in a minute,' she said.

When Franny had gone she opened the chest of drawers. There, under her nylons and pants, was the envelope of pills.

It was fine. She hadn't taken one. She'd resisted. She'd had a difficult night, that was all. Under her ribcage, she could feel her heart beating like a fluttering bird trying to get out. Her hands wouldn't stay still. If she had one, it would calm her, but she remembered Tony's face back in London. The expression of disappointment in her, or rather that she'd once again met his expectations of failure. No, she mustn't give in to it. She pushed the envelope back under the clothes and shut the drawer.

After breakfast, Franny set off on a fruitless 'search for Larry' in the frozen garden, while Malorie set about the Christmas lunch. She had to tackle the bloated, repulsive white carcass of the turkey. She'd pulled the giblets out, rubbed over the pimply white skin with margarine and shoved it in the oven, and was now peeling and chopping mindlessly when shadows moved in the white square of the kitchen window and she shouted out, stabbing the knife into her finger.

A face had been there, definitely a face. An old woman in a brown hat. She was going mad, there couldn't have been anyone there. She wrapped her bleeding finger in a tea towel and chopped another carrot. But she *had* seen someone. It must have been the old woman from the cottage across the lane. A brown face, wrinkled and scrunched up, like a prune, swaddled in layers of cloth. She was gripped by an urge to look.

Heart pounding, Malorie went to the back door. There was no one there but, on the step, a round package. It was a cream pudding bowl, wrapped in muslin. The garden was white and empty. Spots of blood seeped through the tea-towel so she stuffed it in the bin and found a plaster in her washbag. She put on her boots and crunched out into the garden. They could be her footprints from last night, or Franny's.

'They are the old woman's,' she said aloud, to make it normal.

'Franny!' she called. Franny was at the other end of the garden by the drive, looking disconsolate.

'Did you see anyone come to the door?'

'No,' she said.

'Right.' But then, it was quite possible for her daughter to have missed someone quiet. She was always so caught up in her own world.

'What's that?' Franny was looking at the bundle in Malorie's arms.

'I think it's a pudding,' she said, 'for our lunch.' She put an arm around her daughter's bony shoulders. 'I think you should come in now. Why don't you play with your presents?'

The light fled the house and the garden so quickly that it seemed to be a day of only darkness. The lunch was passable. The turkey the grocer had brought was cooked through and the roast potatoes not too soft. Franny was quiet and withdrawn, and though she tried to cheer her up with cracker jokes from the expensive set she'd brought up from London, nothing worked. The figgy pudding was delicious and she made Franny smile when she doused it with brandy and lit it. The blue flame flickered across the glossy brown dome and the sprigs of holly gleamed green and red in the light.

Franny grimaced. She pulled a silver coin out of her mouth.

'Let me see,' said Malorie. On one side of the coin was the head of the King. Not the Queen, but her grandfather, George V. On the other side were oak leaves and acorns and the words SIX PENCE 1935. She held it in the palm of her hand, feeling the sticky crumbs and the weight of it. It was as if it had come from nowhere, an artefact from another world, appearing like a disconcerting magic trick.

'It's lucky,' she said finally and handed it back to Franny, although she wanted to hold onto it. 'Don't lose it.'

'Who's that?' said Franny, looking at the back.

'Just a dead king.'

When Franny went back to her doll's house, Malorie leaned back in her chair and lit a cigarette. The dishes were piled up in the cracked ceramic sink, but she couldn't face them. She sipped the brandy she'd taken from the cupboard and felt the warm sweetness coat her throat. Franny must have put one of the records on the gramophone because she could hear music. It sounded familiar, like the tune from yesterday, the same sad trumpet over the crackle of the old record. There was a creak from the upstairs floorboards. She downed the brandy and finished her cigarette, stubbing it out on the debris of leftover food on her plate. She could slip off now, while Franny wouldn't miss her. Franny *wouldn't* miss her. That was the truth.

In the bedroom, Malorie caught fragments of the same slow jazz. There was only the doll's house to distract Franny from the lack of her father and her dog. Earlier, she'd managed to find a weather forecast from the transistor but what it said hadn't been reassuring.

Norfolk has been cut off from the rest of England. All main roads leading westwards are impassable as far as the Cambridgeshire border. The RSPCA says it has received so many calls for help from farmers in the county it doesn't know which way to turn.

The suitcase where Franny had found the newspaper clipping and where she'd found the two notebooks and the bag of bones was under the windowsill, but she'd searched all through that, found everything there was to find. A sound above her – the scuttling of the rats – and she felt the pull of the attic. She was certain there was more up there. More writing, more artefacts. The attic was stuffed full of crates and boxes. There had to be more evidence of Rosemary's life in them.

Up in the attic, she felt she knew the spaces now – the shape of them, the map of their contents: the old cot, which she avoided looking at; the boxes of children's clothes, which she had glanced at but didn't take out. Right at the back, near where Franny had found the suitcase, was a space she thought she'd looked in but could no longer be sure. There, tucked under the furthest eave, were about half a dozen small boxes. Her hands felt for the contents and touched the thick layer of dust on the top. By now, her eyes had adjusted to the dark enough to see that they were about the size of a shoebox and in each was a clutch of papers. By the light of her torch, she hurriedly scanned each box and found family documents.

Deeds of sale for the land, receipts for furniture bought, a marriage certificate (Richard Wright to Louisa Mulcaney 1912); birth certificates (Philip Richard Wright 1913, Sebastian John Wright, 1914, Rosemary Louisa Wright,

1916). Rosemary must only be what – forty-six – about nineteen years older than she was. Settling into middle age. There was nothing that seemed to belong to Louisa, no record of her earlier life. There were death certificates (Philip Richard Wright, 1913, Sebastian John Wright 1914). They had only lived for a few days. These were Richard Wright's records, not his daughter's. But in the same group of papers was something that belonged to Rosemary herself. Someone must have mislaid it. It was another birth certificate for a child. Richard Charles Lafferty, born 21st January 1933. She'd had a son. Malorie had a sudden violent sensation that she shouldn't be seeing this – she'd jumped ahead in the girl's story and Rosemary hadn't told her directly. But that was ridiculous.

There was a bang from below, and Franny's disembodied voice cut in on her thoughts. 'Mummy? I finished the doll's house. I want to show you.'

'In a minute,' she shouted down.

She heard Franny sigh and the sound of her footsteps returning down the stairs.

There was a sheaf of other papers. And a death certificate. Her body shivered with cold as if a draught had swept through the room. It was the death certificate of her boy. Died 15th February 1934. He'd barely lived. Cause of death: Encephalitis. She didn't know what that was. The dim light in the attic shifted. She shrank back against the suitcase. Her skull was pressing down on her brain. She had to leave; to get out. 'Please,' she said, aloud, 'I need to go.'

Then, as quickly as it had come, the pressure was gone again. There were no ghosts watching her. It was just dust and paper and age and there was one last box with shapes like notebooks inside. Her heart beat fast. She took out two of the books. But they were the wrong shape. *Damn.* They were Agatha Christie novels. What if it was just a box of useless books? But this was *her* box at least. Rosemary's. Further down, underneath a knitted blanket, her fingers finally came to what must be the hard ridged edges of another notebook. She smiled, alone in the attic, and felt the air settle around her as if waiting. A faint sound like gnawing on wood came from near her ear and she jumped. The top of her head banged against a beam and she felt like Alice in Wonderland, too big for the house. Soon her head would pop out the top of the roof.

Malorie slid out of the attic without looking back, clutching the book, and went down to the sitting room and the finished doll's house to stoke the fire back to life. She was cold and she needed light and warmth and real things to feel and touch. Franny wasn't in the room and the gramophone was silent. The doll's house was lit by the firelight and the soft glow of the candles on the tree. In the sitting room of the house, a doll man and a doll girl were sitting on the sofa. The doll woman was in the kitchen, separate. Next to her, a doll baby in a doll cot, with a tiny painted yellow whorl in the centre of the forehead. The second child to make the family complete. She watched the flames rise and grow and held up her palms until they began to prickle with heat. She should take Franny back to London, she should leave her with her father. She'd become fixated on this girl from the past when she had a real girl, here, right now. There was no Rosemary.

And yet. She'd felt the girl's hopes and fears as she felt her own. The flames dipped and smoke drifted out. She *was* real. She *had* been real. If Malorie could only read the last notebook. That was all. Then they'd leave. Oh God, where *was* Franny? It was getting late, the darkness was coming down again.

In her fur, Malorie went out of the front door but there was no sign of her daughter on the drive. Instinctively, she looked over to where the strange little cottage was sunk, but there was no obvious sign of life.

'Franny!' she called, and held herself still to catch a response. There was only the wind in the trees. A well of panic flaring, she rushed around the side of the house and saw a gash of red from Franny's scarf in the grey half-light. She was standing at the back of the garden, looking down. Malorie's heart plummeted. It was the grave, the pathetic pile of snow where she'd hidden the dog. *Oh God, please don't let Franny find out.*

'Franny, it's getting dark, come in. I'll make tea and you can show me the doll's house.'

In answer, Franny turned and trudged back. She could see no sign on her daughter's face that she knew what was under the pile of snow.

In the bedroom that night, Malorie dug herself further under the covers to find a patch of warmth. She could see Rosemary, drinking champagne at her wedding; Rosemary walking towards Franklin, sprawled, waiting for her; Rosemary writhing with pain – on this very bed. Perhaps, she thought . . . perhaps. If Rosemary was only forty-six, maybe she could find her . . . she could give her back her journals. Talk to her.

She switched on the lamp and sat up. The door to the wardrobe was ajar. She'd not hung up any of her clothes, it hardly seemed worth bothering, but now she had a need to look inside it. She got up swiftly before she changed her mind and swung it open. There was nothing in it apart from a few blankets and bits of cloth at the bottom. Kneeling down, she picked them up, and gasped. In her hands she held a long, delicate piece of white lace that had been chewed by moths. She held it up to the lamp and the light shone through the holes, making it look like the pattern of a snowflake. It was her veil, she was certain. Rosemary's veil. She was communicating with her. All these clues: the shell, the stone, the bottles, and now this. She was telling her – *This was my life.*

Malorie snatched up the third notebook. As she did, a piece of paper fell out on to the bed. It was a page of thick, creamy writing paper with a letter written in an elegant sloping hand. It read:

Dear Rosemary,

I am so very sorry for what has happened to you. I have found it difficult to reconcile the sweet country girl I knew with what you did, and I feel some sense of responsibility for not seeing sooner that you were obviously deeply unwell.

Father and Mother are extremely distraught as you might imagine. They are selling Old Hall and never want to set foot in Norfolk again.

I leave for Rome tomorrow. It sounds as if there are exciting things occurring over there and I want to be where the action is. The Italians are bringing modernism to Africa and I feel Italy and to an extent, Germany, is where all the really modern thinking is happening. Gerald is still trying to pin me down to marriage but he's tied to his work for the bank. I'm going to put him off for a bit longer. I crave newness. Perhaps I shall meet an Italian instead.

I hate writing like this. I hardly know what to write. I do hope you enjoyed the books.

Yours,
Hilda

'What you did.' But what *was it* that she'd done? The date on the letter was 15th March 1935. 1935. She picked up the first notebook and read again the first words. *March 1935.* This letter was written *then*. But it said nothing about what Rosemary had actually done, nor what had happened to her. She had no choice but to read on.

Scanning down the first page of the notebook, Malorie saw just a few short paragraphs about the pregnancy and marriage. Flicking the pages, she looked for a reference to the baby. Rosemary wrote of her enduring silence and growing stomach. By the beginning of 1933, she wrote that she had been just as abandoned and sequestered in Old Hall as she had been in the Marsh House. And there was less there for her than there was here. Malorie's eyes scanned the pages looking for what she knew was coming and found it. The handwriting sloped unevenly across the page, splashes of ink spattering the paper, spreading sometimes in dark stains. She began to read in earnest. *I am listening*, she thought. *Tell me.*

28

I see the two of them in the garden where she'd played. The girl she'd made from snow was still there, frozen in time. I see the two of them, one at the door and one at the edge of the garden, not far from where the mother hid the dead dog. Both standing with the same hunched up shoulders as if they were ready to fight. I don't think either of them could see how alike they were.

THE THIRD NOTEBOOK

29

It took me nearly a week to write the last journal and now it's the second week of March and I don't know how much longer I have. So I must get on and come to my boy.

It wasn't long into the new year when the pain began. A New England was coming according to the guests gathered in their tuxedoes and silk dresses at Old Hall that New Year's Eve, but after my shape and expectant condition had been cooed over, I'd pleaded tiredness and gone to bed early. Much later, Franklin lay next to me blind drunk, but he didn't try to touch me. By then he was repelled and fascinated in equal measure by me and my shape. 'I can barely get at you,' he'd say, or, 'You remind me of one of the sows on Blacker's Farm.' Then other times he'd fondle my breasts, swollen as they were. He even put his mouth to one once and looked up at me with his pale blue eyes, daring me to pull it away. His teeth snagged on my tender nipple but I didn't move. I knew better than to rile him. He licked around the pinky-brown circle and I thought of how once, long ago, I would have been delighted with this, with the almost-painful sensation of his tongue and his teeth on the tenderest parts of me.

As if he knew what I was thinking, the fingers of his right hand pushed harder into my breast but I closed my eyes and thought of other things. Of Janey's garden running down to the marsh. Of me and my child (a girl, I hoped) picking herbs for her pot. Soon, he was finishing himself off with his other hand. He didn't ever want to be inside me. He didn't say why but I knew he thought it was somehow wrong and I was relieved for that reprieve at least. I kept hold of the thought that it would be different after my girl was born – Franklin and I could return to how we used to be.

When the real pain came, low down and deep, Franklin and the rest of the Laffertys were all residing at the Hall because the colonel had become interested in game shooting and it was the season then. They sent me to bed for most of January for my confinement. For my benefit they said, but I knew it was for the next Lafferty, not for me. My rings were cutting deep into the skin of my ring finger, but no one would let me cut them off. At first, the pain was welcome when it began grinding into me because I thought it would be over soon and I'd be released from the prison of the bedroom. But it was not soon.

They sent for a local midwife, a woman the doctor knew, but she wasn't Janey. She was a cold, unsmiling woman who told me off for standing up. In the eye of the agony, I called for my friend. I cried and screamed and told the doctor I didn't want a strange woman touching me. There were whispers outside the door and she came at last.

Janey held my hand, put cold compresses on my forehead and muttered charms under her breath. Everyone else stayed away. It got to be night and the baby hadn't come. The grandfather clock downstairs chimed midnight, then one, two. Sometime after it stopped chiming, the baby was drawn bawling out of my body, ripping me apart.

I can't remember now the raw feelings of the baby being pulled out of me, or the blood loss I was told I suffered, or even what he looked like, because all I remember feeling was a strange disconnect between the writhing, groaning animal who'd given birth to a boy (Oh, how they were pleased) and the rag of a being still lying in the bed. Janey held the baby up to the window and inspected him, saying, 'Thank the Lord for that. He's taken after the father.' I supposed she meant they would be pleased that he looked like a Lafferty. She paused. 'He'll not have the gift of seeing, not being born at the chime hours. But he's alive and crying.'

When they finally brought him to me – briefly, as it was clear I wasn't to be trusted with him – he was scrawny and angry and had a bright red face that reminded me of Franklin in a rage. The wet nurse they'd hired took him away quickly to the nursery and Janey had to leave. Janey stroked my hair and my face was wet with tears. When she left, I turned my body to the wall and wondered when love would come. I could see no connection between me and the squirming creature that had been taken out of me. My breasts were aching and sore and began to leak into the sheets. When the doctor came to examine me, I clenched my teeth and waited for his freezing fat fingers to get out of my soreness.

He covered me up and turned to speak to Lady Lafferty who was hovering in the doorway.

'She's damaged but she'll heal. She'll recover. Not straightaway though, mind. Give her a couple of weeks, my lady.'

A couple of weeks until what? I soon found out.

The Laffertys wanted to baptise him early so I was barely recovered when we had to troop with the baby to St John the Baptist's again. I still had little interest in him – the wet nurse fed him and they brought him to me swaddled in a blanket, his small head poking out, but he still looked like a miniature, pinched, red-faced version of Franklin to me. He had Franklin's fine nose, almond-shaped eyes and rosy lips. There was nothing of me in him that I could see. He cried whenever they gave him to me and I just wished they'd take him away. The nurse would fuss around and say 'he's just thirsty', or 'he must need changing', or 'the poor mite is hungry'. It was always something. I had no interest in anything – my baby son, the world carrying on outside the windows of the house, or even myself.

Finally, the day before the baptism, Hildy, up from London especially, said she was going to take me 'in hand'.

'Darling, it's time to buck up. You've done your duty.

You've given us Dickie and that's marvellous but there's no need to be morose. And look at the state of your hair.'

I was reading in the library – I often did, as no one else went in there – although I'd run out of mystery novels and had been forced into reading the dull books on their shelves. Luckily I'd found a Wilkie Collins, probably left by a visitor, and was pleased to discover it had an element of the mysterious about it too. Not that I was really reading. My mind kept drifting off and a servant would ask me if I wanted coffee in impatient tones as if they'd asked me more than once. Hildy dragged me upstairs to her room, which had an enormous window overlooking the disused farmland all the way to the woods. She sat me at her dressing table. It was true, I looked terrible. My face was sallow and queasy and my hair, still long, fine and black, was greasy and tarnished. She began brushing my hair, cleaning my face and applying rouge. At first I looked like a painted corpse – bright spots of rouge on my deathly pallor – but she kept working at me and by the end I did at least look alive, albeit an unnatural form of life.

They named him Richard Charles Lafferty, my father's name and the colonel's. I wasn't given any choice; at that time I didn't much care. He didn't cry at the baptism, which was strange. The new rector looked down at me and smiled kindly.

Franklin must have thought my revived appearance was a sign that relations were to be resumed. That night, he came to my room and lifted up my nightdress, feeling around under there. I clenched my legs together as if I could repel him, but he caressed the insides of my thighs and made me flinch.

'Don't you want me anymore?' he said in a little boy voice and looked up at me, supposedly hurt.

'Of course I do,' I said.

'Well you're not showing it,' he said.

I had no answer to that as it was quite true but I let him carry on and, although it was sore and I bit down so hard on my bottom lip it bled, I didn't cry out in pain because it would have annoyed him and I would suffer for it later.

It's funny, I don't remember a lot about the rest of that year. After all that's happened, it's receded and remains a series of scenes, like a set of still photographs. One of them is the time when Franklin turned up at the Hall in a Blackshirt uniform. I knew from Hildy that Mosley's first wife, Cimmie, had died suddenly in May and he'd gone off to Europe with another of his mistresses. It made me feel sick and uneasy, the way this role model of Franklin's treated his wife, who'd borne him three children. At the same time, I'd read in the newspapers what Mosley's party was up to. The press wasn't wholly complimentary, but I did see a copy of the Daily Mail which the colonel left, and they seemed to like them quite a lot. If I thought about it at all, I thought they looked rather silly in their new uniform, a bit like a pretend army, a version of the Blackshirts in Italy or the Brownshirts in Germany – or was it the other way round? But until that summer I hadn't thought about it much at all. And then Franklin arrived, dressed in the uniform. He picked up Richie and tousled his hair and all the time I had a niggling feeling of unpleasantness. He was attractive, as always – his golden skin and hair shone, and the uniform of black high-neck shirt and black breeches suited him, but it was not him. It was a costume, a show, and an ugly one.

I jumped up and took Richie from his arms.

'Why are you here dressed like that?' I asked.

'Dorothy's organised a rally over near Hillington. Trying to drum up support in the county. You and the boy could come. It'll be something to see.'

'But why do you need to be dressed like that? It's a political party, not an army.'

'Mosley thinks it instils a discipline in the ranks. The women's uniform is rather swish too, you know. You could get one. On second thoughts, no, it wouldn't suit you.' He bent down and pinched my cheek.

I pictured Franklin with a female Blackshirt. 'I don't think it would be good for the baby,' I said.

Throughout that summer he would come and go, to one rally or another, sometimes with the colonel, sometimes without. He seemed to be enthralled by it. At first, I think it was what his father wanted for him, but then, when he was singled out as a bright young hope for the party, he began to enjoy the admiration, the attention, the purpose. He would repeat odd things – 'A healthy and mighty race must have roots deep in the soil of a native land' – although his only concerns in the country were sport and the meetings. He knew very little about the country. There were rumours among the servants that he had a mistress at the party HQ but I tried not to listen.

I asked Hildy once about what she'd said to me, the night of the wedding.

'Oh, Rosie, you don't need to know.'

'Please,' I said.

Her mouth twitched. 'It was just a bit of a fuss kicked up by a girl's father, that's all. I think Frank threw her off – and she – oh, I don't know – she got herself into trouble and ...' She stopped and put her arm around my shoulders. 'Darling, don't. Don't be like that. He does adore you, you know. We all do. You're the only good egg in all of this blessed country as far as I'm concerned.'

Still I tried to ignore it, to tell myself that he loved me. I had to, for Richie's sake.

Another memory I have is of that Christmas. It was a picture-perfect, snow-covered, icily beautiful Christmas.

For a gift, Hildy – who had taken to wearing a brooch with the fascist symbol on it, a kind of lightning flash – had bought me two beautifully bound Agatha Christie mysteries that she'd found in London and I was so grateful I almost cried. They were The Sittaford Mystery and Peril at End House. I liked the title of the latter because it reminded me of the Marsh House, but the former was of particular interest because in that one, it snows on Dartmoor and a terrible murder is committed in a remote place. I thought what a perfect mystery plot it would be for all of us in this huge old mansion to be cut off from the rest of civilisation. But which of the awful characters surrounding me should be the murder victim?

I ate their food and drank their wine and slept in their house. I played with their heir, my son, on the rug before the fire and showed him the candles on the Christmas tree, watching the sparkle of them reflected in his big baby eyes. I listened to their tattle about Diana and Oswald and what a beautiful pair they were, although it was 'still desperately sad' about poor Cimmie, as Lady Lafferty said, and it was a 'terrible shame' about how he had treated her. I thought how small and lowborn and rural I was compared to such people.

Early in the new year, with snow still on the ground, we were out in the garden, the baby and I, he snug in his woollen hat and coat, and I in mine, when he wriggled in my arms and kicked his legs. Willingly, I put him down and there on the snow-covered lawn he began to walk, his short little legs waddling one after the other leaving pockmarks in the snow. I ran forward to catch him and, tottering, he fell at my feet. I picked him up and his beautiful eyes, shaped like his father's and yet so trusting, stared into mine. Up until then, Richie had been fussed around by the servants, ignored by the family and, shamefully, by me. I blamed him for making Franklin stop loving me. I blamed him for making me stop loving Franklin. But that day, with the look of trust he had in me, I thought then that I should love my baby.

I began to get used to the idea of Richie, to accept that I was a mother. I was *his* mother. He called for me, that was one thing. No one had ever done that before. No one had ever seemed to want or need me. I started to ask for him to be brought to me and I read to him from books that had been brought to the house at my request: Peter

Pan and Alice's Adventures in Wonderland and a whole set of Beatrix Potter. I think I enjoyed reading to him more than he enjoyed listening, but it soothed him when he cried and soon he began to look at the pictures and point at the silly animals dressed in hats and tailcoats. Franklin would sometimes appear while I was reading, Richie in my lap. I knew what was expected. I had to give Richie to the nurse and go upstairs. I shut my eyes and my ears to the rumours and tried not to picture him in the black costume.

30

I'll tell this part quickly because it still hurts. I've been putting it off but I have to do it. To put my hand in the fire.

In the late winter, I began to go to the Marsh House whenever Franklin was away. He was often in London on party business, and I spent more time by the marsh. It made life bearable and took away some of the loneliness. I could see Janey, walk with her along the creek. Richie would be carried on our backs or totter between our hands on the beach. She would tell Richie the stories – all the old folk tales she'd told me when I was a child – 'The Green Children', 'The Dauntless Girl' (that was my favourite) or 'Sea Tongue' – and I could be a girl again. Richie's favourite was the part in 'The Dead Moon' where the boggarts came out of the marsh. His eyes would light up with excitement whenever she said, 'The naughty boggarts scampered across the marsh', and we all laughed. 'Moon,' he said, pointing with his fat finger to the sky. It was his first word apart from 'Mama'.

It wasn't long after I moved us home to the Marsh House that he got a fever and a rash and he had to be quarantined in my old nursery for fear of contagion. I especially was not allowed near him, in case I contracted the disease. The doctor was brought but pronounced him over the worst and said he should be 'right as rain' soon enough with liquids and fresh air.

One day in February – a miserable day in my memory, though perhaps it was as bright as a summer's day, who knows? – he was playing at my feet in the nursery. The fever was past. I came to the nursery every day now because I could be with him rather than anyone else. I was reading and was immersed in the novel (it was The Woman in White, which I had stolen from the Laffertys' unused library) so I don't know how long he was like it, but something made me look up – a bird passed by the window, I think, and I heard Smutch howling at nothing from Janey's cottage – and I saw that he was asleep on the rug. It wasn't his nap time and he'd seemed well enough that morning. His cheek was pink and his blond curls stuck to his sweaty little forehead. I nearly cried out but then I noticed his chest swelling and falling.

'Richie,' I whispered, and felt his head. It was hot. His bud lips were slightly apart and his breath was wet. The fever must have returned. I picked him up and he was like a rag in my arms, his little arms flopping down at his sides. I remember he was heavy and it made me think of a 'dead weight'. I ran downstairs, past Fairbrother mopping the floor and out onto the front drive, covered in frost. Perdie began to bark as if she sensed my panic and ran along beside me across the lane to Janey's where I banged hard on the door.

'I was coming to see you and the babby, Rosie,' she said, but seeing him, and without another word, she took him off me. She cooled him down with a wet cloth and put something on his tongue. She lay him on a blanket in front of her hearth, attended to by Perdie who whimpered next to him. Old Smutch stood guard at the door. Richie opened his eyes finally but there was a filmy glaze over the surface and he didn't seem to see me. All I could see was the reflection of the fire flickering on the glaze of his eyes.

'What's wrong with him, Janey? He was better. He's been better for weeks.'

'Fever's got in him again,' she said. 'But it's stronger now.'

Over the next few hours we kept watch over him. He woke up at times and babbled but he never seemed to see me. One time I thought he'd be all right, but he slipped back into his thick sleep, his limbs heavy and his breath rasping. Have you ever heard a baby with a scratching breath? It is the most hideous sound. Unnatural. I don't know how long we sat in our vigil but the shadows lengthened over his sleeping body and it grew dark in the little cottage. Janey lit the oil lamps and the shadows guttered and waved, grew into hideous forms and shrunk to stuttering animals on the walls.

The pink light had faded to dark when Perdie began to whine and pressed her paw to his side. Smutch set up a mournful howl. I knew something was wrong with how Richie moved – he'd descended so far down into his sleep that Perdie's paw didn't rouse him at all. But I was paralysed by the horror of what it meant.

Janey stood up. 'Take him home,' she said. 'Best if I go fetch the doctor.' I had never heard her mention a doctor before.

I pleaded with her. But she lifted him up and put him in my arms, took hold of me and pushed me out of the door, into the night, with my baby. I crossed over to the Marsh House.

That's where he died. The rest of it spooled out before me and I could only watch, helpless. The doctor came, but it made no difference. It was too late.

'No,' I said. I kept repeating 'no'. It was the only word I had.

They took him away and put him in a box and buried him at the church on a bitter, grey day, but it was as if they'd buried something else – an animal, a doll. Maybe nothing at all. Not the beautiful creature I'd had torn out of me.

Janey said later that he was 'too good for this world'. And perhaps that was true because it wasn't his fault he looked so much like his father. None of it was his fault. All the anger I'd felt towards his small soul had evaporated like hot air. I'd allowed myself to love him and now he was gone.

31

'She lost her babbies too, she did. It's something else you've got in common with her,' Janey said.

'What happened to her, Janey? Why has no one ever told me?'

She frowned. 'I don't know what good it'd do you knowing. It ent a happy story, poor child.'

'I'm seventeen now, and I'm married and I'm a mother myself. I was –'

I was fingering the silver locket around my neck in which I kept a lock of his golden hair and tears came, choking the back of my throat, making me cough and splutter. Everything ran with liquid – my nose, my eyes, my mouth. She drew me to her and I sucked in the familiar smells of cloves and rosehips and soup broth until I came to a juddering stop.

'I want to know,' I said, and looked up into those small bright eyes with the fiercest glare I could muster.

She sighed. 'All I know is he sent her away not long after you were born. She were sick, you see, sick in the head. Wouldn't eat, would hardly look at you, would go off walking all the time. Got so bad your father sent for a quack. But I never knew where they took her, Rose, he'd turned against me by then, blamed me for her sickness, said I'd cursed her.'

'He'll never tell me,' I said. But I saw what I could do, what I should have done years before.

I waited until he was out on business and locked the door of his study from the inside. I rifled through his correspondence. He was not a meticulous man, and there were sheaves and sheaves of paper, mostly bills, unpaid. And one of them was a letter with the address marked St Andrew's Hospital. My heart jolted painfully. The anticipation was so great I could barely breathe. The letter said little. The condition of your wife remains stable. She enjoys walking in the grounds and painting. Platitudes – awful, meaningless platitudes. It was her, though, I was sure of it. And she was alive. But instead of a great feeling of consolation and joy, I found instead an immense sense of abandonment came over me. She had loved me so little that she'd left me here, alone with my father; she'd left me motherless. What kind of weak creature would allow herself to do that? Where was she, all those times I needed her? And another, terrifying thought hit me – that I was as weak as she was, that whatever it was in her was in me too. I could no more be a mother than she could. I took the little shell I'd thought was from her and flung it out of my bedroom window.

32

Malorie stopped reading and closed her heavy eyes. The temperature had dropped and she was cold all over. In the bedroom on the edge of the marsh, she lay on her front, with her face in the pillow, sucking in her own damp breath, her back to the room. She dropped the notebook to the floor. No shadows could get to her. It didn't matter anyway, all the shadows were inside her head.

Think of something else, think of something else she repeated but it was impossible. The dark blots in her mind swelled and grew and merged until they became all there was. She could feel herself being enveloped by them, their soft forms surrounding her. She fought against the well of darkness. It wasn't the same. Her grief was not an all-encompassing chasm like Rosemary's – the loss of a child, the desertion by a mother – just a great murky mass of darkness. There was nothing to get hold of.

Sound was coming from somewhere like waves in a storm. Her face was wet. She reached out for a handkerchief but when she lifted it to her face it was the old lace wedding veil. She wiped her eyes with it and stared up at the ceiling with red-sore eyeballs. She was too tired to think or to grieve. By the door, a shadow appeared.

A pressure of air, something solid but invisible pushed her back against the bed.

'Leave me alone,' she moaned.

She shrank back into the bed. There was a flicker of light at the edge of her eye. If she didn't look it would go away. But her head turned. Standing in the dark of the doorway where the shadow had been was a slight figure all in white. It was the same face she thought she'd seen at the sitting room window. Rosemary's face. She was wearing what looked like a wedding dress and a veil – the veil that Malorie was holding in her hand – and her small, translucent hands were on her belly. It stuck out, protruding, the swollen belly of a woman in the late stages of pregnancy.

Automatically, Malorie's hands went to her own, empty stomach. Her gaze rose as if pulled there, from the body to the face of the figure. Rosemary's eyes stared back at her, the inky-green-black of a bottomless sea. They seemed to see right into her and through her. Then a blank. There was nothing there. Just the door. She tried to keep her eyes open, she wanted to keep on seeing. She fought against it but sank deeper into the black sea of sleep. Sleep crept into her brain, drawing her into its soft darkness. Sleep was merciful and full, thickly black and deep.

33

Midwifery they call it now. I brought out so many babbies into this world, hauling them, dragging them into the light, screaming, squalling. And sometimes they're quiet and it's them you ought to worry about. He were a beautiful child, a blessed child. I wished he would bring her joy. And that he did for a short while.

After the child's death I didn't have much heart to go to the church on St Mark's Eve to see what was coming the next year. I were afraid of what'd appear to me. But I did go. I just didn't share what I saw with no one. Perhaps I ought to have done, now I think about it.

34

To the Sea
Boxing Day

The curtains were open and a watery yellow light filled the room. It was so cold the windows were rimed with frost inside. Malorie pulled herself out of bed, put on her dressing gown and breathed onto the windowpane, but her breath was white and made no impression on the ice. Her fingernails scraped letters onto the frosty pane. R – o – s – e. She stopped, confused for a second, and quickly wiped the window until the letters were gone. She shivered and thrust her hands into the pockets of her dressing gown. In the pocket was a scrunched-up piece of white lace. Her eyes swam. She saw the girl with the veil staring at her. A feeling like the wash of a cold sea flowed through her. She took the white lace and thrust it to the back of the top drawer. It could be anything, it might not be the veil the girl had worn. Her mind was confused between the notebook, the dreams and reality. She'd had a nightmare. Today. Today was reality.

The sky was a clear light blue and the ice-crusted snow shimmered. New snow had been covered with a thick frost. It was the first time the sun had shone since they'd arrived and it filled her with a fragile hope. They could finally go to the sea. She would tell Franny about Larry. No, she would tell her a white lie, a kind lie – that he'd run away. She'd promise to buy her a new dog. She would salvage what was left of Christmas.

She dressed quickly and hurried downstairs. The ground floor smelled of toast. Franny was munching in the sitting room in front of a fire.

'There's no tea,' said Franny, 'the water's off.' Oh God, the pipes must have frozen – it was a miracle they hadn't before. She had no idea where they could get water from. It was yet another thing that she couldn't cope with.

'Why didn't you wake me?' she said, then regretted it. She had to start again. 'You made breakfast by yourself?'

'Sorry,' said Franny, her face downcast. 'Are we going today?'

'Don't be sorry. Yes – but we haven't been to the sea yet.' It was too soon. The sea was so close – there at the end of the lane – she could see it from the bedroom. It couldn't be unreachable.

'After that?'

'Yes,' she said. 'We'll go after that.'

'But what if we haven't found Larry? We can't go home without him. We can't leave him here.'

'Darling.' Malorie knelt down by Franny and took her cold hands in hers. 'It's possible that Larry's been run – run away. He's probably very happy where he is, but we might not be able to find him.'

'But you said you'd find him.'

'Sometimes people say things that they want to be true but they can't make them be true.'

'You shouldn't have promised.' Franny's face was drawn tight in grief and anger. She tore her hands out of Malorie's and, grabbing her coat and boots, ran out of the house.

'Franny,' she called after her, but she'd gone. There was no sign of her daughter in the garden, but her hunched angry shape was trudging away towards the marsh.

The bitter wind made Malorie's eyes water and she wasn't sure if there were tears mixed in with it. As they headed away from the house, she felt as if someone was watching from one of the windows. She made herself face forward. The sky was heavy with the palest grey. Her feet crunched on the iced, packed snow on the path to the creek and, above her, birds – black terns she thought they were – wheeled, calling, squeaking. The whole world was a monotone; only the red of Franny's scarf provided any colour. At the end of the lane, they came to the creek running in a muddy gully to the right, alongside the line of trees on a slight rise, bare branches reaching for the sky. The two of them stopped. Franny's eyes were red-rimmed. She should say something to her, find some words of comfort. As they stood there, a formation of large birds like geese flew above them out towards the marsh, making a honking noise.

In a quick burst, without looking at her scowling girl, she said, 'Franny – I have to tell you – I found Larry. Darling, he – he must have got scared by something and I think he got very cold. So cold his heart stopped. I, I made a grave for him in the snow.' She looked down and her heart tore with pain. The anger on her daughter's face had been replaced by desolation and she looked so young suddenly that Malorie had no choice but to reach out for her, to wrap her with her arms. Franny was stiff, unyielding, but she leaned her head against her mother's fur coat, her small body wracked with tearless sobs.

'I should have told you earlier,' she said.

'Poor Larry,' said Franny finally, withdrawing from the fur. Then – 'I want to see him.'

'He's sleeping, darling. He's peaceful now.'

'He's not sleeping,' she said petulantly.

'No, not sleeping. You're right. But look, why don't we go to the sea since we're here? We're not very far away.'

'All right,' said Franny.

'It must be this way,' she said, relieved that the first cut was made. It was still far away on the horizon, but she could smell the salt in the air. Tentatively, she began picking her way along the thin scrubby path that seemed to lead through the marsh to the sea. She thought – one slip and you'd be ankle deep or worse in black, icy seawater. They crossed a small wooden bridge over another creek. The path seemed to disappear into nothing.

'What are we supposed to bloody do now?' The whine in her voice sounded like a child's. How ill-equipped she was, to be a parent.

'I'm tired,' said Franny.

'We can't be far,' she said, plunging forward along what could have been a path once – a smear of stone and mud between clumps of shrub and grass. She had to show Franny the sea. That was a normal thing for a parent to do. Closer now, she could see the tufts of the low dunes ahead and the pale-yellow gleam of the sand and the grey line of the sea. To the far left of them were the hulls of old boats, the blue and red paint, faded and mottled and peeling off. Now and again they came to another little creek with the stumps of rotting posts in the mud. Some of the creeks stopped dead; some were longer and wound across the marsh, but they were thin and lined with scrub that they could jump across. On either side of them were pools of black water like open sores. What nasty things lurked there? You wouldn't want to be lost out here at night, that much was true, like the poor cockler, stranded as the tide and the fog came in.

They tramped on until they came to a creek that was much wider, gaping and deep in front of them.

'How can we cross that?' said Franny. Perhaps they should turn back. It was filthy out here.

'Oh come on, we're nearly there,' she said. 'Listen.'

It was true. She could hear the faint shush of the waves above the sound of the wind brustling across the scrubby marsh.

Franny said, 'Look.' She was pointing below them. There, slightly hidden down in the gulch was a wooden board that served – could serve – as a bridge from one side to the other.

They lowered themselves down to the tiny bridge and scrambled back up the other side, slipping slightly in the slick mud. But now, after a few more steps, they were finally there and the beach opened out in front of them – a pale expanse of sand extending as far to the east and west as she could see, encrusted in patches of ice – and beyond, the white rim of the shoreline, the seal-coloured sea and a thin mist clinging to the water.

Wind from the sea whipped up the sand, and seaspray flicked over her face. She turned away to protect her eyes.

Further up the beach, Franny was picking up shells with her mittens off.

She left her and walked down to the sea and along the line of the shore. She watched the foam lick the sand and retreat, leaving a line of scum the way a snail leaves a trail of slime. There was something shining there. She leaned over, holding her hat down with one hand, and scooped it out of the wet sand. It was a shell, a shell with a pink interior, like the one Franklin had given Rosemary. She held the delicate, brittle object in the palm of her hand and it was funny how it made her feel closer to the girl in the notebooks, as if this very shell had existed in both her world and Malorie's.

Her parents used to take her to the coast when she was little – but somewhere else, she seemed to remember, where cliffs of great dunes fell tumbling to the beach, but otherwise it was the same long, wide sandy beaches and the same brown North Sea that turned grey-blue in the sun. It had been a thing of ritual, the trips to the beach: her mother with her headscarf tied tightly under her chin, and her basket stuffed with egg sandwiches carefully wrapped in paper, a bottle of pop for her and a flask of tea for the two of them. And best of all, a vanilla sponge. They would sit for hours on the sand, her mother reading one of her terrible romance novels (Malorie thought, as soon as she was old enough to be dismissive), her father dozing with his trouser-legs rolled up and his hat covering his freckly face. Alone, Malorie would dig huge holes, pick up creatures in the rock pools, gather a collection of shells. She watched the other children jumping off the dunes and splashing in the sea, but she never had the courage to do those things herself. She never made friends with the other children at the beach – she was wary of them. It pricked at her heart, the image of herself as a child, standing apart from the romping packs of other children, screaming with delight in the water. And here was her own daughter, accompanied only by her mother picking shells on a beach, alone. At the end of the long day, sandy-mouthed and salt-flecked, her dad would wipe her feet with a towel. She remembered looking down at the pinkness of his scalp through his bright wispy hair as he knelt at her feet, and the comforting largeness of his hand as he led her back to the car. Where had they been? She wasn't sure now. It could have been here. She remembered dunes, cold sea . . .

In the far right of her vision, something moved beyond the dune, back on the marsh. The dark figure looked familiar. A rounded shape with a creature the size of a tiger. It had to be the old woman and the enormous black dog. Malorie raised her hand and called, 'Hello!'

She thought that the figure – the old woman, she was sure of it – nodded in response but she wasn't sure. The mist rolled in from the sea and she seemed to melt into it.

'Hello!' she shouted, but the old woman had disappeared.

Slowly, Malorie walked back to Franny. 'Did you see an old woman, Fran?'

'Where?'

'At the other end of the beach. She was walking a black dog.'

Franny screwed up her forehead. 'Maybe,' she said. 'I saw someone but I didn't know who it was.'

It *had* been the old woman, thought Malorie. She remembered the girl in the shop telling her about the sea here. You could only go to the beach when the tide was out. She'd said that when the tide came in hard a spit of sand was often cut off from the rest of the land, stranding anyone stupid enough to be out there. Was the sea any closer than when they'd got here? They'd hardly been here any time at all. But when she thought about it, she had no idea of the times of the tide. Had the old woman been trying to warn them just now?

'I like the beach,' Franny said. 'Larry would have liked it here.'

'Franny, listen. I'm going to get you another dog. As soon as we get home.'

'I don't want another dog. I want Larry.'

Malorie watched the white wisps of her laboured breathing in the cold air. She didn't know how she could go on. Go on without Tony, without her parents. It was too much to bear.

'Mummy, what's the matter?'

Her cheeks were warm and wet with tears that stung. 'Nothing,' she said, wiping them with her glove. 'I know you want Larry, I'm sorry.' Franny looked down at her feet but she didn't say anything. Behind her, the sea felt close.

'Let's get back,' Malorie said, afraid of the tide coming in and cutting them off. She could imagine the mist thickening and the tide rolling in and not knowing which way was land and which way was the open sea. You could scream and scream and although they might hear you, no one would be able to find you. She picked up her pace, away from the sea-mist.

As they walked back the way they came, the mist merged with the thick cloud and snow began falling again, light flakes at first, then fatter and fatter. Franny's form was thin, her brown bobble hat moving up and down like a coconut on a shy, her red scarf flying out behind her, a streak of red on white. Rather than her usual slouch she was jumping and hopping across the creeks and clumps. She was quite agile, Malorie noticed with surprise, and she thought how little chance Franny had been given to be a proper child – to have adventures and to roam about free. How little she'd even noticed her own daughter. A wave of guilt came at her like a sudden gust of wind and she rocked back on her heels. She began to run, splashing and sliding in the mud.

When she caught up with Franny on the road, she laughed, 'Look at the state of these boots!' Both their pairs of boots were covered in a slick of shiny black mud, which was now overlaid with dots of snow. Underneath the slimy, pale-brown mud of the marsh lay another layer, an ooze of black. She imagined the bog creatures crawling out of the gullies and pools on the marsh, slick and dripping with black mud. She wouldn't let them get her. She took hold of Franny's small, mittened hand and squeezed it. Her daughter looked at her with surprise but didn't pull away.

By the time they came to the lane to the house, their coats and hats were covered with snow and their faces wet with it. She gripped Franny's hand tightly. The trees at the end of the lane were mere charcoal sticks in the whiteness.

Through the falling flakes, someone was walking towards them. Malorie could tell by the way the person moved that it was a man and that he was carrying something in a sack. Franny's hand slipped from hers.

'Hello!' the man called. 'I was just coming along with some –' He stopped. Malorie, walking ahead, realised it was the grocer. His weather-beaten face wore an expression of such shock a shivering pulse of cold ran through her and she stepped back away from him.

'What is it?' she said.

The man gaped at her for a further instant then, frowning, he put a hand to his forehead. 'T'aint nothing. I could have sworn – No, no. It was just the way you looked, coming along the lane. It's just this blessed snow getting in my eyes. Must have been.'

Her lips twitched in an approximation of a smile. She didn't like the way he'd looked at her. 'You were bringing something to us?'

'Yes, right you are. That I was.' But he remained staring at her. 'My daughter – she said you might be needing some coal. I brought you a drop of it with the turkey but what with all this weather, I reckoned you might need some more.'

It was Malorie's turn to frown now. 'Thank you,' she said. 'It's very kind of you, but we're going back to London today, so I'm afraid we won't be needing any more coal.'

The man looked up to the sky, frowning. 'You'd best be off then is my advice. Road's going to be impassable soon, way it's coming on.' She had a recollection of the man's voice on the radio: Do not travel unless it is strictly necessary.

'We certainly will,' she said, keen to get away. 'Thank you again.'

'I take it you're not from round here, then?'

'I'm from Norwich,' she said, 'but we live in London.'

'London,' he repeated, drawing out the syllables, making it sound like a different planet. 'Right,' he said. 'Right you are. It's just – I can't get over – No, it's nothing.'

She could feel the presence of Franny next to her, tugging on her hand. 'Mummy,' she was saying, 'come inside. I'm cold.'

'Best be off then, before it comes down worse. You be careful, now.'

'Yes, thank you, we will, Mr –?'

'Bayfield,' he said.

Bayfield. The name was familiar. It was the name above the shop of course. And, she realised, it was the name of the boy in the journal who'd bullied Rosemary. He was real. It was like seeing an apparition, or a fictional character come to life.

'Did you know a girl called Rosemary who used to live here?'

His face turned inward, frowning as if she'd said something terrible, and he began to back away. 'I did. Yes. Long time ago now. What do you want to know about her for then?'

But she didn't answer. She had a strong urge to keep the girl in the notebooks to herself.

'I did wonder if you might be a relative or something,' he said, peering at her curiously.

'A relative? No. But – actually – I'm here because of my father, Harry Skinner. Do you know him? He gave me a picture of this house. The Marsh House.'

He frowned again. 'That name don't ring a bell. Sorry, afraid I've got to get off on my rounds.'

She stood watching him go, deflated by the fact that no one knew who Harry Skinner was. But this man, Bayfield, had known Rosemary. He *was* the boy mentioned in the diaries. Though Rosemary had hated him and in some strange way she felt as if she was betraying her by talking to him.

In the house, they hung their wet coats in the kitchen and let them drip onto the flagstone floor. Malorie told Franny to get packed up. She took down the notebooks from above the wardrobe and sat on the bed, holding them in her lap. She couldn't take them with her – how could she? – they weren't hers. Yet what was the alternative? She couldn't bear the thought of leaving Rosemary and the unfinished notebooks. But that was weird. She'd become too attached to this girl. The whole story was far-fetched. She'd allowed herself to become obsessed with it and all along, the writer – whoever it was – had been manipulating her, making her believe in this preposterous world of Fascist sympathisers and witchy old women. And she'd allowed the eerie old house to make her feel unsettled. She'd confused the two things – her own real, actual grief and sadness, with that of a chimera, a made-up person. And even the funny old woman wasn't that strange when you thought about it. She was probably just an old busybody. In fact – Malorie's brain lit up – that was it! The old woman had been trying to put her off. She'd been trying to spook her the whole time, making the odd noises she'd heard and planting the notebooks so Malorie could find them. Maybe she even wrote them. God, she'd been such a fool – a credulous fool. There was a woman, yes, but it could be anyone. The woman was no doubt trying to spook her because she thought Malorie was going to buy it! She, Malorie, must have looked like a typical up-from-Londoner. They hated them up here in the sticks. Yes, the man had been friendly at first, but she didn't like the way he'd reacted to the name Rosemary. It made her feel uncomfortable, having read about him in the journal, which may or may not be true.

It was impossible now to verify the truth of anything in the notebooks. Either way, the sooner she and Franny got back to London, the better.

Not knowing what else to do, she stashed the books under the bed.

When all the cases were in the car and the two of them were too, their combined breath fogging the windows, she heard Franny's voice from behind her.

'We can't leave Larry here. He'll be lonely.'

She stopped herself saying *No he won't, he's dead* and swallowed. 'I'm sorry, Fran, we can't take him. We can . . . come back.' She didn't even believe herself. She turned the key in the ignition.

The tyres spun. The car didn't move. There was a spluttering, churning sound as the engine turned over.

'Franny, you're going to need to get out and push.'

'Mummy, I can't!'

But she did as she was told. The tyres spun again, she thought the damn thing would never get out, but then there was a sudden release and the car sprang forward along the drive, pulling onto the road, spraying white on both sides. A moment of suspension, of perfect emptiness, the snow coming down sideways onto the ice-encrusted oval of the front windscreen, the wind cursing through the trees and her, driving in her furs. Then the wind dropped, snow fell vertically rather than horizontally. She turned as if to say goodbye to the house but she could hardly see it for the thickness of the snow.

'Mum!' she heard, from far away outside the car.

Too late, she slammed on the brakes; the car slid. A wall of white came fast towards her. The car came to a thumping halt. It had skidded into a hard barrier of snow.

The drift was too high to see over. They left the car there and returned to the house with their cases, dragging their heavy feet back up the road. It was bad – she knew logically it was a bad thing – but her instinct was an uneasy, giddy relief. They had to stay. She would have no choice now but to finish the notebooks and, in that moment, she didn't care if they were made up or not; she had to read them.

As they entered the drive, Malorie could have sworn she saw smoke curling up from the chimney of the cottage.

35

Mother

That night, they ate leftovers from the Christmas Day lunch. She melted snow for water and hoped it would be safe if she boiled it for tea. While she made the tea, Franny had gone and kneeled at the snowy mound where the dog was buried, leaving bits of leaf and stone as an offering. When she came in she was subdued and agreed to play cards but hardly spoke. Malorie tried to find music on the radio, but the white noise was too thick. When Franny went into the sitting room to read, Malorie stayed in the kitchen drinking wine. The third notebook was waiting for her back in the bedroom where it belonged. She could feel the pull of it but she was holding off, too. She wasn't exactly sure why, but she both wanted to be back in Rosemary's world and was wary of it. She was thinking about the little boy who'd died in the house and the girl's mother, rotting in an asylum. Her mind moved to her own child.

The birth had been a breeze. Everyone said she'd done very well, she had a lovely, healthy girl and look, isn't she dinky? Such a dainty little thing. But she, the mother, was afraid of the baby. It was a tiny, scrawny animal that relied on her. When they tried to get the baby to latch onto her breast, Malorie had felt repulsed at the sucking of the baby's mouth, the violent yank on her nipple. The baby wouldn't stay still and spat out the milk. It dribbled down onto her dressing gown. Eventually, the health visitor said words like 'failure to thrive' and 'bedrest'. They took both of them away to a maternity hospital. When the baby was taken to the hospital nursery, Malorie felt only gratitude. Every time they brought her back, the baby's screwed up face broke into a yowling wail and Malorie had no idea what to do to stop the crying. They gave her baby formula and she tried to use the bottle, or a dummy, or her finger. She tried rocking, stroking, jiggling the baby up and down on her still-tender belly, saying soothing, cooing sounds. None of it seemed to work. Each time, she would gladly hand the baby over to a capable-looking nurse and they would take her back to the nursery, judgement in their eyes.

Tony said they had to give the baby a name. Did she want to give the baby her name, Mary? No, she said, Mary was her given name and she'd taken her middle name, Malorie, as soon as she'd left Norwich for London. What about her mother's name? She made a face. No. She couldn't fix her mind on a name for this baby. In the end, Tony suggested Frances, after his grandmother. His mother would like that. Fine, she said, and fell back into longed-for sleep. She couldn't seem to keep awake after they gave her the Luminal. But something would inevitably wake her, dragging her out of the quiet – the clattering of a trolley, the cheery good morning of a nurse, the yanking open of the curtains, the wailing of the baby, or someone else's baby. Once, in the middle of the night, she was woken by the sound of crying. It was soft crying, not a baby, a woman's sob. She lay there thinking that if only she had the energy she could call out to the woman, to say *I'm here. I know what it's like. You're not alone.* But she was afraid. Eventually the woman sniffed and stopped and the ward returned to its temporary hush.

The days stretched to weeks and the weeks to months. A nurse at the mother and baby unit told her that her time was up. By the time they left, she couldn't imagine how she was supposed to look after the baby on her own. Every day and night in the flat with the baby while Tony was out at the club was a trial. Malorie didn't like thinking about those years now. Once, she was in the park when Franny was a toddler – she must have been walking because she wouldn't go in her pushchair. She'd stiffen her legs and cry if Malorie tried so they'd walked to the park, a scrubby rectangle of dirty grass and a few swings on a concrete patch near the flat. In the park was another mother with her daughter, who was about the same age. She couldn't actually remember how old Franny had been then – why couldn't she remember? This other mother was neat and smartly dressed, with a daffodil-coloured spring coat and sensible shoes. The woman wasn't as pretty as Malorie; she was probably older than her too. Malorie had only been about twenty-one then. But the woman looked happy. Radiant – that was a word they used about new mothers. And the baby looked happy, chubby and healthy. She remembered thinking *How have they done it?* How did the mother know what to do? She picked up Franny and shoved her roughly into the pushchair. The baby had set up a forlorn cry instantly and Malorie had marched out of the park, tears welling in her eyes, full of rage at the perfect mother and her perfect baby, at her imperfect, hateful child and her own inadequate, terrible self.

Her mother visited and tidied, washed up, prepared the bottles and complained about how dirty London was. Malorie was grateful to her, but her mother had no words of advice to give her on how to bond with her child and returned to Norwich without any promise to return. She tried hard not to think about how much her father would have loved being a grandfather; he'd only missed her birth by months.

Mostly she avoided the other mothers in the area. Their friends, Clemency and the others, didn't have babies. Malorie would take Franny with her to the parties and put her on a pile of clothes. Or she'd hear Franny crying while she was trying to dance and stones of guilt and hate would fall heavily into her gut. Once, she was stumbling out the door of a party when Tony held up a squalling baby.

'I think you've forgotten something.' His face was full of disgust.

On the way home in the taxi, she said, 'She's yours too.'

'What kind of mother are you?' he said.

What kind of mother was she? It was a question she asked herself.

Franny turned from a difficult baby to an isolated child. And here she was, eight years old and sullen, friendless – only at ease, it seemed to Malorie, with her feckless, insubstantial father, who seemed to prefer being in his bloody club to being with his daughter. She could hear her own whining in her head. *It isn't fair.* But it *was* fair, that was the cruel truth. A lonely person had bred another one. That was all. And why wouldn't their daughter prefer her father's company? He was more *fun.* Her disgusting self-pity was feeding on itself. She was sick of her own sadness, growing and growing inside her like a choking weed, clogging up her every waking thought, until she loathed everything and everyone.

Tottering slightly, she picked up the half-empty wine bottle and her red-smeared glass and took them upstairs to the bedroom. The house creaked and a thin wind cried in the chimney. It was late and she should sleep but she wasn't tired, she was buzzing with nervous energy.

What kind of mother was she? One who had never known her own mother, even at the end, when she'd been dying. She remembered the papers her mother had given Tony, the last time in the hospice. She'd avoided thinking about anything left behind, unwilling to acknowledge the emptiness left by her parents' deaths. It seemed easier to ignore it than to engage with it. Theirs was a history she didn't want. But – what if it told her the connection to this house? She thought of all this tangled mess of inadequacy and rage and blame. Of secrets carrying on and on from one generation to the next, and accepted that finally, she should just look at these papers. He'd said they were in the suitcase. She had it with her now, the same one she'd taken to the hospice, which she'd hardly bothered to unpack. It must be there.

Her fingers were stiff and cold as she rifled through the piles of jumpers and vests, and found it, still there, tucked at the bottom. She fumbled with the large brown manila folder. She flicked through the sheaf of documents, letters from the bank, that sort of thing, the detritus of small lives that no one wanted to deal with. And an envelope with the words *To be opened after I'm gone* written on the front. For God's sake, Mother, that was an unnecessarily emotive way of putting it. Why only then, for goodness' sake? Why not while she was alive? Inside it were official-looking documents. But there was no letter, no explanation.

Her face and neck flushed suddenly with heat. A strange sensation of falling. Adoption papers.

A baby, named Mary Skinner. Parents Mr and Mrs Skinner. Nothing else. No place of birth. It was her. She could hardly breathe. The date of adoption, 3rd August 1935. Her birthday.

There was a photograph attached by a paper clip to the certificate. A swaddled, dark-eyed baby and a smiling woman in a nurse's uniform. On the back it said *Mary, three months, with Mrs Babbage.*

She understood it was her, that the baby in the photograph was her, in the way she understood the moon circled the earth. But she did not *understand*. And then very quickly, in a rush of knowledge, she did. Her mother's drawn face in the hospice. The way she'd looked at something out of the window rather than directly at her. The room began to spin. She made some kind of guttural groan, staggered two paces to the window and opened it to the night.

She thrust her head through the window. Snow fell lightly on her hair and her upturned face.

Her head was teeming. Who was this Mrs Babbage? Maybe she could find her. Who were her real parents and why had they abandoned her? Her mother. Her *mother*. The word itself had changed. She felt like laughing.

She thought of all the years when they could have told her. Her parents. Her mother. Her father. Her *dad*. Her heart seemed to physically ache with the pain of it like a knife wound, plunging again and again. Her mother's words filtered into her head. *I can't tell you. It's too late.* She was the shameful secret. *She* was.

A musical note floated up from the living room downstairs. A single low, mournful trumpet. She must be imagining it. It was the song again, the song she kept hearing. She put her hands over her ears but the song was still there, faint but audible.

She ran down the stairs and into the living room where the gramophone sat innocuously on the sideboard. No sound came from it.

Suddenly exhausted, she flopped onto the sofa. You've suffered a terrible shock, she said to herself, the way someone would to a victim of a crime. It was a terrible shock. But also, what she felt was a small sense of relief that she'd belonged to another mother once, and a dull sadness that she'd been so horribly ungrateful that they'd chosen her, looked after her as their own. And a gnawing, aching feeling that she would never be able to say to her father that she'd loved him. Why hadn't they told her? Why hadn't they let her know she was chosen? And the question which bothered her the most: *Why* had they chosen her when they obviously found her so bemusing? Why had her mother never let her know she was loved? And the impossible realisation that it was because she wasn't.

36

It began in thirty-four. Around the summertime. A hot one it was.

She were eighteen then, still a mere sprite of a thing, hardly grown. Bit like the young one in the house now, only angrier. She could get a right mard on, that Rose, when she wanted to. Both got them narrow greenish eyes, like cats. It were a funny time, cos in one way she were glad, back at home with me and her father. But she'd lost that baby of hers and she began to act like an animal building its nest. She'd always done it, the nesting. When she was younger, she used to pick bits of rubbish off the shore and bring them back to her room – bits of tidewrack what had no place in a home – dried seaweed, tree roots, old bits of blue fishing line, that kind of thing. I don't know why she did it, 'cept she had a liking for the sea. Then her father got rid of it all when she was married. But it were different this time I'm talking about. She'd walk down to the marsh every day, and right across it, to the sand and the sea, picking up gruesome things, strange things. Bones, mostly. Then that boy came and got her and he started taking her back to the hall. I knew what he were playing at. He ought to have left the poor child alone, but he were always sighing at her and whispering sweetness and buying her fancies. And she didn't have her baby no more and I reckon she didn't know what else to do. I tried to tell her, course I did, but you can't tell nothing to a dreamy girl like that, she'd gone away from me, or that's what I thought.

Anyway, she were bound to him. There weren't much I could say about that. I know in some places people hop about in and out of each other's beds and there were those what did that then, I can assure you. But there weren't options for her like that, left out here in Norfolk. She might as well not have existed. It were a hop-pole marriage after all – cos she'd been with child.

Every time he went off to London she came back here to the Marsh House, but I didn't like the look of her. She were getting thinner if anything and that don't make no sense when you think about all the fancy food they had at that hall. Bones sticking out, hollow cheeks, like she were sucking cochies. It weren't right.

'Are you eating?' I say to her.

'Of course I am,' she says, but she don't look at me straight. 'I'm just tired, that's all.'

By then she never talked about him no more. All the shine had rubbed off him, revealing a cheap, empty pot underneath.

We were in my garden. That were alive with my bees and so hot the birds had gone quiet. We were sitting on the back step – her legs sticking out, brown as nuts they were, but her face had a sick look about it like she weren't getting no nourishment.

'You'll always be able to come here,' I say.

But my words didn't seem to make much impression on her. She barely nodded, as if she didn't believe what I was saying and I wondered what was going on with that husband of hers to make her so sad. And it reminded me of Louisa after the babbies died, and again when Rose was born. Like some sickness had got into her and was poisoning all that was good and true. I should have seen it coming, the way she was then.

37

Snowdrift

27th December

It was dark and Malorie didn't know where she was. Blearily, she hauled herself up onto her elbows. She was in the living room. There was the tree she'd cut down, there was the fireplace, the mirror above it. She couldn't remember why she was there. A cold draught was coming from the door. Her head ached and her mouth was dry.

An icicle of light jutted out into the hallway. The front door was open a crack and through it, she glimpsed white outside. There was a sprinkling of snow on the hallway wood floor. She had thick socks on and her dressing gown but the cold from the door was icy and penetrating.

Like a sleepwalker, she moved towards the open door. Outside, snow was falling in thick flakes. It was already in high drifts, stacked against the boundary hedges, heavy on the branches. It was so unreal. She stood, bewitched by its cold magnificence, until she noticed a sudden movement from the darkness in the opposite trees. A swaying, a fall of snow brushed off the tree. Staring at the white garden, she remembered the dull shock of the papers, the sense of disorientation. As she stood there, she wasn't at all sure whose body she inhabited. Was she Mary Skinner? Malorie Cavendish? Or someone else?

She went up to the bedroom. No sound came from behind Franny's door so she went back down to the kitchen to make a pot of tea and cut the leftover bread for toast. They were soothing, these automatic, small movements. She twiddled with the knobs on the radio and eventually managed to find a local station. The words drifted through the familiar dense wave of white noise.

. . . railway line between Sheringham and Holt is closed due to the overnight snowfall but British Rail assure us that it will be up and running soon . . . Snow drifts up to three feet high on parts of the coast . . . the Wensum in Norwich is iced over . . .

It went on like this, in and out of range, giving up little snippets of the icy conditions around the county. Malorie tried to imagine skating on the river. It sounded magical, like something from Narnia. They'd gone boating on the Wensum once, taken a pleasure boat from Pull's Ferry to Thorpe St Andrew, she aged about ten and her parents (her *adoptive* parents) already old in her eyes. It was not like the trip on the Broads on the *Dancing Light* that Rosemary had written about, she'd been a child with her parents, but in some ways, it was not so very different. There was something about being on the water that took you out of time. The boat had been called – she strained to remember – it hadn't been given a name. Her father fussed about the stern, while her mother sat clutching her handbag and refused to look over the side at the flowing river, or look up at the birds in the branches of the trees they passed. Malorie had loved it, but it had only been that one time. She asked herself again with a flare of resentment, why had they chosen her? Had she been a terrible disappointment to them? In the pub at Thorpe, they'd sat on the grass with bottles of pop. Her father had a beer and did tricks with his hands to make her laugh. It had been wonderful, time away from themselves. The fizzing of the pop up her nose, the hum of other people, glittering water just a few feet away. But swans had come up from the river and her mother had shouted at her to get away from them, so they'd gone back up to the pub tables. It was always that way. There had always been something that irritated her mother. Something that *she'd* done.

The lights in the kitchen kept flickering and humming. It seemed incredible that they were still working given yesterday's blizzard. She'd run out of the milk she'd brought on Christmas Eve and even if the house received deliveries, which she doubted, they wouldn't have been able to get through. She reboiled the melted snow for water, drank the brackish tea black again and nibbled at the toast. She tried to see herself as a child, eating toast with her parents, a normal childhood, a typical breakfast scene. But she was always picking at something. Eat up, her mother would say. She was always trying to get her to eat. A rush of anger and pity ran through her – for her mother and for herself.

Something her mother used to say came to her. *You were such a slight baby. There was nothing to you.* She'd said it as an accusation, as if it was Malorie's fault. Now she thought of it, it made sense. Her parents were short, stocky people. Her slightness, her insubstantiality, must have seemed like an affront – a constant reminder that she wasn't theirs. And she didn't have the blonde hair and blue eyes that all the other girls seemed to have. She was a dark, dull mouse with pond-coloured eyes. The other girls plaited each other's hair. No one touched hers. It was only when she went to London that she'd had an awareness of herself as desirable.

She ought to move, to go and look at the car, see if there was any way out. There was no need for the two of them to be marooned out here for another day. Christmas was over. There was no point staying any longer. Her body felt heavy, as if the weight of her mood was dragging it down. A thought, slow but sure, like a slug, slipped into her brain. Her daughter.

Upstairs, it smelt strange. She turned right instead of left at the top of the stairs and went into her empty bedroom. As if it had been a dream, she saw herself opening the window to the night air and thrusting her head outside. The window was now closed, but through it she could hear the groaning of the trees in the wind. It was nothing but whiteness and white noise. Ice patterned the inside of the window and outside, wind picked up the snow and sent it in whirlpools and tornadoes as far as she could see. The room faced north, out to the sea. Something, down in the garden where the trees must be, was moving. Shivering, she wiped the window and – yes, she was sure now – someone *was* on the edge of the garden. It was like déjà vu – a memory flared of seeing someone like that in the night, a white figure. It was probably one of the dreams she'd been having while she'd been here. She was about to prise open the window when she heard a cough behind her, and she returned to the light of the day. Franny.

The funny smell came from her daughter's room. It smelt of sweat and liquorice. It made her gag and she put a hand to her mouth. Franny was lying on the bed, the covers half thrown off. The bed was small and high but in it she looked shrunken, younger. For a second Malorie was reminded of her daughter as a baby, a fragile form of skin and bones that had shocked her with its vulnerability. Where Franny's skin was visible – her lower arm, her neck and face – it was pale and blotchy pink in patches and covered all over in a sheen of grease.

'Franny, what's wrong, are you ill?'

The girl's eyes were rimmed with grey and large and sunken in her small head. She nodded and tried to speak. 'Really tired,' she said.

'Don't speak, don't move,' she said, and rushed back downstairs to fetch a glass of water and then back up to her bedroom for the pills. Had she forgotten to give her dose to her last night? She tipped the tiny pills out onto her palm and picked one up in her fingers. It was tempting to swallow one herself. One swallow. Gone.

She tried to lift Franny up but she was limp and heavy. She held the glass to her daughter's parched lips but Franny only took a tiny sip and jerked her head away as if a fly was sucking on her blood.

'Have a bit more, sweetheart, you need it.'

But Franny shook her head. 'Don't want it, Mummy.'

'No, darling. You have to take the pill. Open just a tiny bit. Come on now.' She slipped the little pill in between her lips and held the water glass to her mouth again. Franny swallowed then shuddered, coughing.

They were for her own good. It had been Tony's idea at first. Franny had always been a worrier – shy, withdrawn – and he wanted her to be more confident, less moody. He thought the Luminal would help. Malorie had gone along with it. And really, what was the difference between giving her those pills and the herbal remedies that people like Janey gave out? But in her heart she knew she hadn't been paying enough attention to her daughter. She'd been too wrapped up in her own pain.

'It's all right, darling. It'll be all right.' She held her palm to her daughter's head and it burned.

Franny convulsed and vomited over the bedspread – a vivid pink pool spread over the wooden floor and the sour, noxious smell of vomit overrode the stale odour of illness.

'Oh Franny,' she said. Franny had tears in her eyes. 'It's all right love, it's all right.' She stroked her daughter's damp cheek, fetched a bucket and a bowl of water and wiped her mouth and chin.

Above the bed, the sampler looked down on her. She felt that she knew the figures depicted in it as well as she knew herself. They were more real to her than anyone else. Staring at it, she noticed something she hadn't seen before. The tiny images in each of the four corners weren't patterns as she'd thought before, but pictures. A shell, a tuft of grass, a wave and, disturbingly, a skull. She had to get Franny out of this room. It was the room itself that was making her sick. She knew this didn't make any sense but lifted her gently out of the bed anyway. The boy had died here. She saw it suddenly, as clearly as if she'd been there: the baby dead in the bed and the dark-haired girl kneeling, rocking, keening. She shut the door on the pink room.

The girl's body was light in her arms as she carried her across the landing. There was so little of her. Malorie laid her down on the bed in her own room and stayed with her until she fell into a fevered sleep.

'Mummy's here,' she murmured, over and over again.

38

That morning, the day it happened, there were a last blaze of summer heat before the autumn came. I walked Smutch along the marshes and beach and it were so hot he sought out any shade he could. Slunk off to lie under the wreck of the old mussel flat run up on the dune. Normally he's out there pestering the oystercatchers and sanderlings. Not on that day though. We weren't out there long, the poor animal was too thirsty. I were at the cottage in the afternoon with the drapes shut to keep out the burning. I remember I had the back door open to the garden and it were buzzing with bees and jaspers and crickets. Smutch was slumped right out on the floor and he'd snap his jaws now and again at some fly teasing him. When I went out in the garden to snip the herbs for the pot, the sky was still blazing blue and nothing in it. The sun was high up, glaring down on us. The cuckoo clock someone gave me for helping cure an old boy's warts chimed and cuckooed two, three, four. It got hotter and hotter. I fell into a doze on the sofa and was woken by a banging on the door.

I rubbed my eyes, stretched and cranked up my old bones to open the door, but before I could, she came flying in. Door weren't locked, never is. It were my Rose, in a right old puckaterry. She were all red-faced and fly-blown, hair in a tangle, jabbering away at me, all duddering. She were talking so jumbled I couldn't make out what she were saying. I sat her down and gave her a glass of water and made her catch her breath. At last she started to make sense.

She said he was sick. Vomiting all over the drawing room and he's lying on the floor, not moving. She couldn't get him to move. Said something about the marsh fever.

She stared at me then with those glass-green cat eyes and for a second there I doubted what she was saying, so fixed and hard they were.

But she pleaded with me to come so I followed her across the lane to the house. I had a horrible doom feeling.

39

Poisons

Malorie peered out of the bedroom window but the blizzard wasn't abating. Tony would blame her for this. He already blamed her for all their misfortune. But they couldn't travel now, not with Franny feverish, even if she could get the car out of the snow, and she didn't believe she could. She could go to the village to get help. Ask the man. George Bayfield. She couldn't go the way she and Franny had gone the first day because of the snowdrift. It felt like many weeks ago although it was only – what? – a week? No, it was five days ago. Only five days. She'd hardly seen a soul since then. She stood staring at the window, rocking back and forth on her socked feet. All this pretence, this effort to be a proper family. She didn't know how to do it. She had failed at everything. She took out the white envelope with the pills. It was nestled in the white lace veil. Just one. She would take just one. She needed to calm the racing of her heart. It was easier to be numb, to take all the feeling away. She had tried to not need the pills but she wasn't strong enough. Could she take two? She put the envelope in her pocket for later.

She swallowed it down with water.

Nothing happened. She sat on the floor of the bedroom with her back against the door. Her mind was a blank. Good. It was better to be a blank than have that weird electric intensity coursing through her.

A moaning sound came from the bed. She sat up straight. At first she thought there were two figures in the room. Someone else sitting on the end of the bed. A white dress. She fell against the doorframe, and looked again. It was just the old dressing gown in a pile. The window banged against its frame but Franny didn't wake. She had no idea how much time had passed. She had a vague recollection of eating breakfast and then confusion. A blank.

The wind outside seemed to rise up. Snow battered against the window. Shadows from the low lamplight in the room waved and then the light went out completely. Malorie cowered in the corner of the room. It's the wind, it's the wind, she said in her head.

She tried to switch on the lamp but it didn't work. Downstairs, she tried the hallway lights, the kitchen. Nothing. The power was off.

Snow was still falling and it was hard to tell, but what light there'd been outside seemed to be fading away. Her watch said nearly two o'clock but it seemed incredible, as if time itself was being twisted by the house. How could it be so dark this early? How had the time disappeared? There was no sound outside except the pattering of the snow against the window and the agonising creaking of trees being battered by the blizzard.

Malorie pulled her scarf tighter around her neck. She was alone again, no Tony, no Franny, no dog. What had happened to the dog? She struggled to remember. Light was fading and she thought *I must get out there now* – before it goes completely.

The draught from under the front door sliced across the room and she shrank from it. She was supposed to do something, but what it was she couldn't remember. Above her, she heard the faint scraping of the rats as they moved around. She shuddered. She felt her eyes move up to the ceiling, her body pulled towards the book. The third notebook. In all the confusion of the snowdrift and the papers and now Franny being ill she hadn't finished it. It seemed imperative that she do this.

After fetching the book from her case, she returned to the warmth of the living room. The tree sat in the corner, dark again, the candles unlit. She lit a candle and stuck it to a plate and it made dark, dancing shadows on the ceiling. She poured herself a glass of brandy and made up the fire. Matchstick on matchstick, struck with trembling fingers, flamed then went out, until finally, one of them caught and the fire came to life. The gramophone and the records were there but she didn't put one on, there was enough noise in her own brain, a whirring that would not rest. The slow heat of the fire spread across her upper body and the brandy burned inside. She was shattered, but her heart was racing. The drugs weren't working. In her hands she had the third notebook. The firelight flickered and cast a stuttering light over Rosemary's handwriting. It was like looking at an old friend. There was comfort here, in these pages, someone to listen to, someone to talk to her, someone whose life was infinitely worse than her own, someone who made her feel less alone. She looked at the words greedily. She wanted to suck them up and swallow them, like food. And she thought, if her father had wanted her to have the photograph of the Marsh House, perhaps it had something to do with *her*, rather than him. There was nothing in the notebooks that would suggest that. But it didn't matter anymore. She just wanted Rosemary to keep talking to her.

There were a few pages of writing about the rest of the summer of 1934 when Rosemary wandered the marsh, collecting things, including a strange, elongated skull of an unknown animal with its teeth intact, and taking them back to her childhood room. The ink was darker and spots flew across the page when she wrote about Franklin's visits, as if the pen had been pressed hard on the paper.

But then after a few lines of this, the handwriting changed and became scrawled and sloping and almost indecipherable.

THE THIRD NOTEBOOK

continued

40

After Richie's death I hardly went to Old Hall. Franklin was rarely there – he was often away travelling on behalf of his father at rallies and meetings around the country. Whenever he wrote, he was quite sure there was a great support building in the country, the Daily Mail was right behind them and victory in next year's election was assured. I asked to go home and the Laffertys and my father agreed that it was for the best, at least for a time. The high-ceilinged, bright rooms of Old Hall reminded me of Richie's babyhood and the winter I'd begun to love him. There was no comfort there. The Laffertys were not the sort of people to discuss what had been lost and he wasn't spoken of. Now Richie was gone, there was little to bind me to that place – the marriage so hastily arranged seemed to have been dropped as quickly as it had begun.

There was little comfort at the Marsh House either, but its gloomy rooms and lopsided, low walls suited me. It was my fault he'd died – I hadn't loved him enough. I wanted to punish everyone and everything that wasn't my baby; this darkness, this damp dreariness was all I deserved. I walked every day out onto the marsh at low tide, and trudged on and on until I reached the sea. I hardly saw a soul but Janey. Father was busy with his work and didn't notice the time I spent away from the house. The only person who offered any solace to me was Janey. She was the only one who'd known my mother, who knew me. I wrote a dozen letters to Louisa, my mother, never sent. I burned all of them, unable to find the right words to speak to her. I could barely forgive myself, let alone her.

I look at the person I was then and I want to shake her, to shout in her ear that she is letting life go by, wallowing in the pit rather than crawling out of it. There was still time then, to have found her, to have made it better. But I didn't know how little time I had left.

The seasons turned and although I didn't think I would, I began to notice the changes. Spring came and the black terns flew over on their way to breed. The marsh evolved from brown to green. I was hardly thinking, or feeling, just being part of the earth. I began to collect remnants of the dead: the perfect white, delicate skull of a bird I found stripped clean; a broken bone that reminded me of Richie's ear; the scaly skin of a dead eel; the skeleton of one of the rats caught by Rogers' traps; a black mermaid's purse with the translucent foetus of a baby skate still visible within it. In time, my bedroom, the room where I'd been a girl and where my son died, became a kind of mausoleum of the marsh. I gathered up the fragments around me. Day after day I walked, my only companion the curlews overhead and the changing sky. The landscape was as flat, as low, as bleak as I was, but it was mine. My mud, my coarse grass, my murky water. In the summer, the sea lavender turned my marsh purple and I felt the sun on my back. My fingers had withered and the rings fell off but the locket was always around my neck, a constant reminder of my short-lived son.

If they could have left me like that, none of this would have happened. But it couldn't last.

It was a warm airless day in late May. I'd walked all along the tidal creek to the beach as I did every day. I was bent over, knees in the sand, stroking a smooth stone when I felt the shadow of something behind me. There was a clutching at my waist and I screamed, buckled and collapsed forward onto the sand. My teeth crunched, I choked. I sat up, spat sand out of my mouth. The spring noon sun was high in the sky behind my assailant, creating a burning halo of light.

After an initial second of terror, I knew it was Franklin. There was no one else in the world who would dare to touch me like that. No one else who – and for this I was grateful – who wasn't hushed and awkward towards me, after Richie.

'I've missed my sweet girl,' he said, crouching beside me.

'I'm not sweet,' I said.

He laughed. 'No, but you are mine.'

I didn't answer. I put the stone into my pocket.

Franklin held out a handful of brightly wrapped sweets. 'Bonbons,' he said, 'from Paris.'

I shook my head, although my mouth was salivating.

He laughed again. 'Don't be silly,' he said. 'I bought them for you.'

I always had a sweet tooth. I took a bonbon from his hand and unwrapped the shiny paper. They were little balls coated in a white powder. When I bit into one it was sugary-sweet and hard like caramel toffee and the white powder tasted of lemon sherbet. It fizzed on my lips. I was taken back to long ago when I was a young girl and my kind governess, Miss Cannadine, would bring me sweets on a Friday and I would devour them all, each one more delicious for being completely contraband. 'You mustn't ever tell your father,' she would say, smiling at me indulgently. And I never did. It's funny but the only other person who ever bought me sweets was Franklin. He was clever like that.

We ate his bonbons and he told me of Paris, Rome and Berlin. It sounded so foreign, so exotic – it had nothing to do with me and my dead boy. But he took my plait in his hand and stroked it as if I were a pet and I fell into a sugar dream, lulled by the soft crash of the waves, the hot sand under my feet and the rhythmic touch of Franklin's strokes.

He kissed me on the top of my head and murmured 'Rosie,' into my hair, and where his lips touched my hair stood on end, electrified at the roots. Eventually, he pulled me up and we walked, me still half in slumber, along the beach. The sand was wet and hard-rippled from the outgoing tide and there was nothing all around us apart from the mudflats and creeks to the left and behind, and the sand stretching out ahead of us until it faded into the glittering sea. As Cabbage Creek came into view, dissecting the beach, a dark shape appeared beyond it on the sand. Coming closer, I could see it was a grey seal. Close up, you could smell the sweetness of rot. I thought of the sperm whale I'd seen once when I was a child, a huge grey beast beached at Titchwell that we'd all gone to gawp at. I'd touched the side of the poor half-dead animal before Fairbrother had shouted at me to come away. But I remembered its skin was cut with lines like an etching and I'd looked into its eye, the size of my own head, and seen the distress there. Some of the other children were mucking about throwing sand at it but their mothers shooed them away. The men tried to keep the beast wet before the tide came in to take it away again. It died before the tide came and rotted out on the beach for weeks and weeks. The bones of that whale are still there now, like a great shipwreck.

I thought of the tiny toad's bones floating away under the Rose Moon.

I thought of Richie's small bones buried under the earth in the graveyard.

Franklin pulled me away from the dead seal and we retraced our steps along the beach to the creeks of Stiffkey and the Marsh House. He had to go back to London soon, he said. There was an important rally in Olympia. At the gate to the house he took hold of my shoulders and said, 'It's all over now.' I didn't know what he meant. Did he mean he and I? I had a moment of terror that he was releasing me. 'You mustn't be morbid anymore and hole yourself up here with only an old witch for company. Come back to the Hall with me.'

He meant Richie. My allotted mourning time was over and he intended to keep me.

'It's not over for me,' I said.

'There's no point moping about it,' he said, his beautiful pink mouth twisted in distaste, and I had never felt so far from him then. How could he not feel the pain I felt?

'How can you be so cruel?' I said.

'It's not cruel to say you're doing yourself no good wallowing like this,' he said. 'And it's no good for me, either.' His face softened. 'I miss you. I miss my sweet Rose.' He stroked my hair. He held my hand in his, rubbing the skin on my fingers. 'Where are the rings?'

'They were too big, they fell off.'

I had an unexpected, wild idea. 'Can I come to London with you? And to Paris and Rome and Vienna and all those other places?'

He looked amazed. 'You wouldn't like that to-ing and fro-ing, Rosie. You're too good for the city.'

'How am I too good?'

'You wouldn't understand,' he said, and touched his fingers lightly along my temple and jawline, making me shiver.

So that was it then. He wanted me as a country plaything and no more. I went back to Old Hall when he was there at weekends and returned to the marsh when he went back to London. The rings were resized and I had to wear them again. I noticed Franklin didn't wear his but apparently the Lafferty men didn't wear them. I submitted to him, and sometimes, when he was gentle with me, as he mostly was, I was reminded of the kisses he gave me years before when I was fifteen, before I was married and had borne and lost a child, and all of that had taken away the simple delight I'd once felt in him. There were times when I wanted him again; I allowed his touches to block my mind, I even craved them. But each time he went away, I returned to my marsh.

I found out soon after he came back to me that the rally in Olympia was a disaster. There had been protests, the Blackshirts had acted like thugs and the entire thing had descended into violence. In The Times, a witness described what he'd seen: 'Five or six Fascists carried out an interrupter by arms and legs, several other Blackshirts were engaged in hitting and kicking his lifeless body.' I haven't forgotten this. It stuck in my mind. 'It's just a nasty element,' said my father when I asked him about it. And Franklin used Mosley's words to me in a letter. 'We never start fights, we only finish them.' But all I could think of was my husband in his black uniform and shining black jackboots and how pleased with himself he'd been, and what kept repeating in my head was a picture of one of those smart, black boots smashing into someone's skull. It was not him, I told myself.

Later that month, I read in Father's newspaper of Germany's purge. 'Herr Adolf Hitler, the German Chancellor, has saved his country', the paper reported, but I read that over a hundred political opponents had been killed. All the papers seemed to think this was a necessary 'clean-up', but how is killing people cleaning up? The Führer himself called it 'The Night of the Long Knives', which did nothing to quell my growing unease.

I waited until the dead seal's flesh had completely rotted and went back to collect its skull. I washed off the sand in the kitchen sink and placed it on my windowsill. Every night when I was at the Marsh House, I'd look at its gaping eye sockets and ask it what to do. How I could find a way to recover my love for Franklin.

41

That summer there were boat trips on the Broads and beach visits, but when he came to see me in the country, we were not the same. I knew there were other women in the city, though how many, I didn't know. He continued to be preoccupied with the party, which he said was tearing itself apart about 'the Jew problem'. He'd complain sometimes about the thugs, certain elements of the Blackshirts, as Father did, but when I said wasn't he part of all that? he would fob me off as if I was being stupid, tell me I wouldn't understand. He treated me like a child, but I wasn't a child anymore.

Hildy was mostly absent as well. I think she was wary of my grief, and perhaps she was bored of it too. I wasn't the pet they used to play with.

Something else was different in me too. I was nauseous in the morning and my breasts were tender. I knew I must be pregnant again. I should have been glad – it was what everyone wanted. Surely it was what I wanted too. A boy to love, a child to dote on. But this sickness felt like a sickness throughout my entire body – rejecting the very idea of a baby. I couldn't see how I could do it. How could I give birth to a child after what had happened to Richie? How could I love another child? My belly, which had been his so recently, still belonged to him. And – unarticulated then but I think now – I was afraid that a baby would upset the precarious balance of my relationship with Franklin.

There were no outward signs, no protruding belly. If I acted quickly, no one would ever know.

'I can't have it,' I told Janey. 'It'll destroy me.'

'Don't be all dramatic,' she said, 'normal as anything, having babbies. Women do it all the time.'

'My mother couldn't do it,' I said.

She frowned, making all the lines on her face scrunch up. 'That weren't her fault.'

'What if I'm the same? What if I'm not meant to have babies?'

'Don't do nothing stupid now,' she said.

'Then help me,' I said.

Down even lower than the cottage and closer to the marsh, Janey had a small garden that she called her 'medicine cabinet'. It had lavender, thyme, costmary, arnica and lemon balm, rue, valerian, cowslip and yarrow. And many more but I can't remember all their names. Certainly in the summer, as it was then, the air was full of the competing scents of these herbs and plants. Under the twittering cacophony of the birds, the pinks and purples of the echinacea, foxgloves and the dusky nodding heads of the poppies stuck out above the greener, prettier plants. There were even the shining dark leaves of a mandrake bush which Janey dug up once a year to use for invigorating potions. We were here for none of those though; we'd come for the pennyroyal.

Janey picked some of the small, bright green pennyroyal leaves and crushed them between her fingers and the most wonderful peppermint fragrance was released. We gathered up handfuls of the puffy lilac flowers and returned to the kitchen for Janey to make the tea.

I'd taken many of these herbs before, like my cold remedy/love potion, and wasn't worried. It tasted fine too, just like peppermint. She said that to have any effect I'd have to drink a few cups of it and by the end of the third cup I was sick of it and my stomach had begun to gurgle.

'You take care of yerself, my girl,' she said, with her hand warm on my head, when I said I better go home or Father would be wondering about me. 'Come back straightaway if you're taken bad. Now all it should do is bring on the bleeding, but if there's too much of it, or anything else rum, you come straight back, you hear?'

I promised I would but I was feeling nauseous by then and just wanted to lie down. At the Marsh House, I told Father I was unwell and went directly to bed.

I plumped up the cushions and bolsters and tried to read one of my precious novels, but the print was too small and began to move across the page like a procession of drunk ants. The pain in my stomach came in waves, and when the wave crashed I was pinned back in the bed, unable to see or breathe. I told myself I didn't mind;

I wanted the tea to do its work. Let the blood come. Let the blood gush out of me, taking the poor creature with it. But the worse the pain ground into me, the more I was afraid. What if it didn't work? Or if it did and took me with it?

Once I felt a warm rushing between my legs and thought it must be coming. Helter-skelter I ran to the water closet along the hall. Through the little high window, I could see the pale blue of the sky but it felt like nothing to do with me. My stomach contracted. I bent over, clutching my belly. Nothing else. Nothing came flowing out of me. I had a strong urge to lie down again.

'What's ailing you?' said Fairbrother, with no hint of sympathy, as I hurried past her on the landing, but I just shook my head at her and rushed back to bed.

In the small mirror on my dressing table, I caught sight of myself. It was as if someone had drained all the life out of me. My pupils were so tiny in my irises, I looked like a staring ghoul. Crawling back into the bed, the pains in my abdomen increased in severity and frequency and I curled into them. I began to feel as if I was being punished. My face and neck were clammy, but my hands were cold and I couldn't get warm. I must have groaned, because there was a knock at the door. Someone was there, then they went away. I lost time and consciousness. At one point, I thought Janey's big black dog, Old Smutch, was licking my face. I cried out and buried myself in his fur.

The pain was even worse than labour – I felt as if someone had dug a knife inside me and they kept twisting and twisting. I thought I would die of it. It was a cruel reminder of what I had gone through to give birth to my lost boy. Each time it eased, I felt the sweat roll down my face and I was aware of light and movement, but when the pain came again it was worse for the relief. I forgot what was supposed to be happening and I forgot who I was.

They must have called the doctor because someone or something was pressed into me and I screamed so loudly, Janey told me later that she heard it in her cottage and she thought my time had come. She knocked hard on the door until her knuckles were bruised, but Father hissed at her to 'Take your black magic away from my door, you've caused enough trouble already.' I don't think he was referring to the tea I'd drunk but something to do with Mother.

'He always had me wrong,' said Janey when she told me later, very quietly as she never liked to draw attention to what she did, but I knew she was frustrated by the way people like my father misunderstood her. All my life, people had been visiting her damp little cottage for remedies, or future-telling, or to ward against some terrible misfortune. Few people thought of her as a witch, but my father did. He barred the door to her, so she was forced to return to the cottage.

'I watched out for you, child,' she told me, and perhaps she did because sometime on the day following, I woke from a dream in which Smutch was carrying me on his back and my uncontrollable shaking had stopped. The pain had eased to a normal stomach-ache and I drank some hot water. It was Dolly who gave it to me, Fairbrother having given up nursing duties. 'She said you were cursed,' Dolly said.

I thought that Fairbrother, for once, was right. I'd been wrenched back from the edge of death but the bed wasn't drenched in blood; no menstruation had been brought on. Not even a drop. It was still possible that the tea had killed the growing form, but I didn't believe it. It was stronger than I was, this thing inside me.

It is hard to recall now, the curdled emotions of that time. I worry that what I've told you is shocking, but I can only tell you how alone I was. I could not conceive at that point, in my dazed state, that anything good could come of it.

Within a week I was up again and in Janey's all-in-one room with my head in my hands. Father had issued orders that I wasn't allowed out, but I woke early one morning with the dawn chorus. I thought if I slipped out then, before anyone else was up, I could see her.

'You didn't give me enough,' I said. But I couldn't really blame her, I knew the herbs were notoriously tricksy and imprecise.

'And let you leave us? You nearly did as it was,' she said, stroking my hair.

I didn't try to persuade her to help me again. I think I knew that what was growing would cling on no matter what I did. And I couldn't stop it now; I wasn't even sure I wanted to. I'm glad now, that it didn't work. It's important you know this.

42

Some time in late July, on one of his visits, he took me out
in his new motor car. He wanted to show it off, to parade
it to gawping villagers. It was a Silver Eagle, in what he
called 'racing green'. He was in summer whites that day,
rather than black, and wore a white cap like the one he'd
worn on the boat trip two years before. Despite all that
had happened between us, the sight of him still gave me
prickles of heat.

I hadn't seen him for a while. I think Father had
conspired to spin some tale of illness. They must have
told the colonel, Lady Lafferty and Franklin and any
other nosey parkers that I was contagious. In my darkest
moments, I think that the sad thing is that if I had died
from the pennyroyal tea, it would have been a relief to
them all.

But when he drove up to the house and honked the
horn, sending Perdie into spasms of barking, I looked
down from Father's room and saw him with his arm slung
over the car door, his pristine white suit shining in the

sun. He'd taken off his driving gloves and the sunlight glowed on his tanned wrists and hands. It bounced off the white linen and the shiny polish of the car and shone back up to me in the dark house, a beacon of beauty. A chink of light in the darkness.

So I called down that I was coming, dressed in one of Hildy's old dresses with a fashionable low waist which hid the fact that my waist had expanded, and emerged onto the sunlit driveway.

'I'm taking you out,' he said. 'Mother said you could do with a jaunt.' His mother had suggested it then. But he smiled at me and squeezed my knee. 'You do look a bit unwell.'

'I'm fine,' I said.

We drove along the coast road towards Cromer, the same route we'd taken years before on that first day out. I didn't feel as if I was the same girl who'd been in the back seat with Franklin then, the girl who was thrilled by the touch of his hand on my bare leg. It was almost the same scene – the yellow of the wheat in the fields, the blue-grey sea, glimpsed in snatches of brilliance, the red dots of poppies – but he was driving now and I – I was changed.

We stopped for a picnic of wine and crackers in a field just after Cromer. I could only take a mouthful of the wine. It tasted sour and thick, like drinking blood, and it made me nauseous. The sun beat remorselessly on us and I wished I could lie down and sleep. And although he was still beautiful, when he laid me down in the wheat, and pulled my skirts up, I had to stop myself from crying. The crushed, spiked heads of the plant scratched at my underside, and the ground was dry and hard beneath me.

There was the smell of the hot earth and the sharpness of his cologne. I turned my head away from his silhouetted form in the tall spikes above me and the violent red of the poppies, and concentrated on watching a beetle crawl slowly over the cracked soil. I closed my eyes, the light struck my eyelids and all I could see was a vivid orange, like the colour of a blazing sun bleeding into the sea.

43

I haven't got much time left to write this so I'll tell you what you really want to know. You'll be able to judge for yourself whether or not I am guilty of the crimes they say I am. I feel I owe you an explanation. Not so you can forgive me, that's too much to hope for.

There was a day, late in the summer. We were eating strawberries and drinking lemonade in the garden of Old Hall. Franklin made me open my mouth and put a strawberry in between my lips. I felt like a stuck pig with an apple in its mouth. Ready to be eaten. He reached forward and touched my ankle, making circling motions on the bone. It tickled and I shivered.

The summer was almost over and you could feel the change in the air. The wind was cooler from the east and the colours were turning on the marsh – the purple fading to a pale blue violet. My body continued to alter as well. Under my dress, the faintest hint of a protrusion. At first I did nothing. I carried on as before, collecting my bones from the marsh, until at the end of August, Franklin summoned me to Old Hall.

'You're looking healthier, Rosie. Almost back to how you used to be. The little girl I corrupted.'

I looked across the long lawn down to the river Stiffkey, the pasture on the other side, and the trees on the slight rise above it. I saw the glade where the summer house was hidden and remembered how he'd forced me a long time ago, before we were married. And I knew he would carry on doing this, again and again, while I grew fat with children who would die or thrive. It didn't matter – either way, there would be nothing else for me. I wasn't expected to do anything apart from breed for him, for them. He would go to London, to Paris, to Egypt, it didn't matter where, and keep his mistresses and his prostitutes. Even Hildy would go to London for the season and marry someone interesting – or even not marry – and she would travel too. But not me. I would stay here with my swollen legs and my ruined womb and no love for me from anyone except Janey. All I'd wanted, I see now, was someone to love me as I imagined my mother had. But no one had.

I pulled my shawl around my shoulders, but there was no breeze that day. The trees were still.

'You'll stay here tonight,' he said. 'And the day after tomorrow, your father and I have business in Cromer.'

'What kind of business?' I asked, but he gave me a sharp look.

'I'm not sure that concerns you, my strawberry pudding.'

I frowned at him. 'I'm not a little girl,' I said.

'Oh, I beg to differ,' he said. 'That's exactly what you are and how I want you to be. And if you ever become anything else I won't like it at all.'

'Are the girls in London young?' I said, some worm of boldness wriggling in me. 'The ones you have?'

He pinched my thigh, quite hard, leaving a pink mark. 'Some of them,' he said, biting the head off a strawberry. 'None as sweet as you.' He spat out the green top of the fruit into the silver dish on the table. 'Some of them are rather grand, you know. Real ladies. Bored of their dull old husbands. And some of them are as common as anything.' He winked at me. 'Does it bother you?'

Stupid tears sprung to my eyes. 'But I thought you loved me. I thought I was special.'

'You are special. There's no one in the world like you, Rosie.'

'You ruined me,' I said quietly.

He laughed. 'That's rather melodramatic. And anyway, I do love you in my own way, if that's what you want to hear. It's just . . .' He opened his arms out and gave me a helpless smile. 'I can't help it. Come on,' he said, tired of the conversation, 'you can't mind that much. It's normal for men. Even your father needs . . . distractions.'

'Why did you marry me, Franklin?' I said.

He stared at me for a bit, his lip twitching as if he felt like striking me. 'You know why, don't torture yourself.'

'Because of our baby?'

'Yes, that. And because I'd been naughty in London and Mummy wanted me out of harm's way.'

'What did you do?' But I didn't want to know the details. I got up so quickly that I spilt lemonade down my dress but I didn't stop. I ran down the lawn to the river. It was warm and still, hardly a breeze rustling in the trees, and the river trickled invitingly, dots of light dancing along it. I took off my stockings, held up my dress and got in. The water was pleasantly cool on my feet and ankles. I remembered what Hildy had said about some incident in London and it made sense.

A shadow behind me and Franklin's voice. 'They warned me you were like your mother. Mad as a hatter.' I stayed looking down at the water running over my feet, green and soothing. I heard him laughing and then a splash. 'But that's why I like you, you're my wild girl,' he said, and I turned around. He was in the river. Completely naked. It was impossible not to gasp, for my hand not to fly to my mouth. He opened his eyes wide and cocked his head to one side, as if daring me to be shocked. I took my hand away from my mouth and tried to stare at him coolly, but my eyes were pricking with tears. His body was golden from the summer sun, from beaches on the Côte d'Azur and sun loungers in hotels. The dappled river light fell over it, creating a filigree of green and dark leaves. He came towards me and drew me to his naked body.

'What would your mother—'

'My mother gave you to me. I can do anything I like, remember,' he said, and planted his lips on mine.

I could feel him pressing against me, his bare flesh through the thin material of my summer dress. We were shielded from the eyes of the Hall down there in the river and Franklin knew it. He pulled up my dress and half-lifting, half-shoving me, he put me up against the muddy bank of the river and pressed down on my hips again and again until it was done. I gritted my teeth and thought about the roots of the trees I was up against, imagined the roots growing up into me and through me, sprouting out through my ears and nose and mouth. At the end, when his body shuddered against mine, I looked up to see his neck arched back like a swan's and his face glowing, lit up by sunlight, his expression one of exquisite torture.

'I've muddied your dress,' he said after, pulling his clothes back on. 'You look like a kitchen maid who's been dallying with a gardener's boy. I rather like it.' He ruffled my hair. 'Don't be a misery, Rosie. For God's sake. You used to be fun.' I began to cry then and his face darkened. 'Not that,' he said. He stalked off to the house and I was left to follow behind.

That night he was rough with me and pinched me again. He whispered into my ear that I was his. I owed him this. I belonged to him. The more I turned away, the harder he pinched and thrust.

In the morning there was a pattern of purpling bruises blooming on my skin.

I didn't breakfast with the rest of the family that morning. Instead, I got up early, leaving Franklin sprawled across the bed. The sun was already warming the grass, and I ran back along the vale to Hollow Lane and to the Marsh House, a confusion boiling in me so explosive, I thought I would vomit a lava flow of rage.

'I can do anything I like,' he'd said, and I thought *But I can do nothing I want. Nothing at all.*

In my room, I tried to read but I could hardly concentrate. It was a hot, still, silent day, too hot for the birds. Perdie lay whimpering, afraid of my mood, at the foot of the bed. I tried to close my eyes, I tried to drift away somewhere else. I would feel calmer if I slept. But I couldn't stop my limbs from twitching, my mind from flailing around for something, anything to do. I hurled myself off the bed, flung open the window to stagnant, warm air. Perdie barked, expecting a walk. How could he hurt me like that? How could he do it knowing I'd given birth to and buried our son? How could he sleep with other girls, other women, when I could do nothing? The unfairness of it was a bitter taste in my mouth.

I wanted to hurt him back, but I was powerless.

Down below my window, the great black form of Smutch moved slowly in the shade of Janey's garden.

Janey. The poison. An idea was forming. It did not have to be drastic, but I could damage him, as he'd damaged me. Make him ill, give him pain as he had given me pain. My breath came faster and my pulse quickened.

I'd already got the arsenic from Janey before he'd come back – I lied to her about Rogers needing it for the rats – but until then I hadn't considered anything other than taking it for the pregnancy. I don't even know if I was really going to use it for that. It was under the sink in the kitchen, forgotten about.

I could just put a drop in the sugar. It would be easy, I had read about it in the Agatha Christie books. No one would ever know. Only I would know. I would know I held something over him, some power over him. I gripped the windowsill as the sun blazed down on my face. It could be done. Yes, sugar in his coffee. The tiniest drop, just to make him suffer. Perhaps he would be sorry, then. He thought of me as a child, but I was not a child. Not anymore.

So on that day, the morning after the river, when I saw the bruises on my legs, and the red marks of his fingers on my upper arms where he'd held me down, I remembered the poison and it seemed as if it was waiting for me.

44

The following morning, the day of the journey to Cromer, I brewed a pot of coffee for the travellers. I put out a cup for myself as well. Normally, Dolly or Fairbrother would have done it but Dolly was busy with laundry and Fairbrother was away visiting a sister in Sheringham. So no one bothered about me making coffee and Dolly was grateful if anything. I brought the tray into the living room myself. The morning light was coming in through the windows and the whole room was alight. The two of them were smoking and talking in the pair of leather chairs either side of the fireplace. I placed the tray on the coffee table in front of them and knelt down to stir the pot. The spoon clattered loudly against the edge and I hoped they didn't notice that my hands were shaking.

'Thank you, Rosie. What a lovely wife I have, don't I, sir?'

'When she behaves herself,' said my father.

I poured the coffee, concentrating hard to make sure I didn't spill any, and they resumed their conversation about their plans for the day. Franklin was going to drive the Silver Eagle to Cromer and they'd have a meeting at the printers where they'd thrash out a copy of the new manifesto. (This was for the great Oswald.) Then they'd repair to the Newhaven Court Hotel for lunch.

Into Franklin's cup, I poured cream and stirred in a spoonful of sugar but it dissolved immediately. I added another. I put just the cream into my father's. I stirred and stirred until all the sugar must have dissolved. I sat back on the sofa opposite the fire, enjoying the sun on my face and drank the coffee I'd poured myself. No sugar. It was too hot and I scalded the roof of my mouth. I waited. They chatted on, not including me in any way. But this was preferable as I'm not sure how much I could have spoken. I could feel my heart banging against my ribs. Finally, I watched Franklin drink the coffee in two long gulps. I waited.

'No cakes this morning, Rosie? I'm disappointed.'

'I haven't had time,' I said.

'Surely you have something tasty for the road for us men of business?'

I watched his face for signs of distaste or sickness but there were none. He was brushing his trousers, a sign that he was about to get up, but just then my father made a face and said, 'This coffee is rather bitter, Rosemary. I'll have to have a spoonful of sugar.'

I sprang up. 'Let me,' I said, and gave him the tiniest amount into his cup. I sat back, my heart pounding.

Franklin was standing up now. 'Good God, do you really have nothing for us to eat, Rosie? I'm famished.'

'I'm fine, Franklin,' Father said, raising a hand. It had almost been a bark, which he'd softened right at the end.

I could see he was irritated by this young, flamboyant layabout, but he was bound to him as much as I was. It was the colonel's money that was funding the fascist propaganda and without it, my father's business would have floundered.

'All right then, I'll make some biscuits quickly, before you go.'

'That's my girl,' said Franklin, grinning at me. I'm sure he would have whacked me on the backside like a horse if my father hadn't been sitting right next to him.

In the kitchen, I hurriedly mixed sugar, flour and butter, egg and vanilla seeds and patted them into rounds and laid them on a greased tray for the oven. It took less than ten minutes. By the time they were standing by the car in their coats and driving caps, and Franklin in his leather driving gloves, I handed him a batch of still-warm biscuits wrapped in a cloth. He kissed me on the lips and waved from the car, as if he was the perfect gentleman, a loving husband.

For the rest of the day, I lived in my head. I walked down to the marsh with my dreams. I cannot remember what I thought about, if it was anything at all. I took a pork pie and a cheese sandwich wrapped in cloth and ate them out there on the dried-out marsh grass, in the full glare of the sun. I walked and walked, along the path that ran along the bottom of the marsh, away from the village, towards Wells, enjoying the solitude, revelling in it, and only came back because I realised the sun was now quite low in the sky. Dolly had left for the day and Perdie started up a high-pitched whine when we got back to the house but I gave her a bone and she was quiet.

It was worse, much worse than I'd expected. Now, I don't know what I'd expected. I didn't even know if it would have much effect on him at all. Since then, I've read about poisonings from last century and the terrible effects it has on the victims, but I didn't know all that then. It was, perhaps, something fantastical. One of my presents from Hildy two years ago had been Mrs Christie's The Thirteen Problems. In one of the stories, a man dies from arsenic poisoning. It's possible I got the idea from that. Then again, she uses lots of other poisons in her novels. In her first novel, The Mysterious Affair at Styles, it's strychnine. And in Peril at End House, it's cocaine in a box of chocolates. But I didn't have either of those. Arsenic was just what I had.

In acute poisoning, what arsenic does to a body is this:

It makes the victim experience 'extreme nausea, vomiting, abdominal pain, and profuse diarrhoea'. I'm quoting here, from the coroner's report. This is what happened to Franklin.

He arrived back at the house, brought there by a man who'd found him at the hotel. There was no sign of my father. Franklin was sickly pale and could hardly walk and was clutching his stomach, doubled over in pain. I knew it was the poison, that it had worked far too well. I held him, together with the man, and we took him into the house, and laid him down on the sofa. The man was desperate to leave – afraid, I think, of the appalling state of Franklin, and of catching it from him. I was seized by a sickening fear of what I'd done and a dizzying feeling that it could not really be happening.

For a moment, I looked down at my young husband, at his wretched, writhing body that had so recently been proudly displayed to me. A knot in my stomach twisted and I felt faint. He grasped hold of me in his sweaty hand. I knelt down and could smell the garlic on his breath. He was trying to say something to me. It might have been 'biscuits', but I put a hand to his hot forehead and extricated my other hand from his clutching grip and said, loudly –

'I've got to get help, darling.'

I trotted to Janey's. I didn't run. I wasn't thinking. I was in a daze, like a ghost.

'What happened to him?' she asked.

'I don't know,' I said, the words coming slowly, painfully, 'he came back from Cromer clutching his stomach and he could hardly stand. He collapsed in a hotel according to the man who brought him back. I don't know what would have happened if he hadn't—'

'Start from the beginning,' she said.

'I'm afraid, Janey,' I said, and I was. 'I'm afraid he's going to die.'

'He's probably got a bad stomach upset. You called the quacks yet?'

'No, I didn't think it was that bad. I'll try now.'

I ran to the telephone in the Marsh House but the line was busy. Janey appeared behind me in the hallway.

'Tell me the whole story now, Rosie,' she said to me. 'And where is he?'

I indicated the living room, but I didn't dare go in. 'He – he came here to see Father this morning before going on business to Cromer. He was going to Father's printers to see about getting some leaflets printed for the BUF and he had a cup of coffee then, but I don't know what he ate for breakfast or for lunch – he could have got anything at Cromer. I don't know! He could have had a bad crab or whelk, couldn't he?'

She nodded, walked past me into the living room. I stayed in the hallway. 'I suppose he could. Who brought him here then?'

'A man from the hotel. He said Frank had come in looking green and holding his stomach, then he'd tottered and fallen. The man brought him here as there's no one at the Hall.'

'So he can't have eaten or drunk anything at the hotel, can he? And you don't know about nothing else, do you?'

'No!' My voice high and loud. On the sofa, Franklin's breath had become rasping and the smell was so bad I knew it was coming out of him.

She took over then. I'd known she would.

'I'll see to him now, Rosie. You run to the village and call for the doctor from the public phone if yours ent working. Tell him to come quick.'

As I was running out, she asked me, 'Where's your father?'

Then I remembered my father hadn't come back with Franklin. It was odd – I'd seen him leave, but not seen him return. But I'd been on the marsh all day.

I heard Franklin moaning in the living room and a rank smell wafted through the door. I turned away, afraid, and opened my father's study door. He looked like he was sleeping. On his desk, surrounded by papers, his head was sunk. A thick, bitter odour of faeces filled the room. I gagged and covered my nose and mouth. There was no movement from my father's body. I didn't want to get any closer to the reek but I had to. I lifted the hair on his head and saw that his eyes were open, staring, unseeing, completely cold. I let the hair fall back down. Then I noticed that on the desk next to his hand were crumbs. They were biscuit crumbs, the biscuits I'd made and given to Franklin. My father must have taken them from the kitchen when he'd returned. He must have had lots of them. I must have mixed the tainted sugar into the biscuits.

All this was going through my head in a quick succession as I stood there in the quiet, dark study, the setting sun casting orange daggers across the wooden floor. Flies were buzzing around my father and I wondered how long he'd been like this. Then slowly, oozing out of me like pus, a realisation: I had to make a sound.

The bodies were taken away and the Laffertys were summoned and it was a nightmarish whirligig of a night. I couldn't cry. When they were gone – I'd said I wouldn't go back to Old Hall, I didn't have to anymore, I decided – I stayed at Janey's cottage. Much later, that night, she asked me straight out if I'd used the arsenic and I told her the truth.

I just wanted to make him ill. I hadn't intended to kill him at all. At that time, in the molten heat of grief and horror, I wanted to make him suffer so badly he wouldn't be the same person. I'm sorry.

45

So I were there when he died. I knew then it would lead to no good.

It were all quiet in the Marsh House. All hushed and dark out of the hot day. That miserable mawther, ol' Fairbrother must've been off cos there didn't seem to be anyone there at all. Smelt funny though. In the sitting room it were all bright from the sun setting and I couldn't see him at first cos it were in my eyes. But I heard a moaning from the sofa and I bent over to get a better look. It were the Lafferty boy all right and he were in a terrible state. Barely moving apart from now and then he'd go into a kind of spasm, like a fish what couldn't breathe. His pretty face was greenish-grey and he were all a muckwash, sweat rolling off him like an old cheese. I leaned over him and his breath were rank with puke and stank of suffin sweet and rotten.

I loosened the boy's collar and he looked up at me with his milky eyes and I knew he'd not got long. The doctor would never get here in time. The nearest quack was old Harrison *in Wells but no one from Stiffkey ever went to him. They all preferred Dr Lacey in Blakeney who was more lax in collecting his debts. Personally I never had much truck with either of them, but I knew she needed to do something with herself so I sent her off. Whatever she thought about the boy, I didn't think she ought to see him like that. He were snatching at the air by the time she went and it were awful to watch. They all thought I was a witch, but I weren't ever a bloody magician – I couldn't do nothing for him, he were too far gone. It were coming out both ends and all I could do was make it a little more comfortable. I got a pan to put under him and took off his soiled trousers, wiped the mess from his mouth and cooled his forehead. But then he went into a series of fits so severe, he gripped onto me with his young, hard fingers and I saw the fear in his eyes. Whatever he'd done – and I knew some of what he'd done – he didn't deserve that end.*

I heard the front door opening and I shouted at her to not come in, but to find her father. He had to be somewhere nearby. Then I heard her scream. It was a shocking thing to hear. I had the boy fitting and gasping for his last breaths in my arms, and I hear this blood-curdling scream.

I couldn't do nothing. The boy was dying. I called out, 'Rosie?' And all I hear is sobbing, a sort of choking-crying. Finally the boy shuddered out his last gasp and fell quiet. I laid him gently on the sofa and put a blanket over his body. I heard her blarring from across the hall and she were standing in her father's room.

46

On the marsh

The notebook went on for a few more pages, still in the same rushed scrawl until it came to an abrupt stop, followed only by a few short, scrappy lines at the end of the book. But Malorie couldn't finish. She felt sick, dizzy. The smell of Rosemary's father's dead body stung her nostrils and she could see the dead man's gaping mouth, hanging open, a black pit, like the frozen dog's. Her soul was sick. Sick to your soul. She understood what that meant. There was something rotten that had been hiding in front of her and here it was revealing itself. And it was inside her, it had infected her.

She dropped the notebook and fell back in her seat, drained. Her lip trembled and she realised she was about to cry. She let it come.

Against the window, the soft thuds of snow, and in the chimney the howl of the blizzard. It had started up again, stronger than before. Her candle was still lit and it shone a low light onto the ceiling. The cracks on the ceiling became the branches of a tree that grew and grew, twisting across the plaster. Her eyes followed them, crawling across the ceiling. She needed to sleep. With an intense relief, she remembered that she'd put the envelope with the pills in the pocket of her blouse. How many had she taken? What did it matter now? She washed a couple down with the last of the wine.

A scream woke her, jerking up into the darkness, staring. An orange glow. Eyes. No, there was no scream, no eyes. It must have been the wind or the screaming cockler calling for help. Dark outside. Light coming from the fire. Slowly, her vision adjusted and she saw that there was no light coming through the thin curtains. Her candle had been extinguished and was a low white stump deformed by globules of wax. The embers of the fire burnt dull orange in the grate. No heat came from it now and the room was as cold as if the snow had come inside.

On the worn red rug on the floor next to the sofa, the notebook lay where it'd been dropped. Arsenic poisoning and the agonising deaths of two men. It was unreal – a piece of fiction. The girl, Rosemary, was living out an Agatha Christie fantasy. The more she thought about it, the more she thought that must be the case. It couldn't be real. The 'account' was made up. None of it had happened. It was just the scribbling of a bored girl who'd been denied an education. She clutched at this idea and smiled uneasily in the dark, empty room. She was Malorie. She was real. The other girl was fiction.

Next to the notebook lay a white mass of lace. The veil. She lifted it to her head and stood up, curious to see what she would look like. In the mirror was the wan face of a girl with a snowy waterfall cascading behind her, cold as if snow was actually falling on her hair. Tentacles of ice on her skin. She dropped the veil.

In the notebook, Franklin had died right here where she'd lain, a horrible, ugly death, everything pouring out of him, dying in a pool of his own effluence. She shuddered.

There was no human presence here. It was how you feel when you are entirely alone. The rooms stretching out in their space. But there was *something* here, something else, a memory. A shadow memory of the people who used to live here. That was all it was.

'You're not real!' she shouted.

As if in response, the radio in the kitchen crackled into life and she heard a voice – *Vehicles have been abandoned on roads as the drifts are now up to fifteen feet in* –

I'll gladly surrender – a mournful voice. *My life* –

That sound wasn't coming from the radio, but the record player. The slow, sweet trumpet got louder and louder. She put her hands over her ears but could still hear it in her head. She ran back into the living room. The gramophone was blaring with the trumpet and the voice. How could it? She hadn't even wound it up. She grabbed the record clumsily off the turntable and it broke. Jagged pieces of black shellac fell to the floor.

In the hallway, she could hear the hiss of the out-of-tune radio and the cry of the blizzard in the trees.

She rushed up the stairs. In the bedroom, Franny was asleep, curled up in a foetal position that grasped at Malorie's heart. Across her daughter's face the blizzard created wildly moving shadow-fingers that seemed to be clawing at her. She put a hand on Franny's forehead. It was clammy and warm. The girl's breath was shallow, hot and moist against her palm. What if Franny was really ill? What if she had a dangerous fever? She had to get to the village to get help, fetch a doctor. She thought of the baby that had died here, in this house. The little boy with the blond curls. If anything happened to Franny – it was too awful to contemplate. Tony didn't trust her with their daughter. He would take her away from her if he could. In a burst of anger and fear, she picked up the envelope and swallowed another pill.

Down in the kitchen, the back door was open and hanging on its hinges, banging and letting in the chill air. Malorie stood staring at the snowy gap. Had it been open just now? She was sure she'd shut it. A door slammed behind her. She spun around. The front door must have been open as well. In the shadows of the twilight, the yellow flowers on the walls were the colour of nicotine; the tar-coloured vines twisted up the walls and towards the door as if they were reaching for the outside, and the light. In the dead time of the night, the house was telling her to leave. The ceiling was pressing down on her. She needed to get out. She had to get help for Franny. The walls were very close. Her head was pulsing. Out. She must get out.

Malorie snatched her fur coat from the banister, pulled on the boots she found by the back door and scrabbled around for the torch in the kitchen drawer.

Outside, snow spun. Ahead of her in the beam of torchlight, a great clump of snow dropped from a tree, spraying white, as if someone had brushed past it. She ran, stumbling in her silly, city boots. When she got to the gate, no one was there, but footprints led to the cottage across the lane where smoke rose from the chimney. There was no sign of any other footprints. She looked left and right. To her right was the snowdrift, the stuck car, the way to the village. To her left, only the marsh. At the end of the lane, where it met the marsh, there was a stumpy line of trees, warped and stunted by the salt and wind. There was a path at the end of the lane that led east. A memory surfaced. She'd gone that way before, when she went to the church. Now, as she peered along the torch beam towards the sea, a shadow moved in the trees. It might have been an animal. A flash of white. A bird? A fall of snow? She stumble-ran towards it.

Reaching the snow-laden trees, she heard a crackle in the icy undergrowth and at the same time, a crow swooped up, calling *cree-aa, cree-aa* into the swirling snow. Her eyes and the torch were drawn upward with its soot-black wings in a grey-black sky.

She stood now, unsure of which was north, south, east or west. There was no sound of the sea, no sound apart from the rush of the snow and the shriek of the wind across the marsh. At least she presumed it was the marsh because she couldn't see. The world was reduced to a whirl of whiteness circling her head.

She heard ice cracking in the creek then another crack from close by. A thin figure was standing in the woods. It was her again, the dark-haired girl. Malorie's throat clamped in fear. She would see her. She turned off the torch and the swirling white night closed in, as the bird screamed above her.

She turned to run but there was nothing beneath her feet and she fell, her arms flailing, unable to grab hold of anything, wheeling through the air. She tumbled down the bank into the creek, sprawling awkwardly, her leg twisting to the side. An urge to scream gurgled up in her throat. Her mind was closed.

Someone was calling. She tried to shut her ears, to listen only to the soft patting of snow on her face. An icy wetness seeped into her back. She didn't know why she was there. She'd been trying to do something. Something important.

Who was making the noise?

Someone was close by, breathing on her, hands under armpits, lifting her.

'Franny?'

It was the dark-haired girl, it was Rosemary. She tried to speak again but her throat was closed.

She had to see. The torch. Her fingers searched until she touched it, where it had fallen. She shone the torch back the way she'd come to the dark stacks of the chimneys of the house, poking above the hedge. But there was no girl. Frantically, she swung the torch around her, throwing a band of light into the darkness, but she could see no strange girl.

Franny. She had to get back. Her daughter was ill. She remembered now. Her daughter was ill.

She tried to stand but a shock of pain ran up through her right leg. She couldn't stand on it. Wincing, she put all her weight on her left leg, leant forwards to the muddy edge of the creek and with effort lifted herself forward and hauled herself onto the lane. She kept sliding and slipping down. The pain in her ankle was intense. She must have twisted it, falling. Halfway down the lane, she stood stock still in the dark, bent over, feeling her own laboured breath pushing against her ribcage. An owl hooted. The back of her head jabbed with pain. She looked around to where she'd been and there was something there, some mass of darkness moving towards her.

Hobbling, stumbling, panting, she slowly dragged her sore ankle along the lane. She felt the presence of the girl behind her. A shape appeared at the entrance to the house. A stout woman dressed in brown.

The woman moved towards her through the shadows. She didn't say anything but Malorie felt a force, like a strong wind, pull her to the house. Inch by inch the chimneys of the house got closer until finally she reached the drive. She stopped and got her breath, turned to look back, but it was completely black, no girl, no woman. She hurled herself to the porch and, lurching, fell across the threshold to the hallway, slamming the front door shut.

A doctor. She must get help. The phone. She picked up the black earpiece of the old candlestick phone and held it to her ear. She strained to hear the dialling tone.

'Hello?' she said, into the mouthpiece. '*Hello?*' There was nothing, no tone. The line was dead.

47

Breaking glass

A voice was coming from somewhere. It sounded familiar. It was someone she knew. Shakily, she stood up and saw a shadowy form in the old mirror on the living room wall. Limping towards it, she saw it was a young woman with dark hair, very straight, and small features and pale, olive skin. She knew her. The large eyes staring back at her were the eyes of the girl in the photograph. It was Rosemary. Herself.

Something came out of her mouth, some lost sound.

She was on the floor of the room.

Darkness. Someone above her. She opened her eyes.

A face was above her. It was the old woman, the one she'd seen so many times. The wrinkled face was close to hers. Close up, Malorie could see that her eyes, small and sunk into her head, were dark brown and shining, like a rodent's. Her hair, poking out from under a brown felt hat, was fluffy, like animal fur. Her skin looked soft, as if lit from the inside, and her small snub nose seemed to be twitching. Her neck was enclosed in a brown woollen scarf, tightly wound. Malorie thought of the voles her father used to catch and kill in the garden in Norwich, because they spoiled his lawn – their soft, brown fur, tiny black, bright eyes and short stubby tails.

She remembered now – the woman had been there on the lane. So had the dark-haired girl.

Watch out there, girl, sound fit to wake the dead.

This sound seemed to come from the old lady but it sounded far away, not in the room at all.

She struggled to stand up. Someone had lit the candles on the tree. The room was a vision of the cosy-glow family Christmas that she'd been yearning for, but the shapes the candlelight created on the walls were like the shadow puppets of ghouls and bog creatures and sprites. On the glass-topped coffee table were cups and saucers – the remains of a tea she didn't remember having. The gramophone was playing a soothing song, a jazz trumpet.

Round the walls the blizzard roared. The front door banged repeatedly and then the back door in the kitchen began to do the same. The candle flames guttered; the shapes became monstrous on the walls. The music began to jump and trip. The night was turning against her.

Watch out there, girl, you're shaking like a jelly. Janey's voice was talking to her. It was muffled now, overlaid with an excited chattering that she thought was coming from her own brain.

There it was again. The young woman's face in the window. A shadowy pale head with eyes like stagnant pools staring at her. Above the hearth in the old, rust-stained mirror, the same face, wavering. Rosemary's face.

Come on now, girl, don't take on so. That's your face in the glass. Just your face.

The old woman was saying something else because her mouth was moving but it was just a distant hum. Another voice was in her head , a younger one –

Purple bruises blooming like pus. Asked for it. Drinking blood.

Opening her eyes, the face – her face – Rosemary's face – had multiplied. She was in the coffee table glass. She was on the old woman's face. The pale oval reflected back at her from the window, from the mirror, flickering in the candlelight, a snow girl with eyes of coal. Malorie put her hands to her eyes. The face was still there behind them.

She picked up the nearest thing – one of the notebooks – and threw it at the mirror. It hit the glass and bounced off, falling at her feet. The face was still there. She picked up a china cup and threw that. The mirror cracked and splintered and the face became hundreds of tiny shards of white and black. The face was still there in the window, a whole moon-face with black-green eyes, staring. She pulled back her arm and threw another cup at the glass. The window shattered, the cup shattered, and hundreds of pieces of glass and china fell to the wooden floor as droplets of tea rained across the room. Now through the hole in the window there was only the darkness of the night and the white of the snow. Finally, she picked up the notebook again and smashed it down into the glass-topped coffee table. A hairline crack appeared and spread into tiny lines and fragments, like a spreading tree. A moaning was coming from somewhere, a keening like the high notes of a trumpet.

On her knees, glass all around her. Glass in her hair. Someone put their hands on her shoulders to steady her as she trembled. All the time the bulk of a body – the old woman – kept hold of her, intoning words over and over in a low breath.

My girl. My girl. S'aright now.

She wanted to say *What is it?* But she couldn't speak. Her jaw was locked.

Calm yourself girl. I'm not leaving you.

– Let her go, Rose. Leave her be. It's time to go.

I won't let go of you.

Again, her brain was filled with the girl's voice.

> *Purple bruises blooming like pus*
> *Asked for it*
> *The coffee is bitter*
> *Poppies like spots of blood*

Her body rocked with a force streaming, coursing through her bones. The ends of her hair static with electricity. The old woman held her so hard she felt her bones would break.

Rosemary screamed in her head, stronger and louder.

> *Cream and sugar biscuit crumbs*
> *Just for you*
> *Flies buzzing*
> *Orange daggers*
> *Blood, blood, blood*

The old woman's hands around her head, earthing the current, subduing it, sending it back into the ground.

Her skull was going to explode.

As if a valve had been opened, she felt a pop in her ears

and the pressure released. There was a high, thin screech like a screaming child.

Silence.

Snow fell softly against the window.

She's gone. It's just you now.

All feeling left. She collapsed onto the floor. The antique red rug was littered with broken glass next to her eye and the dark red cover of the notebook lying where it had fallen.

From the floor, she felt Janey's lips, like a dry leaf scratching on her cheek. A swash of brown fabric as she disappeared out of the door.

And someone's small arms around her, tugging her back to herself.

'Mummy.'

Just before she fell into the darkness, she saw green eyes close to her own.

48

Witch, Old Witch
28th December

A ceiling, buckled and mottled, undulations like the sea. Watery light across it. Morning. Cold. A bitter winter morning. Where was she? The house on the marsh. The Marsh House. Images came rushing in – a tumult of fragmented memories – the sampler with the girl in plaits, a snow-girl with coal for eyes, pebbles on the beach, a frozen dog, an Edwardian photograph, a cot in the attic, an axe, Franny vomiting. An old woman with shining brown eyes. Black wings in the snow. It seemed like something she'd dreamt. A too-vivid dream that wouldn't recede and kept lapping at her brain. She was still staring at the patterns of mould on the ceiling. She had a weird sense of abandonment, a tugging empty feeling, like the vacuum that had been left behind inside her when her mother died.

Malorie pulled a blanket around her shoulders and sat up. Her ankle twinged. The sight that greeted her was hard to understand. She was in the sitting room, hazy in the weak winter morning light. Wax had dripped down the side of the extinguished candles on the tree and dropped in white pools to the branches of the fir so it looked like it was covered in a glutinous snow. The curtains were drawn across but they were gently rising and falling and from behind them came a chill air as if the window was open. The mirror was cracked. Bad luck. In her head the lines from the poem appeared – *The mirror crack'd from side to side;/ 'The curse is come upon me,' cried/ The Lady of Shalott*. Shards of glass were scattered across the rug and the floor. Something had happened. She strained to remember. The blizzard. Outside in the dark. It was too strange, too surreal to be true.

And Franny? Franny was ill.

A noise. It came again. It was a knocking, a knock on the front door. Then the sound of feet crunching on deep, frozen snow. A shadow passed behind the thin, gauzy curtains of the living room window and Malorie pushed herself against the back of the sofa. A tap on the window and a gasp, a mutter and an eye appeared in the gap between the curtains. The eye caught hers. Malorie froze as if the eye had pinned her.

But then the head drew back and a hand waved.

It was a woman, Malorie saw, an older woman with a preposterous furry hat, like a brown cat sitting on her head, an unflattering, squashy version of her own black Russian hat, and a large coat with fur around the collar. The woman was waving a leather-gloved hand towards the door. Malorie realised she wanted her to open it.

Unfolding her aching body, Malorie stood up shakily. An icicle of pain pierced from her ankle up her right leg. What had she done to it? She still had on the same clothes she'd been wearing yesterday. Her sweater smelt stale. The smell of stress and distress rose from her skin. Her left foot fell on something sharp. Bending down, she picked up a bead of glass from her sole. She tried to smooth down her crumpled skirt and knotted, sticking-up hair.

At the door, it wasn't the woman she saw, it was Franny, poking out from behind the woman's bulk, dressed in her coat and hat.

'Mummy?' she said, small and hesitant.

'Why are you in your coat? Where've you been?'

'I was scared. I went to get help.'

'But you were ill,' she said, 'you were in bed.' She pulled Franny to her and grasped her daughter close to her chest.

'It's gone now, Mummy,' said Franny, breathing into her chest.

Over Franny's head, the woman beamed at her. 'Mrs Cavendish? I can't tell you how wonderful it is to find you alive and well. It's been so frustrating not being able to get hold of you for all this time. What on earth happened to the window? Was it the branch of a tree in the storm? I'm sure you've been wondering where on earth you've ended up. Can you believe this weather? Isn't it remarkable? It's not been like this since forty-seven. You would've been a child then, that would have been a lot more fun. I imagine you've been having a fine time of it, haven't you, dear?'

The last was addressed to Franny, who was tucked under Malorie's arm. Malorie blinked at the woman. The sun was rising directly behind her outline but its weak rays reflected off the blanket of snow and directly into Malorie's eyes. She raised her hand to shield her sight and tried to understand what the stranger was saying.

'Sorry,' she said, giving up. 'I don't understand. Who are you? Have you come about the house?'

'Yes, dear. Although I wouldn't have made it through if it wasn't for the wonderful men, they've been working marvels, bless them.' She gestured behind her, at the drive. 'Now, do you mind if I come in? I was supposed to have done an inventory days ago.'

'Pardon?'

'For the house. Check all is present and correct. I know it's a bit late, but better late than never is what I say.' She'd shouldered her way in by then and was standing in the hallway looking around her, already totting it all up. 'We'll have to see to that window right away. Can't have the snow coming in.'

'Please. You haven't told me who you are.'

'So sorry, I let my words run away with me, dear. My name's Mrs Pollock. Like the fish. Mr Poke of the agency sent me to meet you when you arrived, but our dates must have got mixed up because I thought you were coming on Christmas Eve and he told me it was the twenty-second, and anyway, I couldn't get here on account of the snow. I called a few times but the line kept getting cut off. Probably because of the storm. So I must say on behalf of the agency, we're very sorry to have left you stuck out here, and Mr Poke is quite annoyed with me but it was quite impossible. The road from Salthouse has been completely closed for days. I said to him, I said I'm sure you'd understand. Decent people would understand. I was on my way over here, when your daughter came flying down the lane, with an alarming message about you, my dear.'

Malorie's head was aching, just above her right eyebrow, a vicious stabbing pain, increasing in intensity.

'Yes,' she said, not understanding anything.

'You seem, if I may say so, somewhat disorientated. Can I get you anything?'

Malorie swayed slightly. The woman's hat really did look like a cat.

'I'm fine,' she said.

'I am intrigued though, dear, how you got into the property without the key. Was there a spare under a pot? Though goodness knows why there should be. The agency would never do that. Terrible practice.'

A key? Yes, there had been a key. Now it seemed odd, but she'd not thought about it. She'd assumed it was what people did in the countryside. Trying to ignore the pain above her eye, she thought back to when they'd arrived at the house. The bloody car had skidded and she'd arrived flustered and fed up. She remembered that clearly.

'Excuse me?' said Malorie. 'Do you mind just waiting here for a minute? I need to just check on something.' She looked past the woman to the lane.

The woman in the hat was looking at her askance. 'Madam, I really think that you ought to wait here. The men are coming. You should probably sit down. You look terribly pale.'

'I'm fine. Fine.'

With the blanket still wrapped around her shoulders, Malorie crunched down the snow-covered drive to the lane. The night rime covered the trees with a sparkling coating of frost. The sky was a pale, luminous blue and wherever sunlight fell on the white encrustations of snow and ice it was a flash of pure brilliance. All was deathly quiet except the distant sound of shovels on snow and the hum of men's voices. She crossed the lane with a sense of foreboding as if – and she couldn't explain to herself why this came to mind – as if she would find the old woman who looked like a vole, dead in her cottage.

Above the cottage the sky was clear. No smoke came from the chimney. She stood outside the door for a full minute before knocking. Something was stopping her. It wasn't exactly fear, daylight had robbed her of the horror of last night. Franny had recovered. For herself, there remained the overwhelming sensation of emptiness.

Little flickers of memory were coming back from the night – the old woman holding her, her papery hand, the voice saying the same thing over and over. Her own ghostly face in the mirror, but she wasn't sure what any of it meant.

She knocked on the door. It was important to say goodbye at least. The old woman had been there last night. She had touched her.

No one answered and she knocked again.

Still no one answered. Her bare head was cold and no warmth came from the morning sun.

She raised her hand to knock again when she heard the crunch of heavy feet behind her and a man's voice at the same time –

'Ent no point knocking on that door, Miss. That's empty that is. Far as I know.'

She whipped round, heart thudding. It was the man from the shop, George Bayfield.

'But . . . the woman who lived here . . .' She couldn't finish.

He touched his cap as if he was about to tug it in an old-fashioned sign of respect. 'I thought you were supposed to be leaving, last time I saw you, 'fore the snow come down.'

'We got stuck.'

'I can see that.'

She didn't like the way he looked at her, sizing her up, examining her. She didn't know what he wanted from her but she had to know at least one thing.

'Mr Bayfield, would you mind telling me who used to live in this cottage? I'm just curious.'

He squinted up at the old cottage. 'For as long as I can remember there was a spinster living there. A cunning woman some of the old folk called her. Name of Jane Gidney. Folk always called her Janey. I was afeared of her as a kid. All us kids had a rhyme about her.'

He began to chant under his breath:

'*Witch, old witch, what do you eat?*
Little green toads and children's feet.

Witch, old witch, what do you drink?
Poison moonshine and night blood ink.

Witch, old witch, what do you do?
I make potions and curses and I'm cursing you!'

'Funny,' he said, 'I've never forgotten that. It was a chasing rhyme and whoever was "it" sung the rhyme, and when you shouted the "you", you had to catch someone. It were brutal.' He had a faraway, dreamy look in his eyes and said it with relish as if those days were the best of his life. He saw her staring at him and looked guilty. 'We were horrible cruel back then. Kids are though, ent they?'

Malorie's organs were being slowly flooded with cold. 'What happened to her?'

'Awful scandal it were. She were hanged. I remember it well. Not many women were hanged then so it were something special. Quite famous.'

It wasn't possible. But it was true.

Words came out of her mouth without her thinking them. 'Why? What had she done?'

He paused. 'You're telling me you never knew none of this before you came? All what occurred in that house?'

She shook her head.

He tutted, muttered something under his breath like 'Shouldn't be allowed.'

When he answered she felt the crushing, cold horror of something already known.

'She killed two men in thirty-four, that's what. Poisoned them with arsenic. I was the one what found out about it first. The other one though, the young one – it was her what was really behind it. A strange one, she was. More like a sprite than a real girl. Could be vicious, mind, but I felt sorry for her in the end. I always liked her, though she never knew it. It was sad, how it turned out. I never thought – I don't know.' His eyes had clouded as if he was lost in the past.

'Rosemary?' she said, faintly.

The man peered at her. 'That's right. So do you know about her?'

'I need to sit down,' she said. The man in front of her seemed to fold and wave and turn upside down. The sky rushed down on her. Her knees buckled and she felt the path rise and thud into her body.

49

I saw her fall and I knew it'd be that Bayfield. Same as he was when he was a boy, sticking his nose in what ent his business. Still had his beak out of joint 'cos my Rose went off with the Lafferty boy. Still feeling sorry for hisself. That's what it all comes down to in the end: lust and all the foolishness what comes with it. And I thought to myself, Janey, she ought to know now. She ought to know all of it, nothing left out, all the truth of it, what happened. It were time.

50

Cromer

Before she opened her eyes she could hear a gurgling and clanking that sounded like nothing at the Marsh House, and her muscles relaxed into the hard mattress below her. She didn't know where she was, but it smelled metallic and bitter like cleaning fluid and vomit and faintly of burnt dust. She tried to turn over, to stretch, but her legs were bound and seemed fixed to the bed. A dull ache was coming from her right side. It was dark and hot. From what she could tell she was in a small room with nothing on the walls. The only light was a tiny red pinprick but that seemed far away.

Was she in an asylum? Tony had sent her there. He hated her, he was sleeping with that tart at the club. She was mad. He had called her mad. Her throat closed and her teeth ground together and she fought against whatever was binding her to the bed. But she couldn't move. Her arms and legs were fixed tight against her body. She shut her eyes again and lay still, trying to breathe little exhalations through her nostrils, trying not to panic.

Slowly, she remembered certain things. There had been a man dragging her, a voice she recognised. A cup of warm water. A burning taste in her throat. The bright lights in the grey dawn, an ambulance, men's voices, joking. A child. Franny. Oh Franny, where was she? What had happened to them all?

Where *was* she? She wanted to wake up now. It was time. But they must have given her something because there was a weight on her body and in her head that was dragging her back into the drug of sleep. No, she had to know where she was. *Wake up.* In front of her a square of light switched on and she realised that it was in the door of the room. A face appeared. A young woman with a round face and a nurse's hat.

The door opened and the nurse said, 'Are we awake now, Mrs Cavendish? Excellent, I've brought your breakfast.' She turned on the light switch and the strip light flickered on, flooding the bare little room with a fluorescent glare. Malorie screwed up her eyes against the light. Her body was still firmly tied to the bed. The nurse wheeled a little trolley towards her.

'Where am I?' she said, and the nurse gave her a funny look, like you would to a child who had said something incredibly stupid.

'Cromer hospital, Madam.'

'Is it a mental hospital?'

The nurse laughed. 'No, Madam. I should think not!'

Her neck was aching for craning to speak to the nurse. 'In that case,' she said, light-headed with relief, 'please – please can you release me from this bed? I can barely move.'

'Of course,' said the nurse, and dug her fingers in under the tightly-bound blankets and sheets and with a wrench drew them back. Malorie was suddenly exposed to the chest, only wearing a thin hospital gown. She struggled to sit up and pain jarred at her hip. Her head felt fuzzy like it was stuffed with felt and there was an ache in her right ankle.

The nurse fussed about, smoothing corners and putting the tray of unlikely-looking food in front of her.

'Nurse, I wonder, could you tell me about my daughter, Frances Cavendish? Is she here?' Her voice sounded awkward.

'I'll check for you. It doesn't say on the notes.' She gave them a cursory glance.

'I'd be very grateful.' She wanted to shout at the silly cow but she mustn't. They would suspect something was wrong with her. She was safe. She wasn't at the Marsh House. This was a sanitised place with white walls and cleanliness and warmth. Neither was she locked up in an asylum. The strange trickles of memory from the last few days were just bad memories, bits of nightmares. She'd got herself worked up.

The food on the tray was unappetising, but she was suddenly starving. She ate the piece of limp toast, took a mouthful of overcooked beans and then another and another until they were all gone. The egg remained congealing on the plastic tray. She picked up the cold rasher of bacon and nibbled the edge and took a sip of the milky tea they'd made for her. Her eye caught a deep red colour on the bedside table, next to a cardboard bowl. She recognised the bowl from the maternity hospital in London, the kind used for patients' vomit and urine. She focused on the red object.

It was the notebook. How had it got here? She had no memory of taking it with her. Why would she have done? She couldn't have.

For a full minute, maybe longer, she looked at the notebook lying innocuously on the utilitarian hospital table and tried to weigh up whether or not to open it. Rosemary. Janey. The story and the people in it pulsed in her mind, in and out, like a kaleidoscope, achingly clear and blurring to nonsense. Certain words and phrases popped up and disappeared again –

arsenic

flies buzzing vomit

orangemoonshinepurplebruises

These words did not belong in this place. If she left the notebook alone it could fade away and she could live here and now. She could go back to London, find a way to make it better with Tony.

But the red notebook radiated, like a neon sign saying *READ ME*. Rosemary's story hadn't let go of her; it hadn't finished with her. There were more words and she had to read them. She reached over and picked it up and it seemed to glow a brighter, bolder red than it had before. But at the same moment she opened the red leather cover of the book, the door to the room swung open and another nurse came in. She was an older woman in a darker blue uniform, with a pinched, hard face, not like the doe-faced girl who'd come in with the breakfast.

'Mrs Cavendish? Have you eaten your breakfast? Good. Nurse Mackie told me you were awake. Well, I've good news for you. Your daughter is absolutely fine and will make a full recovery. She's weak but there's no trace of fever or lasting damage.' There was a pause. Malorie brightened and she lifted herself up in the bed. The nurse frowned. 'The doctor did say he was going to do blood tests, but he'll let you know about that.' Blood tests? What for?

'When can I see my daughter?'

'She's on the children's ward. It will have to wait until visiting hours. And, I might add, until we're certain you yourself are not contagious in any way.'

'And if I'm not?'

'Then this evening between five and seven p.m. I'll get the nurse to take your tray away. The doctor will be doing his rounds shortly.' And with that, she turned and left, shutting the door firmly.

Now Malorie understood why she was in this room on her own. They'd thought she had something infectious, like measles or flu. Measles. It made her think of the baby boy, Richie. And from there to the last thing she'd read in the notebooks, the anguished, prolonged death of the young man, Franklin, and the girl discovering she'd killed her father. She had a vague recollection of being so horrified by what she'd read that she'd thought it must be made up, a pseudo-Agatha Christie, or a false confession of a disturbed mind. It didn't matter. She and Franny were fine, truly fine. Safe. Now she was no longer at the Marsh House, she might as well finish them. She'd still not read those last few lines in the third notebook. Just out of curiosity. It couldn't do any harm to read them now.

51

That's it then, the end of the story. I hope you've enjoyed it. I enjoyed writing it. I don't know if that's true, I think rather it has come out of me but it's what writers always say, isn't it? I wonder now if I could have been a writer like Mrs Christie. But I don't think I could construct the plots the way she does, full of red herrings and twists and turns. I don't think I have the cunning.

If I had, I'd have got away with it, don't you think? But I was caught. And Janey too, I'm sorry to say, the only person I'd ever loved until now, apart from my son and my mother, but I lost one and never found the other. I'm going too fast, but time is really short now. I feel it every night I look at the sun setting from my cell window. Another day gone.

I'm quite a cause célèbre. I learnt that from the newspapers. It does strike me as strange, that I, an odd girl from a very odd family on the far edge of Norfolk, have attracted the press from all over the world. They call me the Stiffkey Poisoner. Many of the papers have made the link between me and the Laffertys' Fascist politics but I don't think any of this has had a positive effect on the BUF because from what I read, their numbers have declined since that terrible rally in London last year and Mosley's support of Hitler. I'm not sorry.

I can only imagine what this has done to the Lafferty family, because none of them has come to see me, not even Hildy. I thought she would, is that naïve? A package did arrive though. It was postmarked Highgate. Even though they'd opened it (to check for bombs or knives?), the paper wrapping was still partly attached. The Laffertys' London house is in Highgate. I feel it's a clue. Perhaps I'm turning into Mrs Christie after all. The package contained two books. And yes, they were Mrs Christie's latest: Murder on the Orient Express and Three Act Tragedy. I devoured the first one. It was a relief that it was not about poisonings, as it turns out I have no taste for made-up tales of poisons anymore. I read halfway through the second book before I realised what was happening and had to stop. I remember relishing the poisonings in The Mysterious Affair at Styles, but that was a different person, from a different time.

I don't seem to be able to be my real self anymore. I'm not sure I even know who she is.

I didn't have long as a criminal. The police came knocking on the door the day after. They found the arsenic under the sink. I found out much later, at the trial, that the man who'd brought Franklin back from Cromer had told a boy in the village. From the silence of the

Laffertys, I suspect the boy told them and they called the police. They never liked me, the colonel and the lady. I thought Hildy did and maybe I was right. After all, I do believe she sent me the books. I still hope she comes.

I didn't try to lie, I'm a bad liar anyway. I remember getting in the police car and seeing Janey watching from the window of her cottage. I raised a hand to wave but she shook her head and I let it fall. I hoped they'd leave her alone. Dolly came running out of the house with Perdie in her arms yapping away like a mad dog, and they let me kiss her through the window of the police car before they drove off. The police assured me that she'd be looked after but I don't trust them. My hopes of Janey being kept out of it were dashed because at the trial they called her as a witness. It was horrible to see her, away from Stiffkey. She didn't look right with her raggedy old clothes and weather-beaten skin in the pomp and ceremony of the court. I was worried about Old Smutch and who was looking after him. No one would dare to look after that great beast in the village. They were all afraid of him, as they were of her. I started to cry then for all of us: Father and Janey, Old Smutch and Perdie, and Franklin. My lawyer told me to carry on, the jury would have sympathy for me, but they didn't. I was probably too haughty, even with the tears. That's what the village children always said about me, that I was stuck-up. I wasn't, you know, just lonely and shy and angry because no one liked me.

They were cruel to Janey. They called her wicked, a practitioner of black magic and purveyor of poison, and made out that she'd encouraged me to kill Franklin and my father. And when she answered their questions, she was too clear, too sure in what she said.

'Yes, I knew Miss Rosemary as a child,' she said. 'And her mother before her. I was called on to help her, and I did what I could.' But Janey is an innocent in all this. I don't believe she would have ever wanted to harm them.

It worked against her. I think some of the jury turned on her then. They were afraid too, like the villagers. They were afraid she would curse them or something stupid. I wanted to tell the court that Janey had been midwife to countless babies in the village and the hamlets around – myself and my baby included, that she'd healed fractures, soothed fevers and laid out the dead. But no one asked me. Instead they said, 'Did you, Miss Gidney, give Rosemary Wright the arsenic she used for the murder?'

I had insisted on being called Rosemary Wright. I wanted to be who I used to be, not what they made me.

'Not exactly,' she said.

'Please be precise, Miss Gidney. Can you tell the court whether or not you gave arsenic to the defendant, Mrs Rosemary Lafferty née Wright?'

'Well, I did give her some, of course I did. I done it before, plenty of times to others too. For the killing of rats.'

'Was it for vermin in this case, Miss Gidney?'

'I thought so, but –' She paused and the whole court held its breath. 'It might have been for the stopping of a baby.' She looked at me then and I saw she knew.

After that, the court was adjourned and I had to be seen by a group of women to find out if I was pregnant or not. They prodded me as much as the doctor had done years ago, with Richie. Tears ran down my face and I summoned Janey in my head for comfort. I felt her with me, holding my hand, and I stopped crying. And of course, I was pregnant. With you. So that's why I'm here now, writing all this down with you growing your fingers, toes, eyes and ears inside me as I write. It is to you I've been writing all this time, although I've only lately realised it.

I'm the subject of even more press now. Some of them have campaigns for a reprieve. They can't bear the idea of a poor girl being hanged just after I've given birth. In these accounts, I'm a wronged woman, a child who was led astray by an evil witch. There are other accounts though, from different newspapers. Especially the Daily Mail, who've been digging into the Laffertys and their connection with Mosley. In that paper, it's the Laffertys who are wronged, and I have taken their innocent son from them. Mosley is quoted as saying that Franklin was a promising young man, the kind of man this country needs. It actually made me laugh. I do wonder if the Laffertys themselves are turning against Mosley now he's declared himself for Hitler. He's shown himself to be quite a fanatic. The papers say that Diana's sister Unity is a follower of the 'Führer'. I think some women are attracted to men like that – the sort who seem absolutely certain about everything, the cruel sort. I can't quite see Franklin like that, he was too much a pleasure-seeker and I don't even know if he believed in any of Mosley's politics; I don't know if he cared enough.

In these newspaper reports I'm portrayed as a lunatic, the daughter of a madwoman, a madwoman herself, in thrall to black magic and a follower of satanic rituals. People in the village are quoted too, saying how I had no friends and was strange and spent all my time with the weird woman, Janey Gidney.

My pregnancy couldn't save Janey. They didn't wait long to hang her. One of the warders came in to tell me but I knew already. The warder was quite sympathetic. Some of them have been nice to me since it came out that I'm pregnant. Before, when I was awaiting trial, there was none of that. They were cold and hard then. But here, one of them even brought me the newspaper report with an article about it. It said she was suspected of being a witch but really she preyed on innocent minds and corrupted them. Poor Janey, no one had ever understood her like I did. I couldn't save her.

At least I saved you, my baby.

I sat here and wrote this because it was the only thing I could do. I've read my books and I only have this account left. But I don't know what else to tell you because it's nearly over. In my cell there's a small, high window and I watch the sun rise and fall through the bars. I think that whatever happens to me, you'll be here to see the sun rise and set every day, long after I'm gone. But I'm sounding maudlin now. I started writing this account to set it all straight, to show what kind of person he was – not to feel sorry for myself, because there's not a lot of point in that now – but so you would know. Not what I did, but who I was.

I miss Hildy. I wish she'd come.

I miss Franklin too, and the summer I first met him. The Broads, his white suit reflected in the water, him running down to the sea, the first time he kissed me. I touch the sapphire on my finger and remember the blueness of his eyes when he looked up at me, perching in the tree.

20th March 1935

Hildy has written to me. You can read the whole letter, such as it is, as I've kept it. I've read it and re-read it over and over but I still can't tell if she's forgiven me or not. I wonder what you think. 'I am sorry for what has happened to you,' she writes, as if it happened to me not to him, and that gives me comfort, but perhaps I am reading too much into her words and it is just a formality. 'I hate writing like this', she writes, and how I too hate the way she writes. There is no warmth, no friendship, none of our old intimacy. And yet, what can I expect? Her brother is dead and I am here.

29th March

It's not long now. I can feel you kicking at night when I lie on the mattress. I don't know what will happen to me when I give birth. I can't imagine Janey not being there. Sometimes, when I lie on my back with this bump rising up above me, I think I should have taken the arsenic and got rid of you.

4th April

I didn't mean that about taking the arsenic to stop you. I'm trying to think of all the things you would want to ask me if you could, but I'm not sure why I'm writing this now. They'll never tell you who I was. I'm afraid the Laffertys will try and claim you, bring you up as their own, deny me. I'm going to ask if someone else can have you. A kind family who can't have children.

I think now that it was you that Janey was trying to save. It wasn't me at all.

5th April

The campaign is trying to get my sentence commuted to life imprisonment. But that isn't <u>life</u>, is it? It's like an endless death, a purgatory. I read in one of the papers that our old rector is on display, alive but packed in ice, in a glass coffin on the Golden Mile in Blackpool, as if to suggest that he is a curiosity. Which of course, he is. I hate the parasites who feed on such notoriety. Even if they don't hang me, I don't want to take a longer time to die in prison, like an exhibit in a glass case. I don't want to give them that.

Sorry, I'm low again today.

6th April

I think you would want to know that I did love Franklin, and that even in the worst of it, he had some fondness for me too. I didn't mean to kill him, just to hurt him, very much. And I didn't mean to kill my father either. That is the truth. But I <u>am</u> sorry about Janey. She never deserved this. I wish I could – but it's too late to wish for anything now, except for you. You are all I care about now. I love you, what I imagine of you.

The labour pains have started and I need to stop.

Oh Janey, if only you were here. Please come.

I am sorry, Janey. <u>Please forgive me. Please help me.</u>

Oh Janey. Oh my mother.

I'm afraid. Not of dying but of not being able to see you. I want to see you first. I <u>must</u> see you.

52

A Feverish Madness

The rest of the page was blank. Malorie looked up from the book. The fluorescent light above her was pulsing. A hum of voices came from through her door. She needed to get up, to see people, to breathe real fresh air, not torpid hospital air. She needed to see Franny. She needed to read the notebook – but when she turned the pages, they were all blank. There was nothing else to read.

A wave of something like terror flowed through her. How could there be nothing left? She wanted to shout – *Rosemary*. It was true. Or it seemed to be true. She tried to release the tension from her shoulders. Perhaps it was so cleverly done that it seemed real. She didn't know. Her hands were shaking, her heart was racing too fast. It was like something she loved had been taken away from her.

Don't leave, Rosemary. Don't leave me.

*

Later, when she had gathered herself, she heard the door to the hospital room open. A new nurse walked in, smiling, with a doctor behind her.

'The doctor has a few questions for you, Mrs Cavendish.'

'But I'm fine, really. I just want to see my daughter.'

The doctor was young, about her age, smooth-haired, smooth-faced and with a red tie under his gown. He sat at the end of the bed and peered at her kindly.

'Mrs Cavendish, we're concerned about your state of mind.'

'My state of mind?'

'You've been talking in your sleep, saying some – uh – some rather odd things. For example, that there was an old lady who helped you at the house and a young girl in a white dress. From what I can understand, these are figments of a fevered imagination. Now –' He held out his unlined hand and seemed to be about to stroke her arm in reassurance, but rather held it hovering in the air. 'You mustn't worry, these things sometimes happen in young women. A kind of feverish madness. An excess of feeling.' He lowered his voice. 'We know that you had an experience of some disturbance at the house, Mrs Cavendish.'

'No –' she started, but he carried on.

'We wanted to reassure you, there are treatments that can be offered to help with these kinds of neuroses.' He paused, rearranged himself on the bed and focused more closely on her. 'You've had a recent bereavement, I understand. Again, it is not uncommon in such cases for a woman's mind to become – destabilised, even temporarily unhinged. This period of mental fever might indeed pass away of its own accord. But just in case, we thought it best if you were monitored – just for a short while, you understand. I know you live in London?'

She nodded, mute.

'That's excellent. There are marvellous psychiatric practitioners in London. We'll set you both up with a visit when you return home.'

She opened her mouth to speak but it was dry.

'One more thing,' said the doctor as he got up to leave. 'Have you been taking any prescription medication for your nerves?'

Malorie bit her lip. He didn't know. It would be on her records, but of course they were impossible to get hold of at short notice. And certainly not now, with the freeze.

'No,' she said. 'Nothing.'

When the doctor had gone, Malorie took out the Luminal from her washbag and held the envelope in her hand. They reminded her of Tony, of how he saw her. Malorie, who couldn't cope. Perhaps she needed something, but not these. She didn't trust them. First she put them all in the metal bin in the corner of the room. Then, thinking someone might find them, she fished them out again and, one by one, flushed them down the toilet until they had all gone.

53

London

March 1963

The kitchen clock said 9.45. It was already a full hour since Franny had left for school and Malorie was still in her nightdress and dressing gown. She'd made Franny's breakfast – a bowl of cornflakes – and watched her eat while she drank a cup of tea, kissed her daughter goodbye at the front door and stayed there until she walked to the bus stop through the slush and puddles to get the bus to school. Every morning, she'd wait for Franny to turn around and look at her. Every morning since they'd got back to London, she'd return up the narrow stairs to their flat and get back into bed, pulling the covers high up around her neck. She couldn't go back to sleep. Instead, she lay there, trying to ignore the thoughts that came crowding in.

It was just her and Franny for the time being. She'd told Franny that Daddy would be back soon and kept up a show of strength for her daughter, but she didn't know when, or if, he would be back. It had taken forever to get back to

London. They'd had to wait for a slight thaw to open up the roads in the middle of January, before the chill swept around the country again and closed off Norfolk. There had been an awful phone call with Tony. She thought he might have said he'd missed her, that it had all been a mistake, but he was too angry. He'd snarled at her, threatened court. She held the phone away from her ear while he ranted. She realised that too much had happened in Norfolk for them to return to how they were. Her leaving like that had been a way out for him. He lived in the flat above the club in Soho and she took Franny up to his parents' villa in North London on the bus and dropped her off. He'd bought a dog – a fluffy replacement for Larry – but it stayed at the house in St John's Wood. She told her daughter that she had errands to run but mostly all she did was take the tube to Highgate and walk around the snow-covered cemetery looking at the graves. She also knew, because Franny had told her, that sometimes another 'lady' was there, a pretty brunette whom Tony called Babs. She found she didn't mind as much as she thought she would. She had the flat in Pimlico, for the moment at least. He'd not been cruel about that. It was in his name though, it was he who had bought it with help from his parents. They had not yet gone to court to decide what would happen but she thought, she hoped, he would let her stay in it with Franny, at least until she'd set herself up. Once, his mother had telephoned the flat suggesting Marriage Guidance. Malorie, biting down her retort that she herself may need it, said that she didn't think Tony was interested in saving the marriage.

'You don't know if you don't try,' said his mother. 'There are ways of making a marriage work, that look beyond – a man's indiscretions. It would surely be better for Frances if her parents remained together. At least in name.'

What would be the best for her daughter? This was what occupied her every day. The doctor in Cromer had been true to his word and had referred them both to see a psychiatrist. Neither of them had gone to the appointments. She told herself that she wasn't ready, but in truth she was afraid. And she'd said to Franny she didn't have to go to her referral either. She didn't think the hospital in Cromer would follow it up. Not after the chaos of the winter.

They had a silent agreement, she and Franny, that they wouldn't talk about it. She hadn't given Franny any of the Luminal since the night they'd left the house. It had been Tony's idea in the first place, and he was no longer here. Since they'd left Norfolk neither of them had taken another one. She was hardly sleeping and woke each morning with a headache.

The Big Freeze, as the broadcasters called it, carried on until the end of February, fresh snow replacing the old, grubby mounds and covering the city over and over again, until it seemed there would only ever be a winter and it would never be warm again. She hadn't expected it in London for some reason, but when she and Franny returned home, the pipes had frozen and burst and there was no running water. Somehow, though, London still functioned: the roads were cleared by local men with shovels and the milk got through. It was only now, as March began, that the thaw had finally come. But when it came, it was all of a sudden. What had been packed snow and ice mixed with grit and gravel began to melt, causing a torrent of dirty water down the streets. Franny carried on going to school in her wellington boots, sloshing through the puddles.

After ignoring it for weeks, at the end of February, she'd gone to the library, alone, when Franny was at school. At first, she'd put off searching for information on Rosemary Wright and instead looked up what had happened to the BUF. There'd been the famous rally in Cable Street, she knew about that. She read about the king's abdication and the BUF support for him and for the Italian invasion. She read about Mosley and his next wife, Diana Mitford, being interned; most of the BUF disbanding, the failure of it all. He seemed ridiculous now, a bogeyman, a pathetic version of Hitler. But there were plenty who'd believed they were right. They still did.

Finally, she looked up the old newspapers from 1934 and 1935 and read the accounts of the murders in Stiffkey and the trial. Under the yellow light of the machine, she read about the hanging of Jane Gidney, midwife, by Albert Pierrepoint, the famous executioner. Her heart began thumping hard and fast under her ribs. She turned the knob of the microfiche, her legs twitching uncontrollably underneath the heavy desk. Then there it was.

Woman on 'death row' gives birth. – A baby girl. – Healthy. – Whereabouts now unknown.

With shaking hands, she turned the knob.

Stiffkey Poisoner reprieve denied.

She turned again. Then later –

Girl Murderer Dies. Cause of death unknown.

She'd walked away from the library and nearly under a bus she was so disorientated. The rest of the article seemed to hint that the death might have been due to blood loss in giving birth to the baby girl. She thought of Rosemary giving birth alone, no Janey to look after her.

While she was finally dressing, Malorie heard birdsong outside, the first for weeks. Then a clatter and a thud. The post had been delivered.

On the mat was a thick brown envelope addressed to her. The postmark said Cromer. Perhaps it was a bill for the Marsh House. She'd tried not to think about the house since she'd got back to London. She'd focused on Franny. She'd gone straight to the Midland bank and written a cheque, praying that there was money in the account and that Tony hadn't put some kind of freeze on it. She didn't know for how much longer she'd be able to access the account so had withdrawn slightly more than usual, but not so much as to be noticeable. They'd been on visits to the library, tobogganing, even to the centre of town where they'd had hot chocolate in an expensive café off Covent Garden and gone skating together on the frozen Serpentine. Part of the Thames itself had frozen and once they'd watched a man skating on it. She kept a close watch on her daughter for signs of the after-effects of withdrawal, or of damage from the trauma of what had happened to them, but there seemed to be none. She was withdrawn, yes, but no more so than before. And sometimes, in an occasional glance they'd shared, she caught a glimpse of an understanding between them that was new. This morning, for the first time since they'd returned, Franny had turned at the corner of the road and a small smile had crossed her face. It had to be a new beginning. She'd thought, for the first time, that she could survive on her own, that one day Franny would forgive her.

In February, she'd read of the suicide of a young American poet on the other side of London. She'd put her head in the oven, leaving two tiny children behind. Malorie understood. The black forms in her head still came and grew. But she was not going to die – not yet. Franny needed her if she was not going to grow up like her father.

Quickly, Malorie ripped open the envelope, as if she were tearing off a plaster from a wound.

> *Bulwer, Frankling and Reynolds*
> *15 Prince of Wales Road*
> *Norwich*
> *Norfolk NR1 1EF*

Dear Mrs Cavendish,
I trust this letter finds you well.

She scanned the rest of the page and had to steady herself with a hand on the wall to stop collapsing.

With the letter crumpled in her fist, she got herself to the kitchen where Franny's bowl still sat on the table, the mushed cornflakes encrusting the edges. She dropped the letter on the table and made herself a cup of tea. She was slow and deliberate in her movements, trying to remain calm. Leaving the house on the marsh had been the end of it, she'd thought. In the hospital, it had felt like a bad dream. Here in London, it had seemed like something to be put away like Pandora's box and kept shut up. Had it opened itself? Christ, that didn't make any sense. She was acting like she had at that house again. Just read it. Perhaps she'd misread it the first time. She read.

In my capacity as lawyer for the estate of Mrs Louisa Mulcaney-Wright, I write to inform you of her death on 28th December 1962 at St Andrew's Hospital (Norfolk County Asylum) of a heart attack.

Mrs Wright died intestate and we are therefore writing to inform you that, as her only heir, you are now the rightful owner of Swalfield House (known locally as the Marsh House), Stiffkey, Norfolk.

We apologise for the delay in corresponding. This is due to a series of probate issues and problems tracing the family line.

Please find enclosed the deeds to the property and the appropriate keys.

Please do contact me or my associates on the telephone number or address supplied above to discuss this matter further.

Yours faithfully,

Mr Leonard Bulwer-Thorne

Malorie sat staring at the stack of papers in front of her, the letter still in her hand. 28th December. She had been in the house. It was the day . . . Oh. She dropped the letter onto the table. Something fell out. It was a silver locket. She opened the clasp, certain of what was inside. It was still there, a lock of tawny human hair with a touch of gold.

Hardly knowing what she was doing, and still holding the locket tight in her hand, Malorie went up the stairs to her bedroom and opened her underwear drawer. She took out the velvet cloth and the stack of red leather notebooks and, with them bundled in her arms, she returned downstairs. She laid them out on the kitchen table. There was the bone shaped like an ear; there was the tiny skull of a bird; there the scaly skin of a dead eel; the entire skeleton of a rat; the skull of a seal with the huge dark eye sockets, the size of a child's head; there was the long skull of what looked like a boar, complete with yellow teeth.

On the kitchen table, she laid them all out. A song began to play in her ears, a low, sad jazz trumpet. She wondered if she would ever stop hearing it.

Next, she lay out all the documents she'd found or been given. The photograph, still in the old book, the envelope with the adoption documents and now this. There was a birth certificate for Louisa Mulwany. Not Mulcaney like the letter said. Oh. Daughter of – oh. And she thought back. When Rosemary was born she did not look English. Louisa had been – what did they call them – half-caste? – *Anglo-Indian*. She looked at herself in the hallway mirror, trying to see it, this strain of foreign blood that had caused so many problems for Louisa and her daughter. She came up close, put the locket around her neck. It was a shame her hair and eyes were such a nondescript colour. But then she smiled. She thought of Franny's black hair and green eyes. It was still there, even if no one knew; a secret on view.

Behind her shoulder in the mirror she tried to see her mother – her adoptive mother – a young woman picking up a small dark baby, trying to love it. The image wouldn't cohere. She could only see her as she'd been at her death, shrunken and soured by years of hiding the truth. But all that was over now. All they'd been doing was trying to protect her from the stigma of who she was.

Standing in the hallway, she imagined pulling her suitcase out from under her bed, the one she still had from years ago when she'd come to London from Norwich. In it she would place the velvet bag, all of the documents, and her own things. She'd pack a bag for Franny too, go down to the street and open the boot of the awful orange car. It would begin to rain and the rain would putter onto the pavement and the roofs, and the people on the street would look up and open their umbrellas. Her father would step from behind the streetlamp and wave his hat. (Not the other father, she could not think of him as that.) The windscreen wipers on the car would swish from side to side as she drove to Franny's school to pick her up. They'd drive out of London, leaving the tightly packed, grubby buildings, and up on the A11 to the big houses of the suburbs and then beyond – where the rain would stop, and the sun would set behind them as they drove past fields and fields and the road just going on and on. They'd arrive in Norwich late but they wouldn't stop there. They'd be back later. They'd carry on driving as it became night, the headlights two bright beams on the straight, dark road, Franny asleep on the back seat, she

337

smoking with the window down, until the road became smaller and the dark grew bigger. In the car with them would appear an old woman wrapped up for the cold, a sad woman in an Edwardian dress and a small girl with long, dark plaits and green eyes.

And then they would be there.

The house and its ghosts.

Malorie smiled at her reflection in the mirror. She went back to the kitchen and placed the notebooks on the edge of the table. Franny might want to read them one day. They were her birthright. Franny's grandmother's journal. Her mother, Rosemary Wright. Murderer.

54

Up our lane, there's still lumps of old snow, dirty, grey mounds shrinking as each day passes. The trees're dripping with rain and the marsh looks half flooded with the meltwater. Life's coming back. We're still here, me and the dog, clinging on. We're waiting – us and the house – waiting like we was before, back when they come the first time. I don't think it'll be long. I ent sure I'll last much beyond the spring. I'm cold all the time now, despite the thaw, cold and bone weary. I just need to be here long enough to feel the sun and see them back here where they belong.

Smutch starts barking to the sky. Couple of marsh harriers swoop in low over the garden on their way to the marsh. Ke-ke-ke they call, announcing the change in the weather. It won't be long now, Louisa, my love, it won't be long.

Author's Note

This novel had a number of inspirations: the first was the children's book *When Marnie Was There*, by Joan G. Robinson. This was a childhood favourite and I still own my original copy. More recently, it's been made into an animated film by Studio Ghibli. It is the story of a lonely girl who goes to stay with an old couple in a cottage on the Norfolk coast and discovers a deserted house and a mysterious girl who lives there, called Marnie. The novel is a beautiful story of ghosts and friendship and finding out about oneself, and conjures the Norfolk coast vividly. It also gave me the name for my house and the title of the novel: *The Marsh House*.

Another inspiration was the true story of an arsenic murder and hanging from the 1830s. In the real story, one hundred years before my invented one, a local wise woman gave arsenic to a young woman who put it in a cake for her husband. Unfortunately, not only did the husband die but so did her father who ate some of the cake as well. She was found to be pregnant while waiting for her execution and although the child was born, she was hanged in Norwich.

Finally, readers may recognise some of the names of people mentioned in the book. Harold Davidson was really the Rector of Stiffkey who caused a scandal in early thirties Britain. The story is as Rosemary describes in her journal and he really did end up displaying himself in a glass coffin on Blackpool seafront after being defrocked by the Church of England. His death was also tragic as he was killed by a lion in Skegness Amusement Park.

Rosemary's journal also mentions Oswald Mosley and Diana Mitford, who became Diana Mosley, whose affair and subsequent marriage were also hot gossip at the time. Oswald Mosley was famously the leader of the British fascists, the BUF. All the details are from the historical record, although I don't know if he ever came to Norfolk.

All the titles of the pamphlets mentioned in the novel and the quotes from newspapers are real ones.

One more influence on the novel came from the book *The Story of a Norfolk Farm* by Henry Williamson. Before he came to Norfolk, Williamson was famous as the writer of *Tarka the Otter*. Although he arrived in Stiffkey in 1937, so after the time covered in this novel, his story overlaps with many of the places and themes. He took over Old Hall Farm which is adjacent to the Old Hall, and was a supporter of Mosley.

I received inspiration on East Anglian folk tales from many sources, but I would recommend Kevin Crossley-Holland's *Between Worlds: Folktales of Britain & Ireland* for further reading.

Finally, most of the details of The Big Freeze of 1962–63 are historical fact, apart from one key detail: the snow began on Boxing Day, not 23rd December as in the novel. But this is fiction.

Acknowledgements

This novel was partly written during the Covid-19 pandemic and has therefore had a strange genesis. I would like to thank my agent, Laetitia Rutherford, for her calm steering during a time of stress. In addition, the novel has been subject to a series of twists of fate that mean I owe a great debt of thanks to not one, but three talented editors: Madeleine O'Shea, Charlotte Greig and Sam Boyce. I am extremely grateful to each of them for their guidance and expert editing. In addition, thanks must go to all of the team at Head of Zeus, including Kate Appleton, Anna Nightingale, Jade Gwilliam, Clare Gordon and Kathryn Colwell. And I can't forget the designer of the beautiful covers for both my books, David Wardle.

I would also like to thank some amazing early readers and supportive friends: Lily Dunn, Charlotte Packer, Rosie Smith and Lucy Tallis.

Other friends who've been a source of support this last year have been the ever-wonderful Anna-Marie Crowhurst, Gemma Thomas, Jean Stewart and Claire Kendall Muniesa. And a particular and heartfelt thank you must go to all of the D20 writers' group, all writers whose debuts came out in 2020, and who have been such wonderful sources of laughter and sanity during this extremely bizarre and tumultuous time.

Thanks to Jain, whose knowledge of flora, fauna and herbal remedies was an inspiration.

Love and thanks to all of my family in Norfolk and Wiltshire. I must add a particular thank you as ever to Will for his unwavering support, his critical reading and everything else.

This book is dedicated to my children, Alex and Jessie, who both love books and who are brilliant writers.

About the Author

Zoë Somerville is a writer and English teacher.
Born and raised in Norfolk, she has lived all over
the world – Japan, France, Washington – and now
lives in Bath with her family. Her debut novel,
The Night of the Flood, was inspired by the
devastating North Sea flood of the 1950s and is
also published by Head of Zeus.